LIMITLESS POSSIBILITIES

www.LimitlessPossibilities.info

Limitless Possibilities

Learning to Live from the Heart

in this New World!

Kathleen Walsh

Copyright © 2009 by Kathleen Walsh.

Library of Congress Control Number: 2009909119
ISBN: Hardcover 978-1-4415-7111-3
Softcover 978-1-4415-7110-6

All rights reserved. No part of this book may be reproduced or transmitted in any form or by any means, electronic or mechanical, including photocopying, recording, or by any information storage and retrieval system, without permission in writing from the copyright owner.

This book was printed in the United States of America.

To order additional copies of this book, contact:
Xlibris Corporation
1-888-795-4274
www.Xlibris.com
Orders@Xlibris.com
66455

Contents

Dedication vii
Message To The Reader Ix
Acknowlegments Xi
Preface 1
Introduction 5
Message from God 21
Chapter I—Angelic Influences 23
Chapter II—Many Gifts, One Spirit 40
Chapter III—We Have to Say We Love You in a Song! 62
Chapter IV—Soul-Searching 75
Chapter V—Elements in E-motion 88
Chapter VI—Prophecies and the Emerging Power of Light 100
Message from Mary Mother of God 118
Chapter VII—Messages from Markas and Friends 119
Chapter VIII—The Universal Realm 134
Chapter IX—The Lucky One! 143
Chapter X—Universal Olympics 159
Chapter XI—Waking up in the Fifth Dimension 177
Chapter XII—Wait. What? I Don't Understand! 188
Chapter XIII—Orion's Techniques 200
Chapter XIV—The Company You Keep 214
Chapter XV—Catch The Rainbow 226
Chapter XVI—Magic! 239

Message from Lancelot 250
Chapter XVII—Healing the World 252
Chapter XVIII—Healing Eyes of Atlantis 263
Chapter XIX—Dolphins in the Fifth Dimension 269
Message from Mother Earth 278
Chapter XX—Feng Shui 279
Chapter XXI—More Messages from Markas and Friends 293
Chapter XXII—Journey into Wellness 306
Chapter XXIII—Beauty in the New World 335
Epilogue 355
Exercises 361
    Breathing Exercise to Calm and Relax: 361
    Sitting In The Silence: 361
    Connecting To Your Higher Self: 362
    Charging a Stone or Crystal—30 Breaths 363
    Kirunda: Energy Balancing during Transition to Ascension ... 364
Glossary 367
Bibliography & Recommended Further Reading 375
Helpful Resources 405
Index 407

DEDICATION

To Markas, Lancelot, and Orion—I thank you and all of the angelic influences and unseen benefactors for the love you are continually sending to our universe. You may be unseen, but your love is certainly not unfelt. I am forever grateful, thankful, and humbled by all of your gifts and contributions made for this book. I shall always receive them with honor and love as I continue my journey with your guidance and inspiration.

To my dad, who lived the life of *Limitless Possibilities* every day. I thank you for showing me that anything is possible when you find your power within.

To my mom, who taught me to always keep an open mind and an open heart. I thank you, for these without a doubt have been the best gifts that you bestowed upon me.

To my son, who embodies love. I thank you for not doubting me and for your continuing love and support.

To my Twin Flame, whose soul is my soul, and whose love is my love may we grow and evolve in knowledge and wisdom.

And

To the reader, who I wish will read these pages with an open mind and open heart so that you may experience the wisdom and messages intended for your growth and development—all leading you to a place of peace, love, and joy. May you join me in my circle of love. I thank you.

MESSAGE TO THE READER

The suggestions presented in this book are to help the reader journey into a state of wellness. Common sense and wisdom are tools that must be employed to deal with all situations of discomfort, injury, or disease. This book is not suggesting to discontinue or replace traditional medical treatments of any existing condition, either physical or mental. Rather this book is to be used to broaden one's base of awareness and knowledge of energy and how energy affects everyday life and to discover that by what we think, feel, and act, we create our reality. The marriage of Western and Eastern medicines is a wonderful combination to explore healing possibilities. As always professional guidance in all areas of our life should be consulted before adapting, altering, or changing prescribed protocols or regimens.

ACKNOWLEGMENTS

I am deeply grateful and thankful to have had wonderful assistance throughout the writing of this book. The process of listening, transcribing, summarizing, and editing hundreds of hours of channeled seminars initially seemed overwhelming. However, as the work unfolded it became a wonderful labor of love and certainly became a healing journey. I am forever amazed at the dedication the following individuals demonstrated throughout this process creating a priceless volume that is bound forever with love within its pages.

Katherine Thornton, one of the most beautiful individuals that I have ever met, contributed largely to the success of this huge project. Kate came onboard to summarize, edit, and re-present all of the channeled information with clarity, simplicity, and ease. Working through complex information, Kate created a successful format whereby the reader is easily able to discern the knowledge and wisdom from spirit which has been presented as close to the original as possible. Kate, with her dedication and her masterful skills, worked well over three years to complete the information presented from the universe. Her beautiful spirit and the love in her heart has been incorporated so that you feel the book flowing with her love. Kate also participated with me in updating the channeled information so that the reader could have the most current information available.

Lorrie McInerney Moy worked to identify, isolate, and categorize photographs that helped us to understand how the unseen is indeed visible on our earth. Her additional research in countless subjects and/or themes helped me gain a greater perspective thereby bringing me to a place of knowledge. Her many hours of diligence will be forever appreciated as continued blessings arrive for her and her family.

Madeleine R. Coticchia worked chapter by chapter, reading with her perspective of youthful eyes to identify terms, ideas, concepts, or language that may need clarification by the reader. This contribution allowed the development of an extensive glossary so that each and every reader would be able to have an increased awareness, bringing the learning to the greatest level of understanding possible.

* * * * * * *

In addition, I wish to thank the following family and friends for the love and support they gave me during this entire process.

To Theresa, Bonnie, Diane, and Donna, for your love and friendship. I thank each of you for using your gifts to help heal Mother Earth. It was these experiences that provided me with so much of the information that was to be included in this book. Together we are learning healing, growth, development, and enlightenment. May we continue to share in the love in each other's life as I thank each of you for the contributions you have made to my life!

To Kay and Marsha, for your enthusiasm, knowledge, and advice during this journey. I thank you for your continued support and wisdom as I continue to the next phase of my life.

To Lisa, Lorrie, and Lucy, for your continued loyalty, love, and support. Your dedication and diligence at work provided me with freedom in so many areas of my life to be able to complete this project. May you all share in the gifts that will be forthcoming to each of you as the universe shows its appreciation.

To Maureen, Kate, Anne, and Lybbi, women who by their very presence in my life have allowed me to develop into who I was meant to be by supporting me as I stepped into my new world, encouraging my confidence through love, laughter, and tears!

To Jim, Lily, and Grace, for your undying love and support.

To Mesha, Milanka, and Irma. For listening to me and encouraging me and supporting me in so many ways, I thank you. Your belief in me has not only allowed me to grow, but to expand my knowledge so that I can always help others. I thank you for your patience and openness as I have shared all of my comings and goings throughout these pages with you. Your enthusiasm for this project helped me grow in the determination to complete it. I am truly grateful for your continuing friendship.

To all of the Jims in my life, you each have contributed to who I am in more ways than you know. I thank each of you!

PREFACE

Everybody has a story, and today I would like to tell you mine. I only ask that you sit back and read with an open mind and an open heart. I have only in recent years learned how to do that. That is part of my story: how and why I opened up to the beautiful gifts that the universe has bestowed upon me. Am I unique? Yes, we all are! Am I special? No, not at all! What path I have recently traveled on and the gifts waiting for me as I have journeyed down this path are available to everyone. I have learned many, many things, and I intend to share these lessons with all of you with the hopes to help make your journey a little easier. I would like to help you to not only identify your birthright gift but the other gifts available to you as well and then to learn to develop them. You see I have learned that this is part of my purpose here, part of my blueprint.

What is that, you say? Well, I intend to explain everything to you a little at a time, taking baby steps one by one until something clicks. Hopefully I will explain not in boring detail, but my enthusiasm for not only who I have become but more importantly how I have gotten here will help transport you with me to a new place, a better place, a place where we can live in this world, a world where we have learned to live from the heart.

So as my son told me, "You had better tell everyone to get their eye-rolling done right in the beginning of the book!" His love for me is obvious. I will be a little easier on you—you may with my permission roll your eyes during the entire book, and when you are done (if you make it that far) it will be a successful read if during this book you can relate to one small thing, or if you can think differently about something that perhaps has bothered you through the years, or if you can relax your belief system just a little, thus relieving stress in your life.

So I invite you to do the dance with me. We can slow dance when it is serious, or we can jitterbug (now you know I am dating myself) through the parts you know quite well. But also know that during the book we can learn new dances with new partners, all the while enjoying the music, the scenery, creating our own ambience. Our life through these chapters will mimic life—learning our lessons. Some of these lessons will be more important than others, but all the while they will build on each other. We can't learn to waltz if we can't learn to step one step at a time, then throw in the music and go with the rhythm of the energy in the universe. Yes, life is like a dance, our dance as we share this planet together.

We have come to earth during this time of great transition. We are all here sharing our lives with each other, helping Mother Earth move into the Golden Age, the spiritual Age of Aquarius. We sang to it and danced to it in the sixties, naked onstage (no, not me) and, my, did it create a lot of attention! Do I know now what I didn't know then? Absolutely! We are in our final days of our planet's transitioning, which will complete on December 21, 2012. Let me explain.

The Mayans had predicted this planetary shift for the last 26,000 years. We are now all working hard at helping our earth transition into this new energy—the energy of the Fifth Dimension. Wasn't there a singing group by that name in the sixties? How is it that they were named the Fifth Dimension? Did we ever think or ask what it meant? I didn't, and perhaps I should have as I would have been given the heads-up on how our planet was moving into this new fifth-dimensional energy. Perhaps I would have been forewarned or at least started to prepare for this event. Or perhaps I would have done exactly what I did do—lead a life whose day-to-day life consisted of college, teaching, marriage, motherhood, career, and elderly parents.

Did I ask the big questions? No! Did I know I wasn't asking the big questions? Yes! For years I went to bed and oftentimes woke up in the middle of the night hearing the sound of the telephone ringing. I always got up and answered the phone and promptly heard a dial tone. Then one day I read that when someone hears the phone in the middle of the night, oftentimes it is the angels or your guides' way of giving you a "wake up call." Yes, they used that on me and I fell for it every time. After several years (I am embarrassed to tell you that it is probably more than several but less than two decades), I finally woke up and got the message!

Am I a slow learner? No! I was just absorbed in life, participating from the mundane to the mundane: carpools, groceries, laundry, cleaning, ear infections—you know. And then life's surprises: chronic diseases, divorces, and death. Yes, you know the drill. Who has or had the time to look for the answers to the big questions with life happening all around us?

So events occurred, and as the years passed my life took different twists and turns, right into where I am today.

This book is not only my personal journey of my growth, it is also a manual to help you transition from whatever dimension you are in—to bring you up to speed, literally and figuratively, into the Fifth Dimension. You can recognize where you are, and you can find out step by step what ground needs to be covered in thinking, or in feeling or in doing. Or if you are like me, I needed to do the work in all three areas to grow and to relax into unseen and unvisited territory.

Maybe I can help you keep from making some of the same mistakes I made, or maybe I can help you evolve faster, or maybe you will write me and I will learn volumes from you. Whatever approach we take is great as long as we see some forward movement, and as we do this together, as Markas says, we move into a win-win situation. I know we will do fine. We may even perhaps experience moments of greatness!

So who is Markas? Well, please come along and meet my friends and I will explain . . .

Will there be moments of greatness? Oh my, yes. And many, many more to come!

INTRODUCTION

It was early in February, at the turn of the millennium, a cold and gray day in my hometown in the Midwest. As I left work and traveled down the road, I stopped at an intersection about two miles from my home. I had stopped at this same intersection daily over the last twenty odd years. However, something was different that day. I sensed that the air seemed different; there seemed to be a calm, a feeling of peace outside.

My attention was immediately drawn to a large bird with an immense wingspan. As I watched its graceful body gliding smoothly and slowly downward through the intersection, I realized that this beautiful, strong, and powerful free creature was circling. And to my amazement, as he circled his flight path descended down to my eye level, getting closer, closer, and closer until he was next to my driver's window. I looked out of my window and we made eye contact. Within seconds I understood his message: "You are not alone, we love and support you!"

I sat at the intersection, mesmerized, wondering, "Did this really just happen?" Would anyone believe that this graceful creature had spoken to me? Strangely, the answer to this question did not really matter to me. I knew, deep within, that yes, this bird did come to me and he wanted me to know that I was loved. But why? Was this to prove to me that we are all connected? Or was there another reason that this majestic creature came to me? I continued to ask myself questions and was acutely aware that I needed to search for the answers to these and the many other questions that started surfacing but that I had been asking for years.

As I continued my journey home, these questions kept replaying in my mind. In fact, that evening, and for several days afterward, I could not ignore the feeling that my soul had been touched in a way that I had never known before. As I thought about this experience, I found that an inner dialogue began. I began to think about my life honestly and openly, in a way that I do not believe I had ever truly done before. I also relearned to giggle! I was tickled that not only had a special bird come to me with a message, I understood it! How was that even possible? I felt alive, laughing and experiencing a great moment. This was indeed one of those stellar moments that proves to be life-altering. Wow! And then I realized that I didn't even know what kind of bird had visited me. So I ran and found my son's bird species book that he had in high school and identified my visitor as a hawk, a red-tailed hawk! I had never had a feathered friend before, and I thought, well, why not!

My adult life had been one that was comfortable. I was married with one son, and we lived in the same town that we had grown up in. It was wonderful to raise my son and be near family during those early adult years. I had never known my grandparents, so I was grateful that my son would have an opportunity to get to know his. We were also available to take care of our parents as they aged. We became experts at responding to their emergency calls day and night, and I was always grateful that I was close by to handle their needs. Fortunately, I was also able to start my own business and found that not only was I successful but I loved working with people. I had created a career that was helping people to bring beauty into their lives. I had found my niche, and I enjoyed every minute of it. My work was indeed joyful! Life was good, or so I thought . . .

My married life as I knew it, however, was shattered when my husband of nearly thirty years suddenly asked for a divorce. The news came as a true shock, and I had to process this extreme disappointment and hurt as I had never experienced rejection or this type of pain before. I had recently turned fifty and felt that my golden days had now been ironically tarnished. While I was truly blessed that I could remain in my home for the time being, I was no longer certain of my future. I was struggling with my self-image and was surprised at the deep humiliation that I felt. I couldn't stop thinking that I had failed. Every effort I had made to make someone happy had come back to haunt me with this acknowledgement that I had failed. I felt such sadness, such loss. It was truly as if a part of me had died.

If I knew then what I know now, I would have realized that this request for a divorce was the most loving gesture, as I needed to be released from the marriage as indeed the energy had changed. I knew it on so many levels, but simply probably chose not to deal with it as life sometimes gives us enough of a bumpy path that we are using our energy and focus to navigate through the bumps and sometimes the obvious simply gets ignored, or perhaps it was denial or some of both! But this is now with a little dose of wisdom and that was then, so . . .

This sudden, unexpected death of my old life created an urgent need for me to begin a new existence. I instinctively knew that I needed to work toward deep healing in order to reemerge as a new, stronger, healthier, happier, more peaceful version of myself. The question was, how? I could only hope that I would find some part of me to help me become ME again.

I searched and prayed, and deep inside I felt my Self, a part of myself that was my truth, my inner truth. I knew that faith would sustain me and was aware that I would be back, only better, renewed. Somehow faith gave me a peek at security; it was the millennium after all, a new century, a new life.

That being said, it certainly was not an easy journey. I knew intuitively that for me to emerge as a new, positive self, I must get rid of all of the negativity that we are bombarded with on a daily basis. I turned off the television set and stopped reading newspapers. I recognized that the new me would be determined by what I thought, felt, and how I acted. So I needed to be in charge of what I was thinking, and ridding myself of fear seemed to make perfect sense. Every day was a struggle, every day was a challenge, and every day was a lesson. I took the advice of all that "knew" and simply took one day at a time. I made a list of all of my weaknesses and their opposites. I put it on my mirror and every morning I looked at my list and asked the question: "Have I been successful in trying to minimize my weaknesses while maximizing or developing my strengths?" (Of course, I didn't use those words—but you get my meaning!) I was looking for quality here. I updated my list often, finding new weaknesses but also proud that I could add more strengths or at the very least see positive growth. Soon the days turned into weeks, the weeks turned into months, and I was aware of how different I was feeling. The queasy feeling in my stomach and the nervous shaking of my hands started to subside. I observed all of the changes that I felt; I identified each of them and became acutely aware of my feelings, my innermost thoughts, and the growth that was occurring as part of these changes.

I took a look at my surroundings and knew that a huge cleansing was in order. Time to start fresh, so I painted all of the rooms in my home, trying to bring balance and harmony and to simplify the look. I knew that if I wanted my energy to change, it was time to rid the house of any of the sad, hurt, or angry feelings that existed in those walls. Did you know that wood, stone, and other natural materials are all alive? They are, so the energy that surrounds them is also the energy that you live in. I didn't want to live in a home where the energy that existed was all energy from times and events that were no longer me and, more than that, no longer healthy for me. I not only had to heal myself but my environment. Starting new meant that any of my positive feelings could grow and that I would attract similar new friends filled with the same positive feelings that not only I but my home was generating. I didn't know it then but I was learning the Universal Law of Attraction.

I had read that changing daily habits would actually develop new pathways in the brain. In fact, research suggested that these changes could actually increase your brain usage. Therefore, I decided to incorporate this methodology in every aspect of my life. I actually made it a sort of personal challenge to do everything in a new way: I drove to work a new way, changing driving patterns that I had followed for years. I changed my shopping habits, the stores that I frequented, just to look for a fresh way of completing my routine. I changed my eating habits, trying to eat only foods that were natural and organic. I trusted that doing things in a new way would create a new me. I wanted transformation! I wanted to feel differently. I was creating new experiences expanding my environment and ridding myself of the limitations that I had allowed myself to exist under. I cherished these new experiences that I knew would make life interesting and would allow new challenges and opportunities to unfold.

A friend suggested that I measure my growth at the end of a six-month period. I did, and remembering how I felt six months earlier, I was able to compare that feeling to how I was currently feeling. The growth was amazing and I was so proud of my success! I hadn't totally recovered from a fragile and tentative self-image, but the growth was a positive measure for me to see that life was coming alive for me again. Certainly, this was a different life, but I realized that it was still mine! I hadn't lost myself or a sense of myself at all; rather, I was just expressing myself differently. I was open to new thoughts, new ideas, and new feelings. I felt that everything was new to me. I became aware of the fact that the challenge of my devastating divorce was actually the universe urging me to grow and travel down a path that had previously been unknown to me. I couldn't wait to evaluate myself six months down the road—that to me was exciting and of course provided me with the motivation to work harder so that my evaluation of myself would indeed be successful!

I decided that since I had so much free time in the evenings due to my new single status, this was the perfect time for me to read about subjects that

I knew nothing or almost nothing about. I was determined that I would use this time for learning and healing. Was I learning to heal, or was I healing by learning? This was my plan. I made a mental decision to help my emotional body heal, my spiritual side mature, and I felt that my physical body would become healthier as well. I was truly looking for the total package, and was I ever determined to get it!

I began my research by visiting a small neighborhood bookstore that I felt had an inviting and appealing draw. I made it a point to stop there at least once a week in order to soak up the subjects on the shelves. It was a small, independent bookstore that was filled with spiritual books, self-growth books, how-to books, and very inspirational artifacts and gift items, including an occasional class with local experts on various spiritual and metaphysical topics. I spent hours wandering about in order to familiarize myself with the subject matter. I not only exposed myself to what was out there, but then I had to make up my mind as to where to begin. My thought was that I would pick a subject matter and select a half dozen or so books on that subject so that I was reading a broad range of opinions on each subject by renowned authors. I felt that I could take the best of the best, absorb it, process it, and figure out what rang true to me. This approach intuitively made sense to me.

A dear friend had given me a book on angels entitled *AngelPower* by Janice T. McConnell. I had read it and found it fascinating. I decided that angels would be the first subject that I would delve into. I did need a friendly face at home, and I did not want to be alone, so I decided to develop a friendship with the spirits that belonged to all of the angelic faces that I had grown up with in catechisms, prayer books, and the beautiful stained-glass windows and statues in church. The description on the cover of *Angel Power* states that this is "a beautiful introduction to the invisible heavenly host and the immense power of the Nine Choirs of Angels." It is certainly that and so much more!

As I read about the angels and their responsibilities, I began to get comfortable with these beings and saw how the angels affected my daily life. I learned that the angels are available to each of us every minute of every day. All we have to do is to invite them into our life. They are God's messengers and wait for us to speak to them so they may guide us, inspire us, and protect us. While I was familiar with the idea of angels from my Catholic upbringing, they were now taking on a whole new meaning. I was instantly drawn into the feelings of love and comfort that they emitted, and I wanted to experience them on a constant basis! I found these beings exciting and saw that there was so much to learn about and from them.

I began to learn to feel love in spite of the fact that I found myself alone for the first time in my life. It had always been easy for me to give love and to express and show my love, but I seemed now to be able to express love from a much deeper place. I also learned to receive love and, surprise, surprise, I felt loved! My confidence grew and I began to incorporate the angels into all of my daily experiences. I had invited them into my life and they indeed had arrived! My life became full of experiences that were new, exciting, and so magical. I never knew what was going to happen in the course of a day, but I was secure in the knowledge that my newfound friends, my angels, stayed with me, and their presence was felt very strongly by me. I realized that I was never truly alone.

I stocked up on several other angel books, hoping to learn how to incorporate daily communication with the angels and how to encourage them into all areas of my life. The books included many fascinating stories of unusual angel happenings that showed that angels are indeed among us. I was intrigued and curious, and I wanted to see if I could have an angelic experience similar to the stories that Janice had included in her book. I was certain that by learning about the angels, their whereabouts, and my relationship with them, I could develop a rapport with them and soon would see how the angels affected my daily life. It was a goal, a dream that I hoped would soon become a reality!

One wintry evening, very soon after I began my journey of learning about the angels, I was settling in for an early evening at home. I followed my new evening ritual of lighting a candle and listening to a meditative CD while soaking in a warm bath. I closed my eyes and was enjoying the peace and the silence when the bathroom suddenly filled up with the scent of jasmine, the most beautiful jasmine—full and complete. I actually got up out of the tub and went out into the hallway to see if I could determine from where the floral scent was coming. Was I imagining this, or was it real? I walked back into the bath, smelling and enjoying the aroma as the room was full of this lovely fragrance.

I had only recently read in one of the books on angels that their favorite flowers are roses and jasmine. Immediately, deep inside, I knew that I had been the recipient of the kindest and most loving gift. Again, the message that came to me very clearly was "you are loved and you are not alone." I loved the feeling that I was being watched over. It was so comforting. I realized that I was starting to see the miracles unfold in small, small ways— daily events and daily activities. But the impact on me meant so, so much! This was an example of divine timing: what one needs seems to appear at the right time and the right place for the most impact!

I now was sure that I was not alone. This experience reinforced my desire to communicate with these beautiful beings and to include them in all of my thoughts and feelings. I wanted to learn how to see them, to feel them, to talk to them, and to hear them. I began to study the "clairs" (clairvoyance, clairsentience, clairaudience) and realized that everyone could experience different kinds of communication with the angelic realms through their different senses. In fact the more that I thought about it, the more that I realized that I had been having angelic visitations all along. They came, gave love, and I missed it, totally missed it! But in rethinking what I would have called a weird experience or an odd event, not understanding made it weird or odd but now that I "got it" I realized that I had been experiencing beautiful expressions of love since I was a little girl!

Suddenly, I remembered an event that happened in my childhood, something I hadn't thought about for over fifty years. I was one of the youngest on my block, and as a little girl, probably about seven years old, I was at the low end of the pecking order. The older kids oftentimes made me do things to prove that I could play with them or maybe to see how much trouble they could get me in. It didn't really matter to me as I was just happy to be included and to have kids to play with. One summer day I was told to go down to the house at the end of the street, and in the cellar in the basement was a ball that I was to retrieve and bring out for everyone to play with. So wanting to be able to play with them, I gladly ran down the street to get the ball. While down in the cellar, I heard laughing and all of a sudden the door slammed shut and I was locked in. The cellar was dark—no outside window, nor could I find a light. I called out and heard the older kids running up the stairs shrieking and laughing, proud that they had captured me! They just left me there and no one came back to let me out. I lay down on the cellar floor with my legs were drawn up to my chest, wrapped up in a little ball, waiting for someone to find me. Time passed, and I must have fallen asleep when I heard the mother of the house come home from work. I called out to her and she came running down and unlocked the cellar door. I had been locked in the cellar of a strange house all afternoon and I wasn't scared, nor was I shaken. I simply got up and ran up the stairs and out of the house and home. My mother asked where I had been as it was getting near time to help with dinner. I explained that I had been locked in the cellar down the street by the bigger kids. She asked if I was scared, and I remember I just looked at her shaking my head indicating no, but all the while thinking and being amazed that I hadn't been afraid. I actually gave myself credit for being a brave little girl, and of course I played the part well as I accepted all of the apologies of the neighborhood kids as their parents brought them to me one by one. Actually I am sure that I enjoyed all the attention!

But now, for the very first time, I realized and had a clear vision of what had occurred many years ago during that day during those hours I was locked in the cellar. I had lain down on the cellar floor and had fallen fast asleep. No fear, no worry, and I had no concern for my safety—all the while I felt protected. I remember feeling when I heard the mother come home upstairs that it was time to stand up and call out. I did and felt warm wonderful wings unwrap from my body, giving me the freedom to rise. I now clearly understood the mystery of how a little seven-year-old girl could be locked in a dark cellar for well over four hours having absolutely no fear. I had been touched . . . literally touched and protected by an angel. This realization was one of my first of many "aha" moments with the promise of many more to come!

Over the years I have had many angel experiences. Some of these experiences could definitely be put under the category of "life-saving"! One wintry day, I was driving on the highway at the speed limit of sixty-five miles per hour. The car in front of me was probably four car lengths ahead of me when its bumper fell off. Before I even had a chance to react and put my foot on the brake, my car came to a total stop. I mean it went from sixty-five miles per hour to a dead stop (no pun intended here)! It was as if a glass shield of resistance had immediately been erected in front of my car to prevent its forward motion. I quickly looked in my rearview mirror, and I saw a car behind me and a semi-trailer truck right behind him. I saw them slow to a standstill, and the look on the face of the man in the vehicle behind me was so amazed. It was priceless! I quickly asked for help from my angels, to help me start my car and move into the lane next to me with ongoing traffic. I needed help quickly as that lane was continuing to move at the sixty-five mile-per-hour pace. Within seconds, I saw that the cars in the lane on my right as well as the lane on my left were each moving to the lane beyond, allowing me safe passage. It didn't matter which direction I chose, the angels covered all the bases, and I was free to enter either lane, gaining speed as I could. I thanked the angels all the way home, amazed at what had just transpired. My safety, and the safety of all of the cars surrounding me, was quickly handled with the utmost protection. Many nights when I think of that experience, I am in awe at what happened and how I was protected; another miracle performed by my angels had saved the day! Many more miracles have happened which I will describe in future chapters.

I continued learning and reading and even signed up for some metaphysical classes, all the while amazed at all there was in the world to learn about. I realized that all that I didn't know could keep me occupied for decades. This was not only a humbling realization but one that also motivated me to broaden my subjects to study. Before long I was reading books on many topics which had a metaphysical, spiritual, or cosmic bent. I still loved going to my little bookstore, an uplifting spiritual spa, as I felt it had become almost a second home.

One day I walked in and was immediately drawn to the little room at the rear of the shop. There I met a woman named Theresa who I felt an immediate attraction to as if we had been best friends for years. One of her many specialties is aura photography and the reading and interpretation of the aura picture. She had an aura camera and I immediately wanted to have my picture taken. The first photo captured me with three of my angels standing behind me! Theresa was really fascinated as she explained that the angels did not step out of the way but wanted us to see them. She took a second picture, and this time my aura picture showed a totally balanced photo of me with the energies of the rainbow colors in a mirror image on either side of me. This meeting opened me not only to the world of aura photography and its meaning but was to be the catalyst for my future development. Theresa began to teach small development classes on so many of the subjects that I had been studying. But now I would be able to have the practical experience of the classroom helping me to develop my natural skills and abilities. I was so excited to have made this connection.

The first class was very interesting. The class size numbered six, which included Theresa, most of whom felt a connection with the other women in the class. Women they had never met before. They were quick to conclude that they knew each other from a shared past life! Later this was validated as we learned the details of our shared past lives. At the end of this class, we each had a spirit guide or teacher that came to introduce him or herself to us, as well as to give each of us a personal message. The process by which those from the other side came to us was through channeling. I learned that each of us channels, some aware while others may not be as aware. Everyone receives information differently: some intuitively, some through dreamstate, some through visions, and many other ways. The receives are as individual as we are! How, why, and when we receive guidance and inspiration actually makes life interesting and fun! The great masters and of course many other genius and not-so-genius types in all areas of life are all examples of how greatness was really achieved!

My experience was so exhilarating. One of the chiefs of the fairy kingdom, named Eshe, came to introduce himself to me and to thank me for all that I was doing and had done for the world. (I couldn't imagine anything that I did or contributed to the world that would make the fairy world stand up and take notice of me! More than that—just how were they watching?) He explained he came in his capacity of head of the fairies because my soul had spent well over four hundred years in the fairy kingdom. I could attribute my love of nature, the elementals, plants, and flowers to this energy as I had carried it forever within me. He wanted to congratulate me on taking this step and moving forward with my growth. Ah, perhaps this was one of my first lessons to experience the interconnectedness of all things—again it was missed by me at the time, but pretty soon I "got it"!

Then my father came. He had passed away near the end of the twentieth century, and I was glad to know that he was around me and involved with my earthbound activities. He briefly stated that he would talk to me privately after class as he didn't want to take up any class time! He was very formal and spoke very beautiful English—a bit old-fashioned but charming. He came (to those who were able to see him) in a suit, carrying a large stack of books. I guess he was always one to be dramatic, but I hadn't expected his presence, nor that he would come dressed for the part!

True to his word, my father came after class and explained why he was there and what role he would be taking in future classes. He told me that I was directed to meet Theresa that day at the bookstore as it was the beginning of me making connections that would alter my life and allow me to grow, develop, and lead me down the most beautiful path, helping me to understand who I was and the role I was to play during the rest of my time on Planet Earth.

My father was a great surprise, but not unexpected. One week after my divorce—in fact, the first Friday night I was alone—I had come home from work, eaten a light dinner, and taken my evening bath early so I would be able to read for most of the remainder of the evening. I walked into my bedroom after the bath and proceeded to light a candle and sit down to read. I turned around and there sitting on the edge of my bed was my father. His energy was shimmering, not solid or immovable. This essence clearly was my father. This was very believable to me as my father was a very unusual man with many unusual abilities and characteristics. The fact that he had made himself visible to me was very comforting, and I knew that death was not going to prevent him from showing me a gesture of love.

All of sudden I decided to ask him questions. So since the candle was lit, I asked him to answer through the candle. If the answer was yes, he could make the candle's flame jump taller; if the answer to the question was a no, he could quiet the candle and make the flame small. Since he was a well-known engineer and inventor, I reasoned that this would not be too difficult for him. So I proceeded to have a conversation with the flame and was laughing as we communicated in this preposterous fashion. I guess you could say I really "lit" up having him come to my bedroom that evening. In fact, I have often laughed during these last ten years that I have seen him more and talked with him more in death than when he was alive and I was growing up!

I learned that I was a spiritual being (we all are) that had chosen to come down to Planet Earth to experience a lifetime in a physical body. I also learned that I had chosen my parents and my sibling to not only give them an opportunity to learn lessons from me but for me to learn my lessons from them. I knew that we had a master plan or blueprint that had our major life lessons on it and that we drew to us experiences that would help us learn those lessons. Our guides, teachers, and experts would confer and bring us the experiences that they hoped would be the most effective for us to learn from, and if the lesson was easily learned, then the experiences changed so that other lessons could be learned. As each lesson was learned, then that chapter of life could be complete and you would move along on your path. However, if you had the same experience over and over again, that meant that the lesson was not being learned, and each experience presented was more and more difficult until the recipient "got it." I had always wondered why some people get themselves in tons of trouble, and others just have an awareness and the lesson is learned or perhaps a simple experience and then the lesson is learned. Is it because our free will can step in the way and steer us away from our lesson? Or is it a question of awareness? Is it that we don't think that we are part of this school of life and so our awareness hasn't been fine-tuned to pick up on the reason we are having an experience?

Are we so ingrained in our life on earth in our physical body and the person we have chosen to be that we forget the very nature of who we are—a spiritual body having a physical lifetime—and we assume that our life is simply the character that we are playing rather than remembering that we are really just playing a part on this planet?

During another class session my father explained that five of us had indeed shared a physical lifetime together during the days of King Arthur in Avalon. We had been high priestesses and worked with the energies helping Christianity permeate that part of the world. He explained that we were very proficient in our roles and that these classes would simply help reawaken the skills that were deep in our cellular memory. We simply needed to remember! He also explained that we would reconnect our deep bond and work as a group on healing projects. This is in fact exactly what has transpired as the five of us have formed a planet healing group which meets monthly on the first quarter moon to send fifth-dimensional healing energy to the planet to help her heal her natural environment—our water sources, our food sources, and all that constitutes the physical beauty on our planet, including of course the plant and animal kingdoms. We have also expanded this fifth-dimensional healing and send it out to our friends and family and any and all circumstances or situations that need healing. These may be of a personal nature (relationship or career issue) or of a physical nature (health issue) or any other situation that may exist. We also include any and all events that have transpired out in the world, including political, economical, and social and human rights issues. In addition we are honored by many other teachers, guides, and angels who have stepped forward to guide us and to help us to develop our individual gifts while giving us a much clearer picture of the big picture! Some of these guests have given a message that they wanted to be included in this book and their quotes will be identified as such.

Reawaken and remember our skills! Now that notion I had never thought about before. I, in this lifetime, am the sum total of all of my experiences, both good and perhaps not so good. In fact when you think about it since all experiences are necessary for soul growth, the experiences that are learned through many stages of trial and error are not bad experiences as long as the lesson is learned because when the lesson is finally learned that is really all that matters. The judgment shown against how something was done or thought about is so unnecessary. After all, doesn't judgment and critical thinking against who we are keep us in a stressful state? It keeps our self-esteem low, and guilt and condemnation can grow, preventing us from loving ourselves. Since we are fallible beings, it is human to experience difficulties and choices that are not in our best interest. But in the end it is really the lesson that is learned that allows us to grow complete with all of the experiences that got us to this very point. So every mistake, bad thought, as well as every good action and great thought, is incorporated into who we are. This made a lot of sense to me.

And it was during these classes that I was introduced to our class moderator, Markas. Markas was a being whom I shared a physical life with in sixteenth-century England. We sat on council together discussing the social problems of the day. Markas told me that I sat to his right and was a female in that lifetime, and to his left sat another new friend in recent years, Dr. Gwen Totterdale, PhD. Markas came to earth in 1987 as a teacher, helping the residents of Earth to understand the energies as the planet was transitioning from a three-dimensional planet into the fourth dimension and then into the fifth. During these years, Markas and Gwen had become inseparable as Dr. Totterdale became the trance channel for Markas and his group. Dr. Totterdale is highly respected for her work with dolphins, whales, and other marine mammals and has coauthored with Dr. Jessica Severn, books in the areas of teleportation, past-life regressions, and other metaphysical topics. Markas and friends have been giving seminars from 1988-2006 when sadly Dr. Totterdale passed away. Over the years people from many parts of the world and all walks of life have attended the seminars to help ease their transition and learn how to work with the new energies that will comprise our new world.

The classes that I was taking were taught by Theresa, who offered the Markas information transcribed and broken down for learning and discussion. Oftentimes, Markas attended the lecture in the nonphysical sense, and after the physical lecture was done by Theresa, he came speaking through her, offering information to answer questions on the subject matter of the lecture, and then perhaps a personal question or recommendation was offered to each class participant. It was during a class such as this that I was invited to attend the Markas lectures teleconferenced by Dr. Gwen Totterdale.

This invitation was truly exciting as well as very frightening! My view was that "I was just a novice" invited to sit for hours of lecture followed by a question and answer period. The whole process could be three to four hours, with usually six to eight participants. The exciting part was being able to participate firsthand and speak directly to Markas, and I was honored to be invited. The frightening part was being asked to participate with individuals who were well-versed in the information, some of whom had been participating for years and were used to the Socratic method of teaching which was oftentimes used by Markas.

Did I surprise myself! Not only was I able to disseminate the information and understood the concepts and then be able to adapt and translate them in terms of my own life, I was the recipient of such love. Participating was not like high school or college where you needed to "know" the answer. I found fun in the not-knowing! The knowing was drawn out of you by the most loving of questions asked by Markas. Gently and respectfully he helped you get to where you needed to be—until the information made sense to you or you related to his examples—all the while feeling loved and respected. Even the lighthearted prodding helped you to be introspective while thinking things through. If it didn't work from this angle, you were encouraged to approach it from another angle. I was lifted to new heights, and I found my journey to healing was greatly enhanced through this very gentle way of learning how to self-love.

There were even occasions that Markas was available for one on one sessions. I was invited to take one such session, and it was through this means that I learned that I was to put the Markas information down in book format to help people on their journey as they move from the lower dimensions—the first, second, and third through the fourth dimension—and into the fifth. This was on my blueprint—this was what my soul had signed on to do during my latter years to present the information to Planet Earth to help the universe. My head reeled with not only excitement but trepidation as I remembered how I felt when I went to that little bookstore only to learn how much I didn't know. Again naively I assumed that I needed to approach this from a place of expertise—having to know everything before I could write. It was explained to me that the writing would help me to heal and bring me to a joyful place, relaxing me as I journey on my path toward completion, helping me to reach my inner space, all the while ascending the spiral! Wow! There were many, many one-on-one sessions giving me an opportunity to ask questions on the information that was presented over the years and also an opportunity for the other side to update their information so that it could have the largest impact on our world as we know it today.

And so the following chapters are the channeled teachings of Markas and his group. I inquired about the group and was told that there are many such groups that exist on the other side to help the transitioning of the planet and that the Markas group consists of three very powerful energies. The group can expand to however large it needs to be depending on the subject matter taught and which expert/experts or teacher/teachers need to come in to give added information. Primarily, the group of three that are giving the majority of this information are Markas, whose most recent embodiment was a lifetime as a doctor who was a true friend and colleague of Edgar Cayce; Lancelot—yes, the energy of the famous Lancelot of England and of the Arthurian years; and the third is the cosmic influence of a very great and powerful energy, Orion. Orion is the star energy, the heavenly hunter. These three energies constitute the smallest group.

During the last several years, many other beings have stepped forward to offer their knowledge, their love, their hope and desire to help Planet Earth in the most loving visitations. Some of these energies have appeared and indicated they were stepping into my auric field to help me through difficult passages. Others are simply there to hold my hand through the entire process. Some have had past lives on earth and usually present themselves to me in the lifetime that they want me to associate them with. I will identify these beings as we proceed through the book, as the information that they wanted me to have oftentimes pertained to subject matter in certain chapters in the book. I am not only amazed but honored that so much loving support from the other side has come to me to help me gather this information to present to you. The quotes at the beginning of some of the chapter headings are just such an example as they have been given directly by spirit to me to give to you!

The Markas information presented to you in this book has not been greatly altered; rather, the information as originally presented has been kept as close to the original as possible. If words were changed it was to summarize or consolidate a thought package—not to dilute it but just to simplify it. The main ideas and examples have been preserved as they are not only enlightening, but the words are a beautiful example of Markas's personality: charming, intelligent, and extremely loving! My instructions were to keep it simple and to keep it light that the message and the directives that are included as they are digested will simply bring each reader's energy to a higher vibrational level. This is their gift to you, the reader.

The first part of each chapter is the summarized information from a Markas seminar while the second part of each chapter is an expression of my experiences, my thoughts, and my learning exercises as I continue my story of growth and development. It is recommended that a chapter be read, digested, processed, and perhaps even a little work done before moving on to the next. The terminology and the basic thoughts are repeated continually through the chapters—but take on enhanced meanings as they are presented in the context of each chapter's topic. I have written my story from my place of comfort and my belief system, and although this book is not a religious book, I do use the word "God" as our creator to represent the universal energy source or the universal creative source of our planet. My choice of words and expressions come from my place of comfort, and I suggest to the reader that you substitute your belief system, including using the vocabulary that you are comfortable with, as you see fit.

As the book unfolds, my wish for the reader is that he or she is able to create a new future. A future that by what you think, feel, and act brings you to that place in your heart that you come to meet the best of who you are honoring your higher self. That your day-to-day life consists of following your heart as it helps to balance who you are in this world and that by reviewing and studying your decisions, your experiences, and your choices, you become aware of the lessons, are able to acknowledge them and be grateful and thankful that you continue to live a life evolving and growing. This will allow you to live a beautiful life where in every situation you are able to go from good, to better, to best, and perhaps even beyond. It is a wonderful feeling to know that as you expand your awareness, your energy expands and you no longer are your limitations. Your day-to-day life then consists of making choices that create a win-win situation for you and everyone and everything you touch. What a beautiful world for everyone to live in because as we heal ourselves, we heal the world, and that world is a world filled with *Limitless Possibilities!*

So I invite you to come along with an open mind and an open heart and meet Markas and hear what he and his friends have to say!

Message from God

Channeled by Allaesia,

July 6, 2009

You have come as ME, your ONENESS with ME is held in these pages.

For those who wish to absorb ME more fully into their being, you have succeeded and so have the ones who come to ME.

This is your success for your readers shall feel ME and know ME and therefore become ME as they find themselves in these pages.

You are all blessed in MY presence, for it is your love for ME that is all that I need.

Your love for ME is all that I need.

Everyone's success is finding themselves more fully in MY love.

And remember you are attuned to ALL THAT I AM. You are ALL THAT I AM.

MY power is your power, MY love is our love, and MY life is your life.

—God

CHAPTER I

Angelic Influences

I have sent you nothing but angels!

—God

*I need a sign to let me know you're here . . .
I need a hand to help build up some kind of hope inside of me
And I'm calling all angels
I'm calling all you angels*

—Train
Columbia Records

Just as the hit pop song by the band Train states, we can in fact call on the angels! In fact, when you need immediate assistance or when you need to be shown that everything is going to be all right even if you have been jarred a bit, you can and should call on the angels for guidance. These beings will deliver assistance to you and fill you with a feeling of purity and love. While we so often call these beautiful beings angels, for our purposes, we prefer to refer to them as the "angelic realm" or "angelic influences." The angelic realm responds to your request for assistance by sending the most appropriate being to serve you in your time of need. That being temporarily comes into your auric field and steps into this surrounding table of enforcement to help you. So even though sometimes you have felt as if you are quite alone on the planet, you are really not because you do have this special enforcement that is coming up to the forefront whenever your needs require or you desire it.

Let's begin by talking about the angelic realm. This has been identified not just in the traditional Christian teachings but in numerous religions. The various religious traditions refer to the angelic realm by different names, but there are many commonalities in the teachings of the angelic realm. For example, it is often described as consisting of nine or seven categories or thrones, including the seraphim, cherubim, archangels, and principalities. There is also one category that is called a dominion, and there is also a group that we are all familiar with, known simply as angels. What has happened in the past is that religions, whether Christian or Hindu, have tried to formally define these angelic categories. However, this struggle for definition of the angelic realm is in vain as it is not for us to have a perfect understanding of how the angelic realm works—not on the physical plane anyway!

The reason for that is that focusing on defining the angelic realm takes away from the mystery of having a being come to you for assistance during a time of need. When we struggle trying to figure out if this being is coming from the top category or the fifth category or the ninth category, then you are not really getting into the miracle of the whole thing and allowing the mystery of it to raise your vibrational frequency. Another reason why it is important not to get caught up in the definition of the various categories of the angelic realm is that when you are in the physical form you are not able to see the bigger picture. Finally, we as humans tend to fall into competition as this paradigm is often engrained in us as small children through our endeavors in sports or school. This competition has no place in the angelic realm, and so again, the hierarchy of the angelic realm is immaterial. Again, what matters is that the most important being, the one that is most prepared to assist you, is coming to you, and that never fails!

And so it is not important if someone says, "I have a guide and the guide goes by the name of Michael. Is Michael an archangel, is Michael part of the dominion or part of the principality—and what role does he play?" It is more important to understand that Michael is the being that looks out and over this issue of righteousness on the planet. If you have a guide that goes by the name of Speakeasy, it doesn't matter if this being is more highly evolved or less highly evolved than Michael. It only matters that they have gained experience in the area where you need assistance. So that is why we do not talk about levels except to say what dimension of consciousness individuals have gone into. We really do not talk about levels when we are talking about your guides and teachers because that is not what is important; it is their expertise which is important.

You may be familiar with the concept of seven archangels and with the four that are most commonly known. The four most common archangels are: Michael,

Raphael, Gabriel, and Uriel. Michael is known for righteousness. Michael is also responsible for protection against evil, and often Michael is known as the overseer for the other archangels. Therefore, as you can imagine with all of the recent terrorist attacks and planned attacks, he certainly has had his hands or his wings full of dealing with all of that! Michael is the only archangel that can create a miracle in the physical realm. Rafael is the overseer or the CEO of what are called the guardian angels, or what we call your sunshine guides. The guardian angel is a being that watches over your physical wellbeing. So Rafael then is the overseer for that being, and less commonly known, she also deals with travel and can be called on for protection during trips. Gabriel is the messenger angel, the angel that made the announcement for the birth of Christ. This archangel is the messenger although technically angels can be translated into messengers so all angels fit that category. So you might want to distinguish Gabriel as the messenger for good news. Gabriel also deals with justice and making sure that things are justly evaluated and accounted for, as well as with helping individuals to gain mercy for difficult times in their lives. Finally, Uriel means God's light, or god is light, as he was prophetic and a seer and would come to people if a warning needed to be given. In fact, he is credited with warning Noah of the floods. Uriel also brings knowledge about god and god's intentions about man and he is indeed the god's light. Interestingly, Uriel is known to often manifest as an eagle. The very fact that the American national symbol is the eagle is very telling of Uriel's connection to the United States of America. Among the four archangels, the energy must be balanced, so Michael and Uriel are the masculine energies while Rafael and Gabriel are the feminine energies. (This is not to be confused with gender!)

In addition to these four well-known archangels, there are also three others: Jophiel, Chamuel, and Zadkiel. The reason why the others are not as well known is that they spend most of their time in devotion to God. It is difficult for us to imagine this, but these archangels spend their time in constant singing or constant praising of God. To understand why these archangels choose to spend their time doing this, it may be helpful to imagine someone going to college and learning what the school's fight song is. Every time that they hear that song, it creates a positive emotional response and therefore raises their vibration. Similarly, for the archangels, praising God raises their vibration in alignment with those that are in the most purified vibrational state, God being the ultimate. Therefore these three archangels do not do as much in connection with man or with life on any of the planets. They are more connected to the evolvement of their energy so they are aligned with God, and giving back to God the thanks for being alive and for being able to feel these euphoric feelings. Unfortunately we have been taught by many religious institutions that to sing and to praise God all of the time as if God is an angry being or that you need to do it because you are afraid of God or that God is in some way a jealous God and/or is going to punish you. This simply isn't true. You do it because it feels good to you and it is a euphoric feeling and everyone around you benefits, just as the archangels do.

Just imagine all of these beings are throughout the universe, with some of them acting as guides and teachers personally for you! You are connected to these guides not just from this lifetime but from other lifetimes as well. In fact, you have lifetimes where you have built relationships with some of these angels. So you can expect that if you have built a relationship with Michael in the past, Michael is going to come in and serve at least one role for you in this lifetime. If you have had a past lifetime with Speakeasy in which Speakeasy served as a guide for you, it is very likely that Speakeasy would again want to serve as a guide for you because there is so much love between you two. If you have a past life with one of these beings where they were on the planet the same time you were on the planet—you were brother/sister or husband/son or any combination or two close friends—then it is not unusual to expect that they would then come and serve you in the capacity of guide or teacher. Therefore there are some angels that you are closer to than others, just as with your guides.

It is also true that a being can serve as a guide for more than one individual. As a matter of fact, they can serve as a guide for an infinite number of beings. Upon hearing this, you might think that perhaps if they are distracted with others, then they really do not have time for you. However, if you are thinking this way, you are making a mistake of putting our concept of physical time and physical restraints onto nonphysical beings. Time is absolutely not an issue, it is the event or issue that you are in need of help or guidance for that is central, and the appropriate guide will appear to you. If the being is needed elsewhere for another event, that is where the being goes, and it does focus on the event and not the time of the event. So you might think that your event is really happening on Friday, November 5 at noon, but that is because you are on a time-space continuum. In the nonphysical realm it has nothing to do with time, so it might be happening for you on Friday, November 5, but it is not happening at that moment for the being that is assisting you. Remember, this being can assist everyone that is under its wing, so to speak, to protect you and to make you feel pure and to feel secure and to feel loved.

You may be wondering if there are both male and female guides. The answer is yes, absolutely! Are there male and female angels? Absolutely! There are more angels than you can even imagine! Historical and religious texts talk about legends or armies of angels. That is the same thing as saying host of angels which could contain five or ten thousand or twenty-five thousand. Imagine all of those souls and yet everyone feels important. No one feels that they are lost in the sheer volume of angels as they are free from the ego that we are so often enslaved to. Everyone has their task and everyone lives their life to the fullest. All of them feel very lucky and very favored to be in the angelic realm. And that is in part why they are angels—because they have let go of those experiences of competition, of greed, of guilt, of jealousy, of envy; they have let go of all of those things and have healed from them. And so they are ready to move into a position in which they say, "Well, we win as a team or we lose as a team."

In the Hollywood blockbuster movie *Michael*, John Travolta played the archangel Michael, albeit an untraditional take on the archangel. In the film, Michael is asked if there are angels who waste the gifts that they have been given. In response, Michael became very serious and said, "I don't like to say anything negative about the other angels. I don't like to speak ill of them." Why would he say this? Again, because the angels win as a team, they lose as a team. However, the film was not correct in stating that angels have only so many gifts, so many favors, or so many miracles that they can deliver. That is simply not true. The ability to hold the energy of a miracle is what is important, and if you have a purified energy field then you are able to hold those miracles and be able to give them without looking at a finite number. It truly is an infinite experience!

While there is a plethora of angels, when you encounter them, you usually encounter them one by one. There are a lot of souls living on our planet right now, and a lot of them are in dire need of an angel coming to assist them, as most of us have been at one point or another in our life. That is why about 90 percent of the beings that come from the different realms—physical, emotional, spiritual, mental, and fifth-dimensional—are angels. Some of them are entry-level angels, so a lot of guides that you would have would be single-attribute guides or they could be a lifetime processing assistant. Those types of beings are probably entry level. If you have one who is a teacher, then again you are getting greater complexity. If you have one who is a fifth-dimensional healer that is a greater complexity. But about 90 percent of the guides—and you know that you have normally between eighty to ninety or ninety-five guides—about 90 percent of those are angels. Who are the others? The others are beings that you might have had another lifetime with that are not exactly an angel but have had a very strong connection with you. It might be a relative of yours from this lifetime; now that relative could be an angel, but it doesn't have to be. The way that you can tell is to look at the different names of your guides and teachers, and ones that serve more than one function for you most definitely would be an angel.

There are very few exceptions to that. And the ones that don't serve more than one function for you and perhaps a function for somebody that you know, but that is about it—it is likely that that being is not considered yet to be an angel or hasn't yet earned his or her wings. These beings are most likely working toward that and assisting you is helping them accelerate their vibrational frequency.

If you have had the pleasure of seeing the film *Michael*, you may have noticed that there are several truths about angels that are revealed. One such example is the way that Michael dances throughout the film, showing how joyous angels are and how people are attracted to that joy! The character found love and happiness wherever he went, and he tried to teach that to others, in spite of how grumpy or bitter they were. Another example of a truth about angels that is shown through this film is their appreciation for the physical life—whether it was sugar or a big ball of string. Michael found magic in everything on the physical plane. Physicality was not a hardship for him, unlike as we often view it. In fact, he enjoyed it very much, and that is why he wanted to come back to experience that physicality "just one more time." The joy that this character expressed was similar to that expressed by the Dalai Lama—the true joy that emanates from the soul with a pure laughter. Finally, the film showed that angels can come in any form, not necessarily the cherubic vision that we so often associate with them.

Just as it is shown in the film *Michael*, the truth is that being around angels is supposed to be fun. It is supposed to be enjoyable. It is supposed to be a highlight of your life! So if you have a dream and there is an angel in it, that should be something very special for you. If you are meditating and you see the vision of an angel come into your meditation, this again should be a highlight for you and it should be very special. Remember, even if an angel only materializes for a short while, it will stay on earth until his job is done. When you have an angel encounter it is always done with your best interest in mind. It is sorry to say that on this planet not all encounters are done with that intention. It seems that most often the encounter is when someone has a complaint, or a concern, or wants something done his/her way and not in the best interest for you. Fortunately, this is not true of the angels.

An angel doesn't have to physically manifest in order for you to have an angel encounter, it can come to you in a dream or in a meditative state. You will feel the purity and then will feel purified. You feel assisted in whatever way that you have questions or concerns—that is when you know that you have been "touched by an angel." They have their expertise in a certain area and then that is what they focus on. This actually is making a very good claim for the benefits of meditation! You can have a steady conversation with a being when they come in. They can come in groups of about ten or twelve, which serves to indicate just how important meditation is and how certain types of rewards come from that practice.

Our angels also communicate by playing music for us. Certain angels that represent certain duties may play the same song over and over when we are working in that area. Eventually we begin to associate the song with the guide or angel that is sending it to us. When you think about how music lifts us up, and then that our angel has sent it to us, how truly uplifting that is! We have previously mentioned the legends of angels that simply sing in honor or glory to God and how it benefits them. So if you are hearing those songs on an expanded scale, that means so much to you in such a glorious voice. Can you imagine that? When all of them are singing, we can only imagine how uplifting and euphoric it is. So for all of you that are touched by music, and that would be practically everyone, you have that to look forward to. Again it gives you a euphoric feeling beyond that which anyone can describe.

Now that you know that 90 percent—or for some people it might even be close to 100 percent—of your guides are from the angelic realm, it is important to understand why research was done to identify them individually: so that we can understand what they come to assist us in. In other words, a single attribute guide might come for prosperity, or perhaps for general issues about health. If you have a very difficult or very complex health issue, then you can imagine in one form or another Raphael is involved in this and perhaps also Michael, depending upon how that difficulty is encountered by you. You can also look at some of the other beings such as lead messengers. Messenger is another word for angel, and you have lead messengers that come from other realms of consciousness, such as mental realms or spiritual realms or emotional realms, and they deliver knowledge or information to you. There are beings called eternal suns who are messengers, delivering information to or from the birthright angel group. It is beautiful to imagine your guides fluttering about and how wonderful that the more evolved you become, the greater the number are surrounding you because you have more issues and more development that you want to do. You have made it very clear that spiritual evolvement is very important to you, so you attract those beings that can assist you with the myriad ideas and issues that you are involved in.

So again angelic influences should always be viewed as beings sent to assist you in times of need. Sometimes these beings will give you messages in dreams, and if you do not "get it" the first time, they will give you a dream that is a bit more intense, and the third time they will give you a dream that it is even more intense. As Oprah often states, the universe knocks once, and if you don't listen, it knocks louder until you finally answer. The same is true of the angelic influences. And the reason that they do this is to get you to feel that something is going on that you need to attend to. Once either the danger or the opportunity is over and it has been handled, then things will go back to normal. So you should never be afraid of getting a dream that you wonder about whether it is good news or bad news because it didn't feel like it was very good. It is helpful news for you and should be taken as such.

So you should always give thanks for this gift of assistance, which raises the question of whom you should give thanks to. Should you give thanks to the angels? Or do you give thanks to God? Or do you give thanks to the Christ energy? And the answer is that you give thanks to all of them. Because all of them in one form or another are assisting you, so of course you want to give thanks to all of them. And again there is never an issue of jealousy or idolatry that comes from praising and thanking the angels to the exclusion of God or the Christ energy. Remember, you win as a team and you lose as a team. Just by giving thanks you raise your vibrational frequency, and just by giving thanks the wings of the angels fold around you even more tightly and even more securely. This gratitude means that you are closer in knowledge and intention to the angels; you can truly become one with the energies by thanking them. This thankful spirit means that you acknowledge the level of help that you are receiving and how in fact it encourages you to go forward and to handle things where before you might not have handled it if you felt all alone. You no longer feel all alone because you have these angels assisting you. Of course you make the final decision of whether to follow their guidance or not. After all, we all still have free will. However, when you can trust in the righteousness and the intention of the loving beings that have come to assist you, it is so much easier to move forward in the direction they have shown you.

You may be wondering if we, as human beings, can evolve into the sphere where the angels are as we know that they move both within their sphere and our physical sphere. Unfortunately, and as you may have guessed, we have to make a very big leap in order to go into the angelic realm. If you do in fact make it to the angelic sphere, you will transition as a beginning angel, doing very simple things in helping those that are in the physical realm, or even in assisting other angels. As they help other beings, these beginning angels gain a deeper understanding of how things work. They will continue their own development and will turn more and more to God for their own evolution. These angels may want to decide to continue to help beings on the physical realm, or choose to turn their attention to God and study and train with that purified energy. We can think of this as being similar to a PhD program, only you are never going to get thrown out! Using that analogy, if someone is in the angelic realm, it means that they are in the PhD program and that once they graduate they can be a professor; once they reach that level of professor, they may only want to do research while other professors may want to come and help the students (which would mean going back to the physical realm). And it can go either way—they have the choice. So those that have been in the beginning stages of being an angel are being helped by those who have been there a lot longer because that is one of their functions. They will evolve only based upon how they are helping people in the physical realm and what they are doing also for their own development.

The three archangels that we mentioned earlier that you don't hear much about are an example of the angels that have turned their focus to God. The four that we have talked about in more detail—Michael, Rafael, Uriel, and Gabriel—have turned their focus back to the physical realm, which is why you hear more about them. However, sometimes a being that doesn't want to be assisting those in the physical realm will nevertheless sign on as perhaps a teacher to someone in the physical realm. What happens in this situation is that you never hear from them directly, but they will give information to one of the other angels that is in your sphere. That angel will then deliver the information to you. So you may have one who is very high up and wants to turn their attention to God, and yet they have information that would be information for you so they sign on as one of your beings, but you never interact with them directly.

One of the things that people often do not realize is that when you are physical and someone that you love passes over into the nonphysical realm, they have an opportunity to go to a physical place and assume a physical body for just a few moments. Thanks to the healing that is performed by their guides, they get to feel that physicality again, and they feel exceedingly good because they are healed. So sometimes when you hear that someone has materialized on the planet even though they have passed over—for example Jesus walking with this friends after his death—that is what they are doing. They do not want to frighten you but want to experience remembering what it is like to feel good in a body that is functioning.

As we all know, our human experience consists of many experiences that are sad, and events that we oftentimes can do nothing about. When our parents age, and their health deteriorates, their time on earth is simply in God's hands. We cannot, nor can our health professionals, predict with great accuracy when someone is ready to leave the earth. And it is because it is not simply a physical malady that is the determining factor. When someone has fear and is not able to grasp the light and simply release and transition to the other side, it is because that fear holds them back. Their spiritual body of consciousness hasn't been developed enough to help integrate the whole person and help the soul move over to the other side. But for family members and loved ones, watching the struggle of the dying holding on for their dear life is terribly sad. When we participate in this kind of struggle, we are simply living "life 101," and there is nothing that we can do about it. So the more that you can work to perfect your life so that it feels good to you and for you, the more healing this is for those around you. Actually, again as you heal yourself, you are beginning to heal those around you as well. And in the case of an elderly dying parent, he may not get any physical healing from you, but he can get a psychological healing. Perhaps he will not be conscious of the psychological healing, but you can provide one that will allow him to release and move forward to his resting place on the other side.

Furthermore, the more that you redirect your energy back to yourself and help maintain that level of balance within yourself, the more you can help the surviving spouse or siblings deal with the stress of the situation. Remember you really must help yourself to heal and also open up to receive help from others. Let those friends of yours that love you come in and assist you in times of strife, and receive this new energy into your being. Allow it to be the additional nurturing spark to help you keep from letting your energy be drained from you. Remember there is no time here for self-pity—you are just dealing with what almost every child in one form or another must go through. And if it isn't this scenario, then it is the opposite situation where the loved one is taken suddenly, taken before what you would like to say is said. This creates the feeling of no closure or completion. Which of these scenarios is better? Neither one. They are both sad and are the conditions of the human experience. Unfortunately, this is how the transition is designed on our planet until all of us learn how to ascend. And as Markas says, "We don't see that happening, at least not in the near future." While losing loved ones is inevitable, there are things that can be done to help assist in these difficult situations. One such technique is used to send positive energy remotely. For example, a Reiki master can send healing energy long-distance that will help with the overall situation and the ease of transition. Hopefully then the timing will be one where the suffering on earth ceases and the soul can transition sooner rather than later.

We are often presented with difficult situations, and it can be challenging to find the purpose of such events. For example, what could the purpose be for suffering a heart attack? Well, one possible purpose is that the heart attack could serve as a warning. Perhaps it is a warning that the individual takes on a lot of stress and needed to see where his life was taking him. What is the personality of an individual that would take on such levels of stress? He is a pleaser. He tries to please his family, his friends, and his boss in order to attempt to make everyone happy. This warning is to make himself the center of his reality. Initially he might view that as being selfish. However, this is the most selfless thing he can do because he needs to be on the planet for his own development and not the development of others. He must remember not to take on other people's energy; it is not good for him and it is not good for the other person.

Remember, you are never alone. You are always surrounded by angels, beings that long to assist you in your times of need. With that knowledge, we can all walk in peace and confidence to heal ourselves, each other, and the world that we live in.

* * * * * * * *

As mentioned in the introduction, I began my spiritual development shortly after we entered into the twenty-first century. I was introduced to angels when I received a very popular angel book which piqued my interest. I was hooked after reading this first book and voraciously read many, many books on angels. I could not digest the books fast enough. I wanted to learn how to communicate with an angel, how to ask for specific help, how to send help via angels to others, and how to be the recipient of unconditional love—simply by asking! I desired to have angelic beings in my life but was mystified as to how to contact them. Such was my introduction. I dove in, fully expecting to not only meet angels along the way but to receive their love. As Markas says again and again, some things may be "unseen but certainly not unfelt." Angels fit into this category!

Each one of us has a relationship with the angelic realm, and it begins when our soul is anticipating a lifetime on earth. This little soul, before it enters the physical realm, has a spiritual family that consists of many, many angels. When we decide with our guides and higher self that we are going to incarnate to experience a lifetime on earth, generally two angels are assigned to the soul before and at conception. Both of these angels stay with the baby during the nine months of development while in the womb. During birth one of the angels remains with the baby on the physical plane and becomes what is known as the guardian angel or the sunshine guide and acts as the baby's guardian through his or her entire lifetime. The other angel separates and remains on the other side in or with the soul's spiritual family. This angel is with the soul's higher self, and the baby will always have access to this angel through the higher self.

It has been described to me that the wail of the baby upon entering this world is the pain being caused by the separation from his spiritual mother as well as the many angels in his spiritual family. Many times it is at this point that the baby simply decides that the spiritual separation is too painful and wishes to remain with his spiritual family and chooses not to enter the physical plane. The baby's heart just doesn't take hold as it is too difficult for it and wants no part of the separation from this spiritual family. There exists a consciousness at birth, and the babies are aware that they are going into a place with limitations. There is of course the more familiar explanation of the wail of a baby as he or she travels through the warmth of the birth canal and enters an environment that is its opposite: a cold, sterile operating/delivery room. These explanations are both feasible as each relates to the baby and its soul in both the nonphysical plane leaving its spiritual family as well as its introduction to the physical plane. After birth the baby's soul energy has the ability to move back and forth between realms and is continually protected and loved by not only the primary angel but many others as they begin to enter into his or her life. The baby ultimately continues to receive the love and guidance of his or her angels as they begin to fill the circle of twelve that immediately surrounds him.

We have all witnessed or read the many beautiful stories that describe how a baby upon awakening will open his or her eyes and look lovingly up or to the foot of the crib, cooing, and appears to focus on something or someone that elicits a beautiful smile. Who is not to say that this smile is a direct reaction of the baby upon seeing his or her guardian angel or sunshine guide, feeling the warmth and unconditional love being showered upon him or her? This scene is proof that these pure little souls newly arrived on Planet Earth are always protected and surrounded by love and the light of God as they begin their journey with their loving angels in attendance.

We know that small babies and toddlers can continue their connection with and in the angelic realms for many years. They may not choose to break this loving connection. Oftentimes you can hear a little one, unaware of a listening adult, carry conversations on for hours in a language that no one seems to recognize. One explanation for this is that little ones can spend much of their day on the other side if they choose to and will play and chat with other souls that they played with and chatted with while residing with them on the other side. The little children from the other side may also come down and spend time on the earth realm. At some point this connection is typically broken as the earthbound child learns to spend the majority of his time grounded on earth interacting with his physical family. He still may leave (astral travel) but may limit those times to nap times and nighttime while he is sleeping.

Sometimes small children do not talk or communicate with their mom and dad and other siblings. You may hear that a child may seem to be off in his or her "own world." What really is going on is that the child still feels more connected and comfortable with his play friends on the other side and actually is in his "own world," which may be the other world! He doesn't feel the need to communicate here as all of his needs are being met and he is communicating with his invisible friend or friends—who may be guides or angels from the other side that have become a playmate for the child. Many older children may recall having had similar experiences growing up. Many of the details may seem fuzzy and perhaps are not remembered in great detail, but for the one remembering as well as each of us, it is simply wonderful to note that our angels and guides are influencing our lives on earth by helping us feel comforted and loved as well as protected during our early days on earth. This guidance continues on during all of the growth stages that we experience on this physical plane until we die and journey back home.

Identifying angelic energy may happen in a number of ways. As we tell each other heart-filled stories, the comment is often made, "Oh, I feel goose bumps." This is simply your body reacting in a positive way by feeling compassion or love. Your angels love to validate you when your heart is touched, and so a physical reaction is manifested. You may also feel a cool breeze over your arms or neck. I have also felt a lock of hair being brushed off my forehead and simply moved aside ever so gently. Sometimes you can experience the feeling of warmth over part of your body or your entire body. Sometimes the heat is intense and you are very aware that the being that is visiting you is a huge energy and is able to generate this heat within you! For the naysayers out there: no, this is not a hot flash! Looking back, see if you can identify an experience, a feeling, or a touch that you could not define at the time but was special and has left a lasting effect. Deep down you really do know that you were touched by an angel, and so it is fun to revisit that feeling and to keep it alive. If you don't remember such an experience perhaps awareness or keeping an open mind and open heart was lacking and so the experience was missed.

Angels assist us in many ways in our day-to-day world. All we have to do is ask. One day I was shopping in the shoe department of a popular department store. The shoe salesman was assisting me and had brought me several pairs of shoes to try. Another customer was talking loudly, interrupting my conversation with my salesman, and in short was creating a scene. Embarrassed I looked away. That provided a perfect opportunity for the irate customer to snatch my wallet out of my purse. She exited in a hurry, and as things returned to normal, with my salesman apologizing for the scene I had just witnessed, something did not sit well with me. Turning around I noticed my purse was open and my wallet gone. As the department store security came to take down my specific information, I was told to wait for the local city's police, who were already in the mall at another department store where the same theft had occurred earlier.

While waiting I immediately thought to call on my angels. I was traveling in two days and wanted to get home to call my credit card companies to report the theft and to get new ones before I left. Interestingly, I had removed my driver's license from my wallet and had put it in a zipped compartment in my purse. I don't know why I had done that, but I was grateful that I had as without my photo identification card I would not have been able to board the airplane. (In retrospect, my angels were already anticipating this event and my immediate needs and were protecting me from any further inconvenience!) I asked my angels to please retrieve my wallet and to make sure that it was kept safe for me.

The police came, reports were filed, and I went home to make the calls to report the credit card theft. I did take my trip and returned several days later. My son called me from his office to tell me that he had just received a call from the day manager of a national bookstore. This store was located in an adjacent shopping center to the mall where my wallet had been stolen. The manager explained that she was calling him as his business card was prominent in a wallet she had discovered in the store's safe. She further explained that she was calling him as she was not able to find my contact information anywhere in the wallet. She said that she opened the store "safe" and had found my wallet inside. She further explained that she had called the night manager to find out how and why and when this wallet was placed in the safe. The night manager replied that she knew nothing about a wallet, much less how the wallet had gotten into the safe—it simply was there and she thought the day manager had placed it there! I made arrangements with her to retrieve the wallet, and upon her handing it to me, she looked me right in the eye and said, "The weird thing here is that only the night manager and I have the combination for the safe, and neither of us put the wallet in there, nor do we know how the wallet could have gotten in there." I thanked her with the words, "Someone surely was looking out for me!" Well, this may remain a mystery for her, but for me I knew that I had asked my angels to keep the wallet safe for me, and what better place than to have it be safely stored for me in the safest possible place than the bookstore's safe! So with humor my angels had taken their charge literally. We are told to ask and you shall receive. I asked and I certainly did receive!

One really important guide each of us should connect with is our complenary guide. This guide is the one who helps to oversee all of our other guides. The word "complenary" is a combination of the word "complete," meaning whole or entire, and "plenary," meaning fully constitute, attended by qualified members, and absolute. We can connect with our guides in many ways, and one way is to ask him or her to make himself known to you in an unusual way. You could ask the question, "As my overseer, what suggestions can you give me at this time to improve the quality of my life?" And then look for the answer. The answer may come in a magazine article, or in dream sleep, or a book may just find its way to you with the answer clearly inside. A relationship with this guide ultimately leads you to every other guide, angel, or teacher you have. So if you develop a relationship with him, you may simply ask your complenary guide to bring in the appropriate guide for whatever issue you are dealing with in your life: health, career, location, or the emotional guides that help with romance, family, children, and sibling issues. The important thing to remember is that you must invite these angelic influences into your life so that they may take an active role in it.

I always work with the angelic realm when I am out traveling in my day-to-day world, running from appointment to appointment. If I am late or it is raining and I need to get a close parking place, I ask the angels for assistance with saving a parking place for me. I cannot tell you the number of times I have come into an area with limited parking, and as I am getting closer and closer to my destination, I see a car just a couple of parking spots in front of me leaving so that I am able to take that spot.

In addition I frequently travel and must navigate from an entrance ramp across four lanes of traffic to get on the highway in a distance of less than a hundred yards. Sometimes the oncoming traffic will not allow you to enter as they are exiting, so crossing across the lanes to get to the highway lane is very difficult. During rush hours it can be very congested and of course everyone is concerned only about their own journey and not about helping anyone else. So I began to work with my angels to help me and now it is standard operating procedure for me! I always announce to the transportation angels that I will be approaching this entrance soon and to please allow a space for me to enter and move across the heavily trafficked lanes. With rare exceptions as I approach, I literally can see the lanes parting and cars exiting creating an opening space for me to safely cross the four lanes of traffic. I have done this for over ten years now, and I am forever thankful and grateful to my angels for their assistance, and I definitely make sure that they know how much I appreciate them. I could go on and on with similar stories as I know you will be able to. Lastly it is important to know that every time we show our thanks, we actually assist the angels with more grace from above. I am forever thankful and grateful to them for their help, and I am happy that the angelic influences may receive extra rewards for helping me live a life of ease.

When my elderly parents were approaching their last days on earth, I had a beautiful angelic experience. From the time I was a little girl, my mother always made me promise that I would bury her in the most perfect dress—a simple but elegant dark brown dress. I promised and promised and promised. She really wasn't being morose—she just wanted me to pick out the perfect dress in her favorite color. Years passed and that day was approaching. I realized that I had made this promise and now I needed to find this dress. I called every major department store chain in the United States looking for this perfect dress.

One evening, returning home from the hospital, I felt compelled to stop at a local woman's shop not far from my home. Entering I explained to the lady who greeted me what I was looking for. Shaking her head no, she said that they did not have such a dress and wished me well. I left and only got about twenty-five yards when something told me to go back into the store. This time upon entering the owner of the store approached me. I repeated my request, saying that I had been there just a few minutes earlier but was nudged to return and inquire again. Within seconds a broad smile appeared on the owner's face. She asked me to wait and came back seconds later with a beautiful dark brown (my mother's favorite shade of dark chocolate) dress—simple and elegant. The owner told me that the dress had arrived that very day but that she had not ordered it. It had simply appeared and she was going to send it back. I explained to her that it was fairly obvious to me that it was ordered, but not by her nor me, that my angels were my personal shoppers to help me find the perfect dress for my mother so that her wishes and my promises were both honored! Together we laughed and compared goose bumps as I left with the dress that truly was exactly what my mother would have purchased if she had been doing the buying. My angels had saved the day, which allowed me to spend my remaining few days with my mother giving myself the time to adjust to what was fast approaching.

Have you ever wondered what the term "elation" means? It is that feeling in your body through the crown of your head to your heart that is validation that a request made to your angels has been heard and answered. You literally can feel the light rays of the angels coming down into your body and expanding your heart. It doesn't matter whether the light rays are coming to you during the daytime hours or during the dark of night as the angelic light never ceases. It is a beautiful feeling and one that you will never forget. You may also be moved to tears when you experience this feeling—these tears are the ultimate tears of happiness! May you begin to recognize this validation in your life and practice receiving it over and over and over again!

I wish you well in connecting with your guides and inviting them into your life. Thinking back, you will remember an event or assistance that miraculously appeared, helping you out it a small way or perhaps a major way. Ask to remember and you will receive just such a recollection, perhaps in your dream sleep, or it may pop into your consciousness when you are relaxed and least expect it. This is your connection with your angels or angelic influences. Keeping it alive and encouraging active participation between you and your circle of twelve will bring such beauty and ease into your life. In a very short time you will notice how much richer your life is and also notice the unique ways that these angelic influences use to get your attention, to keep you protected and comforted, and to remind you that you are always surrounded by their unconditional love and are never alone!

CHAPTER II

Many Gifts, One Spirit

*Your talent is God's gift to you.
What you do with it is your gift back to God.*

—Unknown

    We are born into our bodies as spiritual beings that have come to earth to have a physical life, to learn lessons, and to heal our emotional body of consciousness. In our current lifetimes, our planet Earth has experienced the greatest and most glorious changes since the golden age. The question is are we equipped to transition and transform ourselves into balanced and integrated individuals who are able to flow with the newest energies that have manifested on Planet Earth? Our kind and loving creator has given each one of us a gift as we have entered this lifetime. This gift is unique to each of us, and during periods of intuitive thought can be easily identified with a little soul-searching and common sense. There are nine gifts from which to choose. We are given one gift as our birthright but have the ability to learn or develop any or all of the eight remaining.

    These gifts from spirit reflect the true love bestowed on each one of us. How we choose to honor this gift is still our choice as we have been given free will. But to integrate our many bodies of consciousness, and to live to our highest and most evolved level, it would be beneficial to identify the gift and to develop it so that it becomes a natural way of life, a life that is adaptable to the many changes that occur on our planet. It has been said repeatedly that our planet is in a constant state of flux. So too must we be flexible and adaptable to handle the change.

Limitless Possibilities

You are spirit having a physical incarnation. So it would only make sense that you would bring with you some of the gifts of spirit. And so you have one that you have perfected, and you perfected it most likely through a combination of a past life plus what you have done when you have been in the nonphysical realm, meaning what you have learned between lifetimes in physical form. If the gift isn't perfected when you come to this planet, you of course need to come with a bit of guidance. That is why each of us has guides and teachers that fill in the gaps in order for this to be an "automatic process" for us.

Because we are all in human form, our lives have created some filters that prevent us from realizing our inherent spiritual gifts to their fullest. A big part of the human experience is to take a look at those filters that are either from a past life that you want to correct in this lifetime or filters from an earlier part of your life in this lifetime. And you want to heal them, to fix them, or to reverse them as they no longer serve you, but instead simply run interference on your ability to realize and practice your gifts with 100 percent accuracy. It is a very valuable practice to concentrate on and to visualize the purification of your spiritual gifts. Learn to "feel things out"; when something doesn't feel right, that is your higher self telling you that you must change something. This could mean changing your thoughts, your actions, or even the circumstances in your life.

Due to these filters, the Christian Bible is not 100 percent accurate, nor are any other religious teachings. Each contributor to the Bible was experiencing a human life, and so they did not see the entire picture, or the "bird's-eye view" that we discussed previously. That is not to say that the Bible is largely inaccurate, but there are biases that are written into the Bible because even though it was the word of God, it had to go through man and there you can meet up against some filters. Again, the more that you allow yourself to recognize and just let go of those filters, the more you become a purer avenue through which spirit is able to travel.

This is why some individuals are able to say, "I talk daily with God," or they might have an identification with God or with the Christ energy or the angels. These individuals have raised their vibrational frequency so that they are able to receive understanding from these spiritual beings. What a wonderful experience—you feel it right in the heart chakra! When you walk away from that experience, you can't prove it to anyone, you can't even really explain what the feeling actually feels like, but you know that you have had this tremendous experience. And that is really what spirit is able to do; the more that you grow and develop spiritually, the more you clear those filters. It is important to keep in mind that your intent should not necessarily be to clean or remove the filters, but rather to be as close to the god-goddess energy as you can possibly be. That is when you begin to free up those weights that are holding you down or pulling you backward and you can really travel upward on the spiritual spiral.

Those of you who have felt the pull toward spiritual things since the beginning of this lifetime have other gifts, besides the one that you were born with, that interest you. You may have felt the pull toward something, or perhaps you had a turn in your life, if you will, toward that gift. This turn is not necessarily a blueprint item in your life or something that irreparably changed your life, but something that you feel drawn to and have spent time exploring. Let's say some of you spend a lot of time on tarot. (Tarot is a divination tool that is used for spirit to bring a message). And so this is something that is a major experience in your life and something that has shifted your direction. You may have been heading in one direction, and then you got interested in tarot, so then you adjusted where you needed to go perhaps a more efficient way of getting there. The gift, while it serves others, also serves you. If we think of our lives and our spiritual quest in terms of good, better, best, and beyond, the gifts from spirit are all in the beyond category. Beyond means that the gifts are beyond the physical world, they are magical and miraculous.

There are many different spiritual gifts, which we will describe here. First are the messages or words of knowledge. Now someone who is operating at close to 100 percent in the area of knowledge has an understanding of how energy flows in and among and through the different parts of the universe. It might not be something that they have said, but it could be the understanding of it, and the understanding makes perfect sense to them. So for example, you might have someone who really has a feel for what black holes are, and if this person is a scientist and a researcher in that area, then you can expect that they would use what they call their intuition to find out how to research this and to discover more about them. This understanding is intuitive to them because of their spiritual gift of universal knowledge. They don't understand why they understand it so easily, why their hypotheses are so accurate, and so they may attribute it to an accumulation of knowledge that they have studied in this lifetime. Of course it is true that if you want to become an expert in something you keep going through the experiences and you keep reading and learning about it, but there is a difference between being an expert and being a master.

If you are a master, you have received this knowledge as a spiritual gift. It is not something that you developed in this lifetime, you just know what you know. This is true for all of the gifts. You know what you know! You can call it intuition, or a "gut feeling," but it really is a spiritual gift. You can find this type of individual in other areas outside of science and research. Individuals who are knowledgeable beyond their education, beyond their realm of expertise, individuals who can explain something in such a way that it is very simple and very easy to understand, these are all individuals who have received the gift of universal knowledge.

Now, you may be wondering, "How does this gift of knowledge benefit the beneficiary?" Well, it gives them direction and purpose for being on the planet, even if they do not use the universal knowledge in their professional life. It is what they give to others, and it is what they have come to understand inside of themselves. Their vibrational frequency accelerates whenever they are able to explain something about the universe to someone else. So it serves them because it accelerates their vibrational frequency and because it is an area of interest for them and therefore an opportunity for pure joy.

The next spiritual gift is the area of faith. Those who are gifted with faith are able to look danger in the eye and get themselves straightened out in quick order. They are able to move through problems, either their own or somebody else's, and come up with very wonderful solutions. They might be complete solutions, or only partial ones, but they are able to do it because they have faith. They know that there is a greater purpose for what is going on on our planet. They don't know exactly what that is as they are not given the bigger view of everything. Their feeling of faith is such that they know what they know and they can translate that into help for themselves and other people. They are able to be there, and they are someone who you would always want to talk to because they don't question that things happen for a reason. Except for a few filters, they don't question the fifth-dimensional idea that everything is perfect even though there is an illusion of imperfection that surrounds you.

What a wonderful gift for those that have the gift of faith! What a wonderful resource to be able to reach up into heaven (figuratively speaking, of course) in order to help others. And if there is unwavering faith, then even if someone is having a very difficult time—on the verge of bankruptcy, or they have had a very traumatic accident, or they are ill in a life-threatening way—they are able to make it through any storm. If you have the gift of faith, you know it at a very early age, which is quite fortunate as it makes traveling through the planet easy. Of all the gifts, faith is the one that makes your journey on the planet the easiest. It doesn't mean that you won't experience problems or difficulties, but it means relying on your faith gets you beyond that storm, whatever that storm is. This is something that deserves some thought, and it is something that individuals would want to develop. Again, faith truly makes this earthly journey much easier as it frees us from unnecessary fear and trepidation.

You can rely on some of the other spiritual gifts such as miraculous powers or prophesy, but none are quite as powerful as faith! Allow yourself to feel faith inside of you, and get an idea of where you stand on a scale of 0-100 percent, with absolutely no doubt representing 100 percent. Remember it is not that you have done anything wrong if you are not at 70-80 percent, it's just that you have been given other gifts. Remember, there is no loser in this situation, it's just that faith may not have been your focal point in this lifetime. Whatever difficulty or hours of darkness you may go through, remember that your faith can not only comfort you but transform a negative situation into an opportunity for growth and learning.

When you go through challenging times, remember that it is your faith that will not only comfort you but help transform you. It is very important that you recognize this: even the most difficult of times can be transformed into good. There is a blessing that comes out of these challenges so that you have then an opportunity for increased visits from spirit, or guides, or teachers. You get visits from these beings, and when the being known as Mother Theresa passed over, her work continued through the hands of others. Figuratively speaking, the work was continued through her hands by the hands of others. The reason that she passed over at that time was that it was getting to the point that she needed to be at more than one place at the same time. One of her strongest gifts is faith, and because she had the experience of being able to gather souls together of like needs on this planet, she is able to so effectively help others with their faith now that she is on the other side. So she does still gather those beings together for purposes of her assistance, her gift of healing. She does it with one group and then another and another. She would not have been able to do that physically on the planet because they were located far and wide. But in the nonphysical way, she is able to more easily develop the technique of gathering souls together.

She might have been able to do it while they are in the dream state or in the meditative state themselves or any number of other ways. She brought together the group that she could, and then was able to give a more powerful healing because her energy was not being challenged by the physical demands of the body. She expressed her area of faith in combination with faith healing. She knew that in passing over, she would be able to serve so many more individuals. By the way her passing over did a lot of healing for individuals who recognized her sacrifice and decided that being in the world or on the planet means that you get so much more when you give. You give something out onefold and it does come back to you tenfold. You give it out one-hundredfold and it comes back one-thousandfold. So with Mother Theresa having this opportunity when she passed over, individuals were again given their opportunity to do what they can do to be able to help the planet for their own growth and development and also to help others, be they the human variety, the planet itself, the animals, or the crystals. But more than help, they know they are here to give at least a partial solution to heal the planet or themselves.

The next gift is the gift of the messages of wisdom. While they both deal with absolute truths, wisdom is different from knowledge. Knowledge has to do with the information, factual correct information, that is given about your universe and parallel universes, including how souls develop, how they move around, and why they go to that constellation, etc. However, wisdom is associated with very old souls. You have probably experienced meeting someone before and recognizing that there was something different about them, that they have a tremendous amount, an unlimited amount, of wisdom. In fact, it has become somewhat commonplace for individuals to look at an infant and say "they have old eyes," or "wow, that is an old soul." Now, were these individuals gifted with this wisdom at birth? That is absolutely one possibility. Or it might be that they are an old soul and they have been developing wisdom over numerous lifetimes. But wisdom comes from those beings, those highly developed beings, who occupy either our universe or a parallel universe.

You can think of knowledge as having to do with facts about what our universe looks like and what parallel universes look like, why they are developed, how long they go on, and all of these things. Wisdom, on the other hand, is the development of you as an individual, the development of your soul. You can develop spiritual wisdom, physical wisdom, mental wisdom, emotional wisdom, and the fifth-dimensional healer wisdom. So you call upon your guides, teachers, those experts, the counselors, the birthright angels to help in case you are not at 100 percent of wisdom. Now 100 percent wisdom doesn't mean that you have all the wisdom, but rather all the wisdom that you need for living on this planet. So if you are not at 100 percent, then there will be, and this is a gift from spirit, certain guides and teachers that are assigned to you to make sure that you are able to operate at very close to 100 percent.

Individuals with this gift of wisdom are those whom you should look to as friends, companions, or life partners as they can aid in your decision-making as you travel through this lifetime. When individuals say "I do not know which way to go," or "I do not know what the best way to care for my older parents is," or "I have a young child who is having a lot of difficulty relating to others in school," what they are truly in need of is the wisdom of the ages. And that is what this wisdom is—it is the wisdom of the ages because there is always new wisdom, so as you develop there will be more things that will open up to you. So the more you develop, the more you will be able to understand the messages of wisdom.

An example of this wisdom of the ages came from all of the parables that the Christ energy told. Christ came into this world with all nine spiritual gifts and chose to use the gifts as he saw fit. So many times rather than saying something in black and white, he would share his message of the gift of wisdom in a parable. As he shared these parables with the apostles, there were many times that they questioned him. You may wonder why they did that. You may wonder, "Shouldn't the apostles have understood his messages immediately? After all, I did." Well, consider the fact that you are experiencing this earthly lifetime two thousand years after they did. You have had all of these experiences in different lifetimes to develop your wisdom, so it is no surprise that you immediately recognize the inherent truth in Christ's parables.

The fourth gift is speaking in tongues. Now you will have those of very religious persuasion say "yes, I speak in tongues. It is the gift that God gave to me." And the truth is that they are absolutely speaking in tongues. But what it means in this day and age is not just tongues but giving voice to the channeling process. So speaking in different tongues or different kinds of tongues doesn't mean in a language that no one can understand, as we often viewed it in the Christian religious teachings. Instead it means that you are opening to give voice from spirit, and that is in the channeling process that can either be a conscious or unconscious channeling or anything and everything in between.

A lot of individuals have this type of spirit communication on their blueprint so that they will become a channel in this lifetime. They may have had some, but not a lot of, communication with spirit, and then they were told at some point of their development, at a certain age, that they were going to open to channel. Some of you reading right now, some of you can understand that. You get it. Many individuals are not masters at it yet, but they might be at the end of this lifetime. They are not at 100 percent, but it was most likely on their blueprint, especially if it is something that is going to dominate what is happening in their life. Or it could be something that they just developed or wanted to develop for themselves, and in that case it is more likely an experience rather than a blueprint item. Still, there are some beings that came in with this

Limitless Possibilities

ability who we would call a natural channel. The reason that there are so many natural channels on our planet at this time is because we went from the third, to the fourth, to the fifth dimension in quick order, and so we needed some direct assistance through these natural channels in order to make that transition smoother and more rapid.

Now you take a look at interpretation of tongues, which is one of the gifts. Most of the individuals who practice this gift are of the religious persuasion. Most of those individuals who do interpretation of tongues, about 80 percent, are interpreting what seems to be a foreign language that no one can understand except them. So you get the message from one who is the interpreter. But for the other ones, the interpretation of tongues is really the interpretation of channeling. Think about it this way: Let us say that you had an individual session with a channel that you know or someone who is well known throughout the world, and you take that audio tape out every three weeks and you listen to it. The more you listen to it, the more that you really get what the message is. So what this means is that you are interpreting the channeled information and you are getting to the deeper knowledge of it. You are getting into the essence of it as you grow and expand. So if you listen to that tape one year from now, you are going to hear things that you won't hear now; the information will resonate with you as you are getting into the essence of what the information is.

Now that we have entered the twenty-first century, this interpretation of the channeled information is relating more and more to the evolution of this planet. Therefore, what people are being given is universal knowledge through channeling. It does not matter if the person receiving the information understands everything as the information is meant to be shared with those individuals who will have a deep understanding of it, those with the gift of knowledge. So what you are going to be finding now in the twenty-first century is that people are going to be hungering more and more for information about what is outside of this planet. So you may find yourself asking for channeled information about things that you have never seen and yet you want to understand. Now, you may be wondering if the person who is channeling can also be the interpreter. The answer is yes. They could have developed that skill as well.

One of the most interesting gifts is the idea of miraculous powers. One of the beings who has that gift is Sai Baba. Sai Baba is one of the better-known beings who was given the gift of miraculous powers. It could have been a gift that was given to him or one that he developed, but it is so strong that it probably was one that was given as a gift that he was already so highly developed in the way in which he wanted to go. Now he wanted to develop and to learn things and so then he was given that gift. There are others as well. Miraculous powers are those things that are accomplished that go beyond your reasoning. You have probably felt the presence of miraculous events in your own life and have learned to be delighted by them, but not surprised by them.

For those that are gifted with miraculous powers, my goodness, what a lifetime to have if you have miraculous powers! The problem is that if you happen to tell people you may be bombarded with requests. If you are not, then your gift is truly a wonderful gift in that you can heal things, you can transform things, and you can create miracles for yourself and for all of your friends. The gift of miraculous powers can be a truly awesome tool when combined with the other spiritual gifts. If you want to develop miraculous powers, you certainly will be able to create miracles. They might not be major miracles, they might not be something that will get the attention of other people, but still they are miracles in your life that you are able to create. However, if your energy is scattered or depleted due to fatigue, illness, or some other distraction, you will not be able to produce miracles. That is why it is so very important that you nurture and take care of yourself, as this is necessary so that you can use all of the spiritual gifts to their fullest. You must concentrate on the purification of your gifts and fully believe that you can in fact manifest miracles.

The gift of prophecy is all areas of psychic development. So when you do table tipping, that is prophecy; when you do a tarot reading, that is prophecy; when you do the pendulum, that is prophecy; when you have precognitive dreaming, that is prophecy; when you have lucid dreaming, that is prophecy; when you use any of the metaphysical tools, any of the tarot decks where your might have the rune stones, or the I-Ching, or the Irish fairy cards, using any of these tools opens up the way for prophecy. How developed you are in prophecy can be seen by the type of answer that you give. Let us say that you use the rune stones, and you get an answer for someone for their query, and so you can read from the rune stone book for what the answer is. If you don't go any further than that, then your development of prophecy is quite low, which is fine; that is all right. But it would be more fun for you if when you are doing the reading you could say, "Well I am getting that this is related to this part of your life. Is that true"? And then they can respond to you and give you feedback so you know whether or not to go further. But by using all of these metaphysical tools, you absolutely are developing the gift of prophecy.

Now if you were given that gift from spirit, then you come in already with information or knowledge of how to helps others and yourself. However, because of the filters that we discussed earlier, it is harder to get to the information for yourself. But if you came with that as a gift, then you will be very highly regarded, and it is probably true that you are doing prophecy for a living. If you came in at 75 percent, and yet this was going to be the gift from spirit, then you will have a lot of guides, teachers, or counselors, a lot of these beings that will be supplying you with information for your development but also to help the client. So if your gift was prophecy, and yet you were not 100 percent developed in that gift, the guides and teachers will help you in your development of it. So you should not be afraid to go forward with prophecy, even if you feel you are not at 100 percent.

The next gift is that of healing. Healers are able to help you bring a negative circumstance or event into consciousness, get it up to the surface, look at it, and because it is your creation, you love it, and then you release it. It is released to God in raw energy so that it can be used in a more helpful fashion. Therefore, what healers do is to transform the energy so that it can leave the body of the individual whose body is afflicted. Interestingly, if there are several people in a group who are experiencing a similar difficulty, then it is very likely that they can all get healed at the same time because it will accelerate their development for the purpose of healing it. This probably sounds reminiscent of when the Christ energy says, "When two or more are gathered in my name, there I am also."

If the gift of healing has been given to you by spirit, you will know it by a very early age. You will feel the pull to lay your hands on people, to meditate or to chant or whatever you feel you need to do in order to help those individuals. When you grow up you are considered different because you have the healing touch, the healing power. If it is not something that was given to you at birth, it can very much be something that you have been developing over numerous lifetimes. So it can still grow and be very developed even if it wasn't given to you by spirit, if it is one that you choose to develop.

The last gift is discernment of spirits. It is something that could be a gift given from spirit, or it could be something that you develop over time as you are doing more things metaphysically. This discerning of spirits could be anything from determining if it is one guide or the other that is with you, or if they are in the room with you at the moment, to deciphering what healing technique would be best for me to help an individual. Then again it can also be used to identify those spirits that can frighten or intimidate. In those cases, you need to turn and face them so that you can help them get on with the movement that they need to make and to discuss things with their guides and teachers. This discerning of spirits is a very wonderful thing to have, and it is something that you can develop very easily over time simply by paying attention to your response energetically. You can use your intuition and let yourself feel the response and determine if the energy feels good or not good. This gift is something that would be a very valuable tool regardless of whatever gift you were given from spirit or whatever gifts you choose to develop.

Because the gift of discernment of spirits is very similar to the gift of faith, it makes your life that much easier! It saves you from taking a lot of wrong directions as it can truly guide you toward what is best for you and your development. Again, it is one that is easy to develop, if you just pay attention.

The guide to call on to assist you with your gift from spirit is called your spiritual companion counterpart. Each person on the planet has their own guide which is part of their own soul. This guide is the one that is most like you spiritually and is there to assist you and direct you with whatever you need. So if you are in a state of confusion, this guide is the one that knows exactly why you are confused and can bring clarity to any situation. So when you feel lost and lacking direction, you simply can go into meditation and call upon this guide and the energy will direct you so that spiritually you can get answers or feel clearer about the direction you should take. This particular guide does not always stand in your circle of twelve, but when you call upon this guide for assistance, the energy arrives in an instant and can come into your circle and give you the frame of spiritual reference you need to give insight to your situation.

There are four companion counterparts, which are reflections of a person's soul as it relates to their physicality, as it relates to them mentally, as it relates to them emotionally, and as it relates to them spiritually. A being or the being that is most like you in every area and every aspect of your soul is referred to as your twin soul. Now the twin soul did not take on this particular area for you because the twin soul has the opportunity to experience in the nonphysical realm what you are creating in the physical realm. Instead, if you have the interest in healing or in knowledge or the interest in faith, it is developed in the spiritual realm by the twin soul initially. It is like a spark that gets you looking in that direction, and then as you are willing to give your energy in that area, so does the twin soul literally come and sit by you and help you in your development. But the twin soul did not want to be limited in the gift that you have been given. The twin soul is an active participant in helping you to create your life and to give yourself the lifestyle that you want.

The twin soul is open to all areas where your creativity has been sparked, including the development of the spiritual gifts. For example, the heart chakra assistant—keeping in mind that all spiritual energy flows in and out of the heart chakra—has knowledge about what you are interested in and can go out and attract in certain experiences that will support your learning in a certain area. That is why that being is connected to you. Every once in a while there will be a teacher or a fifth-dimensional companion that is involved in this as well, but usually it is handled very easily by your spiritual companion. This being assists you with the gift that you are given from spirit for this lifetime. Sometimes this guide will assist you with the other gifts that you are developing, but more than likely you will get assistance for these gifts from your heart chakra assistant. This guide is typically the gatekeeper for your heart chakra. Again, to develop a communication between you and your appropriate spirit guide is a wonderful way to discover, validate, and to help receive guidance for your birthright gift from spirit and the gifts that we are able to develop.

* * * * * * * *

Early on in my spiritual development, I took the class "Many Gifts, One Spirit" to discern which gift was my birthright gift. We learned, as discussed above, the nine gifts and how each presents itself in individuals on earth. As we were identifying those measures that help you distinguish one gift from another, we were asked to simply allow ourselves to be awake to our feelings of how we felt about each gift. Could we relate to one more than another? If so, which one or ones? Did one gift sound natural or familiar and resonate deep within? Could each of us distinguish which gift was our birthright gift? What other gifts did we feel we had developed or were developing in this lifetime? Well, these questions were sure a lot to think about. And I sure needed to do a little more than just thinking to come up with the right answer!

We were then asked to get in touch with our intuitive selves as one means to help to identify the birthright gift. When you call on your higher self through meditation, you can access the information and the information about your birthright gift can be determined. In fact, meditation and getting to know yourself, your inner self, is the best way to determine the gift. It is first important to remove all desire first and not predetermine which gift you would like the most or be thinking which one would be the coolest to have or to have been given. You need to be in touch with who you are and be in touch with your soul and in the state of calmness. Simple meditation practices or simply sitting in the silence or walking in nature are all ways to help quiet the mind, ridding your space from the distractions of life and then being able to listen for the answer. Sometimes the answer comes directly in the form of "knowingness." Other times you simply need to be focusing on other things, and when you least expect it, the answer pops into your mind! We were each asked to go home and think about which of the gifts seem to ring truest to our inner self and to come prepared to the next class to discuss it. We were encouraged to use any of the meditative practices mentioned above to help us determine our gift.

Another avenue we were taught to use that would help determine our birthright gift was to learn how to use the pendulum. The pendulum is a really simple metaphysical tool which is used to help you communicate with spirit. It was suggested that we simply needed to write all of the nine gifts on nine separate pieces of paper and ask spirit to help identify your gift by the simple yes-or-no method. (A pendulum consists of a stone or crystal that typically hangs on a chain that energy may flow through.) A pendulum is a really wonderful little tool to have as it helps to validate intuitive thoughts as well as to give an affirmative or negative answer to a simple question. The pendulum that you purchase should be one that you are attracted to and that you dedicate to one of your guides, teachers, or angels. Each time you use this pendulum, the energy that the pendulum is dedicated to will be there in response to your queries. If you want guidance from several sources on the other side, than each should have their own pendulum dedicated to that energy so that the energies responding are always using their pendulum.

In addition to meditation and the pendulum, we learned an exercise that by simply asking yourself a question you could use your body as an indicator and look to it for the answer. We learned a little warm-up exercise which helped us to determine what feels right and what feels wrong. We learned to quiet ourselves and simply sit with the focus on our entire body. We then were asked to conjure up a scene that was very unpleasant. Asking the questions: What is my body telling me? How and where is it showing me how it is feeling? For me, an unpleasant scene brought a pain in the left side of my neck; ah, the ubiquitous "pain in the neck." This brought a whole new meaning to that expression! Each subsequent quiz brought this same negative reaction by my body, and so I concluded that this was my body's way of showing me or giving me a "no" answer. By thinking of any negative scene, your body reacts to the negative and shows you how a "no" answer is perceived. The opposite allows you to have your body respond to you in the positive. Think of something very peaceful or beautiful and get in touch with how your body is feeling. Then think of a question and put your body to the test. My body consistently showed me a tingling in my fingers when I tested it for a "yes" answer. By exploring the question, "Will it feel positive or negative?" each of us can ask our body to help us answer a question in the negative or positive by observing how our bodies are reacting. This is such a simple exercise to practice and can come in pretty handy when you need to get a quick response to a question. You can count on the answer and will interpret it correctly based on your own unique yes-or-no response.

And yet another way to help us to determine which gift may be our birthright gift is to use color. This should not be the primary way of identifying a gift but could be an additional way to validate information that you have determined from one of the other methods. Again, I repeat, we were warned to be careful not to determine which gift we would like to have and then build a case around it. It may be easiest to ask a few of the following questions, and the answers to them should come from a deep place, possibly after meditation or when you are feeling really introspective. So we asked ourselves: What stones am I attracted to? What are my favorite colors, and what colors am I drawn to? What times am I drawn to certain tones, or certain colors? Is there a correlation between certain events in my life and the colors that I see? What do different colors mean to me? It is always a good idea to keep a journal and write the answers down or any other information that may come in.

Let's say you are drawn to the color blue. You most probably are spiritual or at least on the spiritual path, learning all that you can about this spiritual body of consciousness. This color comes up through your crown and helps you to get in touch with your higher energies. You may be drawn to orange or the greens. Chances are you will be more into education, knowledge, and teaching. You may love the color green and the color makes you feel wonderful and comes to you when you are thinking of others. Green is the color of healers, and it is the spiritual color of regenerative energy and rebirth. Those that see the whites and its many shades and see the fairest, fairest colors of all feel the wisdom coming through. Remember as the body spirals up, the higher up you go. That doesn't mean one color is better than the other, it just means that it is just showing you your gift and is helping you to distinguish it from every other.

Those of you that are coming in with knowledge or for any of the other gifts need to take the colors apart and find out and figure it out from within. The pale blue is from the throat chakra and it is in the area of being vocal; chances are the gift would be the speaking from spirit and interpreting tongue. Purple is spirituality and would represent the gift of faith. Purple and white are the colors of miracles—you are drawing in the white from the angelic realm and using it with the purple or the energy of spirituality and faith. Discernment of spirit would be yellow, your core, and how you intuit or your gut feelings. The gift of prophecy is represented by the color indigo—your third eye or your psychic self. The color magenta represents spiritual healing and is really coming from outside of the body or your eighth chakra area. So you can watch the colors and see what colors you are drawn to, but again this is one means and at its simplest form should be used only as a validation and used secondary to some of the other methods suggested. Colors can and do provide us with a hint of not only our inner self but who we are at our core level and give us insight into the gift that should feel totally natural to us.

Those who have the gift of healing do not automatically see the vision of healing, but their gift takes time to develop as they have to build upon it. Those who have the gift of prophecy and channeling automatically see it. The vision is right there in the third eye because their third eye is open. Those that have to create it to bring it up are the healers. So what is innate and natural to you will help you to determine your birthright. This is why it is so important to do the work—so that you know who you are at the core level, and what makes sense and is natural for you should be factored in to determine your birthright gift.

And of course you can consult the tarot for information on your gift as well as the reason behind giving you the gift. The tarot opens up much history and is able to paint a broader picture of where you stand in the process and why you and your guides chose for you to come in with the gift as given.

So we played with the methods that most appealed to each of us and were to return to class the following week with some introspective knowledge of our birthright gift as well as our impression of all of the other gifts and their meaning. All week long as I was mulling all of the gifts in my mind, and thought about my feelings, my inclinations, my knowing, my inner self, I kept coming back to either being given the gift of knowledge or wisdom. However, I thought, "How can I go to class and say I was given the gift of wisdom. Isn't that arrogance? Or have I let my ego do the walking (talking)?" So when it was my turn to identify my gift, I said I thought I was given either the gift of knowledge or wisdom but wasn't exactly sure. Later I realized all that was requested was an honest assessment of self and an honest response. How silly to listen to my ego and bring irrelevant issues into a simple exercise of discernment! This was a huge lesson for me as I was just beginning to see the role that the ego has in our lives!

I was very pleased when it was confirmed for me that I was given the gift of wisdom. I had been embarrassed to say it, but it didn't matter as I knew that all that was important was how I was using it and to figure out why I had received this gift so that I could figure out how to use it in this lifetime! I learned that this gift had to do with messages coming from an old soul to an old soul. I had felt throughout my childhood and into my adulthood that I seemed to not only "know" things but the "reason" things had happened as well. The subjects or situations were varied and typically about things that I shouldn't really know or that I had learned about. People often made the comment to my parents or to me that I was "wiser than my years." As I was processing the gift I now realized that everything in my life made such sense to me. Another piece of my unique puzzle fit perfectly into place! My relationship with my son was also intimately connected with this gift. The connection between us is greatly increased as my son is very much an evolved soul, so I have been very much involved with his soul in this and many past lifetimes. In my lifetime, I have always tried to key into the wisdom of the lesson or the experience to be gained from it. I have made this step part of the automatic processing of my life. As experiences or events occur, I have learned to ask the question. Sometimes the answer isn't so obvious, but if I keep at it eventually the meaning presents itself.

The definition of wisdom is knowledge applied. Of course I haven't always used this gift with 100 percent accuracy. But to perfect the use of wisdom in my life, I do know that phrase "practice makes perfect," and so oftentimes you need to practice repeating something until you get it right, so I can honestly say that I am 100 percent at practicing perfecting my wisdom!

The other eight gifts I have either fully or almost developed or are learning and newly developing. I have been told that when I started my spiritual development classes, my faith was at 84 percent, which was considered very high for anyone living in the United States. Currently, I have been told that I have achieved the 100 percent level of faith. I have a highly developed gift of knowledge, probably from my education and all of the reading that I have done over the years to expand my world.

I am currently developing the many forms of prophecy. I have learned how to table tip, which means that the energy of spirit actually comes through a special table. You are presented a gatekeeper from the other side that opens the table and allows certain energies to come forth with messages. The pendulum is actually very simple and is a wonderful tool to use for simple yes-or-no confirmation to questions you are posing. The tarot cards are also a simple way that spirit can communicate to you. There are many, many different themes of tarot cards, and I currently am using the Celtic version as it appeals to my strong Celtic background. Channeling is another form of spirit energy coming forth to present information. These different forms of divination are available to help you learn how to communicate with the other side. During learning sessions or during actual use, the energies coming forth are always energies that exist in the love and light of God, and the flow of energies is always protected by the four archangels. My reason for being and doing has always been from a pure heart and for my highest good, and I work solely through and with the love and light of God. Interpreting tongue is simply taking the information from channeling and developing the skill to interpret it.

Speaking tongue and interpreting tongue is really learning how to communicate with the other side and interpreting the information as you receive it. This gets easier every day—as your awareness increases, so does the information you receive.

Spiritual healing is learning how to heal in the fifth-dimensional way and is something that I have learned and consistently use on a daily basis. There will be a future chapter that details the fifth dimension and the role of the spiritual healer in it.

Miracles are also something that I am working on, and there is a chapter which helps to define miracles, manifestations, and how to practice and use these in your daily life.

The most wonderful knowledge comes from knowing what gift you have been given, what gifts you are developing or which ones that are fairly developed that you may have brought into this lifetime with you, and/or which gifts that you may be newly learning about and are working on developing. When you are metaphysically inclined, you have a fairly intuitive feeling for the gifts that you have been given as well as the ones you are developing. It is very rewarding to know not only are you on the right track with you development but that all of these gifts are open for your development.

So in effect it is like a toy store for metaphysicians. The ones that you have been gifted and the ones that you are developing might not be all that you will have. If you find at a later time there is another gift that you are interested in, then absolutely you can go for it! This goes for miraculous powers and for healing. You will have ample opportunity to expand in other areas as well. All of these gifts from God were provided for you as gifts from the Oneness. God is part of the Oneness of us all. As such, we thank Paul for writing and introducing us to these gifts available from spirit.

It is so important to remember that you create your reality, that you create your future with what you are thinking, feeling, believing, seeing, and doing right now. You create your future in your next breath. So if you are an old soul, you know intuitively that you get to create your future. In the Bible, this concept is referred to as free will. Markas and those on the other side call it conscious free will. It is not just free will that you are acting out and doing whatever you want or whatever feels good at the moment, but you are consciously directing what you are believing and knowing to be true right now. You may have noticed that children seem to be coming into this world more and more wise and more and more advanced. That is because a lot of old souls have reentered this earthly lifetime recently, most of them being between one and five years old. The reason for their arrival is that they waited to come in when the planet was getting ready to shift into the next dimension so that they could use their spiritual gifts to help all of us in this current time.

While the terminology associated with these nine gifts may vary by religious tradition, they are in fact universal in nature. For example, if you discussed the nine gifts with a group of Buddhists, they would understand them, just as a group of Christians would. Therefore this part of the Bible transcended one religion as it is applicable to all who are part of the spirit, all part of the connection, so they have each been given one gift, so that no matter what religion one follows, they will find that this is within the framework of their religion. So for those individuals that say, "Well if you are into metaphysics, you are not a Christian," it may be helpful to refer them to the part of the Bible where Paul discusses the gifts of the spirit.

Today many Christian churches, at the conclusion of their service, offer healing to those who are in need of it. You can also hear different ministers referring to "revelations" that they have had, as well as members of various religions speaking in tongues or interpreting tongues. Again, all of these things are truly universal as they pertain to many religions as well as are one of the footholds of metaphysics. However, metaphysics is also practiced by those that are spiritual but not necessarily religious, meaning that they do not practice a particular creed or religious tradition. What you may have noticed is the changing tide in spirituality as it becomes more attuned with what individuals are experiencing and craving, regardless of whether or not it fits into a particular religious mold.

This changing tide has brought forth a resurgence in many things from ancient Eastern practices, including healthcare and anything with a spiritual or metaphysical bent. Alternative medicine, a huge variety of healing classes, yoga, tai chi, and many others have become increasingly popular. Why now? It has been described that as the world is currently transitioning, the veil that separates the earth plane from the higher vibrations has continued to thin so that communication between spirit and man has not only increased but has become increasingly easier to sustain. Many, many individuals throughout the world have sensed and felt that they are more connected to the other side as they experience moments of awe and wonderment as spirits or deceased loved ones make contact or they see or experience something formerly unexplainable. Individuals have felt the desire to learn and to understand as their hearts and minds have been tugged at, nudging them to discover or to reawaken their abilities.

This climate is exactly what drew the five of us in my planet-healing group to explore and discover what we had come to earth to do. Let me introduce you to my four healing partners and tell you a little about each of them, so as we journey through this book, you will be familiar with who they are and who they have become. When we each began our development classes, we were all pretty much at the same level with the exception of Theresa, our teacher. Theresa clearly lived her gift and had been developing prophecy during her lifetime. We all had one commonality: we were all drawn to spiritual or metaphysical topics and were interested in developing ourselves to be helpful to not only ourselves and our families but to others. I think each of us was experiencing a wakeup call, and since each of us is a unique personality, the methods used to wake us up were very different. We all were employed outside of the home at jobs having nothing to do with this newfound interest, so our development needed to occur in the evenings or weekends while juggling family and other responsibilities. Some of us had read more than others, so the level of exposure may have been different, but interestingly we were all drawn to taking Reiki classes, all unbeknownst to each other. So a healing class seemed to be everyone's starting point. We each discovered that by taking a risk and learning something new, we not only learned a great healing skill, but we began to individually develop our confidence. We now knew that we each felt that we had something to offer and that we had found another avenue to put ourselves to good use. We could contribute to the world in a new way. This shifted each of our worlds as we reaped the benefits of how our change in consciousness and our new activity helped us to experience this new energy and a new flow of energy. Each of us grew differently as the process began.

Identifying and growing into our natural birthright gifts and the additional gifts each of us have developed and are currently developing have been fascinating to watch and to assist each other in. Two of the women, Theresa and Diane, have the gift of prophecy, which means they clearly are visual and can see and receive information through their opened third eye. They easily receive by spirit and receive information through channeling, and they can bounce the information off each other. Theresa is an expert aura photographer as well as teacher and healer. She works with light touch and crystals, and her healings are beautifully directed by spirit. She is always open to drawing in new healing tools to expand the impact of the healing. Her work with color harmonics and the etheric weaver is another way for her to gather more information about the person she is healing. When you have experienced a healing by Theresa, you feel relaxed, rested, with your chakras all aligned and spinning in the same direction and close to the same tempo as possible, and your energy flow is even and complete. In other words, you feel magnificent!

Theresa had been a student of Markas for many years and thus became a very dear friend of Dr. Gwen Totterdale. Her spiritual and metaphysical development has grown from channeling to trance channeling, and the information she brings forward for her clients is healing, comforting, and helpful. Her clients have wonderful experiences, and as they do, so does Theresa! Diane has the same gift of prophecy but manifests it differently in her life as she is an expert animal communicator. She not only communicates with animals locally and all over the world, but heals them as well using either the fifth-dimensional healing or a Reiki healing, or a combination of both. She has developed her own methodology of healing by incorporating tuning forks and colored lights. Her ability to receive with her physical senses as well as her advanced intuitive receives makes her an unusual healer. She is dedicated to our animal kingdom as well as the entire planet, and our planet healings are greatly enriched by her participation.

Diane's gift of prophecy is being used to heal not only human beings and human situations but also animals. Her love for animals has given her the catalyst to be a very powerful healer. She is able to move quickly into her capacity as a fifth-dimensional healer and can put herself literally at the side of any situation that needs healing in an instant. Her energy is defined very clearly as coming from the fairy realm, where the love of nature and animals, her enthusiasm, and her playfulness all are evident in all of her healings, clearly using and incorporating her personality with her birthright gift.

Bonnie was given the natural gift of healing. Bonnie comes from such a pure heart and participates with the purest of intentions, and thus her healing energy is beautiful. Bonnie is assisted by a beautiful angel from the highest realms named Angel Helen. She also is assisted by Edgar Cayce and Jesus (to name a few)! Working through Bonnie, these highly enlightened beings come in and through her create a healing energy replacing the existing unhealed energy. This unhealed energy is then sent into Mother Earth for transmutation by God. It was an amazing and exciting experience to watch as Bonnie learned to call on wonderful healers from the highest realms to assist her in working with divine energy on this planet. Not only is the planet lucky to have Bonnie, but our group has definitely reached the highest heights with Bonnie's presence.

Donna received the gift of interpretation of tongue, which she has been using to interpret thought packages that she receives. Donna is a wonderful healer, and a very strong Native American energy walks within her. Donna brings many insights to the table and uses her Native American influences to help us with meditation through original and impromptu journeying. We each have gone on her journeys only to receive one more miracle, more awareness, and more answers to life's big questions! Walking with Donna during a journeying exercise is always fun as you never know who you are going to meet along the path! We have each experienced wonderful visitations from wonderful energies, all coming to supply unending quantities of love. Donna's physical healings are unique as her recipe for healing is different from the others'. She not only is a Reiki master and works with colors and light, she also incorporates the etheric weaver. Donna brings drumming to the table as an expression of the very essence of life itself, helping clients reach new depths of their soul and new places within to connect with the pulse and divine knowledge. Interestingly, as a young child growing up, Donna remembers that she was never ill. She had the natural ability to heal herself, and intuitively she used this precious gift to keep herself well. As she has grown in her role as a healer, she has remembered many experiences from her childhood, allowing her to understand the true and deeper meaning of healing.

Our group has many mentors, and we were honored that we were named Ones That Flow Like The River by Conquering Bear. He has come forward to assist us with the healing we send out to the planet, the planet that he cared so deeply about and fought so passionately for as chief of the Lakota Indians in the mid-nineteenth century. This man of peace and this strong warrior is our mentor! Imagine that! He has told us that he chooses to remain on the other side and will not reincarnate on this earth plane in a physical body as the pain is too great. He prefers to use his gift of wisdom, his love for the planet, and his strength to guide those of us who are here trying to help in whatever way we can. He is truly an inspiration, oftentimes telling us stories from his famous lifetime to help us understand the significance of events in this lifetime. He draws from a place of strength, which is obvious, but he also comes from a place of love, which is inspirational. Conquering Bear has visited our planet healings often, offering advice on how and what we can add to our evenings to make our healings stronger so that we send out the strongest possible healing energy to Mother Earth. He has reminded us that our healing ritual should include elements for all areas of our earth, and that abstinence from food is mandatory before our healing as sacrifice adds power to the intention.

Conquering Bear gave me the following quote for the book to illustrate not only how the power of our group relates to the name he bestowed on us but also describing the synergy of a group in the context of fifth-dimensional healing and nature.

"Everything you touch, when you have your fifth-dimensional energy will blossom and grow, and you can heal the world! Like a river, you all flow in different ways and go different directions, but you all come back to me, the main river. This is where your strength lies when you are together.

To do your healing, you must be together for this power that is in each one of you manifested together becomes an unstoppable river, flowing strong and fast to wash over the world."

Conquering Bear presented each of us with an Indian name that represented our spirit and our essence. We are truly honored that we are the recipients of such love and cherish the responsibility as well as the love and healing abilities that have come to define our purpose. As members of our planet healing group "Ones That Flow Like The River," each us on many levels or dimensions has experienced this shift in consciousness through developing our gifts, enabling the fifth-dimensional energies to flow in and through us like the river! So, Conquering Bear, we thank you for all your love and support as we live each day as a new day, exploring new ways to honor the planet that you loved and cared so deeply about. Thank you from Wise Owl, Walks with Animals, Moonbeam, Morning Dove, and yours truly, Sunshine Rising!

CHAPTER III

We Have to Say We Love You in a Song!

Music washes away from the soul the dust of everyday life.

—Berthold Auerbach

Let's consider what needs to be healed so that we can take the gift of music and allow it to do what it does best: heal us from the inside out! As you may be aware, we each have a body of consciousness for each of the dimensions that we have evolved to. So if you are a three-dimensional person, you would have three bodies of consciousness. Each of these bodies of consciousness has an inner child. If you have transitioned into the fourth dimension, you would have four bodies of consciousness and thus four inner children. Likewise if you have evolved into the fifth dimension, your inner children number five. In fact, throughout our text, we will use the terms *inner child* and *emotional body of consciousness* interchangeably. So as you have reached adulthood, some of your inner children may be happy, and some or all of them may not be. These inner children have stayed at a level where they truly are unhappy and thus affect you by moving you off of your center. This creates an imbalance. It is the responsibility of the adult of you to parent the inner child to bring him/her to the healing place, a place of love. By taking a good look at who we are at that inner level of our inner children, we can determine what area or areas we need to concentrate on to heal.

Our physical body of consciousness may have an inner child that has suffered abuse or grown up fearful from the events that have happened in his/her life that he/she has never recovered from. If you ask yourself how this little inner child is, you intuitively can determine its state of physical well-being. Picture your inner child at a time frame when you were between three and five years old. What do you see? How does this inner child feel during these early years? If you sense fear, then fear needs to be converted to love. If you sense unrest, then unrest needs to be converted to comfort. If you sense sadness, then sadness needs to be converted to a state of happiness. The adult in you needs to spend quality and loving time with this little inner child. Talking, singing, and dancing would be a great way to start giving the inner child the warmth and caring that he/she needs and is the beginning of healing.

As our planet shifts from the fourth to the fifth dimension, you may notice that you are suddenly dealing with old hurts, both consciously and unconsciously. It is really not affecting your physical body of consciousness, but rather it is the inner child within your emotional body of consciousness that is really feeling the changes. Breakthroughs do happen, and when they do we want for you to remember to just relax and to breathe because everything is perfect, even when you feel uncomfortable, even when you cannot see the big picture. Now *perfect* does not mean things will not change as things are constantly changing. There is nothing on our planet that remains the same, including each of our energies, collectively or individually. So everything is in a constant state of flux. Sometimes you feel it more profoundly than at other times. Again, everything is perfect. That does not mean that it is not going to change, but you can trust that it will change in the perfect way that it is meant to.

Your thoughts, what you are thinking right now, create your future. So if you are not aware of what you are thinking, this is the time to be very introspective and take a listen and observe what is happening inside of you, and that is something that none of us have been trained to do. You have been trained to go to the external stimuli rather than taking that quiet time not to get answers but to learn what is happening inside of you. So if you want to know what is going to happen in your future, get in touch with what you think right now. Deepak Chopra has said that you have "thousands and thousands of thoughts each day." So the good news is that you have all of this energy running through you. The challenging news is that the next day you might have thousands of thoughts, but most of them were the same thing that you were thinking the previous day. And what you really want to do is sort through this. Ask yourself, "Does this serve me? Look what I am thinking, look what I am feeling—does this serve me?" And if it doesn't, do not judge it, just embrace it, thank it, and release it, and it will automatically go home to God so that it can be put into a much more useful thought.

We must be consciously aware of the fact that blessings are in everything! Each challenge or problem that we face is actually a beautiful opportunity to work through it and receive a blessing through further development and understanding. Often our inner child becomes afraid when faced with these challenges, and the energy surrounding the experience can become fearful and negative. Therefore we must be cognizant of the fact that you attract what you love or what you fear; whatever you are focusing on, you will attract. It is crucial to remember the principle that your energy brings in exactly what is inside of you.

As stated earlier, we will use the term *inner child* interchangeably with your emotional body of consciousness. Now, just to make sure you are very clear on this, you do have four or five bodies of consciousness. But we are going to address just the emotional body. You also have your spiritual body of consciousness, your mental body, your physical body, and if you have reached the fifth dimension, your healer body. But this is for the emotional body. And you get the picture of the inner child in your mind's eye, in your third eye, your vitae chakra. Normally that child is somewhere between three and five years old, and you have this image of this being who is just starting off in life. Remember, now that you are the adult, you are the parent to this inner child. It is your job to help guide the child so that if he/she becomes afraid, you are right there to help him or her. If the child is confused, you are there to soothe the confusion.

It does not matter whether or not your parents nurtured and protected you, it only matters if you are going to do that for your inner child. You want the inner child to have the safety to explore life and not be afraid. And the last thing that you want is for the inner child to shut down as a way of protecting him or herself. So here you are, the adult, and you have all of these challenges, experiences, and thoughts affecting you. All of these external stimuli can cause you to become overwhelmed and afraid, and the fear actually takes over the body. That is when the spirit guides step in. How often have you been in the middle of something that has been very upsetting for the inner child and you, the adult, when all of a sudden you see a phrase, or you hear a song, or something comes on television, or your friend calls you and says exactly what you need to hear at that minute? You will probably feel a sudden sense of relief and feel that everything really is going to be all right. See you have a lot of big brothers and sisters, the spirit guides, who are helping your inner child! Now the guides do this not to let the adult off the hook but to help you with your emotional journey as that is why you came to this planet at this time for this lifetime, to experience emotionality.

There is a joyful woman, whom we will call Susan, who consciously nurtures her inner child on a daily basis with great success. Susan and her older brother were taken from her parents at an early age due to the fact that they were terrible alcoholics who unfortunately had neglected the children for many years. Susan went to live in a Catholic orphanage and was sadly separated from her brother. However, she never allowed the difficulties of her circumstances to make her bitter, even when she learned of her father's death by reading the obituaries as a child. Instead, she intuitively knew that she had to nurture her inner child in order to heal the emotional wounds that had been inflicted upon her. To this day, she is known to do such whimsical, "childlike" things as sing nursery rhymes, read children's books, and blow bubbles in her garden. She can often be heard saying "this is for my inner child," or "I never sang this song as a child, so I am singing it now." For Susan, children's music has truly played an integral role in healing her inner child.

As we discuss the inner child and the role that music plays in nurturing that child, it is important to remember that we are here now, at this very place and time, in order to develop ourselves wholly. If you wanted to develop only mentally, you could have come in the 1700s or even the 1800s; if you wanted to develop only the healer body, the fifth-dimensional body, you could have done that in the next century or later on in this century. If you wanted to only develop spiritually, you do not need a body at all. So you came in this body on Planet Earth, at this time period, because this was the greatest transformation emotionally that you would be able to experience. So the guides are there then to help your inner child because that is a very prevalent aspect of your life. And yes, you want the good times—the good, better, and best times. And yes, that is what your guides want for you. However, remember that you are the one that takes the steps, and every time that you feel afraid, it does not mean that you are going backward, it just means that you are not going forward. Remember, this life is all about choices. To not do something is a choice; to not move forward is a decision.

When your guides come to you, it is to help your emotional body and also to get the attention of the adult. When you are driving in the car or flipping the remote control and you are trying to distract the inner child who is feeling pain rather than talking to or being with the inner child, your guides will often come to you to get your attention in order to show you that the inner child needs your attention. There are other reasons why you have these big brothers and sisters in the form of your spirit guides that send messages to you. We called this chapter We Have to Say We Love You in a Song because there is something about receiving message through music that sets off endorphins in your body. How often have you had a difficult situation that you maintained your composure through until the music came on and you felt the tears start to flow? The music truly releases your emotions. It is there for you to use your emotional energy to help you create what you *do* want. Your emotions are not limitations. They are tools for transformation. You can use your emotions to create what you do want!

The impact of music is great not only because of the lyrics that songs offer, but because the music itself releases an energy inside of you that is profoundly rewarding and healing. Those individuals who deal with physical healing know that the songs that they listen to can have a therapeutic value. The music is so important because it will set off this release inside the body which is the time of transformation. So when we talk about tears of sorrow and tears of joy, the tears of joy will more often than not follow tears of sadness. You can probably think of a time in your own life when you have heard a song that makes you cry tears of sadness, then after that purge of tears, you cannot believe how much better you feel. The music has truly acted as a cathartic tool, leaving you much more joyous in the end. This is due to the fact that you have allowed yourself to feel your true feelings rather than hiding behind the television or finding other ways to distract yourself and to silence your inner child.

You may be wondering if there is a particular artist or song that should be used for emotional healing. The answer is no, you must find what resonates with you, what brings you into an emotional state of awareness. This doesn't have to be *the* only song, but what is one song? Asking yourself this question can be a great exercise to use to get in touch with your emotional body of consciousness, or your inner child. Pay attention to songs that inspire you, songs that elevate your vibrations, songs that help you to understand, and songs that just simply make you feel good. Remember, not all songs are for all individuals, but when a song feels good to you, then paying attention to it is both rewarding and healing!

As the early rock-and-roll groups began to sing in the second half of the twentieth century, teenagers and adults alike began to view their emotionality as something that was obvious, and lyrics and music took on a whole new meaning in our culture. For the first time, this new rock and roll developed a following by individuals who could relate to their music. Many, many artists became popular, providing the necessary release for the emotions that were expressed during these growing-up years. The planet was in the third dimension, but the energies were transitioning to the fourth dimension, and emotionality was the climate that everyone became accepting of little by little. This emotionality continues in the music of today, from Phil Collins to Train to Elton John to Shania Twain.

Music can be an excellent tool in bringing up memories. Memories are stored in your solar plexus, and ordinarily because individuals find that life at times is very difficult, we tend to remember negative memories with great clarity. But positive music, the tune and/or the lyrics, can force you, in the most loving way possible, to bring up those other memories which are the memories associated with love, joy, and peace. You do not feel anything until it gets to the heart chakra, and music greatly speeds this process. It can encourage you not to judge yourself harshly for past deeds done or not done, but instead help you tap into beautiful, powerful memories and to let them come up into your heart chakra. That is where you use the energy. When we spoke about using your present-moment emotions to create your future, that is where they are. So if you say it is very hard for me to let the good times into my memories and into my heart chakra because right now I am so afraid, the music will help ease them up so that you can build on them and create a more positive future through these beautiful thoughts. Because we create our future with what we are thinking, feeling, and experiencing in the present moment, it is easy to see why music has been around for so long on our planet in one form or another.

Unfortunately almost everyone on this planet views himself or herself in terms of their perceived imperfections. You may think, consciously or not, "Well I can't get too happy" or, "I can't live a life in a false reality," and what happens is that there is a disproportionate amount of unfavorable memories that come up compared to the favorable memories. So the songs, especially the ones that either inspire or take you to a time of peace, are instrumental in helping you to use your emotions to create what you do want. All you have to do is to let them in!

Oftentimes you will read or hear in the metaphysical world that if you are having a difficult time you should sit down and meditate. However, that will only address your spiritual body of consciousness and sometimes that is not enough—it is not the main area that needs to be addressed. Rather, the main area that so often needs healing is our emotional body. If you allow yourself to use music or to talk to your inner child, you will see all of these emotions bubbling up to the surface. That can be transformational and a very strong healing approach.

When dealing with the memories and corresponding emotions that are brought up through music, there are some important things to remember. First of all, you are not your past experiences. Instead, you chose these experiences before you even came into this lifetime in order to learn valuable lessons from them, to become a more evolved spiritual and emotional being. Secondly, you bring them up, these memories, both painful and joyous, in order to heal your inner child.

As an exercise, begin to think of songs that have touched you emotionally or spiritually throughout your life. These songs should help you to spin naturally up in your spiritual spiral, elevating your vibrations and helping you transition from dimension to dimension. Try to visualize this spiral and ask yourself, "What songs can raise me up to my potential, or help me step into my sovereignty?" The third dimension carried with it the energy that individuals were to perform to another's expectations. When you are able to break out of that thinking and begin to stand alone, you come into your own power, and then you are spiraling upward by reclaiming your sovereignty. Emotionally you are able to reconnect with who you really are and not who you felt you had to be. All of this interconnects and forms this integrated spiral in which your energy is going upward. When you go up in the spiral, you get to see the bigger picture, and things will fall into place because you have greater understanding. When you are at the ground level, you see each tree in the forest; when you spiral upward, you still see the forest, but you are not bogged down by the details, which in many cases are actually the belief systems of individuals with which you are in contact. So you are not trying to make them wrong or invalidate them, your energy is spiraling up so that you see the bigger picture and therefore you can make more informed decisions.

As you think of songs that have particular meaning for you, remember that you can create your own opus by selecting your personal favorites and adjusting them as your needs change. You can create a mantra of sorts by changing certain song lyrics as the situations in your life change. For example, you may have an emotional reaction to the song "I have to say I love you in a song." You may change the lyrics to be "We have to say we love you in a song" in order to remind yourself that your guides are with you, that you are never alone. You should remember to be flexible and to not be afraid to modify lyrics as your needs change.

In keeping your inner child in your heart, nurturing and healing him or her through music, and beginning to vibrate upward on the spiritual spiral, you can begin to create the life, the future of your dreams!

* * * * * * *

Even in the beginning of my spiritual journey, I did not go to bed at night with my new favorite books without intuitively knowing that I needed to read them to beautiful music. The angel books that I was reading needed to be read to music that lifted my spirit and was as ethereal as they were. I purchased several lyrical CDs that were inspiring, emotional, quieting, enlightening, and that resonated with me on a personal level. I also purchased a record system that had the capacity for many CDs and simply turned it on when I came home from work and let it play throughout the night. The music changed as I healed. I loved listening to Enya and Sarah Brightman, and then I decided it was time for men in my life! So I discovered the magical qualities of Josh Groban, Andre Safina, and Russel Watson. My world became one with the world of sound and vibration, and I allowed this beauty to fill my entire house. The healing nature of music became apparent, and I still continue to expand and explore new music as my life takes new twists and turns. Today I am continually touched by U2 and Sting, and of course, the list goes on and on.

In exploring how we all move with the music of life, let us go back to the early days and explore the role of music as it relates to healing. Understanding this brief history brought some clarity to my questions about why and how music is a valuable healing tool. Let us begin with the Celtic bards. The Celtic bards were known as master teachers, using a tale and an instrument to bring forth ancient wisdom. Claire Hamilton in her book *Tales of the Celtic Bards* creates a beautiful exploratory event of the magical centuries of bards and druids. Complete with CD, she re-creates the tales and music that bring the drama and truth to your heartstrings. Each tale is unique and evokes different emotional responses within the listener. The traveling bards held their audience captive, creating magical moments drawing their audience into the truth while singing lyrical poetry to a harplike instrument. The tales could be recounting chivalrous explorations in the otherworld, oftentimes presenting gods and goddesses as their main characters learning and presenting lessons to their kingdoms. The tales had elements of magic as the bards related them and were oftentimes accompanied by the druid teachers of the time. The countries known today as Ireland, Wales, and Scotland were the part of the world that the Celtic bards toured, educating the populace with their ancient myths passed down century upon century.

As defined by the Romans in approximately the first century, the druids were considered the most refined, learned men, capable of great decision-making in the areas of justice and finance while adept in medicinal arts of healing and the magical, occult practices. It took twenty years of study to become a druid, and only after serious and completed studies and rigorous appraisal was a druid accepted into this select society. The word *druid* means "knowledge of the oak." Their word and law were not written but spoken. Ogham was the cryptic druidic language. Many of the original tales have been recorded and savored for all to hear. The tale, the knowledge, the ancient wisdom, and the music have preserved the flavor of the time presented in a scholarly way, giving advice both secular and spiritual. In later centuries, the philosophy of Pythagoras has been determined to have greatly affected the teachings of the Druids.

Other cultures throughout the world use music to be able to reach that healing place. The Native Americans have incorporated music by the use of rattles and drums as part of their rituals. These rituals were performed by individuals for personal healing, or by the group. Healings were performed for the land, for all of the elements of nature, for the animals, and for the tribesman. The Native Americans learned that "rattling" and "drumming" reaches a place deep within where healing can occur. Today the secrets of the shaman have been shared as there is a resurgence of getting back in touch with the ancient and authentic rituals to reawaken that part of you and bring forward all of the knowledge that has been stored within. Traditional songs and chants have been performed for centuries by all native or indigenous tribes. Shamans often created their own "power song" to help them get in touch with their power within. These songs were often impromptu and changed regularly according to the feelings of the moment and what needed to be accomplished by the singing of the song. Powerful and strong, the shamans handled all of the spiritual, philosophical, and psychological healings that were required by their tribe, incorporating music as the healing tool.

Dr. John Diamond has written countless books describing his personal journey of healing through traditional Western medicine, expanding to alternative medicine techniques for a person's total wellbeing. One of his books is entitled *The Way of the Pulse Drumming with Spirit*. He states that Hippocrates called music "the healing power of nature!" The music is the tool that helps create the healing life energy within the body. If something is not balanced, drumming could be the tool that helps bring the body back in sync. He further explains that the word *pulse* indicates movement and that when you connect with your pulse, the ensuing movement flows with the ebb and tide of the universe. As the universe flows, so does the pulse within you. Scientists have long studied that the pulse within is the same pulse of the ocean; the tides move the flow in and out. The catalyst for this movement is the moon. As she moves, so do the tides, so does the pulse, and the continuity of life continues. This continuing energy flow of the universe begins to be part of who we are, and we become part of the flow of the universe. This is a wonderful example of the "oneness" that we are with the universe.

I had the pleasure of meeting a gentleman whose spiritual journey has taken him down the path of using ancient healing techniques to heal what and all that needs to be healed in his clients. His commitment to helping people of all ages and all paths has opened areas and explorations for him to discover that all of healing comes from within. Through his guidance and his use of these ancient techniques, his clients have discovered that all have the commonality that allows the "oneness" of the universe to provide the love and support that is longing within. The universe has helped him to provide many different kinds of healing. His warm and apparent openness has brought him to a place in his life that he can acknowledge the wonder and the awesome connectedness with the "all that is." He takes his cue or cures from nature to lead the client down a path of wellness. One such healing technique he employs is facilitating drum circles in the community. I have attended them and was amazed how the drum reached individuals, allowing them to receive personal insights as well as personal healing. By stripping down to the primordial and allowing the heart to beat to the beat of the drum, you have experienced yet another connectedness to the universe. This experience helps one to connect to their God-given life energy, the life force of the universe.

If you think about the first sound that we have ever heard, we would all agree that it was our mother's heartbeat. So to drum is innate within each of us. In some cultures today, when a woman is going to give birth, the tribe brings a drummer into the area where she is giving birth, to drum to the mother's heartbeat so when the baby is born, he isn't separated from the sound of the mother's heart. In addition to simply being common sense, the purity and innocence of this action is what makes it truly real. Attendees to the drum circle that are expecting mothers proclaim that their unborn baby truly loves the drumming! All of the indigenous cultures had as their focal point: the drum. A village without a drum is a dead village. It is a way to communicate village to village even though the dialect is not understood. The drum has one voice, and it is understood universally.

This gentleman has taken his drum to local VA hospitals and facilitated drum circles there. His initial observations were confirmed by a wife of a patient with Alzheimer's disease who announced that for the first time in a very long time her husband had called her by her name! This is yet another miracle to be acknowledged and witnessed in our everyday lives. There seemed to be some short-term as well as long-term memory improvement. The drum circles were enjoyed and successful because the souls of the participants were reached. Even for a short while, a memory revisited is precious. Families were reunited, and the underlying feelings were ones of gratitude and of being blessed.

Our primal need, the rhythm that we wish to experience to feel connected to each other, is difficult to find in our society. Today we have become so separated; as technology has advanced, we no longer feel that connection within our communities. The drum pulls us back to that primal time when we were a community, a village. In addition to the older patients, the drumming has shown amazing success with autistic children as well. They love to beat on the drum, shake it, make noise, and they are all participating in the circle. The children are no longer separated, no longer feel like they are an outsider, but rather they experience the feeling of being one with the group, the village of drummers.

The Eastern cultures have long realized that chanting and musical vibrations have allowed one to reach the oneness within. Tibetan monks spend hours chanting a particular note to create a sound that reaches far within their soul. This sound has a correlating vibration and, when achieved, can raise the energy level to a higher or heightened state.

Deepak Chopra, in his book *Perfect Health*, reiterates the importance of balance and harmony in our lives in order that we may create for ourselves perfect health. His wellness center, The Chopra Center for Well Being, teaches patients a primordial sound meditation. This meditation is based on many thousands of years of beliefs that sound within the body when unaltered maintains a healthy state and that disease may in fact be sound that has gone awry. This is of course an extremely simplified layman's explanation, but the point is made that it is the sound or vibration in the body that the body not only listens to but can create wellness.

Others may use tuning forks to help return a healthy vibration to the body and to help reset or retune the body. Again a simplified explanation is that the tuning fork sends out a vibration that the body listens to and can actually alter a vibration within the body.

My healing group has done healings on many individuals. We are all Reiki masters, and oftentimes a friend or a friend of a friend comes to us for healing. We each have a specialty and we each heal differently. We began to incorporate the drum during our healings, and we found that the sound used vibrated right into the depth of the one being healed. When the session was over, again and again positive comments were made by the recipient that the drumming sensation vibrated right through their very being, allowing the person to travel down a path deep within and awaken refreshed from the experience. Occasionally a visual experience would be felt by the person being healed that perhaps came as an answer to a question or simply a guide or a totem coming to offer their love and support, all the while providing comfort to the part of their spirit that was feeling the fear created by an imbalance.

Have you ever heard of an angel harp healing? I have met an extremely talented and beautiful healer, one that channels the angels as she plays the strings of an angel harp. As you lie down, the angel harp is set upon your torso. The harp is played and the sound and vibration are felt deep within, through your body into the deepest part of who you are. The harp sends the vibration through you, releasing what needs to be released as your angels' love and guidance comes forward, explaining what is occurring and why. The experience is one of a kind, and while magnificent, it is the vibration that helps us to heal.

Each one of us is a healer and can heal is or her own body. So as healers, the very simple techniques such as rattles, drumming, or tuning forks may be employed which help to bring the body into a state of balance. Any of these items are readily available either at local spiritual or healing centers or online. We know that our bodies have been created in perfect simplicity; unfortunately, it is our input, our lifestyle, our stress, our emotional states that have taken simple perfection and replaced it with a complexity of imbalances and diseases wreaking havoc within, creating both physical and mental disturbances.

Creating your own opus is such an easy and most efficient way of listening to your music which only you relate to in order to heal you! Today everyone has easy access to a wide variety of music. As you look at our culture, it is obvious that music is enjoyed by all ages as you observe the number of I-Pods, and even cell phone rings creatively or humorously employ songs identifying individual callers. Everything is possible as technology has made every song from every time period by every musician available! As you create your opus by choosing music that is meaningful to you, your emotional state can learn to relax and de-stress. If you have had many emotional ups and downs with love interests in your life but never dealt with the pain of separation, it would be valuable to listen to music that helps bring back those difficult moments as it is only when you bring things up to the surface that you can heal them. Only you know what song or songs were "your songs" or songs that were current at the time that tap into the memory. So you begin to help yourself heal by picking up on those feelings, revisiting them, and acknowledging or identifying the emotion created by the event, learning how to embrace that emotion, and releasing it to God. So being mindful of your music selection is going to help make a successful healing. When the hurt is processed, then perhaps you want to heal by listening to some "feel good" music. This you may want to be life enhancing and soothing and lyrically beautiful. A song that makes you feel wonderful.

When I was starting to do the work on myself, I found songs that really touched me and made a CD for both my home and my car. Each song I chose allowed me to take a trip down memory lane and heal the emotion that I found dangling! As other hurts surfaced, other songs were found, and the musical journey proved to be a healing journey. I learned not only that it was okay to go back to that place and time but that it was a mandatory journey if one is to expect healing to occur. I also learned to let myself cry to a sad song, to allow myself to experience the angst, and to bring myself back to a better place, releasing anything that did not feel like love to me. The not going down the path is what keeps the emotion unhealed. It isn't easy, but with a little courage, focus, and determination you can heal yourself so completely. I can't emphasize enough that the trip down memory lane is so worthwhile, and not only do you feel proud that you took the journey, but as you feel the benefits within, you know that the journey was not only the right journey but a necessary one.

CHAPTER IV

Soul-Searching

*Light is the magnet of hope and reason that
brings the soul closer to the essence of being*

—Spirit, 2007

You are fifth-dimensional and the planet is fifth-dimensional, but you haven't always felt in sync. The reason for this disjointedness is that souls are developing at different rates. There are a lot of souls that have remained three-dimensional, and some perhaps have shifted into the fourth dimension but have not shifted again into the fifth dimension. So you have been living in a world that doesn't feel fifth-dimensional because most of the participants are not fifth-dimensional. Now one of the ways that you have been called upon to overcome this is to use your powers of creativity to consciously create your surroundings. While that meets with success, it feels as if it is a lot of work. It feels like it is a lot of effort, and you were hoping that when you got to the fifth dimension the processing and learning would be effortless.

We are not going to talk here about techniques that you can use to bring things into your life as you already know how to do this. What we are going to talk about is allowing this process to be easier, to be more fulfilling, and to be more playful; not about trying to fix anything, or even trying to learn anything, but rather allowing the energies of a fifth-dimensional status to permeate not only your body but your surroundings. So it is not a technique; it is not even what we call a process. It is just a manner by which you live life with greater ease and with less of the effortful learning process.

The way that you do this is with a team, a nonphysical group of beings that surround you that are going to be coming into your energy or your auric field. These energies are going to be coming in on a ley line that is just to the right of your heart. As you know, you have many ley lines going throughout your body. The one that you are probably the most familiar with is the line that connects your chakras. If you have done acupuncture or acupressure or have studied massage, you know that there are many, many ley lines that run throughout the body. But what we are talking about is creating a path directly from your front area coming to you on the right side of the body near to your shoulder, really just to the right of the heart. If you look at the feng shui of the body, that part is your spiritual knowledge area.

This team of spiritual beings will consist of some that you recognize and some that you will not. As you think about this, can you feel the pulse of this concept? You may be able to feel their souls come marching along the ley line into your auric field. Among these beings there will be a lot of what we call the fifth-dimensional counselors. You might also have some teachers coming in as well as some of your major guides. Your team is going to be defined as time goes on, and you will be made aware of it in the appropriate timeframe. You actually will not even go through a process of learning who your team is, although for most people, we will talk about a few members of the team. Instead, you will just have the thought that they are around, and you will begin to feel their entrance into your auric field.

At the same time that you are allowing this to take place in your auric field, you will notice that you are suddenly receiving the nourishment and the support that you have been longing for without having to ask for it. You will feel as if you are completing certain parts of your auric field. So if at the same time you are feeling in terms of good, better, best, and beyond, you might be feeling better, going into best, but not yet at best and beyond. In some circumstances you will feel another ley line that comes into your auric field; this one comes to the left of your heart chakra at a diagonal. These will be some of your benefactors, the unseen benefactors. These benefactors come in on the left shoulder, the left arm, and the left lung area. Sometimes you might feel the ancestral benefactors, or what the Hawaiians refer to as the *Hamakua*. These benefactors do not necessarily have to be relatives that have passed over, but they can be a type of guide—perhaps a lifetime processing assistant or a major arcana guide, your companion counterparts, or your twin soul or any number or beings. They remain unseen in terms of not being known by your consciousness. This can happen at different times during the day, and when it happens you begin to feel more comfortable inside your body as a fifth-dimensional being on a planet that is fifth-dimensional. The key here is that this assistance allows you to not require beings around you to be fifth-dimensional. So what this does in a sense is broadens your auric field. Think of a baby that you love very much. Now, imagine how you would want to surround that baby in a very warm white blanket. If there were diseases going around, you may want to wrap the baby in even a few more blankets. The same is true with your auric field. These beings help to thicken the auric field around you to protect you from your surroundings. Now you don't have to invite them in as you will just feel what we call the pulse of their energy coming to you.

Your soul, which sits right behind the heart chakra, will begin to bring forward these vibrations as you feel the perfection of all things. You will feel this because again your auric field is getting wider and wider and wider. Some of you may remember a fourth-dimensional technique where you were to feel your energy getting bigger and it would fill the room, and then it would fill the house, and then it would fill the block that you lived on, and then upward to even the state that you lived in. That was an exercise in consciously expanding your energy. This, however, is quite different. What we are talking about now is to simply consciously breathe and trust that these things are done for you because our powers of attraction are much greater than they have ever been. What you want to attract to you is the concept of ease in this process so that things will happen upon you. You will feel as if you are in the perfection of a fifth-dimensional reality regardless of what is going on around you. It feels as if the world fades away into the distance; it fades further and further and further. Now it won't happen all of the time, but it will be happening for you more and more. All that you have to do is to be conscious of it to a certain degree and then relax and smile and feel yourself in that state of wellbeing.

Begin with trying to feel your heart chakra. Then see if you can get a sense of the perfection of your soul right behind the heart chakra. The heart chakra is in fact driving the automobile that is your soul. Get a sense if you can feel it. As you get a sense of it, you may also be feeling those things in the body that don't feel perfect. That is because whenever you feel the sense of the soul, you will automatically feel those things inside of you that don't feel perfect, whether it is worry, disappointment, or unforgiveness.

In reality all of this is fear. You are afraid of certain things happening, and you are afraid of certain things not happening. You are afraid of certain people around you. You are afraid of certain people that are not around you but still have an impact on your life. You are afraid of what is coming or what you don't think is coming into your life. These fears become an open wound. This open wound may cause you to slip out of the fifth dimension and into the fourth dimension. Some of you might even feel that you are slipping a bit more, into a three-dimensional way of handling these fears. But remember that everything that you need to heal this wound is already here. It is all just energy. Whether or not your hopes or fears come true is all based on energy.

The fifth-dimensional way allows you to feel the energy without having to do the processing. Your willingness to feel the energy is very similar to your going outside when all of a sudden it starts to rain. You determine that you can do one of two things: You can either stand in the rain and feel it, or you can make a run for it and try not to let the rain hit your body. So a lot of times you want to protect yourself from the energy. Other times you say, "I just am going to go ahead and feel it, it is just energy." But when you talk about doing soul-searching, you are in fact searching for the perfection of the soul inside of you and you are trying to match that perfection with your experience of life.

The only thing that stands between the perfection of the soul and the perfection that you feel in life is the intensity of fear. That is the only thing that keeps you from having a perfect life. It is not what has happened to you, it is the fear of what may or may not happen to you. That is the fear that is preventing you from feeling the perfection of life. So here you have a perfect soul, and you live on a planet where you have learned about fear through your experiences. Again sometimes you are afraid that something might happen, and other times you are afraid that something is not going to happen that you would like to have happen. So there it is in a nutshell: fear is what is preventing you from feeling the perfection of your soul, and this fear is reinforced because you live on a planet where the majority of people are two-, three-, and four-dimensional.

Now you have some people who are very advanced fifth-dimensionally, and you have a few that are even sixth-dimensional. If they are advanced in that way, they are never going to cause you a problem. They are never going to cause ill will to happen to you. They do not operate that way. So your feeling the lack of perfection gets reflected in having to deal with individuals who don't know what love is yet. They do not know how to live in a win-win world. It is either about their competition or lack of knowledge, but they feed on the fear inside of you. The wise person lets himself or herself know that that fear is there. It is there; it is taking up a part of your energy because you feel it and you focus upon it. But remember, it is just energy! So rather than seeing this fear as being evidence of something that you are doing wrong or that you are not doing enough to fix it, simply see it as energy. That neutralizes it, so don't be afraid to look at it and say yes, "That is what my open wound is about." You may have several of these wounds, and remember that you do not have to do any processing to fix them. Just bring your fears into your awareness so that your fifth-dimensional body of consciousness can begin to dissipate it and free yourself from that fear.

The fact that you do not have to consciously process your fears is a beautiful gift of the fifth dimension. Again, you simply bring your fear up to the surface to allow it to start to dissolve. You may even state your fears out loud so that the power that it has over you begins to dissipate. Then ask for the fears to be removed. Or as you feel your team come in or as you feel your unseen benefactors come into your auric field, you might even say to one of them, "I want this removed." And then you wait for the results, you wait for the evidence of its removal. The proof that your fear has been removed can be as simple as waking up in the morning feeling lighter. You feel as if a great burden has been removed from your shoulders. You will feel this way because as you move along in the fifth dimension you are not just going forward, but you are going upward. As these fears begin to subside and begin to dissipate around you, you are going forward. When it is completed you will feel yourself going into an ascension. This will automatically happen; your vibrational frequency will accelerate without you having to do anything about it. You will consciously feel that your energy, your etheric body, is ascending. You are not going to ascend off of the planet, you are simply increasing your vibrational frequency.

Now when individuals do soul-searching, what they want is not just the removal of those things that don't feel like love to them, but they want to have passion in their lives. They want to have passionate lives, and they want to be passionate about everything: about life itself, about jobs, about opportunities. If you are going to feel passion, then what is unlike passion is not going to feel very comfortable inside your auric field any longer. So you are not running from fear, and you are not processing the fear—you just bring it up to the surface and feel it so that you are consciously aware of it and then allow it to be removed.

Now many of you have had a difficult relationship, and you go over and over in your mind a conversation that you had with someone. And it keeps going and it occupies all of your time. You have all of these bigger things to look at, but you cannot get beyond that particular difficulty. It is very frustrating for your guides because they see that you have a soul that is ready to emerge, that you want to go from becoming into beingness. So the emergence is becoming and the beingness is not going outside to try to make something happen. And the beingness is not going over and over and over in your mind a conversation that was problematic for you. It is the totality of your potential. So your guides, these beings that surround you and these beings that have an influence on you, they want you to go into the becomingness as a prelude to being. And it is beyond being human. They realize that you have taken human form, and you are spirit first. If you had only one day to be a spirit occupying a human body, you would probably act very differently than what you do on a day-to-day basis.

You must step into your potential. You must activate the imprint of your soul onto your body. It is your blueprint. And for it to be activated, you can't be going around and around in the same circle over something that has bothered you. There is often a disproportionate amount of time that you spend on things you don't really care about due to some unhealed open wound. You need to remove yourself from the day-to-day babble of the marketplace, from your ego-based thoughts and annoyances, and decide that you will no longer spend time on them. In doing this you live the life that you were meant to live, not the life that you keep saying to yourself that you are going to get to. You are going to be living the life that you are meant to live. It is very easy and very doable to live a life with assistance from our closest beings by just asking!

The purpose of soul-searching is to identify what it is that you are passionate about. It is when these passions are identified that you will make a conscious decision not to settle for anything less. The thoughts will create your future by giving your soul direction. In a very loving way, you can give yourself the direction you need by making up a plan. For example, you can make an open-ended five-year plan in which you are going to have those things that are meaningful to you. This may involve being able to relax the mind (the mental child) and let yourself experience the flow of energy so that you get into what is referred to as your super consciousness, the fifth body of consciousness. This is your fifth body, and this inner child of this body is the inner child that knows your blueprint. You can make a plan by acknowledging that there are certain things that are important to you, and stripping away those things that are not as important to you, so that the five-year plan is filled not with quantity but with quality. And all of this is done the fifth-dimensional way.

You may be ready to have a meaningful love relationship. If you think about the way you would have treated this in the third or fourth dimension, you would have great doubt about how and when and where this could happen. You may have hoped that it would happen, but the fears would be overriding that it even could happen. You could worry that you are not able to have this because you are not going to be able to attract a relationship to you. But you now know that there are beings that are going to help remove these fears, and you are going to begin to live your life as the "fool" in the tarot. And this means being willing to see where this flow of energy will take you. This means letting go of trying to create what you desire mentally and instead allowing your energy to flow and for that which you desire to come to you.

You need to mentally get out of the way so that your mental child who tends to direct does not control you. You are an adult who has the power to allow the universe to show you which way you are going to go and to feel it as a pulse. That is the fifth-dimensional way, through what we call pulsing. The more that you open yourself up and let the universe show you which way to go, the more you honor your fifth-dimensional energy. So strictly speaking it is to think less and to feel more, making yourself an open book in order to go into super consciousness.

This method of moving yourself forward is probably going to feel a little uncomfortable. To think less and to feel more is unfamiliar to you! You have all been taught that in order to motivate yourself, you must think things through and come up with a game plan. This plan works when you are three-dimensional, but it didn't work too well when you were fourth-dimensional. But now that you are in the fifth dimension, it won't work at all. Remember, letting go is the key to fifth-dimensional living!

When you went from three-dimensional to fourth-dimensional living, you were very hungry to be away from feeling like a victim emotionally. So even though it felt difficult many times, you continually asked yourself, "How many times do I have to connect with my inner child, and how many times do I have to remember that self-love is the prelude to universal love? How many times do I have to love myself when it doesn't feel like I am being loved on the outside?" However you were willing to do this because you were hungry for emotional stability. You didn't like how it felt when you were emotionally unstable, you didn't like how it felt when you were emotionally victimized. You didn't like what was going on when you were in a relationship where there was a lot of blame and finger-pointing. You were hungry for emotional mastery, and you got it.

Now in the fifth dimension, which is the realm of the spiritual healer, you want to see the perfection in all things. What you are not prepared for is the infinity of what happens in the fifth dimension because the infinity has to do with feeling love beyond the boundaries of what you felt emotionally. And so it feels as if in the fifth dimension, things are not moving as quickly, things are not understood as quickly, and you are not getting the results that you are looking for as quickly. Part of it is that even though you are hungry for the results, you do not understand the dynamics of this particular dimension. You need to understand the fifth dimension in order to heal others and yourself by seeing perfection where there has been the illusion of imperfection.

It is certainly a challenge to see perfection where there is amongst many on our planet, if not most, the illusion of imperfection. In order to do this, you must turn your attention to the infinity of love. Now, try to wrap your mind around this infinity. It is difficult to do, isn't it? Love is not just what you gave to your parents, and it is not what you are seeking in a lover. That is not all that it is. It is not simply the love that you have for friends that you are aligned with, or soul mates that you have had in this lifetime, or animals that you have loved. Love is what keeps your consciousness alive, expanding and being able to do things that you wouldn't even dream of while being in a physical body.

And that type of love means that you will do great things.

You still want to see perfection, but you will see less and less of the illusion of imperfection because you won't be looking behind you. Now when you look forward what you are going to see is beings that are highly evolved. You are not going to see an illusion of imperfection. This is important to understand—when you truly look forward, you are not going to see the imperfections and have to remind yourself "I am in a perfect world, I am in a perfect world." You are going to see the perfection that was promised to you, and so now it is time for you to turn your attention and to move forward in this way.

So get a sense of that right now. You haven't graduated from the fifth dimension, you haven't gone to a planet where they only have fifth-dimensional beings, but your focus is different. You are now going to go into the infinity of love and feel comfortable. And remember once it happens inside of you, you will attract more and more of that to you. So even though you live on a planet where you have three-, four-, and five-dimensional beings, you will still continue genuinely feeling the perfection. The more you see this perfection, the more you will attract beings of light, which you can think of as sunbeams.

Let yourself imagine the Dalai Lama. Most likely the picture that appears in your mind is him experiencing one of the joyful laughs with which he is so associated. This is so true of many of the masters—they love to laugh! Everything is so delightful to them, nothing is a strain, and nothing is difficult. That is what is intended in the fifth dimension. You are meant to look into life's infinite possibilities rather than looking over your shoulder at the past. The good news is that you aren't learning in the fifth dimension the way you learned things fourth-dimensionally. That felt like a chore, this is a blessing. All you have to

Limitless Possibilities

do is let yourself feel the infinite nature of being. Let that be as real to you as getting up and going to work. Let that be as real to you as having to counsel someone who is having a difficult time emotionally. Let that be as real to you as feeling the presence of one of your guides.

All of us on this planet have experienced a limited form of love. For most individuals, you have never had limitless love. You didn't get it from your parents, you didn't get it from your siblings, and you certainly didn't get it in romantic love relationships. You didn't learn it from teachers, and you didn't learn it from coworkers. In fact, for many of you, the closest that you have come to experiencing infinite love is from your personal interactions with your spirit guides and teachers. However, once you are looking forward and feeling comfortable with infinite states of love, then you begin to attract those things into your life, and all of those things that you have learned about the fifth dimension will come into play. Remember, self-love is the prelude to universal love. You must fully love yourself in order to experience infinite love. Let yourself feel that infinite love and remind yourself that you will never be at the end of it because there is not a finite resolution of love. There is an infinite number of ways for love to manifest. So you have an infinite number of experiences of love waiting for you, with no upper limits!

You may be wondering what happens when an individual wants to experience the infinite love but in fear pulls back and doesn't allow oneself to go for it. A person may pull back because they are afraid to be too far "out there," or they have a fear of disappointment, or they are afraid that they will not be dealing with reality. What they are forgetting, however, is that this is the reality, this is their creation. Infinite love is the antithesis of fear. So when fear arises, as it will, remind yourself that this is simply because you are part of the learning process, you are learning how to live fifth-dimensionally.

In talking about the infinity of love, we also want to mention the role that faith has to play in all of this. There is a level of faith that all of you who are interested in metaphysics have, and this level of faith has to do with the fact that you are on the right path. The path that you have chosen for yourself in terms of your development is going to lead to the outcomes of your desire. These outcomes could be greater states of consciousness of expanding light and the joy and enrichment of life as you go through it. Now sometimes you have faith in something external rather than having a faith in yourself. You need to have faith in yourself, not for a certain desired outcome, but faith in yourself that you have chosen the path that is the best course for you—faith not in your belief systems, but faith in your feelings, faith that there is a reason why you feel the way you do.

When you have complete faith in and about the feelings that you are having, then everything else falls into place. You do not have to worry about outcomes; you do not have to worry about whether or not you are approaching something in the correct way. You can let all of that go and just trust that all of your feelings are in fact guiding you along the very best way for you to approach not only your development but what you are going to experience on the planet.

* * * * * * * *

Learning to navigate into the fifth dimension was an interesting process to experience. After understanding what the fifth dimension is all about and the way to work into it, then it is just a matter of putting your awareness and focus and discipline on what needs to be adjusted or changed to begin to be open to receiving the fifth-dimensional energy.

One of the initial steps that I took was to allow myself to be the observer in my life. When you look at yourself from a different vantage point, you see things that you normally would not see. I also learned that although I wanted to participate fully in my life, I needed to learn the difference between being active and reactive. Once I was able to observe my reactions in situations, I was able to determine whether or not my response was good for me and for others and for the universe. Did the event warrant my reaction? Was I expending my energy appropriately? Was I sending out energy to the planet in a beneficial way, a positive way?

I learned very quickly by simply being attuned to the hows and the whys of the above questions I could learn to compare the difference to how I felt in different situations. At work an event beyond my control could take place, and I could react to it in an irritated or agitated way and afterward feel not very good inside. Taking this a step further—voicing the irritation to my coworkers—was just enough to alter the energy in the office. Besides the fact that this energy was certainly not pleasant to be around, it oftentimes was just enough to be incendiary to my coworkers. They in turn would react to my reaction, and their irritations would spew forth until the entire office was filled with energies that become toxic all around.

So I made a conscious effort to remove the negativity from my day-to-day life. There were thousands of little ways that I displayed my displeasure, or unhappiness, or sadness or whatever other negative emotion that I experienced on a day-to-day basis. I also learned to not join into conversations that were negative or complaining. Instead of making a comment which would add more fuel to the fire, I tried to find something positive to say or make a comment to look at the event from a different angle so that I was being a contributor to my and my coworkers' wellbeing. The difference with how I felt inside was phenomenal. I now understood the phrase "misery loves company." Today when I slip back into my old habits, I immediately am aware of the difference of how it makes me feel inside. As Markas has said often, if it doesn't feel like love to you, simply release it and use a different approach until it does feel like love!

Have you ever considered how the day-to-day banter sends out different energies? When you are out and meet new people and they engage you in small talk, what is the first thing that everyone always talks about? The weather. Yes, there are many comments: I hate the rain, where is the sun, it is too cold, or it is too hot—all conditions that certainly affect us but that we have absolutely no control over. Why do we feel it is necessary to comment in a negative fashion, pulling not only us down but the people we come into contact with? Of course this is true for how we talk about our sports figures, our celebrities, our world leaders, family members, girlfriends, etc. We make disparaging remarks all the time about people that are in our line of fire. What does that say about us? Why do we choose to send this negativity out into the world?

I think it is important to not only understand that the energy we send out is magnified when it comes in contact with similar energy but that that means that we are actually contributing to the negativity in the world. Negative energy does not discern or categorize itself. So if you send out a whining, complaining energy, it does not discriminate against an energy whose basis may have been hate. Negative is negative, and when it all gathers together it just expands and expands and expands. So the next time you think to call someone a name, or tell a story that is hurtful, or participate in a conversation that is gossipy, remember that that energy actually is making the hate in the world stronger. When you understand this simple truth, our personal responsibility for how we present ourselves and how we choose to participate in the world becomes increasingly important.

In a very short time you learn to identify the difference between how you feel inside—do I feel like love or do I feel my inner child inside whimpering or complaining? If you feel the inner child, recognize that it is fear that is making him/her act the way he/she does. What is the source or sources of the fear? So you begin to work with your inner child to identify the fears.

I learned that you live your life either loved-based or fear-based. Love cannot live where fear exists, and fear cannot live where love exists. I needed to make a choice—love or fear? I chose love as I knew it was the only choice. How can you choose to grow into a loving energy if you allow fear to control and make choices for you? I needed to become my own spiritual warrior or move into the leading role of my own life.

I remember deciding it was time for me to have a conference with all of my inner children. So I invited them to a "tea party," an event where they would come all dressed up and with their best manners and their finest behavior. (Any social engagement is acceptable—but I would hold off on inviting the inner children to be on a sports team until they really learn to work as a team!) It was on this occasion that I introduced them to each other, politely citing their strengths but also gently mentioning their weaknesses. It was time that the parent in me parent them! Identifying the sources of fear is the first step toward being able to acknowledge the problem. Next came the hard work, digging deep, sorting it all out, and then addressing the issue with the appropriate inner child. Which inner child is affected by which problem? The emotional issues that surface from time to time come from our emotional inner child. This child needs to feel safe, secure, and loved. The mental child oftentimes just needs to be talked to calmly and logically as she likes to run the show with word games or playing the brainiac in front of the others. This inner child needs to learn to take her place amongst the other inner children and not direct every waking moment.

The physical inner child sometimes just wants attention, and she complains of all kinds of aches and pains, headaches, or whatever ailment she can conjure up. This child tends to react to the emotional inner child and plays off of the fear of the moment. So each of these children needed to figure out they were part of a team. As team players, there are no stars—the rule is you either win as a team or lose as a team. There is an inherent responsibility that each team member must face this fact and own up to it. The parent has the inherent responsibility of each body of consciousness to direct adequate communication and attention to each inner child, helping them to get to a place of love, safety, and security. The ultimate rewards are great. I had to teach myself how to love myself. Little by little I observed their reactions to things and tried to circumvent their behavior. Before long we were all getting along and all behaving very well. I was not only calm inside but loving. What a wonderful feeling to experience!

I had now created this atmosphere within that I was ready to invite my fifth-dimensional counselors to come. I knew of course the definition, but now it was time to implement the learning. I was able to see the perfection where formerly I saw the illusion of imperfection. I could participate in the world by making positive comments about our world or my day-to-day life. I could flip the negative over to the positive. I actually felt my vibrations rising. I felt great inside, and my energy was flowing and flowing.

When you allow yourself to receive these beautiful energies and it becomes a part of your life, not having the beautiful feeling is such a loss. So the better you feel, the more you want to feel that way, and the way you respond to things, the way you think about things, and the way you act allows that feeling to become addicting and your energy expands.

We have learned that energy expands outward and then upward. So what we send out also allows us to grow and spiral upward. You can feel the lightness inside and your heart feels so light and full of life. The energy that you attract to you is also light and full of love. It is a gift to be able to reach this place, and the gift is the gift of love that we not only give ourselves but to the world. This gift has been given to each of us.

I know when I request something from the other side that my request is heard, processed, and answered. Of course, I have learned that the answer is sometimes not the answer I expected. I have learned to relinquish all control and expectations. After all isn't that the way to remain limited? Who am I to decide what the best way is to resolve a problem? The universe has the best vantage point and far greater than mine. The universal energy provides the best answer, and it is simply up to us to receive it. This is another way to develop faith. I just know and trust in the process, and then I am there to witness the results! You begin to live in the flow of the universal energies and begin to receive the gifts that the universe bestows daily. I turned my life into a win-win situation, and I also learned the value of living from good to best to better and receiving from the beyond!

CHAPTER V

Elements in E-motion

*Love the experience, accept the pain that goes with it,
but when love is no longer a gift . . . give it back. If not,
it becomes a burden to both parties.*

—Markas, 2009

Knowing that we are all intimately connected with all of our five inner children, let's discuss your inner child from your emotional body of consciousness in more depth. If you have worked on healing the hurts of your inner child, then you know that this processing can be a difficult experience. Oftentimes the inner child will disappear or simply go away because it was too painful to deal with. However, one lesson that you learned as you began your emotional processing was that there was no way to successfully turn back. In other words, once you gained an understanding of what was driving you and what was causing the sadness or anger inside of you, you knew that you must continue to do the emotional processing not only in order to be successful, but also because you had experienced glimpses of "feeling" better.

We use the word "feeling" specifically because what happens is that your emotions are things from the past that you carry inside of you, be they favorable or unfavorable. When you bring that remembrance up to the present moment, then it is a present-moment feeling. Many times we have repressed those emotions because it was too difficult for you to bring forward those things that felt unhealthy to you, those things that felt as if they were bothersome and that reenacted a difficult time period in your life. It would be the same as if you shoved dirt under the rug; you know it is there because it has formed a tangible lump under the rug, but you simply did not want to deal with it or see it.

But as you began this emotional processing you found that it felt good to complete with something. It felt good to close the door on something that traumatized you in childhood. You had been carrying it around, and it had affected how you interact with individuals in the present time period. Furthermore, as all of these issues are healed, you are able to let your energy flow easier through your body and you do not get hooked on negative things the way you would have done in the past. For example, you do not get hooked into arguments with others or become affected by someone else's inner child taunting you. You are able to, as the expression goes, "let go and let God." That of course doesn't mean that you liked their behaviors, but you were able to say, "I am not going to deal with this because these behaviors are unacceptable." This is a far different approach than to attempt to defend yourself and getting hooked into a lower vibration of energy and allowing yourself to be pulled down.

So as you began to process, you could recognize its benefits. You may not have thought the processing was fruitful or helpful at the time, but on a deep soul level you recognized that to not process would cause you to be stagnant. It is not the processing that causes you to get into the repetitive behavior cycle that makes you go around and around in circles, but rather the refusal to process these things. Remember, the goal in growth and development is a movement that is upward in a spiral motion. If you did not have that emotional healing and had not helped your emotional child to deal with those needles from the past, then you would simply keep going around and around in circles, and you would continue to invite in that which you feared.

So when you handle those emotions, you are in fact handling those fears which are connected to those past behaviors and past situations and past relationships that were difficult. When you handle the fear, then the wound can get healed and you would also begin to feel elements of mastery in the physical realm. In other words, you could live simply and beautifully without feeling as if you had to protect yourself emotionally. You are no longer operating from a base of fear, but you are operating from a base of knowingness. Remember, as other situations come in you would know how to handle them, and you wouldn't need to be afraid or shy away from people or situations as these situations would not be bigger than you and they would not be more powerful than you. As you handled each of these experiences that reminded you of experiences that you had completed, you would handle each new one more efficiently and better than any of the earlier experiences, and you would feel as if you were the center of your reality!

During the time period of the fourth dimension, there were many key phrases that captured the spirit of the time and described the fourth-dimensional evolution. The expressions were all about your inner child such as "you attract in what you love or what you fear" and "there is no competition." You learned that it was best to get out of that feeling of competing with someone or trying to better someone or to get the best of them. These phrases became all-encompassing in this transformation. You actually moved from a state of feeling unhealed and vulnerable to a state where you felt the healing had taken place and so there was the removal of fear. Your guide in this fourth dimension happened to be called your removal-of-fear guide, and once the fear was removed, the guide no longer served as your removal-of-fear guide. Often this removal-of-fear guide would sign on in a new role as another guide for you that exists in the fourth dimension called your expansion-of-love guide.

So the guides in the fourth dimension were your emotional realm coordinator and your temporary removal-of-fear guide and your permanent expansion-of-love guide. You may or may not have been aware of what was going on behind the scenes during this time because your focus was to make sure that you were staying connected to your emotional body of consciousness. It was important that your inner child no longer felt abandoned or pushed off to the side as if he or she did not matter. Ideally you then formed a very close relationship with your inner child and you were able to reach out and comfort this child when he or she was afraid or lonely. This was how you were beginning to teach and to feel self-love. Before, the only way you could get love validated in your life was to have someone outside of you loving you. If you were involved with someone romantically and their inner child was unhealed, the relationship was probably not very good because you could not feel loved.

Before your self-healing, the inner child never had an opportunity to experience that inner confidence and that feeling of love from anyone. This caused the inner child to feel as if they just couldn't fit into the world. When you healed, however, what you found was that your inner child needed a lot of love, had been missing a lot of love, and only you knew exactly how your inner child needed to be loved. This doesn't mean that you won't have spouses, lovers, or close relationships where others will love you in the way that they can and it feels good, but it is certainly not a substitute for self-love. So once you began to interact with your inner child, you began to get this grand sense of what love really was. Once you have that inside of you, even if it was an effortful process, you had to keep reminding yourself if you felt a lack of love to go within and to be with your inner child to see why he or she felt that way. Pretty soon the more you brought consciousness to your inner child, the more it was no longer an effortful process and it began to become an automatic process.

When the world was a three-dimensional reality, most individuals did not pay attention to their inner child. This caused a great deal of feeling lonely and feeling abandoned in love relationships. Often individuals would turn to their spiritual body of consciousness to help remedy this. As we all know, spirituality is very helpful and transformational for those who need to feel a part of the universe and a need to connect with their unlimited abilities through God. So these individuals used their spirituality and turned to religion to help make them feel better. This may have helped them in the short term, but it did not heal them. And be assured there is a great difference between the two. It helped them because they could connect with their God and the saints or spirits in their particular religion, which helped to improve their mood and allowed their guides more access to help them. However, they were still not healed.

The whole purpose of moving into the fourth dimension was to become conscious of your emotional states. Once you became conscious of them, you realized that it was different than spirituality. Those individuals who would condemn metaphysics or would say that metaphysics really did not exist, or that it was fraudulent, those individuals did not make the distinction in terms of healing their emotions. These individuals who use spirituality or a mental approach to put down metaphysics are not healing their emotions. They are simply trying to support whatever their particular beliefs are, and they are standing in judgment of others. It was and is only those individuals that are willing to do the emotional processing required that are able to become conscious of their emotions. These individuals are able to transform their lives and create circumstances in which they are able to see the bigger picture and therefore to help themselves emotionally. As all of this was taking place on the planet, you shifted into the fourth dimension.

You may find it amusing as you look back on the past few years that you probably couldn't wait to get to the fifth dimension because it felt like it was such hard work being in the fourth dimension. Now that you are in the fifth dimension, there is a level of confusion of what this fifth dimension looks like. Even though you may not have healed yet in the fourth dimension, you did know about your emotions, but you do not really know what a spiritual healer is. Nor do you know how exactly that fits into your compass or your directions you take into the world. You may have thought the fourth dimension was difficult because all of your emotions were building up for centuries and centuries from your past lives and from your current one. But when you get to the fifth dimension, you realize that you know how to heal emotionally and how to help yourself get out of the difficulties that you may get yourself into.

You probably noticed that the title of this chapter is "Elements in E-motion," with an interesting separation of the word emotion. The motion that we are referring to is the flow of energy in the fifth dimension. We are talking about taking the emotional energy that has been healed and using it in the flow of energy, the motion of energy that occurs in the fifth dimension. What you have done up to this point in the fourth dimension is absolutely wonderful! This is not a replacement to what you have previously learned, this is an additional process. You are going to be adding into your life in a very simple way, in a very present-moment way, and these elements of e-motion are going to help your inner child to take a more prime position in your life. In other words, you are not going to heal your inner child and shove him or her into the closet. This healing will help your inner child to develop a level of maturity and a level of enlightenment.

Emotionally the objective is not only to heal, but to use your emotions to bring emotional wellness into your personality in order to better relate to your spouse, your children, and other individuals. And to do this in a way that makes you feel confident, that allows you to feel the self-love that you deserve so that you do not enter into relationships from a standpoint of being needy or commanding attention by seeing how you can get love from someone else through manipulation. As you well know, there are many individuals who are still doing things this way, but keep in mind that they are not happy! It is old-fashioned in the sense that those old techniques are less and less effective as the planet gets further and further along away from a three-dimensional train of thinking. Not only is it old-fashioned, it is even beyond just that by being a three-dimensional experience.

* * * * * * *

As I think back to my early childhood, I see that I grew up with a lot of fears. It doesn't seem to matter what we are fearful of as a fear is a fear and left unattended can be paralyzing. I remember from the time I was a little girl my mother was deathly afraid of mice. She told the story again and again about an event that happened to her when she was in her twenties. She and her coworkers were attending a company picnic at an amusement park near Lake Erie. One of the younger men found a little mouse and thought he would play a practical joke on my mother. He with mouse in hand crept quietly behind her, tugged at the back of her shirt, and dropped the mouse. Screaming and horrified, she fled the picnic. Every time she repeated the story, the fear swept over her face, reliving that initial reaction of panic. For years this fear controlled her life and also affected my life as she was terrified that a mouse would somehow get into our house.

From the time I was a young girl, her obsession with cleanliness made my life miserable as the list of chores that I needed to complete each evening after dinner got longer and longer! She was a perfectionist, so I lived with the constant fear of receiving her heavy hand if my job was not done to her satisfaction. She inspected every kitchen countertop for any morsel or crumb that may have remained after its being both wiped down and washed. In addition, after every meal I swept out the floors in three connecting rooms so that they would be free of any invisible speck that might entice a little mouse to visit! Over the years, this fear never subsided but grew as she repeated the story again and again. I used to wonder (I would not have dared utter this thought out loud) "how could she be afraid of a little mouse?" Sadly, she never overcame her fear, and when she died at the age of eighty-seven, she took this fear with her to her resting place.

Have you ever heard the expression that the "apple doesn't fall far from the tree?" Well, similarly, I fell into the same fate. One hot summer morning when I was about seven years old, I awoke early to the sound of the milkman. We used to get milk delivery (in glass bottles no less) to our milk chute at the far end of our garage. I got out of bed and dressed in my long summer nightgown and in bare feet proceeded to the garage. You entered the garage from the kitchen, and as I stepped into the garage, I distinctly remember the door slamming behind me. I worked my way around my mother's car to the milk chute. I remember sensing some movement on the garage floor, but wearing a long nightgown I could not see the floor that I was stepping on. Something made me stop, and I pulled my nightgown to my knees to see where I was walking, and there on the garage floor were seven or eight snakes all moving in different directions. I remember they were different sizes and different colors. I screamed and ran straight ahead to the double garage door in front of me, throwing it open (we did not have garage door openers in those days) and then pulling it right back down behind me.

I was amazed to have found the strength to open and close the garage doors. I quickly remembered that if I let the snakes out of the garage and they escaped into the grass, I would never be able to play on the grass again. I ran down my driveway and turned down the street, running in the middle of the street screaming. A neighbor came out of her house to find out why I was running down the street screaming in my nightgown! I told her what had happened. I was very concerned that my mother would have awakened to my scream and the noise of my opening and closing the garage door and that she may have followed me out to the garage, experiencing the same scare that I had. So I asked the neighbor to call my mother and warn her. Immediately my mother woke up my nine-year-old brother, a boy scout at heart who spent most of his summer days in the park or the valley near our house catching tadpoles, salamanders, and yes, snakes. My mother just didn't know that on this occasion he had brought them home with him. The box that he put them in wasn't strong enough and they had escaped. My mother instructed my brother to pick them up one by one and take them back down into the park and let them go.

This event was a nightmare for me. From that day forward, I could not go to bed without getting up and looking under the bed for snakes. Sometimes I would get up and look three and four times in the middle of the night to check under the bed. I tried to sleep with a light on, but my mother put an end to that after a couple of days. When I got quiet and was ready for bed, I could visualize the snakes and actually hear and sense their movement on the concrete floor, revisiting that initial experience night after night. This fear stayed with me well into my adult years. In the fourth grade in science class, we oftentimes would stand up and take turns reading from the chapters. One science class period, as one of my classmates was reading our current chapter, as she finished the page and we turned to the next page, there exposed was a full page of a picture of a jungle. There right in front of my eyes was a python wrapped around a tree, in full living color! Panicked, I screamed, and the book went flying on the floor. Terrified, I pretended I had just dropped the book and quickly picked it up as if nothing had happened and hoping I wouldn't get called on to read. I remember being so scared that the teacher would call on me and I would have to stand up and read the paragraph with the snake in clear sight. Quickly I removed a couple sheets of penmanship paper from my tablet, and folding them over the color page, I created a cover that blocked the page with the snake from my view. I had humiliated myself in front of the class, and luckily I did not get corrected or punished, but suffering the humiliation was minor to the feeling of panic and fear that I had re-experienced.

The following year, my mother and father treated my brother and me to a movie. We were allowed to walk to the movie theatre and walk home. We would cut through the park near our house to save some time. As we were walking, I saw that on the path in front of me were several snakes sunning on some stones. Screaming in panic I again jumped back; my brother, not being afraid, simply removed the snakes from the path and we continued on our journey. I begged him on the way home to take another route so that I would not see the snakes again.

Years went by, and anytime I was out walking in the park or on the lawn, I always watched exactly where my next step went. When I would cut through the park alone, I was sure the snakes were there just waiting for me to appear and would run at lightning speed, stopping at nothing. The fear kept safe deep inside, but I knew at any given moment it could and would appear. Going to movies as a teenager and a young adult, I always kept one eye glued to the screen and the other eye ready to hide in case the scene being filmed was going to have a surprise in it for me. I thought I was doing great, and I was now well into adulthood and I hadn't run across a snake in many, many years when the popular movie *Indiana Jones* came out. Everyone was talking about how wonderful Harrison Ford and Kathleen Turner were and so I went. No one of course had prepared me for what was about to appear on the screen. Terrified that night after the movie, I went home and immediately looked under the bed, a fearful activity that I had long since suspended but in an instant returned.

It really bothered me that I had allowed this fear to stay alive within me. So I decided it was time to do something about it, and I came up with a game plan to help me overcome it. My goal was simple—I simply wanted to be able to see a snake on TV or on the movie screen and not have a physical reaction. I wanted no feelings of panic, no sweaty palms, and no hot or cold sweats. And so I started little by little, watching the nature shows on the TV. Intellectually I knew that the snakes were on the TV and not in my living room, but unfortunately this knowledge did not help me solve the problem. It was my little inner child that needed to feel safe and secure. Somehow she needed to get herself to a happy place not picking up fear or panic. Little by little, with baby steps, I worked at it and worked at it, forcing myself to look at TV and the big screen! I actually trained myself not to react and came to a point that I could see a snake on TV or a picture in a magazine and visually be fine with no physical reaction from my body.

About fifteen years ago, I was invited to the opening of our local zoo's rainforest. I loved animals and I was excited to see this new facility. Moving from display to display, looking through the glass at the vignettes recreating the different species of animal life in their natural venues, was fun to see. I hadn't thought about my fear in years, so I had no reason to think that this evening was going to somehow jar me right back into the past. As part of the opening party, zoo trainers were wandering around with various animals to let people take a closer look. I was walking on the winding trails through the displays when the line stopped moving forward. While waiting I heard someone walking behind me. Turning around, the zoo trainer was walking directly toward me in this narrow path with a huge boa constrictor wrapped around him. In a split second I bolted, a grown woman running through the line, excusing myself through the entire display until I made it outside gasping for breath. Feeling trapped, my inner child had panicked.

My fear had simply lain latent, waiting for an event, another test to see if I had mastered the fear. The answer was no. I have continued to work on this fear, and when I walk through the pet store I always look at the snakes behind the glass windows—from a distance. And remarkably I have also seen real snakes in my yard and have mastered being able to watch them slither through the yard, creating no physical reaction to my body. I am sure that I will continue to work on this issue throughout my entire adult life, and I look forward to the day that I master it. I think about my mother and her fear and I think about mine. I learned my reaction of panic from my mother as I had observed my mother with her fear.

We all have fears that hold us hostage from enjoying ourselves and perhaps having a quality of life free from panic. These fears do not have to be like my mother's and mine, as spiders and bats can be equally terrifying! There is a whole world out there filled with things to be fearful of. Many individuals have a fear of flying while many young mothers must face a fear of travel as they journey off with their spouses leaving their young children behind. Whatever the fear, the reaction stems from the same place. We all have an inner child that needs to be calmed so that the panic can dissipate and the fear is removed. Working with our inner children allows us to begin to heal. I have learned in these last years that sitting with my inner child and recognizing her feelings and allowing them to be expressed gives both her and me the opportunity to heal.

So looking deeper within ourselves, we need to make our inner child feel safe and secure. It doesn't matter whether the issue is a childhood fear like the ones I have been dealing with or a painful or hurtful experience. Many of us have had very difficult childhoods, complete with abuse on many levels. The depth of this hurt from abuse or perhaps the fear of abandonment is so huge in one's mind that the emotional body is never at rest, never to experience peace or able to trust. The fear of my earlier example appears to be simply an inconvenience that one must live with as opposed to the paralyzing and traumatic event or events that come from abuse creating permanent damage generally in one's life as well as in all close relationships. There is no comparison between the two, but there are similarities to the hurt that the inner child experiences and the aftermath of fear that follows. This can and must be healed to bring yourself emotionally to a state of wellness. To experience a harmony and balance in the body, we must heal everything that doesn't feel like love. By beginning to heal our inner children of our emotional body of consciousness, we are moving in a forward momentum, dropping the fears, the hurts, and the pain and replacing them with the calm and peace similar to what we feel after a storm.

So let's begin by being introspective as we ask a few questions that will get us moving in the direction that we want to be going! First, the big question: On a scale of one to ten, "How happy is your inner child?" The answer to this question should be fairly simple. Assessing your involvement with your inner child will help address his/ her level of cooperation.

Continuing then we can ask another big question: On a scale of one to ten, "How connected are you consciously to your inner child?" The answer to this question should be fairly simple but it probably won't be as tons of variables will undoubtedly be presented by your mental body. The mental child can make a big case for you and offer excuses such as your lack of time, the demands of your job, or busy events going on at home, etc, etc, etc. So hush the mental child and ask yourself for an honest evaluation of the time you have spent with your emotional inner child. Of course, it isn't so much about the amount of time that you give to your inner child that is important but the quality of connectedness that does exist during those times that you are spending with him or her. Taking this a step further, it doesn't really matter what the answer to the above question is in terms of time, but it does matter when you are connected, just how connected are you? By answering this question you can give yourself a measure to compare your future visits with your inner child and simply try to expand the time and the connectedness.

Again continuing along this line of questions in order to move in our spiral: On a scale of one to ten, "When you are connected with your inner child, have you been able to connect on events that may have caused you discomfort while growing up? It is easier to begin the connection process when you are simply handling events or emotions that are uncomfortable. This may establish the necessary rapport with your inner child as a level of trust is being built within as well as seeing the results of your attentiveness and hard work certainly relieves some of the stress. This sets the groundwork and begins a way of working with your inner child that is simply taking baby steps and working through the less difficult events in your life by taking the steps one step at a time. I can tell you that dealing with my snake fear was a great way for me to begin learning how to help myself heal. The more I felt equipped to deal with my more insignificant fears, the more courage I had to begin to deal with the events in my childhood that created major fears and major hurts.

The less-serious fears provided the groundwork that needed to be covered so that you and your inner child have learned how to work at a good comfort level. It is time now to tackle a more difficult event. And as you climb the ladder, working through difficulty upon difficulty, recalling those events in your childhood that have left that open wound, the fear dissipates, and you become lighter and lighter. Not only are you healing yourself, but you are beginning to feel pride in who you are and what you are achieving. This pride helps you to achieve a level of confidence. Your strength is born. Your strength may now grow and take on the hardest and most difficult events in your repertoire. It is and was not easy, but learning how to work through the pain—and understanding that I need not be my pain nor my hurt emotions, but that I could see myself as a healthy, healed, and complete person—was the attitude that I needed to adopt to begin taking the baby steps toward healing. Fortunately, I was able to maintain faith in the process, faith in myself and faith from my unseen benefactors to help me through what I knew I needed to work through. Of course, I did not know then that my benefactors were removal-of-fear guides, but I did know that I was being assisted by and receiving major help from the other side. Fear was not going to limit me or paralyze me, and I was bound and determined to put any and all traumatic events behind me, never to affect me again.

As Markas has described, this very process that you have built with yourself within yourself is in the beginning an effortful process. You must consciously set time with your inner child to do the work. Soon after, you repeat the process again and again the effortful process becomes automatic. You may actually surprise yourself that you are able to handle situations where you formerly were unable to in a way that causes no hurt to your inner child and the situation simply dissipates. Thus you can see how this can become a confidence builder. And you begin to carry that grace within you that speaks to those that are astute and intuitive that you come from a place of quiet confidence.

This is a major way to grow and develop, saying goodbye to lifelong fears, feelings of insecurity, numerous hurts that you encountered along the way, and even the momentous painful experiences that have done major damage. Saying thank you and so long to the removal-of-fear guides and welcoming the expansion-of-love guides into your life to help you help your inner child to learn to trust and have faith is another step that feels great—an accomplishment! I knew that I was not doing this work alone—I always felt that I was being assisted from the other side. Knowing and thinking that the damage is not irrevocable but is revocable as you continue along working side by side with your inner child is necessary for you to let go of the pain, giving yourself permission to heal. This work leads to the healing, the healing leads to the ease, and the ease leads to a release that is allowing you to bring yourself into a state of balance. I understood the meaning of love, and I understood the meaning of forgiveness. The state of balance leads you to a general state of wellbeing as you continue on this upward trend, spiraling your way through growth and development.

Will there be lapses along the way? Will you meet someone who will push your buttons and you revert back down that path—that path that you know so intimately because you took yourself there again and again and again? Yes, that may happen. But this time you will not allow yourself to go all the way down into that black hole again; you have tasted the honey, and you have experienced greatness, or at least success in releasing those emotional bondages that you brought in again and again. You now recognize that and simply become addicted to the new you, the healthy you. You now can taste how success feels. And you will not allow your inner child to backtrack. You have learned that you will survive, and you do. You have discovered that "happiness is being within," and you and your inner child continue on dealing with life's difficulties, taking it one step at a time and growing and developing the strength needed to continue moving into the healthiest you: a person who does not want life to rock them loose of their center!

CHAPTER VI

Prophecies and the Emerging Power of Light

Love should be your guide. Be eager to have the gifts that come from the Holy Spirit, especially the gift of prophecy ... When you prophecy, you will be understood, and others will be helped.

—Paul (1 Corinthians 12:1,3)

Today we have come to this point, on this planet, where our fifth-dimensional experience is leading us to what we call an emerging energy or power of light. If you reference the very early religious writings, be they from the Bible or a different religious text, they speak of moving into greater and greater states of light. There is talk about cleansing one's system, spiritually speaking, in order to move into this grand state of lightness. Remember that most of these religious texts were written when this planet was a two—or three-dimensional planet, so there were some basic things that needed to be taken care of immediately. However, now our planet has moved very quickly through the fourth dimension and has emerged into the fifth dimension. We have merged what we learned three-dimensionally with what we learned four-dimensionally, and we have added that to our collective understanding.

A better description would be that you have integrated great portions of what was learned earlier into your fifth-dimensional experience. Once it is fully integrated, then things will look very simple. But as it stands right now, many things still look like they need to be figured out; they need to be solved, they need to be understood, in order to see the bigger picture. But while this is happening, while you are integrating earlier teachings, you are also going back and picking up some other things that perhaps you didn't really fully understand, and you are learning them even though you are in the fifth dimension. So you might be learning something that you didn't fully understand from three-dimensional reality or from the fourth dimension, the realm of emotionality. You are learning it before it can be integrated into your fifth-dimension experience of life. This is really what you have been doing over the past several decades. You have been learning how to live in the dimension of consciousness that has been presented to you.

Now we are not talking about when you shifted into fifth-dimensional reality. We are talking about it being presented to you from the universe. It has been presented to you on this planet. So we are talking about when the planet shifted from three—to fourth-dimensional reality, and then from fourth—into fifth-dimensional consciousness. Things were presented to you, and then you had an opportunity to integrate what you learned and also to go back to pick up on some things that you wanted to learn that were important for your personal experience. Even though you have a cosmic consciousness, you are learning things and you are developing things from your own unique perspective. As you learn things, you can integrate them. Right now things do not look simple; they don't look easy in your fifth-dimensional consciousness. But as you integrate, you will see more and more of this emerging power of light, the emerging energy of lightness.

What does that mean for an individual that is living on a physical planet? Well, you must ask yourself not only why you came to this planet and what your purpose on this planet is, but also is this fulfilling the very aspects of your blueprint, what you wanted to learn? Now you can only ask that from a philosophical viewpoint, because you really don't know what your blueprint is. You know fragments of it, and when portions of your blueprint are completed, sometimes your guides will confirm for you that a certain part of your blueprint is complete. But for the most part, you are in the dark when it comes to your blueprint.

Where would you be and what would you be doing if you weren't on this planet right now? Well the truth is if you weren't in physical form in this lifetime, you might be in another part of the universe, being in a nonphysical structure. Or you might be in another part of the universe, a different planet or a star system, that is spiritual only or is mental only. Or you might be between those types of realities in a different dimension in which you are learning. You may be wondering, "If I am going to learn on the planet, and I need a physical body to learn certain things, is it also correct to say that I need to not have a physical body to learn other things?" The answer is, absolutely! There are certain things that you cannot learn while you are in a physical body because it is too limiting and too restrictive for the type of cosmic lessons that you would be learning.

So while you are learning things three-, four-, and five-dimensionally on this planet, you will also learn things cosmically in another place without a physical body. You may wonder, "Well if that is true, then can I leave the physical body and go into the nonphysical at will?" The answer is no. You will leave this physical body when you have completed your journey here and not before. Instead, you can gain your cosmic wisdom when you are in a sleep state. So when you are in sleep state and you are having dreams, apparitions, or visitations, your guides are teaching you cosmically.

This cosmic learning can only happen when your physical body is not restricting the experience. A wonderful example of this is astral travel. When people astral travel, they experience all kinds of amazing things, whether they remember these experiences or not. Through astral travel they are able to experience cosmic learning in a sleep state. This is possible because we are all multidimensional; while we are in a physical body, we are able to unharness ourselves from that physical form in sleep state. And so when we talk about the emerging power of light, it so often happens that when you take the learning that you receive cosmically in sleep state, it propels you forward into the light.

For example, you may feel as if you are on a plateau of sorts in terms of your spiritual growth. While you are learning things and integrating them, you may feel as though the process is a slow one. Then, all of a sudden you enter a sleep state, perhaps in astral travel, and things are instantly integrated for you! The cosmic realizations that come to you actually propel you forward, not only in a nonlinear way but in an astrological way. So what you are learning cosmically is defined when you look at the astrological aspects of Virgo, of Scorpio, of Sagittarius, and of Aquarius. As you know, there are certain tendencies associated with each of these astrological signs. Let's say that you were born on this planet with your moon in Sagittarius and your rising sign in Leo. Well, there would be certain tendencies associated with those signs. To step into the nonphysical, which is what you do when you are in sleep state, you can learn what these tendencies are, and these tendencies will help you to understand cosmically what a person is all about, what your soul is all about, and what your consciousness is all about.

So you do not have to figure out your dreams, but let those dreams and the dreamlike experiences happen upon you. Whether or not your remember them, you need to appreciate them. Let them be integrated into what you are experiencing as well, and then you will feel as if you are being propelled forward into this energy of light, this energy of light and lightness. The advantage for you being physical is that once you have an integration of something, things do get very simple for you. Things become black and white; they are no longer gray. It is black or white, it is yes or no, and it is something that is clearly defined in your understanding. It is the "aha" experience; this emerging energy of light takes hold of you and you "get it" and then everything is crystal clear.

Think of your own life. Are there things that you are completely certain about? Other things that you are uncertain of, that appear to be gray rather than black or white? Well, this is simply because you have not integrated that particular issue, you have not learned in that particular area. To demonstrate this idea, we will use the example of a dream that is actually quite common. Imagine that you dream that you are told that you are enrolled in a class, and in order to complete that class in the required time, you must take your final exam. The setting may be a college, or it may be a class that you voluntarily sign up for, say, a self-improvement class. You say to yourself, "Well, maybe I really don't want to complete this class." Your guide or your instructor says to you, "But you have no choice. You have enrolled in this, and so we want to give you advance notice. You haven't been doing much in this area, but you are going to have a test." Well, what they are really doing is preparing you that you have been given some understanding cosmically and that you must integrate it into your fifth-dimensional reality so that you have a complete understanding of it so that you will pass the "test."

The area for which you will need understanding in order to pass the "test" may be quite personal. It may be about how to interact with your son. Or perhaps it is about your career and your need to make a decision about which path to follow. You may not know which way to go, and then all of a sudden the light goes on and you do understand. It feels as if you have been given a prophecy. The truth is you have earned it. You haven't been given it, but you have earned it! Whether it is insight into something that seems trivial in your life or something that is a very important part of your life, you will have no hesitation as to how to move forward.

You may be wondering how you can encourage this process in your life. Well, the number one thing that you can do is to be open. You must relax your belief system about the particular area that you are in need of clarity in. For example, if you say "I am not having any luck in my relationship with my son. We just don't understand each other, we cannot communicate, and it seems as if he just brushes me off when I try to get through to him," and you say to yourself, "I have to do what I think is right," well, you might want to just take a look at that belief system of what you think is right and then relax it. You don't have to fix it or alter it; you just need to be open to having alternatives presented to you. Just be open to alternative ways for things to be reconciled. Once you do that, then your guides have an opportunity to present you with some of this cosmic information. All you have to do is say, "Well, I have done it this way up until this point and I am just going to relax that way of thinking. I am not going to judge it by saying that it is right or wrong. I am not going to say that it is accurate or semi-accurate. I am just going to relax it." Once you relax your old belief system, you will find that bits and pieces will come to you from the nonphysical realms that will help you to be guided in a direction where things will at some point become black or white, yes or no, sunshine or darkness.

The other thing that you have to do in order to assist in this process is to give yourself time to just "be." In the three-dimensional reality, you learned how to use your mental attributes because you were taught that that is the way to succeed. So you have these very developed mental bodies of consciousness but are still trying to figure things out. As we mentioned before, you do go through a filter of your beliefs that were built up based upon your experiences in the physical realm. This belief system may be from this lifetime, or it may be from a past lifetime. Our mental children are operating through that haze, through that set of restrictions. So what you need to do is to enter into the process of just being—being aware of what you are thinking, feeling, and doing in the present moment. The more that you are in the present moment, the more that you will not go back and evaluate past decisions, and the less that you will worry about the future. All of you know that you create your future with what is going on for you physically, mentally, spiritually, and emotionally right now. So whether or not you are conscious of the fact that you are creating your future in the moment, you most certainly are. So when you step into that energy of just being, you consciously make the effort to relax your belief system and be open to the word of spirit, to the word of God, and to the word of your angels.

You just need to remain open to new ideas and not automatically assume that they will not work for you or your particular situation. Just trust that the information or guidance that you need will come. It might come in dream state or in daydream state for you. It might come when you are watching TV and a commercial comes on that somehow relates to your particular situation. Or you may turn on the TV and happen to catch a movie that has a very special message for you. Of course being open doesn't mean that you are not paying attention to the physical reality. It only means that if you are spiritually open and aware of the present moment, you can allow the greater wisdom to come to you.

While this "letting go" sounds like a simple process, letting go of our beliefs can be difficult because it is often synonymous with saying letting go of our ego. It is very easy to become committed to your way of doing things and to be determined that others should see things your way. You can get very committed to your style of doing things, and the problem with that is that doing things the conventional way often prohibits us from getting the job done. Ask yourself, "Would I rather be right or get the job done?" If you think, "Well I know I am right, so I know that if I am right I can get the job done," you are beating your head against the wall. Instead, if you let go of that and realize that just as you are multidimensional, so is there a multidimensional approach to addressing challenges that come into your life.

Think of what happens when someone enters a room and turns on the light switch. All of a sudden things become very clear to you! This is what you are trying to do with your own life. You are not just trying to learn your lessons and to integrate them, but you are trying to have a simpler, happier, and more successful life, not to prove anything to anyone else but just to live that life and to have that experience for yourself. So again let us take a look at the phrase "would you rather be right or get the job done?" And perhaps we could restructure that phrase so as not to say get the job done, but we could say would you rather be right or happy? It really just comes down to that. You alone permit or do not permit happiness into your life and your way of evolving into it.

At times it can look like everyone else isn't doing things your way, but the truth is that whether or not they are doing things the "right way" is of little consequence to your reality as you are the center of your own reality. You are the one who holds all of the power as long as you stay in the center. But when you start to look at what everyone is or is not doing and what you think they should be doing instead, you lose your power because you have stepped out of your center—you have stepped into their belief systems, you have stepped into their limitations, and that is from where the frustration comes. So again, would you rather be right or be happy? It is important to remember that you can be happy without things going the way that you mentally think that they need to go. Once you relax those beliefs and you open up to the will of God, remembering that we are all part of God, you allow that which is in your best interest to come to you. You will find that what you receive is actually greater than what you would have imagined mentally because you are free from the limitations of your beliefs and your paradigm. We are not talking about compromise, but rather about emerging or evolving. You let the guidance come in and you end up with something even grander, something that mentally you could not have come up with, and yet it is perfect. Tell yourself that your approach has been one-dimensional in the past, but now you are going to go into a state of beingness and let other ideas or possibilities form in your consciousness. I simply am going to be open to that.

Now, try to remember when you were six or seven years old. You had started in school and you were being influenced not just by your parents anymore, but by your classmates, your teacher, the principal, the structure, the rules and regulations, and also by what you were learning in school. While you were only in first or second grade at that age, think about the pressure that you had! You had to learn all kinds of new things because you were going to take tests that you were told that you had to pass. So you memorized everything from math equations to spelling to basic scientific facts. A few years later when you entered junior high school, you actually understood some things that you had simply memorized before. So when you were learning your addition tables and you were saying two plus two is four and three plus five is eight, seven plus nine is sixteen, you had done previously this strictly by memorization. However you were able to fully integrate this information so that it became an automatic process to recall these facts once you entered middle school, and even more so once you were in high school. The reason that you were able to integrate it was because of all of the experiences that you had through grade school and high school.

Just as you did not judge yourself as a child for the need to memorize information when you were first exposed to it, you cannot judge yourself now that you are an adult that is exposed to new information or a new way of thinking. So do not judge yourself because right now you are in the process of integrating information in the fifth dimension. This is because now that you are in the fifth dimension, you have had enough experience to allow you to begin to integrate information in order to increase your wisdom and understanding. You may find that you are memorizing things that seem to be contrary to your normal way of thinking because the fifth dimension is about spiritual healing, seeing the perfection of all things. When you struggle with this new way of thinking, it can be helpful to repeat the mantra "Everything is perfect, everything is perfect, everything is perfect"!

Sometimes life just doesn't feel perfect. If you are having an issue with your child or are having an issue with your ex-spouse, or you are having major problems with your career, or there is a lack of love in a relationship that goes awry, it certainly doesn't feel perfect. Of course no amount of telling yourself that it *is* perfect is going to make it feel perfect, but it can make it feel a bit less wrong. If you stick with it, you will find that you will begin to have experiences that help support this new fifth-dimensional information. Again, all you have to do is to be open to it, consider anything to be a possibility, and stay open to all things. Then you will begin to see that things take a very dramatic turn, things get lighter. The understanding is like a snap of the fingers—*snap*, it is there! Even though it may not look like what your mental child thought it should look like, you got the job done. You are happy, you are not frustrated or without knowledge, you now get it, and the relationship takes the turn for the best, the career takes a turn for the best, and all things begin to take the outcome that you want, without using your particular beliefs to make that happen.

All of this leads to this emerging energy of light. Imagine that someone was to tell you that there are fifty languages on the planet and that you get to choose two languages to learn instantaneously. It is as if you have spoken them in other lifetimes and so they make perfect sense to you. But if you want to learn the other forty-eight languages, you will have to memorize them. If this is the case, you probably will not want to learn all of the forty-eight languages. You would probably evaluate the other languages and choose a few that you are particularly interested in and learn to speak those few languages instead. This is what happens when you come to a physical incarnation. A couple of things are going to come very easily to you because they are big things on your blueprint and you want to have the skills in order to move forward in that area. These interests will differ from person to person as each of us is drawn based upon our blueprint. You are drawn to these other areas, but you do not come in with a mastery in that area, and so you begin to study and mentally memorize the information around that subject.

There is an expression that states that "happiness is not needing to know what is going to happen next!" You certainly want to be happy in as many moments of your life as you can. When you have difficulties, it is virtually impossible to be happy because it doesn't feel perfect, it doesn't feel like love, and it certainly doesn't feel as if you are getting things the way that you would like them. So what happens then is that the difficulties become your reality, and it is very difficult to receive prophecies for yourself. You can do it for others, and in fact if you are operating as a psychic, a channel, or an intuitive, your own life might be a complete mess, and yet you can receive very accurately for someone else. When there is this gray energy all through your life, you can still be a very clear channel for others, but not for what is happening in your life. In fact, when you are in the gray area it is very difficult for someone else to read your energy. And it happens sometimes that a psychic is not able to read your energy because it is as if there is a wall or a block. Well, it is that gray energy. While you can't talk yourself out of it, you can evolve out of it.

Once you allow yourself to be open up to this energy of just being and you allow things to come to you, you will begin to have these "aha" experiences. Things will start to get black and white, and then it is much easier to see what your next move is going to be. You will be able to receive prophecies for yourself, and it will become much easier for you to see in what direction you should go. Focus on this and understand that it is not that your mental child is going to be pushed aside, it is just that he or she is going to be taught to relax as there still is a lot of information that needs to come to him or her. And so it will be a learning experience for your mental child, and mostly the learning will come from your fifth body of consciousness, the spiritual healing body, and the superconsciousness.

As part of this integration, things in your life will go from impossibility to possibility, possibility to probability, and probability to actualization. In this paradigm, what we are saying is you are going from confusion into understanding, understanding into enlightenment, and then from enlightenment into wisdom. When you go from confusion to understanding, you are going from not knowing into a form of knowing. When you go from understanding into enlightenment, you are going into the perpetual state of knowing, wisdom, or cosmic consciousness. The expression "there is nothing new under the sun" is really about this cosmic consciousness. It is infinite and it is already in place. To have the gift of prophecy is to go from confusion to understanding to enlightenment, or the perpetual state of knowing. That is where we want to go in every area, in every aspect of our lives. Think of how the Christ energy was able to ascend. He had the knowingness, he had this perpetual state of knowing, he was enlightened. That is why he went into the light body of consciousness. When he was on the planet and he was walking amongst the multitudes, he was doing a lot of healing as well as teaching. He took fifth-dimensional form because he was able to show instantaneous healings and he also was given the gift of prophecy. His biggest contribution was helping individuals by setting the stage for them to recognize that we are all part of God. So it is time to forgive, it is time to say that if a particular belief system doesn't match with mine, I may need to relax my belief system. When you do that the anger goes away, as does the need to be right and any confusion.

As Christ walked among the people in order to heal and teach them, he shared himself with those who were open. He didn't do it for the Pharisees, he didn't do if for the Scribes, he didn't do it for those that were plotting to undermine him. Again, you must be open in order to receive the blessings of the spirit. The mark of a fifth-dimensional entity is that they remain open regardless of how rigid or how developed their belief system is.

There is a synergy between future events and evolving into this energy of light, becoming the light, allowing that to flow. It is like being in a greenhouse when the sun comes out and the sun's energy is able to be absorbed by you because even though you are in a structure, the light is able to permeate through. So there is a connection, a very strong synergy between future events and your experience of being a lightbody. That synergy is developed or perpetuated when you stay in the present moment and allow yourself to enter into the state of beingness because you cannot only predict future events, but you can alter them. I choose my reality, my future, based upon what I am thinking, feeling, experiencing, and believing right now. So if I want to change a prophecy such as my son and I going our separate ways, I can be present in the moment and open to greater states of wisdom, going from understanding to enlightenment.

You have probably met someone before who is truly such a pleasure to be with that everyone around them is drawn to them. You may wonder what it is that is so attractive about this particular person. Well, it is most likely the power of lightness inside of them. Just being who they are, they are able to attract people as well as happy circumstances because they are in this experience of light. Each of us must ask ourselves, "Am I one with light as far as I can take it?" If not it may be because of a gray area in your life that forces you to live in confusion. Your mental child may be saying, "This concern that I have, these problems, they are too big, they are too overwhelming." But there is a solution. There is a solution that is to your liking. Relax and call upon the will of God, which you are of course a part of, and give thanks for what you have been given and ask God for the assistance that you need. Then trust that what you need will come, and that they will be unfiltered by your old rigid belief system.

Traditional religious teaching tells us that we must have faith in order to receive God's blessings. We do not dispute this as we must have faith in God as well as faith that we will receive the wisdom that we need. However it goes much further than that. It is saying that I am part of God, I am one aspect of God, and if I am part of God, and God has solutions to everything therefore, these solutions will come to me. If you don't have a love interest in your life and desperately want one, there is a solution. If you don't have good health in your life and really want it, there is a solution.

You may be wondering how this relates to your blueprint. Well, perhaps your blueprint doesn't call for a love interest. Perhaps your blueprint calls for you to have a certain illness so you can help others in that area. Does that mean that you cannot request certain things? Absolutely not! You can make a request not so much to revise your blueprint, but the way to accomplish the blueprint. An example would be that on your blueprint, it calls for you to have the love of your life for ten years or fifteen years. This may not sound fair as some individuals may have the love of their life for fifty years. It has been determined that you are going to have the love of your life from thirty years old to forty-five years old. Then for whatever reason, the love of your life is going to pass over early, there is going to be a splitting up in one form or another. After that you do not have any other major love interest on your blueprint. But here you are at forty-seven years old, and you are saying, "I know what I had, I loved that, and I want to have that again." All you have to do is say, "I still want to accomplish what is on my blueprint. I just don't want it to feel lonely by missing love." Even if your blueprint is that you are at a time that is critical for your career, you may be able to accomplish this blueprint career item and still find love by finding a love interest that is so involved in your career of choice that you work together for the betterment of your career. And so you go about the process of accomplishing your blueprint differently; rather than doing it alone, you do it with a love interest. So it allows you, this process of being open and allowing this information to come in, to adjust not necessarily your blueprint but your approach to accomplishing it.

When you look around this planet, it does not appear to be a very healed planet right now. It doesn't look like a fifth-dimensional planet as there are all kinds of illnesses and biological, humanitarian, and nuclear threats. But remember that if you are the center of your reality, all just passes you by. It doesn't mean that you do not have compassion and you don't want to work for change, but you don't for one minute believe the illusion of imperfection. Why? Because you are the center of your reality and it feels very powerful in the center. Don't be afraid to let yourself know; it is the not knowing that creates the difficulty. It is the not knowing that perpetuates the confusion. Let yourself know so that you go from confusion into understanding on the way to enlightenment.

During the fourth dimension, individuals could take stress energy and relax with it and convert it into strength and from strength into success. In the fifth dimension, we don't talk about going from stress to strength, but we do talk about going from confusion to understanding to enlightenment. Confusion has to do with the fact that the fifth-dimensional reality is being lived by a lot of individuals who are not fifth-dimensional. That is not a judgment—you simply come to an understanding that the fifth dimension is still at the mercy of those who live on this planet. You cannot go from confusion to understanding outside of yourself because most individuals are three—and four-dimensional. It is only necessary that you don't believe the illusion of imperfection that surrounds you. You could be attacked in any number of ways by the threats of the outside world. So why aren't you? Because you are the center of your reality and that is the reality of lightness. And if it isn't a reality of lightness, it is going to be. It can't be any other way.

Now this leads to your role as spiritual healers, and not all of you are going to be actively doing spiritual healing, but you are all going to be doing spiritual healing in your own lives. And that is going to be reflected in the circumstances around you. So metaphysician, heal thyself, know thyself, and at the very least you will be making a contribution by getting yourself into this energy of light. Those of you who are true healers will want to be doing this actively as this is your metaphysical role. And you do this by gaining the clarity going into enlightenment, and so then are you a stronger vessel, so then are you a more enlightened vessel. If you look at the alchemical tarot where they talk about how vessels hold different things such as water, power, or gold, whatever the vessel holds, you too are a vessel, and you will hold whatever is on your blueprint for you to hold. The question is, "Am I on my blueprint or not?" Until you move beyond that, I know that I am on my blueprint because this feels like love doing fifth-dimensional healing work. I am doing it, and every time I do it, I know that more light is opening inside of me, making me more able to help others. Imagine then how much more is available inside of you when you don't have pockets of gray area. Imagine how much of your potential is untapped but will be tapped into when these gray areas clear up. When things get crisp and clear, black and white, yes and no, sunlight and darkness, imagine what is available to you!

* * * * * * *

The process of integrating your five bodies of consciousness seems like a difficult feat, but in reality with focus and determination it is very doable. When we begin this process, we have learned that two states are necessary: to be open and to just be!

Throughout our childhoods, each one of us has experienced difficulties in learning. My childhood was relatively harmless, or so I thought. I grew up in the fifties, a time of simplicity when parents knew what their children were doing every minute of the day. We had a short rope (mine was the size of my jump rope), and if you were allowed to "play" after school, that rope extended only within the neighborhood close to home, a walking or biking distance away. School was a big part of our life; in fact, school and schoolwork was our life! Many of us have horrible memories of how we suffered in school through a certain subject or a discipline that was confusing and frustrating. I remember being sick (I had the two-week measles) when my third-grade teacher was teaching multiplication. I returned to school after being absent for ten school days only to discover that I missed out on a totally new concept called multiplication. The teacher was calling out math facts from her flash cards and the kids in my class were calling out answers. She called on me, and I not only did not know the answer, but I did not understand what the lesson was even about. My face turned red with embarrassment.

I hadn't been introduced to the concept of multiplication. It was a total mystery to me. I remember feeling totally out of step with the rest of the class. I don't know if I had ever experienced that feeling before as learning was easy for me as the work was not difficult. I went home dumbfounded and wondering how I was going to figure this out. I asked my father for help (big mistake!). My father sat me down and tried to explain multiplication in the way that he understood it. He was a math genius who was an inventor and an engineer. He probably was also a frustrated college professor, and so he began to give a very advanced discourse on the principles of math! I listened politely as I would have been scared not to, but also remember being fidgety as I did not understand anything other than I was very sorry that I had asked for his help as I knew he wasn't helping at all! I not only felt stupid but now felt frustrated!

I believe that this was my first experience in feeling truly frustrated. I then went to my older brother, who told me in a tone that only siblings can have for each other that I probably would never understand it so all that I really needed to do was memorize the answers so that I was able to give the answers on drills and tests. So now I was not only feeling stupid, but insulted as well. He then proceeded to instruct me on how to make multiplication flash cards and taught me how to memorize them. After learning the easier numbers, I went back to school feeling that I could bluff my way through by giving an answer, but I knew that I did not understand multiplication the way that I was supposed to. Every night I went home from school and really worked very hard at memorizing the math facts, and eventually I was able to get all of them memorized. I got by by memorizing correctly and answering accurately during our drills and tests, but I knew that I did not know multiplication the way that I should.

The following September, school began with us taking a multiplication review before we began learning division. I remember sitting in the class and looking at the blackboard and seeing for the first time what the multiplication process meant, and now I understood the entire process. I was happy that I knew the answers to the problems as it made my math homework go quickly and I was able to answer easily in the math drills. But for the first time, "I got it." I clearly understood the multiplication process. On another level I also understood the difference between learning by memorization and knowing the mathematical principles and process. It took a while, but I worked with it and now it had become part of what I knew; it was black and white, right and wrong; it was clear. I had integrated something into my knowingness, and this had allowed me to have insight and clarity on a foggy issue! My mental child was happy as I had moved from confusion to understanding. My physical child was happy as I had moved from frustration to understanding. My emotional child was happy as I had moved from being scared to becoming confident. My spiritual child was happy as she finally had all of her siblings happy and now she could relax. Today I see that all of these little inner children had moved from a place of probability to possibility and then to actuality.

Now please forgive this very simple example of a young child experiencing her first feeling of frustration in a learning situation. It certainly must have created stress in my early life as a student because to this day as I am repeating the story, I am surprised as I am re-experiencing all of the feelings as if it happened only yesterday. Deep within my memory I still have a very clear picture of my feelings that obviously need to come up to the surface for healing. I am sure everyone has had a similar situation in their childhood, whether it occurred in a classroom or on a sports field, and can remember experiencing feelings of frustration or perhaps even feelings of inadequacy while trying to accomplish what was felt at the time to be impossible.

Do you remember that kid in your class that during recess or gym just was not able to "get it"? Perhaps they couldn't understand the game of baseball, and when they caught the ball they were so stunned at their success that they didn't know what to do with it and everyone else just started screaming at them! Or the kid on the soccer field who, just starting out, really didn't have the concept of the game and began running the wrong direction, away from his goal, to everyone's chagrin. Or on the basketball court with everyone running up and down the court, the ball is caught, and instead of it being passed to the forward to take the shot, our novice player takes the shot, totally missing the basket. All of these and the embarrassment felt in the many hundreds of humbling experiences that we have both witnessed and participated in as we were growing up, trying to learn the ropes, have left little wounds. A small weight that left unattended to festers over the years and is the beginning of the weight that is held deep within.

Moving into the preteen years, those awkward years when everyone either looked lanky or chunky and felt insecure because of braces or pimples or both! You either wanted to grow or you had grown too tall, your hair too frizzy or too straight, a mousy shade of brown or worse (mine was called "dishwater blonde," and isn't that a pretty disgusting description?); no one ever happy with the way they looked, the way they talked, their parents, or their siblings. Everywhere we turned we saw something better and something we would rather be; ah, the impossible dream. Listening to that little voice that reminded you that you were not good enough, pretty or handsome enough, not smart enough, or not good enough or not good at all. And it didn't matter where: the classroom, the athletic field, or hanging around home. Some of us growing up disappointed in what we were and wishing and hoping to be something different. These are little ways that showed that we really didn't love ourselves, leaving little indelible marks. Little hurts that more often than not got submerged or pushed down, down deep inside, adding to the small mound of existing hurts, adding to the weight felt deep within.

Then came the teenage years, the times when almost everyone had their first taste of cruelty. Perhaps the cruelty wasn't intentional, but it still was felt and it hurt. First love, or wanting a first love, but being hurt by your best friends as they plotted and planned against you so that the guy you wanted to go out with was set up with someone else. Or the shy, gentle soul that takes a long time to get the courage to ask someone out to a school play or dance, only to be treated as if he or she didn't exist. Hundreds and hundreds of events at school: copying someone else's homework, or cheating on a test, or perhaps not standing up for someone that was being treated cruelly, or other experiences that we all witnessed either firsthand or from a distance that left more indelible marks that took up residence in the body, and not in a good way. Looking back at these years, doing things that didn't feel good, or perhaps saying or doing something that you knew just wasn't right, all adding on top to that already existing pile of hurts, your emotional body of consciousness getting heavier and heavier. Does this sound like fun? No wonder why most people hated high school!

Now let's visit those young adult years: perhaps college or even during our first job, we all experienced a situation that was a challenge to a moral code that really wasn't set in place yet. Perhaps the purpose of the experience was to test us to see how we felt about ourselves and what we truly believed in. We were given an opportunity to step up to the plate and defend out beliefs. Or did we cave and allow our beliefs to be washed away and opt to keep the peace so we would be accepted by others. We were just beginning to learn how we felt about our world and how to express ourselves. It was trial and error. Thinking back, did you earn kudos by doing the right thing, or are you disappointed in how and why you answered that challenge?

Our twenties and thirties were the times to develop into adulthood and beyond, times to dedicate to our careers and to the role that we chose for ourselves: wife, husband, mother, or father. It was the time to see ourselves in relation to our small world or to our community. Learning how to set the example for those we were responsible for and beginning to think about asking the big questions, starting to absorb some of the answers . . . all the while we were walking around with a weight pulling us down, yearning for the days when we felt lighter-hearted and wondering where the spirit and passion had gone. This weight really wasn't about the responsibility that one takes on with age, but rather what was unseen and lying deep within, weighing our spirit down. I believe the old term was "baggage"; now our young people use the word "issues."

So it is time to begin the work. One by one, our memory brings up an episode or an event which needs to be mulled over, or a song on the radio reminds us of a teenage conflict, or a lost love, and we begin to process. We bring the event up and allow ourselves to feel it and then we love it and let it go. It is really all about learning the lesson that this event is here to teach us. Once you "get it," you can step aside, and having learned the lesson, you can put yourself in a different place, albeit a better place. Your heart gets lighter and lighter. You work bit by bit, little by little, through your forties and into your fifties. By now it is time to be asking the important questions, and it is time to let the sun shine in! You see yourself, the totality of who you are as you exist and the totality of who you want to become, and your spiritual development begins. In our younger days, we mistakenly began to seek answers outside of ourselves; now, being wiser, it is time to learn that all of life's answers are inside of ourselves.

After the clarity arrives, the lightness comes. Is it any wonder that we feel lighter when we can remove the heaviness of an event from our being? Think about any or all of these events from childhood through to the present time and begin to lessen the effect that they have on your being, on all of your five bodies of consciousness. It doesn't matter whether the event is one of the earlier innocent ones, or the simple experiences of those tender hearted teenage years, or something more serious in the young adult or adult years. All of these experiences brought about feelings of frustration, fear, anger, or whatever. All of these events add up and need to get handled. When you begin the clearing and the cleansing, you feel lighter, and then you understand just how heavy your heart and spirit have been. Now it is time to ask the questions: How heavy is the soul? How can light move through a dark, dense body? It is time to let all of the hurts go. It is time to heal.

And so we see the need to remove and clear and cleanse all that we have inside that is weighing down who we are. We must let it all come up and be released. We do not hold onto any memory with any guilt, any hurt, any sadness, or any other negative feeling that may continue to reside within. It is time to let it all go, time to release all hurts, time to move into a new paradigm of clarity by relaxing a belief system that keeps us limited. The hurt is replaced with light, the guilt is replaced with light, the sadness is replaced with light, and you become the lightbody that you were meant to be. The emerging power of light replaces all the darkness and heaviness that existed. You become light and reach that "grand state of lightness" that Markas speaks about in the beginning of this seminar.

Now let us fast forward to adulthood and affairs of the heart. I clearly remember over the last ten years how my heart has recuperated from the sad and heavy experiences of these later years. Nothing really, really major, just a compounding of hurts and disappointments that life brings to us for learning and subsequent growth although, at the time, I was not so wise in the ways of the spiritual world. Today I am able to view these events from a spiritual perspective. I have developed my spiritual body of consciousness and my spiritual healing body of consciousness. As you shift your perspective and invite the inner children from these two bodies of consciousness to participate in your life, your life is richer on so many levels.

So working on my emotional body of consciousness, I began to heal past hurts while teaching my inner child to feel love and to feel safe and secure. My mental child also must find her place, and I realized that I needed to teach her that she is a valuable body of consciousness and that her opinion does matter. Keeping her mentally active is not a problem, but keeping her controlled so that mentally she is not running rings around the other inner children is a problem. But when she realized that I loved her and that I do value her voice, her opinion, she became happy and content. Sometimes she needs to be assertive, but mostly she needs to learn to be respectful of her siblings. She is after all simply one fifth of all of my bodies of consciousness, and as such the other bodies all deserve equal time. The physical body reacts when the emotional body freaks her out and the mental body makes her nervous. Headaches, stomach upsets can all be blamed on these out of control siblings. This is when the adult must put a hand out and say "Stop!" in a loving but authoritative voice. It is up to me and to you, the parents of these inner children, to ensure that all of our five inner children are loved and feel safe and secure. When you have achieved this and they are all friends, then you have begun to integrate them into the totality of who you are and the essence of who you are is moving toward being complete, an adult that is balanced and centered and lives life in an harmonious way. You begin living in the fifth dimension as a fifth-dimensional being!

A lighter, more enlightened being, one with wisdom who steps into her space on earth with her five inner children all contributing to the whole; this is the time when the other world comes to your world and begins to educate you in cosmic ways. This is when the world of beauty, magic, and miracles begin to flow. This is how the world of prophecy arrives, complete with all of the tools at your disposal. You can pick and choose what is meaningful to you.

My exposure to the metaphysical and spiritual world through the many books I read gave me a whole palette of subjects from which to pick and choose, and little by little I developed my interests. I also requested my spirit guides for direction so that I could read in areas that they knew I would be experiencing down the road. I took classes on sacred geometry, astrology, reflexology, yoga, meditation, and breathing. I also took classes that emphasized various healing modalities: I became a Reiki master and a color harmonics therapeutic light healer. I took spiritual development classes that identified and taught the use of many metaphysical tools such as channeling, table tipping, tarot interpretation, pendulum usage, all the while sharpening my intuitive skills.

Today there is a myriad of ways out there for you to begin to develop during these challenging and chaotic times as we move quickly toward the beginning of what is being referred to as "The Golden Age" in this twenty-first century, the age of spirituality. So explore your area for metaphysical shops, your community center, your library, and the Internet and see what interests you and what you are drawn to. As we are getting closer and closer in time to the planetary shift of 2012, more and more people are getting it. The earth's energies are shifting from matter to a higher vibrating energy of spirituality. This impetus will continue at record speeds (not quite the speed of light), and as record numbers are experiencing the shift and new paradigms are created, lives will be lived more fully and more beautifully with love from their hearts.

Message from Mary Mother of God

Dear Reader,

Many people feel like they have been abandoned. This is not so. I am with you always, and I will never leave you. Some things must change first: There will be sorrow and there will be times of great joy. There will be times when food will be hard to find, and there will be times of great plenty. It is a circle, but it is the circle of love that binds us together and will forever. Remember I will always be with you and you may call on me. Those in need will be blessed. Always call on me. Prayer is the answer. Pray every day. Pray as you do your daily chores and pray as the children walk to school. Prayer will keep you safe. I love you all, and I love the world. I have not abandoned you and heaven has not abandoned you. These are lessons you must learn even though they seem hard. All of these things have come to pass before—it is the circle. [Mary holds out a white rose.] The rose signifies beauty, birth, and death—that is all in the circle. Remember me when the rains come and remember me when the wind blows; pray to me and I will protect you. Prayer is your greatest gift, love your biggest asset. Countries whose value is only about money will not prosper. Only those who put love first will flourish. Many countries understand this, and many countries are currently in the process of changing. The governments are beginning to see the light. Religion should be in school. How will the children learn if we do not teach them? This is important. [She lets rose petals fall so that they cover her feet.] As the rains cover the earth, think of them as rose petals falling from the flower, still beautiful but still destroyed in some ways. Remember rain can nourish or it can destroy. Do not lose faith. In the end faith and love is all you have. Love is first. Love is foremost. Love each other and you will be loved by the world. Take care of your neighbor and follow the prayer: "Do unto others as you would have them do unto you."

Channeled May 1, 2009

Planet Healing

CHAPTER VII

Messages from Markas and Friends

There is No Room for Judgment.

—Edgar Cayce (3/31/06)

We are sent messages from the universe all of the time, in so many different ways. One way in which you can receive messages, which may seem odd at first, is through the constellations. The night sky may reveal things to you either by directly showing you an image or in an obscure way so that it is left to the viewer's imagination to really understand what is coming through. Very similar to direct communication with spirit, it does not come always in the form that you most readily understand it. The reason for this is simple: your guides are here in order to grow and to expand your consciousness, and if everything is put in the same form, in the same time, and in the same manner, there is little opportunity for growth.

Remember that, as is so often true in life, less can be more. Rather than trying to analyze and interpret parts of the cosmos that you are able to see, let your mind wander to look upon the beauty that is presented. Your mental body of consciousness will have ample opportunity to analyze and categorize. It is much more important for you to just allow the beauty and power and the overwhelming presence of the universe to reveal itself to you in its way and in its fashion. This thought is echoed in the Bible when it speaks of the goodness of God and the need to surrender to God. When you surrender to the vastness of this experience, it encourages personal growth and spiritual expansion.

You should also feel free to pose questions to the night sky. Remember, however, that you must surrender to the timing of the answer and the format of the answer. Think back to your days as a test-taking student. Some of you preferred to have your tests in multiple choice, and others preferred simply true or false, and some liked to write essays or to be able to work things out longhand so you could get some partial credit even if you couldn't get the complete accuracy in the answer, and others preferred not to write at all but to speak, and others preferred not to take a grade but just to have a pass or no-pass decision. And so it is that the universe has an infinite number of ways to answer your questions, and if you remain open, the understanding and the wisdom will come. It will either come immediately because it is in a format that is preferred by you, or it is going to come eventually as you grow and learn and expand your consciousness.

As you learn to accept messages as they are given to you, in the format that they are given to you, your healing can begin. Once you let go of your mental framework and expectations and then you get down to the business of playing. Because you recognize that everything is perfect, things come to you when they are supposed to come to you and not when you think they are to come to you. Now for some that might be a disappointment, but for most of you, you understand that you have spirit guides that are fifth-dimensional counselors and that these beings are there to help you. Their job is not to frustrate you. Their job is to assist you, and sometimes you don't understand why they operate the way that they do, but if you trust in God then you see the story behind the answer. And what lies behind the story is the wisdom. And what lies behind the wisdom is the energy of God. And that is where you are going; you see there are an infinite number of paths to get to God.

Even with these messages from your guides, there will be times when you feel that things are not going in the direction that you would like them to, when you are frustrated and you are feeling alone. This is the time for you to let go and let God proceed and let the bigger plan take effect. If you do this, you will begin to see how things miraculously fall into place. Sometimes individuals run from what they fear, rather than moving toward it. That is a huge difference in perception, a huge difference in how an individual lives his or her life. Recognize the things of which you are afraid. You do not have to defeat the fear or overcome it right away. Just bring it up to consciousness and recognize it. Allow yourself the realization that when you run from that which you fear, not only does it waste your precious energy, but it creates greater fear.

When you begin to feel fearful, stop, recognize the fear, acknowledge it, take a breath, and then focus on what you do want and begin to move toward that.

Don't wait until your back is against the wall to do this. Instead, consciously choose to look at your fear and recognize that it is a part of your creation; you are attracting to you that which you concentrate on, why make it your fears? When you consciously address your fear, you will find that that of which you are afraid often will simply dissipate. The removal of this paralyzing fear will allow you to concentrate on what it is that you do want and to manifest that into your life.

When you live your life on the physical plane, you have opportunities; sometimes they look like difficulties, and sometimes they look like problems. If you begin to see them as opportunities, then you begin to play with the possibilities. Remember when you seek truth, truth will find you; when you seek truth, knowledge will be yours!

Once you have control over your fear, you can move into more important matters, such as spiritual healing. Now, why is it that sometimes those who think they want to be spiritual healers really want to receive a spiritual healing? Do they want to receive the spiritual healing as part of their path in order to become spiritual, or is it that they have a fifth body of consciousness, the superconsciousness, which comes to them as a person moves into the fifth dimension? Of course, the fifth dimension is the realm of the spiritual healer, who heals by seeing perfection where there has been the illusion of imperfection, or heaven on earth.

When looking to receive messages from your guides, whether it be about spiritual healing or not, remember that they are cheering you on, but it is for you to gain the wisdom and the understanding because that is why you come to the planet, for learning and for fun. But remember the learning is written in the form of what is appropriate for your blueprint items, literally what is on your agenda. Focus on the big picture rather than worrying about trying to receive a message in a certain format. Do not concentrate on one particular goal as your scope will be much too small for the vastness of the spiritual realm and your own spiritual growth. Instead, remember that it is the process that you live that is crucial, and those that live the process with an open mind and open heart receive more than they thought was even available.

While discussing the topic of receiving spiritual messages, it would be nearly impossible to not bring up meditation in prayer. There are, however, important differences between the two. When you meditate, you are centering your energy, and you are stepping into a state of peacefulness. You are allowing glorious and wondrous things to come to you. You are setting the scene for things that are good, better, best, and beyond to come to you. So meditating is getting yourself centered, relaxed, energized, and less stressed. To pray, on the other hand, is to make a request for certain things to come to you or those for which or for whom you are praying.

Both prayer and meditation are necessary in order for you to advance spiritually, but even more important than their use in this advancement is that they are both necessary in order for you to begin to know yourself as part of God in a physical body. If you think about meditation, what you are really doing is creating a wider and wider space in which to catch the good things that are available to you. So when you are meditating, what you are really doing is dropping the energy of stress out of your energy field. Imagine that you are trying to catch water in a bucket with an opening that was continuously expanding. This would make the task much easier, wouldn't it? Well, the same thing is true with meditation: when you meditate, you are creating a greater opportunity for things to reach you.

If you continue with this particular analogy, imagine that you are still trying to catch water, but this time you pray that there will be more rain in order to increase your probability of catching it. When you pray you are specifically asking for things to come to you and to those for which you are praying. So when you pray you are really increasing the probability of rain, an ongoing rain, a steady rain. You must pray in order for you to attract those things that you wish for to you. When praying, you must come with an open heart, come with an open mind, to become part of the oneness even if for a moment with God, with your creator, with your creative source.

As you can see from our rain analogy, both meditation and prayer are necessary. If there is a lot of rain but you don't have anything to catch it in, you have not accomplished your goal. Or if you do have something to catch the rain in, but only a very small amount of rain comes, you still have not accomplished your goal of catching a great deal of rain. Again, you must use both prayer and meditation in order to increase your vibrational frequency and connect to your divinity.

Another way to increase your vibrational frequency is through colors. Think about the amazing power of colors: the clothing that you wear or the way that you decorate your home and your office; think about the impact that color has as you go through your day and the vibration that reaches you from color. And then begin to let yourself to vibrate with those colors that accelerate your vibrational frequency. The way that the colors affect your vibrational frequency is completely unique to you; allow yourself to feel the emotions that the colors make you feel. Let yourself not only be surrounded by beauty but pay attention and heighten your awareness about the impact of colors; notice that you are able to incorporate a lot of the gifts of color that are given to you through your surroundings when you just take a walk, or go to a neighbor's home, or go on a shopping trip. Now you don't have to make this a job. This is about collecting through the vibration of color, collecting energy to help you.

We have everything on this planet that you need, but sometimes, as we alluded to earlier, it is in a form that you do not recognize. You do not have to figure this out. You do not have to make this difficult. You will never understand why certain things affect your vibration, just know that they do. Help is all around you, not just in verbal form, but that is how you tend to hear it and to receive it through writings, through verbal communications through audio tapes, but all of your senses are available and ready to be activated in order to raise your vibrational frequency.

Now why would you want to do this? The answer is very simple: you want to step into a more conscious state of perfection rather than living in the illusion of imperfection. You want to know yourself as God. So using color, just as using intonation of different voices, or music, meditation, or prayer, everything influences your energy. There is nothing constant on our planet except change. Why is this true? Because you are interacting. You are not your own entity on a planet without anything else going on. So everything affects your vibration. But not everything increases your vibrational frequency. In fact, when you have had too much to drink, it decreases your vibrational frequency. When you have had too much to eat, particularly foods that aren't especially good for you, it decreases your vibrational frequency. Of course when you argue with someone, this decreases your vibrational frequency as well. Again, everything affects your vibration, it is true, but not everything affects it in the way that you would like it to.

Become aware of things such as color, and let yourself be nurtured and supported by things that are all around you. Have you ever had the experience of going shopping for clothing and finding something that appeals to you in every way: you like the material, you love the color, the fit is just right? Well, what is really happening is that all of these things are affecting your vibration.

It is up to you to seek out those things that raise your vibrational frequency and accelerate it, but you do not use that in place of going within and talking with the bodies of consciousness. What is happening to you emotionally? What is going on with you mentally? What are you feeling physically? The more that you gain consciousness, the more you recognize that you have brought certain things into your life to increase your vibrational frequency. Stay aware of these things and look about you, and seek out those things that give you greater states of self-love.

When you think of the things that have an effect on your vibrational frequency, you probably will not be surprised that your place of employment is a significant contributor. Think about your job and ask yourself if it is simply a means of financial support or if it is actually helping you on your path. If it is, that is wonderful. If it is not, then take a look at those things in your job that don't really serve you. Just for a moment, step out of being the participant and become the observer. Ask yourself: if you could be doing anything in the world, what would it be? Where would you be doing it? Allow yourself to feel the first answer that comes to you, no matter how off the beaten path it may be.

If you are not following your heart's desire in terms of your professional path, what better time than now to make a change? Imagine yourself doing whatever it is that you would truly love and ask yourself, "What am I waiting for?" Are you waiting for God to come down and create that position for you? Are you trying to build yourself up before trying to go forward and do it the old-fashioned way? Or are you trying to follow your passion and do it the fifth-dimensional way?

If you are blessed enough to already be doing something that you love in your life, make yourself an expert at it. Don't settle for less, don't settle for an incomplete version of life. Let yourself be an expert in that professional area that you love. Follow your passion. It doesn't follow a timetable, and it doesn't follow the limitations that you have been consciously or unconsciously putting on yourself. As we said before, you are on this planet for fun, so follow your passion with a joyful heart! And remember, if something is in your heart, it is part of your blueprint. It cannot be otherwise.

Think about what following your professional passion does to your vibration. It is not simply about being happy at your job, or feeling more fulfilled, it is all a vehicle to increasing the frequency of your vibration and therefore allowing you to live more fully as a fifth-dimensional being. Imagine how wonderful it is to get up every morning to be so thankful that you did not believe the illusion, that you did not believe what mass consciousness told you. Instead you followed your own passion, listened to your own heart, and chose to do that which you loved; you lived the life well-lived.

Because the planet has shifted into the fifth dimension, it is easier for your guides, or teachers, to materialize. It is easier than it has ever been on the earth plane. However, that doesn't mean that everyone is going to be able to see them. The reason for this is that you need to raise your vibrational frequency in order to see the unseen. It is similar to dogs being able to hear very high-pitched tones that humans cannot hear. You have to train yourself to be in a position to see what has always been right in front of you, right before your very eyes.

Remember that you create your reality, and you create it by using techniques such as materialization, manifestation, and imaging. You create it by raising your vibrational frequency, looking at issues of love and issues of expansion. And so as you come to a place where you are able to experience more, so then will you be able to see more than what you have seen up to this point.

You may be thinking that you are ready to expand, ready to take that next leap. You are not to do it mentally; in fact, you can't do it that way. But the good news is when you follow your heart, these opportunities for advancement present themselves to you. Think of the concept of good, better, best, and beyond in terms of your development; you don't want to just get to the level of good but to that place of beyond, and then you are ready for your next leap, your next level of development. So remember some of your guides and teachers may be ready to materialize. Are you ready to receive your guests?

Another tool in the quest to increase your vibrational frequency comes in the form of health and healing. The most incredible healing energy that can come to you is through crystals and crystalline formations. It is not the only healing technique available, but it is quite powerful. As our planet shifted into the fifth dimension, the use of crystals has become more powerful as the vibrational frequency of the crystals has shifted as the planet has shifted. The crystals will find you. You don't have to debate about which crystal to use. As you raise your vibrational frequency, you will attract to you more powerful crystals and crystalline formations—in other words, crystals with attachments. It is only about quality that I speak to you at this time, not quantity, only quality. Make friends with the crystals that find their way to you. Talk to them as you would talk to a pet or as you would talk to a plant. Talk to the crystals and let them respond vibrationally. Remain silent as they respond vibrationally, remain open as they respond vibrationally. You will see they are part of God's creation of nature.

Nature heals because you are part of God's creation of nature. All of us together form the oneness. And as the right hand would like to help the left hand, as the right leg is needed to move forward with the left leg, so are the crystals and crystalline formations ready to move forward and assist each of you that are part of the oneness. Talk to them, listen and receive from them, and it will assist your healing process going into a state of good health, a state of calmness, and a state of knowingness. Journey into wellness; healing is not about the journey out of illness, even though that is where the focus is on our planet. Wellness is not designed by the planetary influences, by the medical community, or by the aging process of the body, it occurs in the mind. It is mind over matter, not running from what a person doesn't want, but a journey into what they do want.

When you think of raising your vibrational frequency, magic may not be one of the first things that you think of. Picture some of the magical experiences that you have had: perhaps seeing a rainbow, or having a beautiful bird fly directly in front of you, or seeing a cloud formation with a message that you know is meant for you. Of course all of things are part of the ebb and flow of nature. And yet for them to appear in your reality means that you drew them in because you were ready for the gift.

Now it is true that your guides and teachers connect with you in many ways other than nature. But if you think about some of the magical aspects of nature, then you realize that it contains potentially everything that you need for enhancing your connection and receiving your message from spirit. You do not really have to go to a particular vortex or ley line in order to make that connection. You simply have to recognize the signals that come to you and to recognize that they are in fact meant for you.

Now there is a movie that came out quite a while ago called *Defending Your Life*. And in that movie it talked about going to a place called the "past life pavilion." And it is very similar to aura photography in that you would lay your hand on the hand plate and your previous lives would make themselves known to you. Some of them were exciting in a good way, and some of them were nerve-wracking. But in almost every case an experience that the individuals had in that lifetime came through loud and clear through nature. The need for this interaction with nature is a large part of why you came to the earth plane. You choose a physical incarnation to learn to grow and to evolve to go to the next level of consciousness. And so all of these things that guides do are to get your attention or to give you a confirmation that everything is going to be all right, that you are protected, that you are loved, and that you are taken care of.

Your guides do not give you negative symbols in nature. This is important to remember. Many individuals say that they are afraid to communicate with spirit because they fear that their guides will tell them that they are doing something wrong, something terrible, or that they are simply not doing enough. Your guides will not send negative symbols to you, but you may attract them through your fear. When we talk about the magic of nature, we are talking about the beauty and helping you to expand through love and excitement and anticipation.

We also wish for you to focus on simplicity. Our world has changed but the virtues will never change. Simplicity is a virtue that will always hold true. When you really focus on what makes you happy or how to achieve a state of happiness, it really is all about love. What you love and what you can survive on are all of the things that our earth has given you.

The fifth body of consciousness, also referred to as your superconsciousness, is that aspect of you that knows your blueprint. There is a very strong connection between your fifth body of consciousness and your higher self, what we call your spiritual source. While the other bodies of consciousness play a role in your spiritual development, they really play a role to each other while the fifth body of consciousness is a stand alone energy. Now your role in raising your vibrational frequency is not to educate your other bodies of consciousness, but to observe your fifth body of consciousness and let that aspect of you do what it does best: going into a fifth-dimensional way of being. You must observe and let this aspect of you lead you and help raise your vibrational frequency.

In all of this talk about vibrational frequency, what is the difference between gratitude and grace? On our planet there is quite a bit of gratitude, especially for those things that are given to others in need. We are not just talking about material things, but emotional and spiritual gifts as well. So what do you sense is the connection between gratitude and grace? Those who have an attitude of genuine gratitude are automatically in a state of grace. That is very different from a little child that grows up learning that you must say thank you for the food that is on the table, you must say thank you for the good grades that you get in class. Having polite manners is very different from being an individual that feels gratitude for every one of life's blessings. These people feel gratitude because the whole thing feels like love. If you are helped emotionally, if you are helped spiritually, if you are given some insights to help you mentally or for a physical or material need, it feels like love. If in fact your first feeling is not really one of relief but one of gratitude, then you are in a state of grace.

And you know that all gifts come from the god-goddess energy no matter who the messenger is, no matter how it is delivered. It all comes from what you know as the universal source. Those who automatically feel the gratitude and have a joyfulness about them, those are the ones that are in a perpetual state of grace. That is quite a powerful place to be. We would like to encourage all of you to practice gratitude. Then you begin to see the beauty, the excitement, and the magic behind all of those events that led to your receiving the blessing. It is like the layers of the onion. You peel off one layer and you go a bit deeper. You peel off another layer and you go even deeper. Then you begin to feel your world through a feeling of gratitude. Then you begin to understand how elements of your world operate. And your world of course is a microcosm of what the universe is all about and how the universe operates.

There is more good news! As the planet has speeded up, the way to approach the fifth dimension is faster and quicker. There is a faster way to achieve the fifth dimension and there is a faster way to see the results of the fifth dimension. It is an instantaneous blessing!

* * * * * * *

Growing up, in the summertime after dinner, all of the kids in the neighborhood would meet outside and play ball, usually in the middle of the street. Mothers and fathers would venture out after the dinner dishes were done and catch up with each other, discussing the happenings of the day or week. I always loved when my mother talked with the neighbors because she would lose track of the time, and miraculously my bedtime would be later than usual. I remember lying down with my back on the grass and gazing up to the nighttime sky. I was attracted to a cluster of stars that appeared directly above me. I didn't really know anything about the stars I was looking at, I just knew that I loved the hazy but bluish/golden glow that surrounded them. The effect on me was that they were dreamy, intriguing, and calming. I would look for them whenever I was outside.

Years later I still watch this star group, but now I have done the research and I do know what I am looking at and why I am attracted to them. I have discovered that I was admiring the Pleiades, a group of 500 stars, the brightest of which are known as the seven sisters: Alcyone, Atla, Electra, Maia, Nerope, Taygeta, and Pleione. The stars send a bluish light because they are emitting a high-frequency energy. There is some discussion that the Pleiades is moving through a nebula, or great cloud of interstellar matter and gas. The nebula has created some controversial discussions among scientists. Some suggest that the nebula actually is a photon belt and that this photon belt is traveling toward the planet Earth and should arrive in 2012. Although other scientists deny the existence of a photon belt, we can safely say that we have no scientific way of actually detecting the energy that is in this nebula. While others suggest that this photon belt actually consists of the spiritual energy that the Mayans have predicted will be leading the way to the Age of Aquarius, the golden age of this twenty-first century.

In recent years, I have learned that during my sleeping hours when I leave my body for further learning I travel to the Pleiades often. Many nights our souls are taken out by our guides to learn whatever it is that we need to learn or to experience. This is called astral traveling. Everyone has this experience although you may not be leaving your body consciously. It is a way for us to grow and expand our consciousness. If you have ever had the experience that when you awake in the morning you feel very stiff, tired, and immovable, most probably you were astral traveling. Your limbs and arms simply feel dead to the world. It takes a while for you to awaken your body. This is because when you have been out astral traveling, your guides return you to your body and your spirit is simply readjusting into its physical structure. Sometimes as you are returning you can actually float on your bedroom ceiling and see your body asleep in bed. I have had that experience, and it is rather fun to see your body sleeping calmly in your bed. When I saw my body I decided that I wasn't ready to "come home" yet and asked my guides to take me back out for more fun! The next time I awoke I felt very stiff and very, very tired but gradually allowed myself to wake up and get up!

My attraction to the Pleiades made such sense to me as my daytime body was acknowledging the attraction that my nighttime spirit body was visiting! I have learned that my soul has spent a great deal of time on Peleides, experiencing the energy for learning, for growing and expansion. I have also been told that I have a parallel life happening currently on Pleiades, and oftentimes my soul fragment on that planet comes to earth at night to exchange knowledge that my earthly body is learning in this lifetime. I guess you could say that the soul fragments are part of an interplanetary exchange program and I am reaping the benefits from both worlds! This is not an unusual experience—because most of us are not aware of the comings and goings of our soul!

During this transitioning period on our planet, many books have been written about 2012. Some are books written from a place of fear and are filled with doom and gloom. If you are drawn to reading one of those books, I would be really careful not to be drawn into that mindset. There are other books written that are informative as they explain the historical significance of past events as they relate to our 2012. One such book—now don't laugh—is *The Complete Idiot's Guide to 2012: An Ancient Look at a Critical Time* and provides information which will give you the overview to all of the events surrounding the 2012. For the purposes of this book, I would like to provide a very simple summary of the role that the Pleiades has in relationship to the completion of the planetary shift. Please refer to the above book for more of these details. Pleiades is playing a role to help awaken the energy that will be the energy released onto our planet. It is said that the pyramid of Kulkulkan at Chichen Itza during the spring equinox casts a shadow which travels downward toward the base of the stairs where there resides a serpent sculpture. This represents the return of Kukulkan or Quetzalcoatl. This also represents the return of the zenith sun when it passes over Chichen Itza, typically on May 20. The magic of the 2012 will bring the zenith passage of the sun exactly at the same time there is a solar eclipse that aligns with the Pleiades. This alignment represents the opening of the return of the Quetzalcoatl energy.

This energy is the ancient energy emerging into our planet that brings us into what is being referred to as the golden age, the spiritual century coming to life. Lightworkers all over the world are awakening to this and are learning and growing from exposure to the energy on the Pleiades. It is an exciting time, and not only was I drawn to the beauty of this star group, but I was continuing a relationship with the energy of the Pleiades to help me continue not only my spiritual growth but to aid me in completing my blueprint.

Our guides help us to develop spiritually by exposing us to new areas regularly. We think we are going to bed, but actually we may be attending classes anywhere in the universe! This brings a whole new meaning to the phrase "night school"! I also feel there are times when our soul is needed to give love and compassion to others so we extend ourselves at night, joining other souls, moving our energy and our light to where it is needed. One such example is the whitish/golden band that was seen night after night after night around the ground zero area after 9/11. Many, many souls giving a beautiful tribute!

There are many advanced ascended master "after hours" schools that you may attend. You may go for exposure or for advancement when your soul has reached a certain level of growth. This may be considered a reward for your focus and determination to continue to expand your consciousness as well as increase your vibrations. Our guides know what we are to accomplish, and they will help us in every way possible to reach new heights! We only have to be open to the unlimited possibilities and they will be brought to us.

On a day-to-day level we are able to communicate and receive information from our guides in many different ways.

The information that is given to us of course is recognized by us when we live a life of open minds and open hearts. At any given time a message may come, and when we acknowledge it we allow the communications to come forward. Sometimes we don't understand, and we know there is a message and we acknowledge its source but the meaning remains unclear. Several days may pass, and when we least expect it (typically because we are relaxed and not trying to force a meaning), the meaning pops into our head or we experience a knowingness deep inside—we have another "aha moment"! Keeping a journal often helps relate the experience to the meaning, and reading one's journal on a regular basis allows for the meaning to take on new expanded meanings as we see the bigger or more complete picture and so our soul expands. When our world expands, our soul follows suit and we begin to experience the joy of life.

I went to Catholic schools growing up, so prayer was something that I was taught and it was part of my life as a child. I remember lying in bed at night and praying and knowing that someone was listening to me. I don't know if I felt that my prayers were "answered," but I did know that I possessed the faith, that I continued asking and praying for what I either needed or wanted for myself and for what I needed or wanted for my family. Somehow I don't think it was as important that I felt that I needed a resolution to my prayer, but I needed to continue to pray because of the feeling that it gave me. Not only did I feel that I was connected to something larger than me, but I felt that I knew that whomever or whatever I was connected to was in my corner.

You may have heard it said that prayer is asking a question or seeking a request and that meditation is listening for the answer! If this is true, then obviously you can never listen for an answer if your mind is always in a constant state of movement or commotion, always thinking and never slowing down. I believe that that state is referred to by Markas as the "babble of the marketplace"!

So one trick that I was taught to quiet the mind is to simply take a specific time of the day, preferably the same time every day and for a thirty-day period, simply sit in silence for ten minutes: no telephone, no computer, no music—no distractions. As you sit, you allow your initial thoughts and distractions to leave and you become comfortable with the quiet. The more you allow the quiet to become your friend, the easier it is to get in touch not only with your energy and your innermost thoughts but also to the energy of your guides.

Simply request one guide to accompany you during this ten-minute period. As I practiced this new form of quieting myself, I began to really see color. I could see who was coming in and was able to identify the color and connecting it with my guide.

Initially it takes several days to be able to sit for ten minutes. It doesn't sound like it would be difficult, but it is surprising to see how you need to discipline yourself for such a short time period. After a few sessions, you relax into the feeling of what you are trying to do and it becomes easier to sit for the ten minutes. In a few more days, it is surprising to see that instead of ten minutes passing, you have been sitting for twenty or even thirty minutes!

At the end of your chosen thirty-day period, you are so proud that you have accomplished your goal and you are also proud that you have taken the time to get to know yourself, no expectations and no requirements. You simply have given yourself not only the gift of time but the gift of silence. Priceless!

Being in touch with who you are, and having the loving visitations of your guides, helps to raise your vibrations. So when you finish your thirty-day period, you are vibrating at a higher rate than you were before you started.

One of the ways to continue to raise your vibrations is also to be aware of all of your thoughts—and see that they are coming from a loving place. Kindness is important as are all of the positive virtues or traits that we can possess. Losing any of the negative traits is not only critical but mandatory. Acknowledgment is key. Once you recognize judgment or criticism directed either toward others or to yourself, it is easy to simply drop it and flip over to the positive. This may take some training in the early stages, but eventually it becomes automatic.

What is difficult is to recognize the role of the ego in all of this. The question is really what is your ego trying to direct you to say or think or do? And it is really very easy to recognize that it is your ego voice that is controlling you because it is the voice of negativity! Whatever the issue, whatever the complaint, it is the ego voice that is postulating in a negative way. Either you or someone you are thinking about is never good enough, pretty or handsome enough, or smart enough. The ego continually diminishes you and keeps your view of yourself in the lowest esteem possible. If you want to overcome the negative and put yourself and others in a positive light, then you must learn to control your ego voice within.

This is when I learned to have some irreverent fun! Every time the ego voice talked to me in a demeaning manner, pulling the rug out from under me, I would feel a lack of confidence and begin to travel down the path of negativity. It doesn't take much before your attitude becomes negative, affecting not only yourself but those around you as you allow yourself to go down that black hole again and again. I needed to train myself to recognize that it was my ego voice causing trouble and simply trained myself to say or think "Shut the F—k up" at the appropriate time. Then an ensuing giggle would follow . . . because I was not used to talking to myself this way, nor was I used to using this vocabulary! But I needed to get my attention, and get it I did—besides the fact that this was the only thing that I came up with! Now we are old friends, my ego voice and my inner self, and as one old friend to another, we are able to be blunt but honest with each other. My ego voice knows where and how it is to reside in my body and what will happen when it gets out of line! Yes, I have learned to quiet the "babble in the marketplace," perhaps not in the most orthodox way but in a way that works for me. I am sure you can create your own way to keep on top of the ego voice to keep it from getting out of line, all the while having fun with it—taking the heaviness away with lighthearted fun!

CHAPTER VIII

The Universal Realm

*I look no further than I can imagine.
There can be no limits to imagination.*

—Spirit, 2009

Many of you have had the experience of interacting with teachers from the universal realm. You have found that it is a very different arena from either the physical realm or the emotional realm. The primary difference is of course that the focus is on cosmic consciousness. And so the types of beings that guide you in the universal realm come with a grander scheme in mind than just your blueprint. Beings from the physical realm of consciousness want to make sure that you have followed your blueprint, and that you are having all of the experiences that you are supposed to have. But it is different for the universal realm: they actually give you either the existing cosmic information that is on our planet but not really recognized by us, or cosmic information that is waiting for our next stage of development. You really want to see how far along your development has come in terms of your understanding of the cosmos and the understanding of universal principles. By and large, these individuals come not for fulfillment of your blueprint, but more because you are ready for the next step. You are ready to understand how all of this relates back to you and how all of this really relates to this planet.

The universal principles deal with how the universe actually came to be, how the individuals who are on this planet came to be here, what we are creating on this planet, and why we are doing it. So if we look at this planet, we will see that those that are in the more advanced countries tend to have more of the attention of teachers and other beings from the universal realm of consciousness. It is simply because of the connection between the planet and the cosmos. So you might see that those who are doing a lot with astronomy, and those that are doing a lot with the biotechnical field, will have a greater influence from those in the universal realm.

You have several different beings that are coming to you from the universal realm. You have your birthright angel, two eternal sons, as well as other beings who act as teachers. You also have a cabalistic arcana guide as well as some chakra assistants. As you know you have seven primary chakras, and those who have entered into the fifth dimension of consciousness have an eighth chakra that is right above the crown chakra. In addition to these chakra assistants, you have what is called an assemblage of commitment instructor. Remember these titles do not mean anything, except in the manner in which we use them! They explain what the distinctive role that these guides play for you is. Finally, you have the very interesting group called the lead messengers.

The cabalistic arcana guide is a being that you have a direct connection with, and it is fair to say that in one form or another you have shared a past life. Your cabalistic arcana guide is an entity or an energy assisting with your development of the very beginning. You came from a certain place in the universe—you weren't born on this planet; instead, your soul originated in another part of the universe. Let's say that you spun off from your higher self and you became a separate soul. It is your cabalistic arcana guide who was there when you became a separate being. So when your soul arrived, so to speak, you began to develop in certain patterns, you studied certain things, you approached things in a certain way. It is very similar to the way that a child is influenced by the way that they were raised. For example, if you were a Japanese-born person (soul) raised in New York City, your experience would be very different than if you had been raised in Tokyo. You would imagine that your experiences would be different. There would be some similarities, but also very distinctive differences. And so that is what the cabalistic arcana guide brings to you—information about your point of origin, specifically identifying the belief systems through which you evolved.

If you examine how you interact with individuals and how you live on this planet, you will realize that it is in a large part determined by the filters through which you view this planet. Those filters are your belief systems. Now your belief systems aren't necessarily good or bad, they are structures for you within which to receive information, process it, and see how you can relate to it. But sometimes you outgrow a particular belief system, and if you continue to hang on to it when it no longer serves you, then and only then does it become an impediment.

Think of a belief system as this continuum that you are moving through. You have probably already relaxed that belief system as you have developed spiritually. But you have numerous belief systems that you are operating with relatively unconsciously throughout your day. So these belief systems then had a point of origin for where in fact your soul had its initial development. If individuals are interested in family development, psychologists will say that the most important years are the first couple of years in a person's life. Well, from a cosmic standpoint, we wouldn't say that they are the most important years, but significant in terms of the belief systems that you develop. Yes, absolutely. And those belief systems will carry you through from lifetime to lifetime. It could be a lifetime on Planet Earth, it could be a lifetime on, let us say, a different part of this galaxy, or it could be a completely different galaxy, wherever you have your lifetime experiences.

So let us take a look at those belief systems and see if those beliefs really serve you. At some point you might say, well, I really don't want to have any beliefs, I want to come in and experience life in a unfiltered way. But mechanically that is very difficult to do on your planet. Our planet is held together by a construction of beliefs—a belief about gravity, a belief about the passage of time, a belief about the understanding of revolution and rotation of the planets. There are so many beliefs on our planet, but we are able to relax those beliefs and live more metaphysically on what is a physical planet. Because we are all part of the god/goddess energy, we are all perfect. If we accept this perfection as the ultimate truth, then we recognize that we really don't need to go anywhere, to learn anything, to advance in any way as we are already perfect. You may say, "Yes, everything is perfect as it is, and yet I want to gain consciousness. I really want to know more. Even though I am part of this big perfectly formed structure, I still want to know more. I want to identify myself and my consciousness forever, not just for one or two lifetimes, completely and in an infinite way."

If this is the case, you may choose to go to a planet that is spiritual. As we have mentioned earlier, we really are on a planet that is multidimensional; it is physical, emotional, mental, and spiritual. You chose to come to a planet that is a combination of energies because you wanted to pursue that. Now at some point you may say, "I really want to go to a place and have fun. I know that ideally learning should be in combination with fun, but I really just want to have a break. I want to see what it is like to be completely unconscious and have everything go my way and just skate for awhile." You may look and you see people who seem to be having an abundance of fun in this lifetime and ask yourself how they got so lucky. They don't seem to be growing spiritually, doing their work, to phrase it in an old-fashioned way, really making progress. They just seem to have everything handed to them. Well, the truth is that it is one of their lifetimes to experience that kind of fun and joy. Now you don't just get that handed to you. In a sense you earn it. You have enough respect and responsibility in what you have done in other lifetimes that you have earned this bit of a vacation.

You might think that you too would really enjoy the combination of learning and fun in this lifetime. What you really need to do then is to relax your belief system about how it is that you can accomplish your goals. No pain, no gain? Not necessarily. Ask yourself, "Do I really have to be the worker bee? Do I have to do things the old-fashioned way?" The answer may be no, that you can accomplish your goals while having fun and experiencing joy in this lifetime. Think about how you can do things the new-fashioned way. Use your emotions to create what you want rather than feeling as if your emotions are something that you are not able to get a handle on. So when you take a look then at some of your deepest beliefs, ask yourself if you are thinking about it in the old-fashioned way. Ask yourself if that belief system really serves you or not. If not, relax that belief system so that it helps you view your world in a way in which the learning is actually going to get easier and so that you can incorporate elements of play.

* * * * * * * *

Isn't it interesting that sometimes some truths make such sense to you? You don't know why you believe what you do, but you only know that you do. Other truths may not make sense or resonate with you, and still other truths you simply feel indifferent toward.

Is it a wonder that we are all so very different? Each believing a truth or variation of a truth but not really knowing why or being able to explain why we feel the way that we do. Upon examination, we don't understand why or what events in this lifetime or past lifetimes have contributed to this belief system. We can look toward our early formative years and not know why our parents thought, spoke, and acted in certain ways. We may only have a slight remembrance of grandparents or our relationship with them was simply one of nurturing and love. We have never been given the insight of why our grandparents and parents before them had developed the consciousness that made them feel the way that they did. Our parents may or may not have investigated why they felt the way they did from their story within their family. If we investigate this even further, we may realize that there has been no formal learning (consciously) about what we believe either from school or from our family in this lifetime. So much of who we have become has simply been assimilated from the family, friends, and schooling that we have been exposed to. So why do we believe what we do?

If we are a sum total of all of our learning in all of our lifetimes, some experiences may feel familiar and can be identified by us while other experiences feel strangely new—as if we have just arrived in uncharted territory. These experiences not only define us but define who we are at our core. Although we may not specifically tap into the time, place, and date of the how or the why of what we have experienced, we do know that these experiences exist. You can feel that they exist and so you know them to be true.

You may be interested in investigating why you feel the way you do. Perhaps you have an undetermined pain symptom which has become unbearable to live with and the medical profession is unable to help, or perhaps you see that you feel passionate about something that no one else in your family does and you wonder where that passion comes from. Have you ever considered having a past-life regression? A past-life regression may help you arrive at answers to questions that have been bothering you or have become a problem for you. There are very qualified individuals that can help you identify experiences in other lives that may provide you with the very answers that you need that can put to rest questions or problems in your current life.

I have had several past-life regressions and I really loved the entire experience! (I only recommend professional past-life regressions being conducted by a very positive and spiritual individual—so that the memories are all positive recollections.) From the minute I relaxed into the chair, allowing myself to simply float to a place where I could witness several events in several lifetimes, I have felt a deeper connection to my inner self. My first experience was really beautiful. I was taken very slowly and quietly on a journey of relaxation. Once relaxed I was asked to float to a beautiful majestic grand hall, white and marble in construction. Once inside I witnessed many, many doorways, each representing the path to a different lifetime of mine. I was told to simply walk down the hall and when I was ready to select a door and enter. So as I walked along the hallway. I chose the second door to the right. I walked literally into a scene in seventeenth-century England where I was known as Elizabeth Adams. My life as I was viewing it consisted of a very difficult childhood, an escape that

that allowed me to journey to a big city, and a view of me as an adult, happy and prosperous. I learned about the choices that were presented to me. I also recognized many people in this lifetime who gave me opportunities to learn in that lifetime which allowed me to transition that lifetime from difficult into beautiful. Being mindful of what I was taught: it is how you extract the lesson or lessons in a lifetime that makes the regression a successful one as you gain insight into your soul.

In subsequent past-life regressions, I learned that I have had a lifetime in France where I was painted by Renoir, a lifetime in Holland where I was painted by Vermeer, and I have glimpsed myself in many Native American lifetimes. All of these experiences have taught me that we can bring up and review any part of who we are from our cellular memory. I always feel that it is wonderful to see who I was and what I have learned, but I am careful not to get caught up and lost in the details of the lifetime. The value comes from simply understanding that that lifetime afforded me the opportunity in which to learn many different lessons, and it is the acknowledgement of these lessons that is to be cherished. I also have enjoyed the process of regression and how easy it is to retrieve events and information from past lifetimes.

Early on in my developing period, I had an experience that helped me to understand not only the concept of past lives but also how past lives affect how you think, feel, and act. I had gone to a client's home a good distance from mine. When I left for my appointment that morning the temperature was in the midsixties. As I concluded my appointment, a cold front arrived, and I now needed to drive across town in thirty-degree weather with high winds, hail, and ice. Mother Nature reminding us once again that she is the boss—the weather was treacherous. I called in my transportation guides and my angels as I watched cars and trucks veering off the road and landing in ditches. I prayed and asked for protection as I was scared! I drove very carefully and took what I felt would be the safest route. It took me several hours to travel the forty miles to reach home and thankfully I arrived home safely. As I arrived home, I knew I was in for the night as the forecasters were predicting the winds to continue with an accumulation of snow. All night I heard the wind whistling outside, the ice pounding on the windows, and the darkness getting brighter and brighter as the snow was covering the landscape. My home was situated on a bit of a hill with no protection from the north, allowing a northern clipper to be strongly felt as the wind traveled up my driveway, swirling round and round, usually bringing twigs, leaves, and other debris with it. There on the stoop of my back door was a grouping of white feathers totally untouched by the weather. The feathers were pristine, each about five inches and absolutely perfect and all pure white.

I was amazed. What were these beautiful feathers doing on my back step? How were these feathers able to simply be resting there, totally undisturbed by the storm? I gathered them up and brought them inside, fingering their perfection and simple beauty.

Several days later the mystery began to unfold. One evening I went to bed, and while sleeping my dream was a very different kind of dream. It was as if my mind was running a film showing me an entire lifetime of mine. This experience went on for several nights as I witnessed my life as a shaman of an Indian tribe in the Midwest. I remember thinking the "film," for lack of a better word, was unusual as it was similar to the celluloid that movie houses put on a reel to play their film, and the color of the film was all in sepia tones. The first night showed my life as a child living near the Ohio Valley and traveling along the banks of a river with my Native American tribe. I witnessed my participation with my family as we set up camp, fished, and prepared meals. I witnessed myself learning how to survive, all the while being taught to respect nature. There seemed to be a lesson associated with each experience, and the elders of the tribe were continually telling stories illustrating new experiences and new lessons. This was my most favorite part of the day—the storytelling was fun as I began learning the concepts and meaning of honoring nature as well as learning how to love and respect your fellow tribesmen.

Each consecutive night I continued my dream, watching this little Native American girl grow right into adulthood. I witnessed her learning, growing, and developing as I was trained to become a shaman. I was given the name White Feather by my tribe as I had earned it moving into the role of spiritual adviser and teacher for the tribe. (Imagine that!) Today I clearly understand how my spirituality in this lifetime has come from the depth of previous lives. Recognizing my closest relationships from my current lifetime that were important people for me in that lifetime has answered many questions. Individuals played different parts, and I have been able to understand why I was attracted to certain individuals in this lifetime after I saw our relationship and events that connected us in my Indian lifetime. I am also able to see why certain individuals in this lifetime simply do not get along—as they were living lives opposing each other (Native American vs. cavalry), and that energy has carried over, continuing to influence their relationships. I witnessed several very sad events that helped me to understand why individuals can carry over an attitude or a manner which formerly seemed unexplainable. I learned things about myself, and I see how White Feather's life has indeed influenced my belief system and its current thoughts and attitude about things that remain sacred to me. My life is richer for having had this experience.

In addition, I learned how the universe works. It was time for me to wake up to the totality of who I am. My dream sleep provided me with wonderful knowledge and information that my guides felt I was ready to see and to understand to help take me to the next level. Witnessing my lifetime through the manner that I did helped me to understand that we truly are the sum total of our past experiences. My goodness, I learned about my cellular memory. Replaying the details of this beautiful life is simply a very small part of who I am. Our belief system is the sum total of all of our experiences, and that means many, many lifetimes! So when I have been told to bring an experience up and simply remember, I can now see how that is possible. But the gift is so much more than that. I felt the love. I felt the love, the powerful love from the universe! I was not only a witness but the recipient of a beautiful miracle, the universe presenting me with the white feathers—symbolic on so many levels—totally perfect and untouched during the storm was but another validation that miracles do exist and are given to us on a daily basis. I was beginning to understand what it means to be in the flow of the universal energy. I got it!

Today I am constantly being showered with gifts. On special days or perhaps when I am searching or looking for answers, the universe will surprise me with a white feather, validating my thinking, or my experience, for me. I have been gifted them at my business, during my business appointments, and on very special occasions—I may come out and a white feather will be on my car windshield or even balancing on the car handle! I then exactly know the answer to my question, or the reason for the gift. I relish in the connectedness once again as this is indeed another magical gift from the universe.

I suppose that this inner knowing is the one element in us that helps us to understand that logical thinking cannot always supply the answers. If we choose to open our minds and our hearts, and if we truly understand how limiting logical thinking really is, and we are ready to grasp knowledge from our experiences, then we are ready to really get in touch with the essence of who we are. Being nonlinear is the name of the game. How do we do this? How do we open our minds and our hearts and expand the base from which we can draw our answers from? Why should we do this?

Let's begin by relaxing our belief system. I learned very early on that what often is written in stone either shouldn't be or doesn't have to be. The very idea that concepts have to be written in stone is in itself limiting. I am not saying that all concepts that are written in stone should be changed, but what I am saying is that when you have narrowly defined your belief system by an already limiting view, it can never be recognized and relaxed. Remember the expression "never say never"? This example simply teaches us that just when you say *never*, a situation or event occurs that you wished you had never uttered the word *never*! So the lesson is learned, and we decide that it is not in our best interest to be using the word *never* as that is coming from a place of narrow thinking which is limiting. So you relax this thought and consciously say that you are not going to limit your thinking. Not only are you allowing the beginnings of limitation to leave your consciousness, you are actually expanding your consciousness. That is the goal! Only growth can occur, and your soul can evolve when you are expanding your energies that are all around you.

We have an expression that is very popular right now, and that is "thinking out of the box." Scientists and educators recognize that when you step outside of your comfort zone and allow yourself to think outside of the box, you are allowing new information to flow to you and through you. While being comfortable in one way is wonderful and supportive and adds security to one's life, in another way being comfortable can be limiting and possibly stagnating. So getting "uncomfortable" is actually a good thing! I recently read a quote by Reese Witherspoon, "If I am afraid or fearful of something, then I probably should do it." This wonderful statement is an example of Reese putting a value on working through fear and stretching her boundaries. It is such an enlightened statement as the value is placed on the growth that is gained when one is working through their fears. She gets it! By seeing the value of challenging herself, Reese Witherspoon has stepped up to take the role of a contemporary heroine as she is passing on to us another way to gain confidence as we work through our fears to become more complete.

CHAPTER IX

The Lucky One!

If one is lucky, a solitary fantasy can totally transform one million realities.

—Maya Angelou

You are beings who are here to project light. You are meant to project light in your home and in your habitat, wherever you are, and also wherever you visit. It is not just enough that you are a light being, but you must also project light. You don't need think about it, you just are it, and so it projects from your chakras, in particular the heart chakra. It also projects from the throat, or communication chakra, as well as from your vitae chakra. When you project light, you begin to see that the world around you changes. You are here to assist with the transformation of the planet and those on it, whether you help one person or a thousand people. The number of people that you help is not the issue; it is the quality by which you follow your own life's blueprint that is of the utmost importance. It is not by accident, it is not by luck, it is not simply by a stroke of fate that you ended up in the location that you are. You are there to use your energy to assist other individuals, whether or not you are consciously aware of it.

Being a fifth-dimensional being is a privilege and a responsibility, but there are a lot of attributes of living in the fifth dimension that most of us have not tapped into yet. It is very similar to when you first went into the fourth dimension—you were very confused and extremely overwhelmed with emotions. You have probably been overwhelmed and confused with the level of anxiety that accompanies most of the individuals who are living in the fifth dimension.

That anxiety might be emotional, physical, mental, or in some cases, it may even be spiritual. So there are instances, many instances, of individuals who feel that they are on a different plane of awareness than they were previously even though they are in the same physical location. It is reminiscent of the line in *The Wizard of Oz* when Dorothy says "it doesn't look like Kansas, anymore."

The reason why you have probably found the transition to the fifth dimension more difficult than the transition to the fourth dimension is because of the expectations that you may have had. You may have thought that it was going to be easier because you were spiritually evolving and this evolution was supposed to help you to step into the world of the spiritual healer with all systems go. So everything was intended to be moving as if all of your chakras were spinning in the same direction. However when you got into the fifth dimension because of the upheaval, what you found was that what you were doing didn't seem to be sufficient for what was going on in the planet. No matter how hard you tried to be fifth-dimensional, you still had a planet that was not looking very familiar to you.

Now imagine living on a planet where there is no disease of the emotions. If there was no disease of the emotions, there would be no jealousy, there would be no hatred, there would be no hurting of each other, opening up wounds, and trying to inflict harm. There would not be the sadness, there would not be longing, there would not be any of those emotions that don't feel like love. Of course you cannot cure the whole world, but as those who project light, the more that you are cured yourself, the more that your light is effective because there are no blemishes, there are no holes in your energy. The more you are a healed version of a spiritual healer, the more that you are able to help others.

As we have stated previously, you create your reality by what you are thinking, feeling, and imagining at this time. Now you do not imagine so far into the future that you do not live in the present, but you allow yourself to think and to feel and to imagine things that are best and beyond. You do not have to do it all day, you don't have to do it for five minutes; you just have to have a thought and put yourself into that place and imagine what that would be like. Think of the John Lennon song that says, "Imagine there is no heaven." Instead, why don't you "imagine there is no hell on earth." Now just imagining that changes your vibrational frequency. So you may be fifth-dimensional, and you may be 20 percent into it, and back to 10 percent (you can go backward), or you may have moved ahead to 30 percent, but as soon as you begin to imagine these other things, your vibrational frequency will be accelerated. You will not only experience your world differently, but you begin to live in a different world. That does not mean that the world will be healed instantly of course. There will still be individuals on our planet who want to go to war, individuals who continue to plan terrorist attacks, and individuals who withhold love from others. We are not saying that things will change immediately, but trust that they will change.

There are several things that can help you raise your vibrational frequency. One such thing that can be a very powerful tool is aromatherapy. Frankincense is one of the most powerful fragrances for a fifth-dimensional body. Preferences when it comes to aromatherapy are really a unique thing. Some prefer lavender, others lemon or peppermint. Other things that help raise your vibrational frequency include telepathy, transmigration, and teleportation. While each of these things can be quite powerful, they are not as necessary as they were when you were fourth-dimensional. This is because your vibration has already been raised to this point, even when it doesn't feel very good living on this planet.

Now there are some individuals that you know that may switch back and forth between the fourth and fifth dimension. They sit right on the edge between the two, and they go back and fourth. Some of these individuals have been a little frustrating to work with; they may be family, friends, or coworkers. You may also have been involved with individuals who are just in the beginning of fourth-dimensional living, which may have been very frustrating for you. Or you may have family members that are three-dimensional and you have learned how to "let go and let God" while continuing your own development.

You see when you were three-dimensional, you had a quest. You wanted to expand metaphysically, to expand spiritually. When you got into the fourth dimension, it wasn't so much a quest as a desire to master some of these emotional states so that when things happen you could move through them more easily and in a healed manner. So it wasn't a quest to become more metaphysical, it was learning about emotions and how to master them. Then in the fifth dimension you don't have that feeling that you are on a quest, and you don't have a feeling that you are on a mission of learning; in fact, you don't really know exactly what it is that you do in your development as a fifth-dimension individual.

So you may be wondering, "How do I go forward in the fifth dimension?" Well, in the fifth dimension you are becoming; you are not seeking after something, you are not learning it, you are becoming. So your effort is directed in becoming something, in becoming someone, in letting your soul evolve rapidly into becoming something new. But you don't do it by learning, and you don't do it by saying that I am just going to develop my metaphysical skills. You have done that. You can do that some more if you want, but that has very little to do with being fifth-dimensional. Instead, the fifth dimension is all about the art of becoming.

There is a guide that many of us share who goes by the name Aristotle. Aristotle has had a lifetime, not the one as Aristotle that we are all so familiar with, but one in which he entered into the fifth dimension (it wasn't on your planet, it was somewhere else in the same galaxy). He went into the fifth dimension, and then he became a soul who was intent on becoming something. For him the something that he was intent on becoming was an instantaneous healer. That is what he wanted to do. And so he relaxed and let himself be guided on his journey by experts, some physical and some nonphysical. He let himself be guided rather than being taught. It was not a teacher that was sent to him but rather beings, again some physical and some nonphysical, who came in and guided him gently into the arena of being an instantaneous healer.

Everyone who goes into the fifth dimension has the opportunity to become something new, whether we realize it or not. When you become very clear on what that particular something is, then you will begin your journey. You will be given images of who is assisting you. Certain individuals will be coming to you who will guide you, again not teachers but someone who takes your hand, figuratively speaking of course, and helps you to move in the correct direction for what it is that you want to step into being. You may already know what it is that you would like to become, or perhaps you are still sorting through a lot of the filters that you have about what the fifth dimension is about before you can get to the heart or the truth of who you want to be.

Of course there are those who exited this lifetime before they went into the fifth dimension, and there are some who exited the earth plane before the earth went into the fifth dimension. They did either of those things because they were not in a position of becoming something. That wasn't part of their blueprint. But for all of us here at this moment, it is in our blueprint to enter into becoming something new in the fifth dimension. So if you are unsure of what it is that you want to become, take time to talk with your fifth-dimensional counselors. These counselors include Michael, Rafael, Mary, the Christ energy, Lancelot, Orion, and Markas. So take the time to commune with one of your fifth-dimensional counselors to gain some clarity and to ask them to help guide you. Because we are in the physical world, you will have some guides in the physical realm of consciousness that are single-attribute guides. You can have a single-attribute guide for fifth-dimensional living. Or you might have a single-attribute guide for fifth-dimensional becoming. Just remember to look for assistance on both sides, physical and nonphysical.

You will see that the help that these guides can provide will help you to live better in the fifth dimension. You have your own personal roadmap.

And you are charting new territories because the planet has not been fifth-dimensional until now. So what that means is that because you now have a roadmap, you should begin to feel happier because now you have something that you have a passion for and you are becoming it. And again, at the risk of repeating, it's not something that you are learning, and it is not something that you are questing after, it is something that your vibration is entering into. So it will be something that fills you with a lot of passion, desire, and wanting. You will want to know everything that you can about that particular area.

In addition to the example of Aristotle that was mentioned previously, many of us also have a single attribute guide of joy or good living that goes by the name of Persephone. When this being took the opportunity to step into a fifth-dimensional world, she then became fifth-dimensional. Interestingly enough, what Persephone really wanted to become was a being with an extraordinary sense of smell. And so she became someone who was able to smell the very slightest change in something. For example, if someone came into her environment and was getting a cold, she could smell it before the person even knew that they were getting sick because it was different from the normal smell that a being on that particular planet would have. She could even determine if someone was going through a traumatic time through her amazing sense of smell. Remember, each one of us can choose to become something different, something more than we are today. Ask yourself what you would like to become and then be open to that manifesting for you!

In order to be fully fifth-dimensional, you must also let go completely of everyone else's impressions of life. So every time you turn on the news and you hear that this is happening and that this is not happening or that this is a problem or that there is something that is to be afraid of, you must let all of that go. It is dust. It is no more than one person's opinion. It might even become their reality. But you must let it go because it weakens your own reality. Remember, an opinion that someone forms is a belief and an attitude, but it is not your reality. That is not to say that you shouldn't listen to the news at all, but when you do, become very conscious of the fact that you are living in an illusion. You are living in the illusion. The reality is in dream state.

In the dream state, you are not limited by belief systems and by the structure of how things are set up on this planet. Therefore you are able get to the truth of things. So look to your dreams. A lot of your dreams are for purposes of healing, but many more of your dreams are for purposes of tapping into not what is a conditional truth or a fantasy, but one piece of the puzzle that is absolute or conditional. So when you look at the news, don't believe for one minute that that is reality. It is made up of collective opinions by those individuals that are creating their realities, often because they have an agenda. They want something a certain way and they see things very much as being black and white. So they don't want to create a win-win situation. In fact it hasn't even entered their minds that there is such a possibility of a win-win situation.

Therefore in order to live fifth-dimensionally, you must let go of the opinions of others by either not responding to them or not even engaging in them to begin with. If you are worried that you will be too disengaged with the outside world if you don't follow the news regularly, you can trust that the important things that you need to know will be given to you or find their way to you. As an example, imagine that you go to buy a newspaper. As you know, the headlines are almost always about a murder, but let's say that you are particularly interested in the war in the Middle East. You open the paper and you turn to the business section. Then you go into the "softer" news, for example the advice column and editorials. You then peruse the sports section. Your emphasis shifts when you go from one section of the newspaper to the next.

Individuals will read the newspaper in their own unique way. There are certain people who don't want to do anything but read the sports. Some individuals will go right into the softer news and will read about book reviews, new albums, and advice columns. Those that are in business will often go to the financial section just to keep updated and so they can be informed during conversations with colleagues. Some individuals start right at the beginning, read the paper all the way through. Now, just imagine in the state or area that you live in and that 80 percent of the adults are reading the newspaper. Imagine how it is forming their reality! Think of the power of that collective consciousness, particularly of those individuals that are reading the hard news of violent events and difficult environmental and economic times.

You can see just how easy it is to be drawn into the feeling that life is dismal and full of overwhelming problems. But you begin with the self, and if you believe that you have enough understanding and enough power to master you physical reality, then it doesn't matter what is going on in the world and what other people believe and what they choose to act upon based upon those beliefs. It will not influence your reality. As we discussed earlier, your thoughts do in fact create your reality, and so you must carefully monitor that which you are thinking and manifesting in your own life, in your own reality. That is actually very good news, for as fifth-dimensional individuals, you have even more ability to affect change in a positive way!

Another key aspect of living fifth-dimensionally is that you should always have a sense that you are connected with God. Now everyone has a slightly different opinion or experience with God. It doesn't matter if you are Christian, if you are Jewish, if you are Buddhist, if you are a spiritualist or an atheist; people within each of those groupings has a slightly different image or impression of God. The important thing is to know that God is not a being that is far away from you. Your soul is instilled with the part of the god/goddess energy. And this means that in recognizing that you are part of God, you realize that to say that God does not hear or see you is like saying that your left hand cannot talk to your right hand because it doesn't know where the right hand is. Of course your left hand knows where the right hand is! And you, as the connector of the two, can tell you left hand, "Well here is the right hand, go ahead and communicate." This is the same way in which you are connected with God. All that you have to do is pose your concerns, your desires, your questions, or your plan for the future to God and know that you are connected. So do not forget that you came from God and that you have part of God inside of you!

Another wonderful aspect of living fifth-dimensionally is that you will be able to increase your enjoyment of living. When everything is flowing and moving along within the body, mind, and spirit, your reality reflects that and you feel very lucky. *Lucky* means that you rise above the trappings of the market place. It is as if God has His hand in what you are doing, and not only are you doing God's will, but you are living your life to the fullest extent possible. You are making good use of your time exactly where you are. Some people say that you create your luck, and the truth is that you certainly create circumstances where you can bring luck in. But absolutely, when you are in the flow, you feel lucky! Now being lucky doesn't mean that it has to end, as most people say. Often when people have been on what they call a "lucky streak," they actually choose to end it because of how unusual it feels to them.

Now the important thing to note here is to not focus on being the lucky one, to not even to focus on what that means. Instead you need to focus on remaining in that state of God's will and God's grace, not out of fear but because you know that this is where you are meant to be. And of course you feel very lucky from that standpoint. Let your mantra be: "This is where I am meant to be. This is what I am meant to be doing. This is what I am meant to be experiencing. This is what I am meant to feel, to understand and to interact with others. This is the norm, this is natural for me." When you begin to feel that way, then others perceive you as the Lucky One! But you never perceive yourself as the Lucky One. Do you see the difference?

Living in this state of "luck" is what can be referred to as being "in the flow." Now get a sense of yourself and determine where you are in the flow. Right now in the flow, let go of the past, let go of yesterday, or two hours ago, or two years ago; right now in the flow are you 10 percent in the flow, 20 percent, 30 percent, 40 percent or more in the flow? Take a breath and get a sense of yourself and determine what percentage you are in the flow. If you are less than 50 percent, do not judge yourself for that, just recognize that you have had a difficult time in adjusting to your reality of fifth-dimensional living. So let us say that you are around 30 percent; what that means is that right now your potential is still another 70 percent. But operating in the 30 percent range is okay, it is just where you are today. You are 30 percent in the flow. Now you cannot talk yourself into anything greater than that, but you can in a sense become who you are destined to be by focusing on God's grace, allowing yourself to be more "in the flow."

Ask yourself, "If I had my choice, what would I be doing, what would my calling be, what would I become?" When you focus on that, it begins to accelerate your vibrational frequency, and you begin to migrate back into your own energy pattern. If you are not in your flow, it means that others, the mass consciousness, or certain issues in your life will dictate your reality. This is in contrast to being in the flow where you are not really thinking about it, you are just enjoying your life in its totality. So if you are less than 50 percent, don't worry about it; it is not something that you have done wrong, it is just that you have had as hard a time as most individuals have to adjusting to fifth-dimensional living. But once you let all of that go, you will begin to get a sense of being the center of your reality and thus you will get into the flow.

You are probably familiar with the vast work that has been done involving chi energy. The chi energy that flows through you is your life force. So when we talk about getting into the flow, we mean allowing that life force to flow through you. So when individuals are talking about building up a lot of chi, they do this by being in nature, by following their passions, and other fulfilling practices. When you build up this flow, you actually have more of that energy inside of you. Part of your chi flow actually has to do with the ambience of what surrounds you. As you know, you are creating your reality and achieving mastery as the center of your reality. So if you haven't been doing those things that are building up the chi energy inside of you, it is all right; now you will be doing it, bit by bit as it is appropriate for you. And with this there is a tremendous amount of healing that takes place.

If you were to talk to any of your bodies of consciousness, including the fifth body of consciousness, they would all have complaints. They would tell you, "Well this isn't quite right, that hasn't been going well." That is because they feel it, they see, they experience it, they understand it, but it is not quite how they want to experience life. And so there is a lot of healing that takes place as you make the commitment to adjust to fifth-dimensional living. You are going to let go of the past. You are going to let go of all of those news reports that don't feel like your reality. You are going to take on more of who you are and become the center of your reality. And others will see you as being lucky!

You might question how someone can be viewed by others as being lucky while enduring a physical illness or other ailments. But when you begin to create your own reality, all of these things that are limiting are going to begin to just fade away. It is very similar to what Deepak Chopra talked about when he said that your body is never the same from one moment to the next. Furthermore, your body does a complete change in two years. So why is it that people still have heart disease, or they still have cancer, or still have MS? How is that possible when all of the cells in their body have completely changed? Well, this is because your belief system carries the memory and not the body's cells. But the cells will listen to what your beliefs are or to what the mass consciousness beliefs are. Again, this is why it is so important that you let those beliefs go.

That is the difference between third—and fourth—and fifth-dimensional living. In fifth-dimensional living, you just need to drop the curtain on the past and just let it go. You don't have to fight it, just let it go. If you say "well it is too hard," then hand it over to God. Or hand it to your guides and ask them to take care of this particular issue in your life that is weighing on you as it is too large for you to let go of on your own. Allow your old beliefs, your fears, your limitations to truly be a thing of the past. Release them entirely! Similarly, if anyone that you know is having a hard time, send out and project your white light to them. By doing this, you will help others to be lucky as well!

When your guides, your teachers, and your counselors refer to you, they sometimes do talk about you as being the Lucky One. But what they are saying is not that you are lucky because you just happened to be at the right place at the right time. Instead, they say you are lucky because you are getting it, you are understanding it, you are recognizing that you are part of the source of everything that is. That's why we call your higher self your spiritual source—because it is the connecting point from your source to God. So it is your spiritual link up to God, through your birthright angel to God. You are lucky because you are able to overcome or move through your limiting beliefs.

Now a while back we talked about what different tools are for changing your life. We stated that approximately 25 percent was looking at your belief systems and changing those that are limiting to you. Twenty-five percent was the feng shui of the body, meaning that you nurture and take care of your physical body. Another 25 percent is the feng shui of your surroundings, so in both cases we are talking about being in the flow. Your body being in the flow is part of the chi and the chi energy that surrounds you. The other 25 percent has to do with using your metaphysical tools. You can use everything that we talked about in the fourth dimension in the fifth dimension, but it is not as necessary. What is most important in the fifth dimension is that you learn how to raise your vibrational frequency and that you are conscious that what is around you affects your vibrational frequency. Proper use of these tools will allow others around you to call you lucky, but you will know that the truth is that you are in the art of becoming.

As we talk about progressing through to fifth-dimensionally living, it is important to note that it is not relevant how far into the fifth dimension that you are relative to anyone else. It is only important to your own blueprint. One individual may have come in with a much more rigorous blueprint than another person. Therefore we are not competing against one another in terms of our growth and progression. We all have our own environmental and mental toxins that are prohibiting us from developing to our full potential. So there is a reason why your immune system is suppressed. There is a reason why you haven't been living life fully in the fifth dimension. There is a reason why you are not feeling that hopeful. And you really can let go of all of the negative thoughts and beliefs that hold you back for a week, not just for ten days or a month. But if you can begin to live your life so that you are conscious of your interconnectedness with God, you will see changes. There is no way that you can have a less fulfilling life if you begin to live it with you as the center and letting go of the past. You can do nothing but move forward.

You have probably heard individuals say that they would prefer to live in this physical world than to be nonphysical. They are actually saying this because they do not know what being nonphysical is like. In fact, none of us remember what it is like because you came to this planet to be physical. If you remembered what it was like to be nonphysical, a lot of us wouldn't want to be here. In some ways it is the ultimate experience to be nonphysical as you have levels of freedom that you never have when you are physical. No matter how metaphysical you are, no matter if you transmigrate, or you learn to teleport, or you learn bi-location, or if you learn about using your power in the physical realm, even with all of that, you never have the level of freedom that you have in the nonphysical. You also don't get to see the "big picture" until you are nonphysical, both for yourself and for your loved ones. That is why deceased relatives will temporarily come in as a single-attribute guide in a certain area—because they get to see the bigger picture and to advise you as to what to do to get to be best and beyond. When you ponder being physical versus being nonphysical, remember that you are exactly where you are supposed to be, in the form that you are supposed to be in!

While there are not any "good luck guides," there are many guides that will come to you in order to enhance your opportunities in certain areas for which you didn't feel as if you had good fortune. As we discussed earlier, your single-attribute guides focus on one particular topic because you need help in that area. For example, your health guide isn't with you all of the time. The health guide is with you while you are dealing with illness or on your road to recovery. Your career guide is only with you for certain time periods when you need assistance, when you've reached a turning point in your career. Your prosperity guide is only with you for certain time periods when you turn the corner into prosperity and abundance. Your location guide is only with you during those times when you are getting ready to change and to move to a new location. So if you take a look at your single-attribute guides, you see that they come in to help you during time periods of transference or transition. They will help you to get into the flow so that you feel confident that the decisions that you make are the right ones.

Teachers come in for a different reason. They teach you something so that you can then pass it along. But teachers do not come to you because you are at a critical point in your life, but rather because you are at a place now at which they can teach you something new. Your major arcana guides are temporary guides in the spiritual realm. Teachers are in the universal realm, single-attribute guides are in the physical realm. But the major arcana guides come in to give you spiritual understanding about what is taught from the Kabbalah and shows up in the major arcana of the tarot. So again it is not a particularly transitional time period for you. It is just that you are now ready for a new understanding in the development of your spirituality. Additionally, in the emotional realm of consciousness you have the removal-of-fear guides. They are temporary and they come in to assist you with the removal of fear when you are ready to take a look at your fears and release them. As the fears are released, these removal-of-fear guides turn into expansion-of-love guides!

With all of these wonderful teachers and guides ready to assist you, allow yourself to release judgments and beliefs from the past and get into the fifth-dimensional flow!

* * * * * * * *

In reviewing my transition into the fifth dimension, how did I get from point A (my starting point) to point F (my current state in the fifth dimension)? I asked myself: What areas needed the work? Where do I start?

I knew that it was time to start purifying the physical body. My day-to-day energy was low, and I oftentimes felt not only tired but exhausted. This was the perfect place to start. I began to look at my physical body and take note of what made me feel good and what made me feel not-so-good. Is it surprising that my choice of foods were not the best choices? I took shortcuts, and although I did not eat a lot of fast food, I did consume a lot of diet soft drinks. In fact you could say I existed on them. I fell into the trap of consuming empty calories with no nutritional value. I never could figure out why I was so very thirsty all of the time. The more diet soft drinks I drank in the course of a day, the more my body required.

No one can argue that your weight is connected to your self-image. And so when on the emotional roller coaster, your emotional state just transfers itself into your physical state. Some people do not eat when they are in the throes of emotional turmoil, other people eat and eat and eat. I was the latter. The more upset I was or the more emotions I experienced with the ups and downs of my new life, my weight and thus my body followed suit. I saw that I could be nervous about almost anything, and I was. I then had an "aha" moment: the state of my nerves was simply a state of what I was thinking, feeling, and acting. I created this reality and I needed to stop—and stop I did.

I stopped drinking all carbonated beverages! My health guide came in and told me that the carbonated beverages were adversely affecting my immune system! Who knew? Immediately I got off all caffeine and the carbonation and I replaced the diet soft drinks with *water*! Yes, I went "cold turkey," and I never even suffered the caffeine withdrawal's headache as my guides helped me along the process. Ask (for no headache) and you shall receive (the gift of no headache)! Water, the purest of all beverages, not only is the ultimate cleanser of the body but also satisfies thirst like nothing else. Water as it constantly flushes out the toxins also helps your energy levels return. The more toxins that left my body, the more energy I had. This simple substitution to my new drink of choice changed my body immensely.

Eating also needed improvement. My body was seriously reacting to what I was putting in it. I bought good food, and did eat what I considered a healthy meal many evenings during the week, but my body still reacted. I could not figure out why my digestive system would be so upset some days and other days seemed perfectly fine. During one summer I noticed that my body seemed to be expanding; whatever I ate, my body grew and grew and grew. I was supposed to be working on expanding my consciousness, *not* expanding my physical body! I was again experiencing the exhaustion and could hardly make it through a day at work. It was then that I discovered that my body had become gluten intolerant. I quickly learned what gluten is and which foods it is in. I discovered that this toxin has in fact gotten more toxic as food manufacturers were trying to increase their profit margins. The corporate offices were concerned only about their bottom lines and certainly not about ours! Gluten is seemingly unseen (but certainly not unfelt), and so **cheaper and** cheaper gluten was being manufactured in processed foods. It was easier **to memorize** which foods do not have gluten (it is a pretty short list) than the **ones that** do (which is a very long list). And so the removal process began. **Little by little** I substituted, removed, and replaced all of the food in my diet which **contained** gluten. Within three weeks, my body got down to a more normal size, **and** my energy began returning and I felt far better!

Today it is not unusual to see why gluten has become the "buzzword" of 2009. Many, many people, both adults and children, have developed an adversity to toxins. Why, that not only makes sense, it is good sense. Our bodies were not made to be sifting out toxins and poisons that are in our food. We are so careful with our instructions for pregnant women to give birth to healthy babies. We talk a good talk about good nutrition and what makes our bodies grow and develop into healthy children, and children to healthy teenagers, and then teenagers to healthy adults, all the while we are feeding our bodies toxins. The more you eat, the more toxins you consume. It was time that our bodies said: "Enough—I have had enough! Please cleanse and clear me and let me work like I was meant to: a well-oiled machine that needs to be nourished and rested for optimal comfort and optimal performance!"

So my personal mission has been to purify my body. Water and gluten-free foods are my choices. I eat food that has been kissed by the sun. My meals look different than what I was taught a healthy, well-balanced meal should look like, but I am proud to report that I have relaxed that particular belief system right into good health! When you eat healthier and more natural foods, your body will actually be more satisfied and you will eat less. Since good food is more nutritious, your body isn't craving huge amounts of food in order to find any nutrition. Of course, maintaining these good habits to give me good health will always be a challenge for me. I am still aware of the conscious effort that it takes to keep me healthy. I am just saddened that the rest of humanity in our world is not given good food, but that it is something that everyone needs to work hard at to learn and then to try to achieve in this world of fast food and convenience. It simply is not right that good food isn't available to everyone. It should be a God-given right, shouldn't it?

My physical body now healthy, I could move on to my emotional body. Since my emotions were definitely connected to my physical body, I saw that it was time to work with my inner child to help her feel loved. So I began to love her and love her and love her some more. Once I sent her this beautiful love and she received it, she seemed to settle into a happy place. She no longer jumped up uninvited to speak her mind, or react with disgust and express her utter fear about a place or event, and she no longer felt any guilt or remorse. She simply turned into a beautifully behaved little lady who was a pleasure to be around! I made it very clear to her that I was the parent and although I could empathize with the reason why she felt the way she did, or reacted the way she did, bad behavior was no longer acceptable or tolerated. She accepted my parenting with grace and grew in both congeniality and contentment. I had healed her, and she had healed me.

My mental body was easy to purify. My thoughts were reflections of my desires, but those desires were to honor my higher self. So I did not have a huge job to do here. I continued to pursue learning and was keenly aware of all the experiences that came my way, always keeping in mind that my goal was to learn to grow and to develop a more purified life, a more evolved life. My mental body was constantly open to whatever I brought for it to devour. The majority of what I did bring home was spiritual and metaphysical reading materials. I was fascinated with subjects about philosophies of life, psychic abilities, meditations and prayer practices in different countries, our cosmos, and the study of energy and our planet's future. I read, I learned, and I grew.

My spiritual body was delighted. This body was being fed with reading materials that delighted all of its senses. The energy was growing, the body was expanding (this time in a good way), and the soul was in harmony with my heart leading the way!

It was at this point that I learned that I could use my energy to heal myself and to heal others. I knew that my body was primarily energy and vibration. The purer my energy, the purer energy could flow through me and ultimately from me. I needed to learn how to capitalize my energy to become a spiritual healer.

I started to learn different healing modalities. As I mentioned earlier, I began my development by taking a Reiki class, learning how to bring the healing energy through me to Reiki others. I became a Reiki master. I enhanced my Reiki by learning how and why crystals heal. Finding and using the appropriate crystal during a healing brings different healing energies into the process. I then was taught how to use tuning forks, a simple old-fashioned tool that helps your body's energy vibrate in sync to a place of balance and harmony. So I added turning forks to my healing sessions. Then I learned about the use of color lights. I took a seminar in color harmonics. I learned that different colors in use with different geometric forms using different protocols could heal the body by balancing the imbalances within the body. Energy, vibration, color, and sacred geometry—what a recipe for healing! I am always learning and looking for new ways to heal. The combination of any of the above modalities is an ever-changing process that allows the body to use the beautiful healing energy from spirit to help heal its imbalances that we have created. After all isn't disease simply dis-ease? We simply need to bring our bodies back into a state of wellness, a place of ease, a place of balance.

By working with each of my five bodies of consciousness within me, I had cleared and cleansed each and was allowing them to get to know each other. They were meeting on common ground, one that was open and filled with love. They respected each other, creating connections that would last a lifetime. These connections were deep and pure. I had learned to integrate myself and my five bodies of consciousness. We could laugh, play, and have fun as a team. There were no stars in this bunch, but all equal team players who worked together not in a competitive spirit but in the spirit of love. Not one of these parts would bring the rest or any other part down. We grew together. We would and could win as a team!

This winning combination was and is the ultimate goal. To integrate my five bodies of consciousness and to give them the gift of living in a body that is pure and cleansed paved the way for my body, mind, and soul to enjoy a body filled with harmony. This is the body whose energy expanded, and I felt lighter and lighter and lighter. I could feel my body vibrating at a higher rate. I was living in the fifth dimension, enjoying the fruits of my labors. It took hard work to get me here, and feeling the love was addicting.

I was creating my world, my beautiful world filled with love, by how I was thinking, feeling, and acting. Only those people, those events, and those thoughts that felt like love were allowed to enter. I had created a new paradigm from which to live my life. I made a very conscious effort that this world needed to be protected from all things that no longer felt like love to me. I distanced myself from people, events, and behaviors that no longer served me. I was aware of my thoughts and what I was sending out to the universe. I purified my home and my workplace. I wanted to live and work from a place of love. I set the tone. I no longer participated in conversations that did not feel like love. I made no judgments. If I slipped, I simply let go and moved forward: no guilt and no remorse, but simply love for myself. I found that when you set a standard, others rise to that standard. The energy in and around me was purer and lighter than I had felt in years. I was vibrating from a purer place, so my energy was vibrating higher and I was in the flow with it! I know that I am in the flow of becoming, as Markas has described, one of The Lucky Ones!

CHAPTER X

Universal Olympics

Follow not the wrath of the storm, but the calm that follows!

—Spirit, 2007

All of us have had the experience before of waking from sleep state and feeling very down and out of sorts. It feels as if the world is not quite right. Believe it or not, this experience actually has been with each of us for a very long time, for some of us as early as when we were coming through the birth canal. As you were being born, you may have thought, "Well, this really wasn't that good of an idea, and perhaps it would not be too late that I could rethink coming in for an incarnation." If this was the case for you, you will have had episodes of depression throughout your life. Others, however, will have made it through childhood without depression, but as you became older, you began to feel as if you were very limited inside your body. Perhaps you thought that you weren't smart enough, or you weren't compassionate enough or good-looking enough or athletic enough. What is driving all of this is an internal feeling that there is something more that you are meant to be accomplishing, that there is something even greater that is waiting just upon the horizon for you.

You may have turned to antidepressants to help you deal with these feelings of inadequacy. Those feelings of inadequacy may have been preventing you from really living your purpose. You may not be happy on this planet because you are not living the life that would give you fulfillment and enlightenment. All of us have a different story, but often the same thread of confusion and depression can be found woven into the story of our lives. In extreme cases, some of us may have even wanted to die, whether at our own hands or due to a disease, so that the problematic feelings would just go away. More commonly, there are those of us who just shut ourselves away from others by becoming workaholics or having an aversion to leaving our home altogether.

Because there is an opposite to everything on this planet, there is of course a flip side to these feelings of depression or limitation. Those feelings are reminding you that there is more to life. They are reminding you of what it is that you are here to accomplish, what success will mean for you! And this is why we call it the Universal Olympics because in fact you are carrying the torch for all of those who come from the universe, and they might be coming into the earth plane now as third-, fourth-, or fifth-dimensional individuals. Remember, you are the center of your universe! This may sound obnoxious, even egotistical, at first, but be assured that it is not. When you allow yourself to truly believe and accept that you are in fact the center of your universe, the feelings of depression and longing will begin to dissipate, and you will begin to feel unlimited.

So what is it that keeps you feeling limited when you really want to be unlimited? What is it that seems to force you into that feeling of limitation or restriction? By focusing on the feelings of unhappiness or inadequacy or any negative feeling, it causes you to keep the feelings of limitation alive. By looking to and experiencing feelings of happiness, you bring into your life that which creates joy, which gives you the energy to expand in as many areas of your life as you need to. By doing this you are being your own best friend and helping your world to be a joyful one. This approach is both simple and practical and is clearly a much better approach than going to—and paying for—formal therapy because what you ultimately are doing is bringing into your life that which gives you joy. Everyone would love to set out and create joy in their own lives, and it is really just a matter of making it a habit. Identify what it is that creates joy in your life, trust that it and you are unlimited, and feel the joy!

That is not to say, of course, that the journey to unlimited being is without challenges. We all have situations in our lives with our children, siblings, or various members of our family that create dynamics such that you lose a part of who you are and who you have become. Oftentimes when you are with certain individuals or in certain situations, you feel that your energy is zapped as you are pulled back into the dynamic in which you may have grown up. This pull and tug is not only unsettling, draining, and dramatic, but is indeed limiting. You may feel that a part of you is lost or that the part of you that exists now is not acknowledged consciously or subconsciously by other members of your family, which causes you to doubt who you are.

In these types of situations, you must ask yourself how you can create a win-win situation. Setting boundaries within the family dynamics so that your expectations of others, and theirs of you, are clearly defined and stated is one option to help you stay true to who you are and what you want. Remember, you cannot and should not be trying to please everyone. You should not make their differences of opinion your problem. When you interact with family members out of a sense of duty or codependence, what you are really doing is allowing them to be the center of your universe rather than making yourself the center of your universe. You must always make yourself the center of your reality because if you are always allowing others to be the center of your reality, then you will always feel and be limited by them.

Put another way, you must make yourself the center of your bodies of consciousness. The first, second, third, fourth, and fifth bodies must be central in your actions, thoughts, and feelings so that you stay balanced and centered in all situations, even those that seem to threaten your very being. It is these five bodies of consciousness—a little family within, if you will—that you must keep together and not allow to argue with each other. It is not your responsibility to help the family that you grew up in to get along at all costs to you. It is more important that you learn to stay centered and balanced in all situations so that you are your own best friend and remain true to yourself.

Every one of us has times when we have slipped and lost a sense of who we are. When we feel the limitation of depression, we have lost or misplaced what we know to create joy in our life. Each time we feel this way, we need to just stand right up and say to ourselves "enough already—enough!" You must declare that regardless of what anyone else is doing in their life and how it interacts with yours, this is your life to be creating in a way that makes sense to you and is something that is based on love for you. Every time you feel yourself slipping out of that knowledge, go back and make yourself the center of your universe and you will feel that self-love.

This process is called "inner child processing," and what happens in the crux of it all is that you are learning that you are the parent to your inner children. When your inner child feels your love and approval, you will find that you are less vulnerable to outside distractions and more assured that you are in fact the center of your own universe. This process can take a long time, or you might shorten the process by focusing on what it is that your inner children need in order to love themselves and then focus on what that need is.

Not surprisingly, this process is not without challenges. Even when you are sending love to your inner child, there are times when depression may creep its way back into your life, back into your thoughts. Unfortunately it can find its way back again and again. However, the good news is that your efforts are not wasted; for every time that you have an "aha experience" associated with this processing, the depression will come back in a weaker form. You will find that when the depression is in its weaker state, it usually returns for shorter periods of time, and your self-talk will be more effective against it.

Apart from normal day-to-day challenges, you may have experienced a tragic or catastrophic event in your childhood that causes you to slip into periods of depression. So what do you tell your inner child, and how do you help them to accept that traumatic event that acts as a catalyst for depressing periods? When enough time has passed and you find yourself in a safer place, you can then talk with your inner children to help them deal with the event. You can speak silently in your heart or out loud; whatever approach feels right to you is the one that you should follow. You must raise the question to your inner child and bring it out into the open for them to be fully exposed and for them to fully heal. So when you open up the trauma for discussion with your inner child or children, you no longer have the fear of what would or could happen. You have ultimately removed the fear from the equation, and then you can move toward love and to the safe space of healing.

When you encounter something that you are afraid of, we do not suggest that you jump in with both feet. What is the better way of handling a situation like this? Rather than a big leap, start with baby steps! Why should you take baby steps? You can take little steps and begin to introduce the trauma gradually until you feel comfortable over a period of time, and then you can go a little further. In following this approach, your inner child will not be fearful that something has been thrown at them all at once. This of course helps to reduce the risk that you will panic and fall into a depression.

It is certainly worth giving this approach a try with your inner child to gently help him or her through the trauma to reach a place of safety and love. And if you feel that you are going too fast, slow down. You don't have to have all of the answers in a certain day, just maintain a pace where your inner child feels comfortable. When we stated before that you are the center of your reality, this concept promises the complete independence from fear. You are not afraid of anything, and being the center of your reality, you know that you are powerful and are not afraid that anyone or anything could come along and do you harm. Our emotional bodies do not stand in this truth and are vulnerable to fear that someone will hurt them, making it all the more crucial that we nurture and heal our inner children.

Depression always begins in the family. What your family says matters to you, and what they say to you, about you, or for you has an impact on you. For example, imagine that you are an explorer looking for humpback whales. Your explorations bring you to different parts of various oceans, and your job is to try to determine how many whales there were in each of these areas. You might find ten or fifteen humpback whales in a certain area, but you don't know exactly how many more, if any, there are that may be under the surface. Going from the data that you have, you try to extrapolate how many humpback whales could possibly be in the area. You really love this job, and you feel as if you are making a difference because you are helping protect a beautiful creature, a creature that you know has a consciousness and a way of operating in which they create a win-win situation. Imagine that you continue to do this job every day when you are suddenly visited by someone who thinks that they know everything about humpback whales. What do you think your reaction would be? Well, if they came from a place of arrogance, you would immediately be turned off to them.

So how can you help your inner child so that they don't turn off from what you have to say? There is so much you can do with your inner children to help them when they encounter someone that is arrogant or difficult, whether it is a family member, coworker, or stranger. It is your job as the adult to help keep your inner children from feeling that inferior. Your inner child or children believe that things are permanent, so if a situation is difficult, they believe that it will always be that way. Instead, of course, it is just the opposite! Nothing on this planet is permanent, nothing is set in stone. You must therefore continue to build up the self-confidence of your inner child so that you can chip away at the depression that is holding you back and preventing you from realizing that you are the center of your own reality.

If you find that your inner child is reluctant to interact with you, it is always because he or she doesn't feel safe. Therefore if you are not getting a response from your inner child, all that you have to do is just show love for that child. Tell them that they are not going to be put down, shut up, or ignored. Remind them that you simply want to be connected to them, to help them, to be integrated with them so that you both can heal and move forward in love. You will find that you will soon not be the one talking as the inner child will soon feel safe enough to begin speaking to you. Remember, when the inner child feels cherished, you will get rewarded. When the inner child feels hopeful, you will see so many benefits.

So are you willing to try to communicate with your inner child? Let's take a few moments right now to call in your inner children. In other words, bring the inner child up to consciousness; you may even visualize that child sitting on your knee or standing before you. Keep in mind that the inner child, which is again the emotional body, is in the three—to five-year-old age range, so be sure to keep your emotional state in love so that the child feels safe. As you do this, how is your inner child responding? If your inner child hasn't come forward yet, just turn up your love some more!

Each of our experiences with our inner child will be unique. Some of you may experience your inner child sitting on your lap contented, or standing shyly in front of you. Whatever the experience or visual image that you have is, it is yours to treasure; simply continue to give love to the inner child and allow him or her to feel safe. Personally, when I communicate with my inner child, the image that I have is of me on my father's lap. I feel very warm and his arms are around me. I have a feeling of love pulsing in my heart, and it feels like absolutely ideal love. So allow yourself to experience this love, and you too will see that this is not the end all, but that it is the beginning of a dynamic relationship.

Now try to bring up the image of your physical body of consciousness that is the aspect of yourself that feels things physically and physiologically. Then try to bring up your mental body of consciousness, the thinker inside of you. Next, bring up your spiritual body of consciousness, and that is your purified spiritual field. You have of course already brought up your emotional body or your inner child. Finally, try to bring up the fifth body of consciousness, the being or aspect inside of you that is able to see perfection where there had been the illusion of imperfection. Let go of that veil of imperfection and allow yourself to be a fifth-dimensional being, one who feels the feeling of perfection in one's environment. Allow all of those additional four bodies of consciousness to come up and, for each one, take just a few moments to feel love and acceptance and connection with them.

Now all of the bodies of consciousness are supposed to ideally be able to go forward. If you are having difficulty with your physical body of consciousness, how would that manifest? What would your physical body tend to do? Well, quite simply, it would have disease or feel uncomfortable in one form or another in the physical body.

How could you tell that the mental body of consciousness is not in a good flow? This would be exhibited in erratic or irrational behavior. How could you tell if your spiritual body of consciousness is out of sorts? It could be through loss of faith, hope, or love for others. What would be an imbalance for the spiritual healer? That would be manifested in someone who always sees the negative rather than the positive. We have of course already spoken about the emotional paralysis that can occur when the emotional body is out of sync. So if you find that you are experiencing difficulty, first determine whether it is physical, mental, emotional, spiritual, or fifth-dimensional. Once you have identified where the problem lies, you can then work on fixing it and moving forward and toward the Universal Olympics that you want to participate in.

As we talk about feelings of depression, begin to think about how you are feeling right now. On a scale of one to ten, at this time in your life, how would you rank your level of happiness (ten being as happy as you could imagine and one being depressed)? It may be surprising to you to know that just as important as the level of happiness is the variance of the swing in the pendulum. For example, if you are at nine, and if the pendulum were to swing from eight to ten, then you are always in the category of better, best, and beyond. But if the pendulum has a wider variance, it might swing from seven all the way to a ten, it would move you out of the category of better, best, and beyond. It may even swing from a seven to a ten-point-five, going off the scale, but again the variance would pull you down out of the category of best and beyond. So what you are really trying to do is be an integrated being, meaning that you want to have the opportunity to experience life from the standpoint of better and best, and best and beyond, with a smaller variance. So imagine that if you were at a nine and if the pendulum would only swing to an eight and upward to a ten. If this was the case, then you would have a very small variance, with your lows really not being very low and your highs being very high, which would cause you to feel moments of perfection!

When you examine your own life, try to determine on the scale of one to ten where you are currently. If it is a low number, this of course indicates that there is room for you to elevate your level of happiness by your experiences. If it is lower than you would like it to be, ask yourself what is holding you back. What do you need to do to create the joy in your life that will help lift you out of this depression? Have you identified these experiences? Have you been able to incorporate them into your life?

If you are at a four, five, or six, then you are learning to have experiences that are moving toward the level of good. It is your choice to bring these experiences into your life. It is a beautiful experience to be able to see that when you do, you can enrich your life, add harmony and balance, and that the quality of wellbeing is enhanced. For it is your choices that allow or prevent you from moving into the area of good, or moving from good into better, and moving from good and better into the area of best and beyond.

When you really feel that you are the center of your reality, you begin to change your outside circumstances; not by what you do, but by who you have become. This is a more advanced way of doing it which is made possible by the fact that the planet is more advanced than it was five, ten, or fifteen years ago. What happens when you change is that the circumstances around you change, which is the part that your inner child has a hard time believing because you haven't seen hard evidence of it. Remember, as we stated before, there is nothing constant in your life except change! You have the power to direct the change by how you take control and centralize the energies of your body.

There is nothing outside of you that is creating those circumstances or realities that have an impact on you. The more that you nurture and take care of yourself, the more you make yourself the center of your reality, and circumstances will begin to align themselves to you to support you. You may be skeptical and say, "Well, I don't think that will ever happen." Well, it will happen, but not until there is inner harmony with the bodies of consciousness.

Sometimes you need to have validations that will help give you that boost of energy, ones that act like the proverbial "leap of faith." Those validations are so important for individuals who are living on the earth plane and are not able to see the bigger picture. So when you get a beautiful validation, it is something that helps your energy to soar. Awareness of these validations is critical, and you need to be open to receive them when they appear.

Remember, you are never in this alone! Your creativity guide in particular will be with you as you go into this type of Olympic development. This guide knows that your love for that development is going to lead you onto a path where you will be recognized in the gymnastic area, meaning that you will be able to move your energy very efficiently for the desired outcome, just as you would in gymnastics if you were in the Olympics! So remember to keep things simple and stay in a place of love so that your energy is able to move freely and your guides are able to reach you with ease on your journey.

* * * * * * * *

"Depression always begins in the family." Wow, isn't that interesting! As I am processing this, I am taken back to my childhood when I experienced difficult and challenging events in my life. But then who hasn't? We can each take a look at our lives, our families, our childhood events, both good and bad, and wish that we had been given something different. But the truth is that we picked our parents and picked our siblings and even picked many of the events that we have brought into our lives!

Each one of us, before coming into this physical body, with our higher selves and our spirit guides, angels, and teachers mapped out our blueprint and defined our lessons to be learned in this lifetime. We not only selected some of our major experiences or events in our life, we then selected those other earthbound beings that would help us learn our lessons the best. Of course, those beings also have lessons to learn from us. So we become both the master and the student in every situation that we encounter. We learn on the physical level, and then reaching deeper it is recorded and learned on the soul level as well.

Every experience, thought, feeling, and action is recorded deep within. When you look at this system, it is far easier to discover why you picked your parents or your brother or sister and friends along the way. I am sure you have heard the comment about how a set of twins are polar opposites or how all the children in one family seem similar but one who appears to be different and is termed "the black sheep of the family," or it now may make sense why there are two siblings in the same family that are extreme opposites. Each comes in with totally different gifts and goals, but to get to where they need to be, they need to acknowledge their opposite, learn from each other, and then somehow each must find a way to a place of balance. It really takes a great deal of the stress out of our life when we see the why and the how of our birth and its relationships, and it actually helps us deal with self-esteem and confidence issues as well. It actually makes sense to depersonalize your life when we can see things from the big or bigger picture!

How can you depersonalize when it is so very personal? Well, the answer to that we have talked about earlier: how about becoming the observer in your life and seeing from that standpoint why and how you relate to things and why and how things relate to you? Each of us has a story, a very different story that simply speaks our lessons to us. I will use my little story to help give you an example of the thinking that can be applied that may help you free up your childhood memories to a place of better knowledge and then to a place of better understanding. When you remember that knowledge is power, it helps you to see just how the process can move your life and its events, allowing you to expand into a place of wellness.

I was born to parents who were very different and had very different energies. My dad was an inventor, an engineer, a philosopher, an artist. His world consisted of melding fantasy and imagination with scientific and mathematical thinking along with a smattering of philosophy and literature. In short, he was a Renaissance man. My father loved me and I did feel his love. He traveled a great deal, and his job took him to distant parts of the country for extended periods of time. So although he loved me, he was so oftentimes not there. And even when he was present physically, he still wasn't really present. His views of my abilities and his dreams for me I knew at a very early age were totally unrealistic. I often wondered if he loved me unconditionally or did he love me if I fulfilled his dream of what I was to do. I remember asking myself this question often.

My mom was born to experience extreme hardships. One minute she could be very funny and engaging and the next very sad or angry or bitter. In one eighteen-month period of her childhood, she buried her two brothers and her mother. Her father, totally distraught over these events, left her in charge of raising her two younger sisters, ages seven and one. At fourteen not only did she take on this responsibility but amazingly was able to flourish. A wonderful athlete, she became captain of the boy's softball team and continued to achieve great grades. The neighborhood women helped her to care for her little sisters while she was at school, but after school she came home to taking care of her siblings, the house they lived in, and all of its responsibilities. There were times when she did not see her father for weeks at a time. Strong and proud, she did what needed to be done.

Depression years were difficult enough with a family intact, but with her unique challenges, I cannot imagine how she was able to get through her days. This extreme responsibility in her life made her bitter and resentful. She was a teenager by day and an adult by night. Times were bad in our country with the upcoming depression of 1929. Her life was filled with fear and fury directed at the one parent who was alive and who could help her out of her overburdened life. She became so angry at all that had happened in her fourteen short years on earth that she buried her feelings to just get through her days. She never was able to forgive her father for burdening her with all of the responsibilities that she had, and unfortunately her health suffered as a result.

As my mother she was very strict, and her expectations of me were extremely high. There was no disappointing her. You knew exactly where you stood from the get-go, and you learned very quickly what you needed to do to toe the mark. Her expectations made me nervous, and I continually looked to her for her approval. I did not feel any love from her; what I did feel was fear, and I sensed at a very early age that it was expected that I would continually disappoint her. I don't ever remember any compliments she directed to me. In later years I was told by others that she spoke highly of me, but I never heard it directly. I suffered from very low self-esteem, and I spent a lot of energy trying to cover that up!

My mother taught me everything one needed to know about the care and upbringing of the household, complete with all of the trimmings. I could do anything and everything and often did. There were times when she woke me up in the middle of the night to have me rewash all of her clothes or to wake me up to re-iron her clothes. I knew that it wasn't normal for a twelve-year-old to be washing or ironing all night long while she and my brother slept. I definitely felt like Cinderella in the fairy tale, and I knew that nothing I could ever say or do would make a difference or could change anything. My long suffering hours were simply a price to pay to exist in that household.

Even though I felt very much at odds in my family, I had a very strong loyalty to my parents. I struggled looking for acceptance and love, and I never doubted that it would come one day. But at what price and when? I could only guess, and I was almost always wrong. As the preteen and teenage years went by for me, I was increasingly unhappy. I clearly saw that my small family relationships were oftentimes based on fear, manipulation, and dominance. I knew instinctively that my life was far better than my mother's was. How could I complain when she at my age was raising her two siblings and single-handedly running a household while going to high school? The fact that she turned over her household to me to run at about this same age was difficult but not overwhelming. I tried not to complain, I tried not to be miserable. But I was and was just smart enough not to show it.

This little girl was being made into an adult, living and doing things at home for her parents that were far too advanced for her. She no longer played nor had much of a childhood. I became the full caretaker of my mother's household before I turned fourteen. My mother had gone to her doctor and was being treated for depression. She was overly medicated and spent much of her time sleeping. Only occasionally did she interact with my brother and me. My father, safe on a job in California, stayed away during this entire time.

Cinderella and I clearly had parallel lives. I got up early and started the chores before I went off to school. It was expected that I get great grades, so there was no slacking off there. Returning home in the afternoon, I completed homework and finished up chores. I paid all of the household bills, did all the laundry and ironing, bought the food, cooked dinner, and did all of the banking and anything and everything else that was necessary to run the household. Weekends were doing everything that didn't get done during the week.

Of course during all of this time, my mother expected me to get straight As, and the rest of my life was dedicated to chores or items that just needed to get done. I never told anyone at school or elsewhere that my life consisted of all that I was doing. I kept it very much a secret because I knew that no one else did what I did, and I was embarrassed by it. I tried not to call attention to myself.

I knew early on in my life that I was born into a situation that seemed to me to be impossible and off-putting. My father loved me but was never there. The mother who was always there didn't seem to love me. How and what could I do to help them together so that I could have a little love from both? I often wondered before falling to sleep at night how I could make it happen. Should I feign or wish for a serious illness, forcing them to come together for a common purpose, forgetting their own emotional traumas and extending a united front to me—all in the name of love? Would this help me with what I so badly wanted and needed from the both of them? A little girl trying to solve big problems with a fairytale solution!

I would lie in bed at night thinking that these are my parents and I do not want to be like either one of them, at least not their faults. I remember thinking often and talking to myself at bedtime that I was not who they were and that I would not ever be like them. I vowed very early that I would never be depressed and that I knew I could do things differently and end up differently. I felt that if I got married, I would have the perfect marriage and not one like theirs. A little girl thinking big things, wishing, hoping, and praying things were different.

This little girl of my childhood had moments of peace but mostly had moments of fear. Her little inner child was very demanding and kept that feeling very much alive. My life consisted of inconsistent events and emotional outbursts from the parent who was to keep the stability and consistency in the household. Every time something unexpected happened, the inner child became alive with fear.

My inner child was always present and always expressing her feelings, constantly seeking security and love. I spent many hours at night before falling off to sleep quieting her, talking to her, and trying to be calm. Of course, I didn't realize I was talking to my inner child. I did, however, know that I was talking to that part of me that needed love.

My inner child loved telling me how unhappy she was and loved being given treats which would satisfy her for only a short time. During the fifties, which were the years I grew up, yes, we had treats! Occasionally, when you did something well, perhaps you were rewarded with a special treat: a cookie, candy, a brownie, or an ice cream cone. My inner child loved treats! And being the good parent to her, I allowed her to have a treat to help offset her fear or sadness! So you could say that I actually comforted her with not only comfort food but sweet treats as well! This is certainly the beginning of what we call today "emotional eating." We have learned that when we practice something until it becomes automatic, we then become an expert in whatever it is we are practicing. I guess you could say then that I became an expert in emotional eating!

To do something that is not only natural but that makes you feel better must be good, right? Wrong. I copied this habit from my mother, and to this day, when something goes wrong, I find myself going to the sweet thing in the cupboard. Old habits die hard. But the mere knowledge of emotional eating can help stop the urge. I am lucky that my way of helping my inner child was simply food. It could have gone down the path of many more serious things, such as alcohol or drugs or other self-sabotaging behaviors. Today when you look around and you observe the behaviors of friends, family, or acquaintances, there are so many destructive habits that are out there. Each person simply picks the habit that they are attracted to. The trick is not to feel guilty or to judge yourself harshly or to be self-critical. The trick is to be able to love yourself knowing and observing any and all weaknesses within you and then acknowledge, release, and let those habits go until you are whole. There is help around the corner for any and every weakness or addictive behavior; it is all about taking the first step—the first step toward healing.

We all come to this planet with a feeling of low self-esteem, and we all come to learn how to love ourselves. Self-love needs to be worked on every day, and when you are successful, the love of self brings you to such a place of joy and comfort. And this love of self actually allows you to love another. How can you ever love someone else if you do not love yourself? It cannot be done. We think we love others because we think we love ourselves. We only think this way because we choose to think this way. But by an honest evaluation of ourselves, and by taking the role of the observer on how we conduct ourselves in our lives, it may be revealed that we typically do not really love ourselves.

One constant we have learned throughout this book is the importance of healing our inner child from our emotional body of consciousness as well as the inner children from our other bodies of consciousness. This is something that we need to work on every minute of every day. We need to come to a place of love within us and then to a place of love that extends out from within. We then can ask ourselves the questions Markas posed in the earlier part of this chapter: "How happy am I? What do I need to do to create joy in my life? What experiences bring me joy? How can I bring more of these experiences to me?" Answering these questions will help you evaluate yourself and motivate yourself to do the work. And as we have discussed earlier, it is doing the work that takes you out of the realm of possibility and into the realm of probability and then helps you to move forward and upward by going into the realm of actuality by healing your children within.

I intuitively, as a small child, fortunately was able to keep my spirit alive. I believe that faith and trust kept me from disappearing down that black hole we have referred to in this book. I always believed that I would be fine, that I would be happy, and that I would not only survive but be successful in my life. My thoughts, my actions, and my feelings brought me to a place of happiness and kept me in a place of happiness. As I grew as a person, integrating and developing my five bodies of consciousness, my happiness number grew higher and the variance on the swing of my arc got smaller and smaller.

Now that I am smarter and wiser, I understand the value of forgiveness. Forgiveness allows one to heal, and the vantage place that you put yourself in to see and reflect on past experiences in your childhood, or your relationships with siblings and parents, should be a vantage place of understanding and forgiveness. I learned to think about something I had never considered before—not only do our parents come in to work on their lessons, whatever they may be, but they are coming in with a buildup of many past-life karmic lessons as well. These may be two-sided issues. So please consider that if someone is struggling or depressed, it could be that they are trying to make sense of a horrendous lifetime where they have suffered extreme cruelty from another or perhaps they were the antagonist to another. In either event, each and every situation deserves understanding and forgiveness! And you will be glad when you heal these relationships as you never know when the end will be near.

My mother and father lived long lives: she into her mid-eighties and he into his early nineties. Two very different people, living two very different lives and dying two very different deaths. My mother had a stroke late one evening when she was eighty-five years old. The stroke occurred at their home, and my dad, elderly and frail, as the sole caregiver in their home had to handle this medical emergency. This amazing man was blind, deaf, and voiceless—due to the effects of being intubated and on a respirator for almost a year some sixteen years earlier. He also needed a walker to get around as he had partially recovered from a paralysis and a repair from a broken hip. My father found her lifeless on their bathroom floor, a full-sized woman; he was concerned that the paramedics would not be able to all fit into this small bathroom. This eighty-five-pound man pulled my mother out of the bathroom so there would be more room for the paramedics to do what they needed to do! He dialed 911, and after they arrived on the scene, one of the paramedics called me (I lived just a short distance away). After the initial assessment, it was decided that they would take her to the hospital in the ambulance and I would follow. I knew that my mother would never come home again. I knew that she was slowing down to begin her journey home.

The next day I went to tell my dad the sad news. He didn't give me a chance as he simply asked, "Is your mother ever coming home?" Communication was difficult with him, but I was able to help him to understand that she would not be coming home ever again. His response surprised me as he explained, "Well, I will need to make my own arrangements as my body is tired, and if I am no longer needed here, it is time for me to move on. I will be gone within 30 days. Please make sure that you give a donation to St. Peter as I understand he is in charge of the 'pearly gates,' and I wouldn't want to be kept out because we did not donate!" Half-joking and half-serious, I realized that being an old Irishman, he was just covering his bases.

My mom, safe in the hospital, allowed me time to try to figure out how best my dad should live his remaining days. His frailty and his physical condition made it impossible for me in good conscience to allow him to remain at home alone. I needed to explain to him the necessity of moving him and hoped that he would understand. His love for me was obvious as, at that difficult moment, he agreed to be moved to a safer environment complete with supervision. I knew he did not want to go, but he also knew that he could not stay there alone without adding stress to my already stressed life. Here we were, solving life's big issues, and he was worrying about me!

I moved him and got him settled into an environment that he was familiar with as he needed nursing care after his paralysis and his broken hip. Twenty-four hours after moving him, he took my hand and explained he needed to adjust his schedule. He stated that he would be leaving in fourteen days as opposed to the original thirty days. He reminded me again about sending St. Peter the donation and said if I would take care of that job, he would take care of the rest.

My mom was never going to recover from the stroke, and the next week the hospital decided it was time to move her, and so I moved her to the same nursing facility that my father was in. I think each may have known the other was there, but I am not sure. Within a forty-eight-hour period, my mother contracted pneumonia and went into respiratory failure. The facility called me, and riding in the ambulance with her, we took her back to the hospital. After she was processed, she was moved to a room. Walking down the hospital corridor, I heard my name being paged over its PA system. I stopped at the nurses' station, and they put me through so I could answer the call. My dad was in an ambulance and on his way in as well. His fourteen days were near up, and he was making his way home. So on that day, Good Friday, I admitted my dad as well. There was one room available, and that was on the same floor as my mom's, two rooms down. Back and forth I traveled, visiting each, discussing each case with their respective doctors, giving me time to adjust and process what was indeed happening.

Within a few days, the hospital called me at work and told me my dad was in his final stages of life—he had arrived at what they called "active dying." I walked into his room, only to see him handing a coffee cup over to the head nurse. He said to please tell all of the staff that he appreciated all of their care over the years and asked her to thank them. He then thanked her for his "last cup of coffee." He made himself comfortable; grasping a rosary, he crossed his hands across his chest, closed his eyes, and simply lay back into what seemed to be in a very relaxed state. Two hours later, he took his last breath. He in his own masterful way released himself to move into the world beyond. He had done what he had come to do and was now ready to return home.

A week later, a similar call came from the hospital. Gently, very gently over the course of that past week, I talked to my mom and told her that Dad had passed over and explained that she was not ever going to recover from her stroke. I simply told her that she was in charge of her life and her death, and if she chose to move forward, I would honor that as I wanted her to live a life of beauty, peace, and love. I told her that if she was ready to transition, I was ready for her to do that as well. I wanted her to have a beautiful quality to her life, and it was very clear that the aftermath of the stroke, as it was moving her in and out of consciousness, did not provide that quality. I felt that although she did not or could not acknowledge my thoughts, she did in fact hear them and understood them.

I returned to the hospital, and walking into her room, I saw her soul releasing from her body. The most beautiful golden light moving ever so slowly, swirling out of her chest and moving forward. It was the most beautiful sight that I had ever seen. I stood in the doorway of her room, awestruck. The nurses that were with my father when he died were now with my mom. Imagine that! As

I entered her room, one proclaimed that she was so glad that I had witnessed the beauty of death. She said that so many times, sons and daughters are so distraught that they simply miss it. I was grateful that I hadn't.

Two very different people, living two very different lives, dying two very different deaths, each giving me two very different gifts. My dad's death—an experience teaching me that one is always in control of one's life and one's death. The power of the mind, body, and spirit, when working together toward a common goal, can in fact create what one wants. He knew he could release himself, and as he did, I saw that the power that he had within was in fact again serving him ever so well. My mom's death—an experience that was so beautiful as I was allowed to witness the beauty of her soul leaving her body. The gift of that vision I think about often, and deep inside I revisit that feeling of seeing the overwhelming beauty of the golden light of her soul and I stand in awe. Each lived a full life, experiencing moments of greatness and moments of difficulty, challenging times and healing times, each choosing to journey home in a way that made sense to them. A reminder that as we write our story, we also write our ending. Ultimately, how we choose to live our life and how we choose to die brings us to many different states of happiness on so many levels, and it is up to us to create that level of happiness.

When I took this seminar, I was called upon by Markas as he asked, "On a scale of one to ten, what would you say your level of happiness is? One being less happy and ten being very happy." I remember that I took a deep breath and heard myself say nine point five! I actually surprised myself. He paused in the seminar and stated, "We will scan you for confirmation." A moment later I heard Markas say, "Yes, nine point five is confirmed, and we see that the variances on the scale as it swings back and forth are an eight on the low side to a twelve point five on the high side!" Explaining, he stated that my variances are all in the best and beyond category, so that my life and the experiences and joy that I have brought into my life are indeed allowing me to live a life of happiness. You can only imagine how I left the seminar—not only proud that I had lived my little story, learning how to travel down the road, avoiding the bumps, and becoming an expert navigator with perhaps only a smooth road ahead, but joyful that I had worked so hard on myself that I was indeed experiencing those moments of greatness. Yes, I have come a long way, a very long way!

During this time on our planet as we are getting closer to 2012, we see and feel the chaos, and as our planet is readjusting itself, we are all experiencing that time is picking up and going faster, but there are also stages that people may feel that the planet is slowing down. These times are viewed and felt as slower because people are confused, and they simply do not know what to do. Some people are moving as fast as they can to catch up to correct any errors that they have made. They have relied on outside or exterior resources far too long instead of relying on themselves. As the world as the macrocosm has been trying to correct itself, we—as the microcosm—need to do the same. We need to start at home. What works for my family? Forget about the outside world as far as what he has or she has. Everybody is talking about what they are losing and what they haven't got, but what about what you have got? Everyone has so much, and when you are caught up in the material life, perhaps then you are forgetting about all of the good things that you have. Where is the gratitude?

So it is time to take inventory of all of the gifts in our world. This is a major lesson for everyone on the planet who chose to come in at this time. We need to reset ourselves and, if necessary, shift back into the basic values, the basic truths. The lessons will continue to be presented to the world, and the more people that learn them and "get it" will help transition the planet faster and quicker to where the planet needs to be for the completion of the planetary shift in 2012. The lessons will get harder and harder until the gifts that are right in front of us are valued. This learning and readjustment period is how the planet is balancing itself, allowing those that need to move forward to be able to do so. This is the Universal Olympics—each person working toward his or her personal best, seeing and using all of the gifts for his or her highest good, helping raise the consciousness and shifting the energy into the realm of best and beyond, thus making each person or situation the best that it can be.

CHAPTER XI

Waking up in the Fifth Dimension

If you can let go of imperfection, perfection will appear by itself.

—Deepak Chopra, MD

This morning you woke up in the fifth dimension, but did you *wake up* in the fifth dimension? In other words, is your vibration adjusting so that you can step into the role of spiritual healer? The spiritual healer heals by seeing perfection where others still see the illusion of imperfection, so you heal from a base of living in the perfection of all things. This is how you can fix or attune or adjust your vibration to that higher plane of awareness, and in the process live more completely in a more prosperous, abundant way. This does not mean that you will simply be more prosperous financially, but that your life itself will be rich with blessings of all kinds.

You began this process when you were three-dimensional, and you raised your vibration emotionally so that you could step into the fourth dimension of consciousness. During this time, you spent a lot of time processing who you were emotionally. Every time that you did not run from one of your emotions, but allowed yourself to feel it and bring it to the surface, you took a very big step forward and in some cases upward in terms of your shift into the fourth dimension. Although it wasn't easy for you, you did this anyway because you knew that by emotionally experiencing life you were going to empower yourself and then you were going to begin to enjoy life. And so what happened was that you ended up going into a state of knowingness without your emotions. As you know, just because you went into the fourth dimension, it didn't mean that you still weren't going to experience ups and downs. It didn't mean that at all. It simply meant that you were going to be able to handle them more completely and much more efficiently. This planet by its nature has many ups and downs, and you are quite literally along for the ride. Therefore you want to have the sharpest skills possible so that even though things are happening on the planet, they are not happening directly to you.

The reason that you went through the difficulty of allowing yourself to truly feel your emotions, both good and bad, is so that you could step into the fifth dimension. Many of you entered into the fifth dimension before the planet did. If you were one of these individuals, you may have thought to yourself, "I can't wait for the planet to get into the fifth dimension because then I am going to feel more aligned." And there is some truth to that statement, but remember that just because you stepped into the fifth dimension doesn't mean that you mastered it. In order to master the fifth dimension, you have to do things the fifth-dimensional way. This means that you will have moments of mastery in which you allow your emotional body to use the appropriate emotions to create what you want in your life.

A challenge that you may experience in your quest to master fifth-dimensional living is that there doesn't seem to be a strict format to follow. In the fourth dimension there were some clear basics to follow: don't be afraid to feel, allow yourself to go into that feeling state so that you can then move into your power into your strength with the situation. Even if those instructions were not easy to follow, you at least understood what was necessary in order to move into the fourth dimension. But now that you are going into an entirely different dimension, you are probably wondering how to proceed. Well, my friend, we are going to walk you through this process right now.

First, we are going to help you bring your fifth body of consciousness up to consciousness. Now you of course know that you have an inner child who is your emotional body of consciousness, and you have a physical body of consciousness, and a mental body of consciousness, and a spiritual body of consciousness. The problem has been that your spiritual body of consciousness has been trying to move through the fifth body of consciousness, but it is not really his or her area. Their area is spirituality, and that is different than being a spiritual healer. Therefore the first thing that you need to do is to bring up your fifth body of consciousness, also what we call your superconsciousness. For those of you who have not done this before, all that you need to do is to sit quietly and comfortable in a chair and ask your superconsciousness to come forward. As you can see, this is a very simple, very painless process. Do not delay doing this as now is the time that our planet needs fifth-dimensional spiritual healing.

When we talk about spiritual healing, you may be wondering who the first spiritual healer was. Well, Jesus Christ or the Christ energy was the first spiritual healer. As you can imagine, the time during which Jesus lived was very early into the three-dimensional energy. However, Jesus was such a powerful spiritual healer that he was able to heal others by simply laying his hand on them, by looking into their eyes, or even just by the intonation of his voice. He was able to do this because he was and is perfection. Now there are some who would say that everyone on this planet is an imperfect being striving for perfection. However, we would argue that everyone's soul is perfect, and it is more a question of discovering the perfection inside of you. The Christ energy knew his perfection; he knew it the very moment he was brought into the world.

Now, this doesn't mean that you will be able to or that you even should try to emulate any of the great religious leaders. That is not what you are here for or what this learning is going to be about. However, one of the things you can do is learn by looking at the Christ energy how everything moved around him in perfect order. He really was the center of his reality, and things fell into line around him. Because of this, when someone would come to him for healing, he would look into the souls of whoever was coming and would read their energy and then would give assistance as he deemed it appropriate or necessary. Now that the planet is in the beginning stages of the fifth dimension, things may seem to get much more complex before they get simpler. However, keep in mind that this is all part of the perfection; things are being sorted out just as they are meant to. As we have said before, the spiritual healer is one who heals by seeing perfection in all things. They see the world with new eyes and don't see it with all of the problems, difficulties, atrocities, animosities, and differences among people. Of course those things do exist, but you need to be able to look into the soul of the individual that you are communicating with and recognize that that soul is perfect—even if the behaviors are imperfect, even if the actions or what they are up to is imperfect.

Looking at the world with love and seeing the perfection in all things and all people is not an easy task, by any means. It is in fact a learned behavior. So the more that you practice this, the easier it will be for you. As you practice looking at things with new eyes and seeing things as perfect, your energy begins to adjust in a fifth-dimensional way. Now, keep in mind that this spiritual practice is vastly different from that of those who walk around the world in a state of denial. You realize that there are problems, issues in this world, and you allow yourself to feel the emotions that arise in you due to these things. However, you move past them and continue to see the world from the viewpoint of perfection.

As you add each dimension of consciousness, you are moving forward while not forgetting about the previous dimension and the lessons that you learned in it. Emotions can play a big part of this process. This is because you will not only have certain experiences, but you will allow yourself to reflect on them as well. And that is the role of the spiritual healer. So when you have an experience that doesn't feel like love, or one in which you feel that you did not have spiritual mastery, remember that your fifth body of consciousness, your superconsciousness, knows your blueprint and will help you to get centered again. Rather than having your inner child try to fix it or the spiritual child try to rise above it, go directly to your superconsciousness. Do this as the adult, as the overseer of yourself, and interact with your fifth body. As you do this, your fifth body of consciousness will show you the lessons that you need to learn from the experience so that you do not have to go through it again. Your fifth body of consciousness will show you a perfect way to respond to difficult circumstances. After all, the circumstances may not be perfect, but they will create a better, more perfect circumstance down the road if you learn from them and continue to see the perfection in all things.

As you well know, our planet is one of contrast. When you appreciate the contrast, you will find that it exists in every experience that you have had or will have on this planet. When you experience something that is difficult and allow yourself to appreciate the contrast, you remove yourself temporarily as a participant and you place yourself again in the position of the observer. As you are observing the experience, you will work with your fifth body of consciousness, which is one of the best friends you are ever going to have. Bring up the fifth body of consciousness by simply inviting him or her in as we described earlier, and then you set him or her loose. When you do this, there will be a shift in energy that will help you to let go of any negative experiences in your past once and for all. In order to receive this help from your fifth body of consciousness, you need to remain in a relaxed state.

The more relaxed you are, the more present you are in the moment, and the more effective your fifth body of consciousness will be able to be. This is because in the fifth dimension there is no time. There is the illusion of time, but there is no time. That means past, present, and future are all happening simultaneously in this moment. When you get into a deeper state of relaxation, you are able to go into that space of timelessness. And when you are in the space of timelessness, this is when it is very easy to see the perfection because you are not comparing things. You can't compare anything because past, present, and future are all the same moment, so you can't possibly be in contrast. You will find that there will not be a stopping point to your relaxation; you will be able to go deeper and deeper and deeper into it as you do it more often. You go deeper and deeper into present-moment consciousness, and in that state everything inside of you feels perfect. So if you want to see the perfection of things around you, step into the perfection inside of you!

Think about that for a moment: if you want to experience perfection around you, then you must become that moment of perfection. When you think this way, you are really doing so in a fifth-dimensional way. In the fifth body of consciousness, if you want to be and see perfection where there is the illusion of imperfection, all that you have to do is get into a state of relaxation and go as deep as you can into that state of grace, into that moment of existence that feels as if everything is as it should be. Remember that you create your future with what you are doing right now. So when you practice this exercise of relaxation and finding perfection in all things, including yourself, you will attract fifth-dimensional gifts and blessings into your life. When you receive such a blessing, don't think about it, but instead stay for a moment in the feeling tone of it. If you have a moment of bliss or perfection and allow yourself to continue to feel that blissful, wonderful feeling, it will be much easier to attract more of those moments to you.

There are tools that can help you in your quest to get to this state of deep relaxation in the fifth dimension, including aromatherapy. While different aromas appeal to each of us, there are some that are generally particularly helpful for the fifth dimension. These aromas include frankincense, neroli, lavender, and myrrh. The petals from flowers can also be very effective, include those from roses, plumeria, and petaki (Hawaiian flowers). So if the season is right, go out into your garden or go on a walk in the woods and find flowers that have aromas that have a relaxing effect on you. Experiment with various scents until you find out what is the most effective for you in terms of its ability to help you into a deep state of relaxation.

As you work with your fifth-dimensional body of consciousness, you will continue to be aided by your other bodies of consciousness. Your emotional body of consciousness will help you to not run away from emotions but to feel them. Once you feel them, then they are no longer big bad monsters in the closet. The emotional body of consciousness will allow you to feel the emotion so that you can release it and have an empty emotional chalice, if you will, to fill with beautiful fifth-dimensional wine. Your mental body of consciousness will act as a team player and to reorient itself to using the mental skills for materialization, manifestation, and imaging. Use these mental skills to go forward, but do not allow them to try to control the other bodies of consciousness. As the adult, you have to keep helping the mental child to be a team player by giving him or her worthwhile jobs to do and employing his or her energy in a way that is constructive. As for the spiritual body of consciousness, his or her job is to find the moral high ground. This means looking at situations with a very compassionate heart and opening up and allowing yourself to make choices that feel like they are honoring yourself first and foremost, choices that feel like part of your true nature. When your spiritual child is struggling, you must help him or her to be able to make choices that feel compatible with morality and consciousness.

As we described earlier, the fifth body of consciousness is responsible for attracting perfection and helping others to learn how to attract perfection so that all of the bodies of consciousness benefit and experience the life well-lived. Again, you simply need to invite the fifth body of consciousness in. Up until this point the fifth body of consciousness has been helping all of the other bodies of consciousness, but you haven't spent a lot of time with the fifth body of consciousness. This is exactly what you need to do in your fifth-dimensional living. As a spiritual healer, the more that you are in your perfection and the more that you invite in these perfect situations or experiences, the more that you help others by the energy that you are putting out to the universe. Your energy starts to speak for itself so that you are not necessarily healing in an active way, but simply by the energy that you put out by living your life in a superconsciousness way.

Faith is having a level of trust, trusting in the unseen, and knowing that that which you need will come about even if it is not in your awareness. Trusting in the unseen also means expecting the best, anticipating something wonderful without putting a label or a picture to it. This is really the same thing as inviting more love into your life. For spiritual healers, the way that you substantially increase your faith is by allowing it to have an impact on your life. What this means is that all of you came to the planet for a reason; you came for learning and to have fun. Ideally you would like to combine the two! All of you have self-selected into groups of friends, whether it be two or fifty. You self-select certain groups of individuals, most likely because you had an agreement with them before you came into the physical realm that you were going to experience spiritual growth together. Therefore you need to allow others and their miracles to operate on your behalf. In the fifth dimension you are allowing your faith to be raised not by others' stories as much as by their interactions with you.

There are a few fun exercises that you can do to help you to have fifth-dimensional experiences. The first is very simple as it involves any sort of social activity. The next time that you are in a social setting, whether it is going to a game, a wedding, or just going over to a friend's house, allow yourself to truly feel the moment while being aware of the fact that you are in fact doing so in a fifth-dimensional way. Another thing that you can do is go to a restaurant and order something that you would not normally order, something out of the ordinary for you. When you taste the food, consciously acknowledge that this is a fifth-dimensional experience, that you are living in the moment. Next, the next time that you are near a body of water, whether it is a lake, ocean, or stream, look into the water and defocus your eyes and see what looks back at you. This is a fifth-dimensional moment because it will help you to see that you are closer than ever before to having more direct communication with spirit. Some of you may see guides or other spirits that will serve you well. Whatever you see, just be open to it. Finally, when you are at home in the evening, before you turn on the television, just let a channel number pop into your head. When you see the number in your head, simply turn on the television to that channel and see what the message is that is intended for you from your fifth-dimensional energy counselors. While these are all very simple exercises, they will in fact help you to be conscious of living in the fifth dimension.

As we talk about these exercises, you may be thinking that you would still like to know even more about how to have more fifth-dimensional blessings come your way. Well, the good news is that it is quite simple. You simply need to bring yourself into this awareness by finding something that really brings you joy in either the healing or spiritual realm. It might be a movie or a book. For example, it might be a book that fills up your heart chakra and gets you excited about the way that things can be. Just read or watch something that you find to be very uplifting and that rings true to you around healing or spiritual wellness. When you do this, it will help you to see the perfection in all things that we spoke about earlier and will therefore allow you to attract more fifth-dimensional things into your life.

Remember, the fifth dimension is not about being in denial of your surroundings or the challenges that are in your life. You can create balance between the weight of this planet and the lightness of the fifth dimension. For example, you will still have bills to pay and difficult challenges at work and at home. However, the secret about the fifth dimension is that when you embrace all experiences and really understand how they make you feel, you will find that there is no need to control it, fix it, or make it go a certain way. Instead, as you practice the art of living in the fifth dimension, things will very naturally go toward their state of perfection. Again, simply invite your fifth body of consciousness in, relax in the process of seeing everything as perfection, and enjoy the ride forward and upward into the fifth dimension!

* * * * * * * *

This fifth-dimensional feeling comes as a very subtle shift in your ability to live a consciously happier life. I think one of the best exercises that I have done to help me live more fully in the fifth dimension was just allowing myself to acknowledge that each precious moment is perfect. I began by looking at my life and sought out anything that was annoying to me. Trust me, that certainly wasn't difficult! I then consciously made the decision to look at it from new eyes, fifth-dimensional eyes. Once you take away the annoyance and find something positive to say or feel in the experience, you begin to perceive things from a different perspective. So this initial step actually makes you proud that you have been able to see something in a new light, in a better light, a more positive light. Then when you experience this same experience again, you consciously put yourself back into your new framework, and bingo, you have seen this experience again in a positive light. Each time you revisit the experience, your thought or reaction to it is now positive. Ah, yes, practice does make perfect!

Then step back and observe the behavior of others and see and listen to them as they illustrate their annoyances, and you will see that they are reacting just like you used to! Now recognize your growth and witness how annoying your friend's reaction is to you. Removing the annoyance out of your life and reacting to it with someone else is really seeing how your energy is affected by others. You have purified your energy field, and you have also raised your vibrations. Their annoying reaction actually is irritating to your energy field, and once you experience peace, you do not want to backtrack and return to the way you used to be.

I am not suggesting that you judge or be critical of your friend but rather to gain the knowledge of human behavior; I am suggesting, however, that you *can* teach yourself a new trick! I am suggesting that with a little practice, each experience or reaction that you may have felt one way can in fact be changed with conscious effort. The new reaction simply frees you up, and you remain lighter inside than before because you are not creating any tension within. You are allowing yourself to react in a purer fashion with the freedom and thought and from a place of love and not fear. When you practice this and bring yourself to a place of mastery, you are now an example for others as they can witness your lighthearted attitude, your ease, and your energy is engaging. You are *now* a spiritual healer.

Everyone has a friend or a family member that has hurt them. Oftentimes we create an expectation in our head of how and why we expect someone to act, and then when they do not perform the way we want them to, we are disappointed. When such a situation occurs, you have two options: no longer continue the friendship so that you are not putting yourself in the position of hurt (this may or may not be practical as it is hard to dismiss friends and family from one's immediate circle) *or* to continue the friendship and participate from a new place with a shift in your consciousness. How do you do this? One very easy way is to simply look for the lesson in the experience.

There are hundreds of examples that are irritating, annoying, and hurtful that every one of us experiences in our daily lives that we could change if we simply looked at them from a different vantage point. Can you relate to any of these experiences? Here is a short list: you continually invite your friends or family to dinner, and one guest regularly shows up one hour late; you take a friend for an afternoon of lunch and shopping only to hear later that she has taken out another friend of yours for lunch and shopping and excluded you; you share information with a coworker about a project that you are working on, and the coworker presents it to her boss as her work; or you are at a party only to see your good friend coming on to your husband, and your husband is actually enjoying it! In addition, have you ever loaned a friend money because he or she is in a financial crisis, and instead of watching the money being spent in a responsible way, you witness the money being spent for foolish and lavish items? Then you become sorry or angry at yourself for being generous and wish that the other person could just learn their lesson the hard way! Sound familiar? Lastly, you lend your friend a new sweater, or your neighbor a lawnmower, or your car or whatever, and who hasn't had the item returned ripped, dirty, broken, or dented? Ah, yes, life's little irritations. We can, however, turn them into a win-win situation!

I am sure that all of us can think of a similar experience if they are not able to relate to one of the ones mentioned above. These little experiences can be very hurtful and damage a relationship, destroying the trust and responsibility that one friend or family member has with another. Our daily lives are no longer peaceful as the annoyance takes on a life of its own, making us seethe inside every time we think about it. Life is far too eventful on its own, and we certainly don't need to keep petty annoyances alive, making us feel sad, disappointed, or angry.

So let's transform the hurtful experiences by dealing with the emotion and sending it off for resolution. Each experience has touched off a feeling or a response that needs to be addressed. Remember, we are looking for "easement" in our physical body and not anything that can create "dis-easement." We have been taught that we can bring the feeling up to the surface and deal with the emotion and then put it to rest.

Now let us learn how we can handle the experiences in the first place so that we turn a hurtful experience into a positive one without creating any negative emotional response. How? By looking for the lesson in each and every experience. So let us look at the earlier scenarios and see how you may have handled the situation and then let us learn how you should have handled the situation, creating a win-win for everyone involved.

Let's deal with the irresponsible, selfish friend or family member that is always coming to dinner late. (Okay, so I did use a few descriptive adjectives—but they are certainly not judgmental!) Do you: A) Tell him or her that the time of the dinner is really an hour later so that he or she actually arrives on time? B) Not invite him or her anymore. C) Understand that he is operating on his own time clock and proceed without him so that no one is inconvenienced, and when he arrives, he eats the dinner as is—cold or hot, whatever. And the answer is? C. You have made peace with your guest and accepted him the way that he or she is—and are learning the lesson of tolerance and patience along the way. If you chose either answer A, are you simply becoming an enabler? Or if you chose answer B, friends are not irreplaceable—he either is a friend or he isn't!

Your friend that you have taken out for an afternoon of lunch and shopping hurts you when she takes out your friend for lunch and shopping without including you. Do you: A) Call her and tell her you were hurt because she didn't invite you? B) Immediately call her friend and invite her out for lunch and shopping and make sure that your friend hears about it. C) Invite your emotional inner child out for lunch and shopping instead of the above and decide she needs to understand the meaning of the terms *jealous* and *possessive*. And the answer is? C. Your inner child actually has her emotional dander worked up, and she really needs to feel loved while she is being educated in the meaning of a couple of unbecoming words. If you chose A, you have expressed yourself, which is healthy, but you haven't gone far enough to the root of why you are hurt, and that is what needs to be handled. If you chose B, you are simply playing games, and if it was wrong when your friend did what she did to you, isn't it just as wrong when you try to get her back? This act certainly isn't coming from a place of love.

Should we talk about your best friend and your husband? No, let's skip that one as she obviously isn't your best friend and he's in the doghouse! Perhaps they deserve each! Let's move on to the next one.

Let's talk about the work scenario when your work has been "borrowed" by a coworker and presented as his or her own. A) You call a meeting with your boss and explain what has happened. B) You resolve never to share your work or ideas with anyone as people cannot be trusted. C) You call a meeting with your coworker, the "borrower," to explain the meaning of the term "borrower." And the answer is C. By calling a meeting with your coworker, you are defending your work as well as sticking up for yourself. You learn your lesson and see that the resolution has taught you something valuable—your self-love and self-worth are more important than presenting a side of yourself that is less than who you are. If you chose A, you absolutely can explain to your boss and hope that it won't be interpreted as "sour grapes," but you are not solving the problem where the hurt originated. If you chose B, you have joined the "OSC" or organization for skeptical and cynical people. You have bought into the fear and have allowed it to alter your judgment and pull you from a place of love. There is no room for another negative person on this planet!

So you get the idea. There is always a way to handle something so that it becomes a good, better, or best situation. By learning how to think things through and then by acting with that knowledge, you have turned the experience into a win-win situation, all the while honoring your higher self. The lesson is not lost on you, and perhaps a lesson was even learned by the individual you are in contention with. The most important thing is that you "get it." You don't need to worry about the other person as that person is not the center of your reality—you are at your own center. And as such your focus is to maintain and bring you back to your true center so that you may live from your center, thereby maintaining the power of who you are.

CHAPTER XII

Wait. What? I Don't Understand!

One man can make a difference and every person should try.

—John Fitzgerald Kennedy

We are all existing and trying to move forward in our spiritual growth on this planet. It will not surprise you to hear that we are all having difficulty in the fifth dimension, just as we did in the fourth dimension or before we even engaged in such mental processing in the third dimension. While we are trying to move forward, we really need to be trying to move upward. It is not exactly a spiraling upward although you do want to accelerate your vibrational frequency, but rather moving on higher and higher planes of consciousness. This is a difficult process because it can feel like you are literally going uphill. Well, that is because that is exactly what you are doing—you are going uphill!

Now, to make things even a bit more complicated, it is not that you should just stay in the same place and move upward. Instead you need to be moving through your life on an uphill plane. You may be wondering how you can possibly do all of this without feeling as if there is a tremendous amount of effort. Now learning does take effort, there is no question about that. The thing is that individuals are trying to learn things the old-fashioned way, and every time you do things the old-fashioned way, it is going to feel as if the motion that is moving forward is moving in slow gear, in the slowest gear possible. That means that you are trying to move forward rather than upward. You probably want this struggle and wasted effort to stop, so let's fix it together!

First, concentrate on your breath. Close your eyes and relax and go back to doing just some normal but conscious breathing exercises. Right now get back in touch with the energy that is in your body. It should feel different than it has in the past because you are in a different place in your life. Now again, with your eyes closed, try to open what we call your psychic screen and let pictures, images, and colors, whatever it is that wants to come through, come through on your psychic screen right now. What do you see? What do you feel?

As you feel your energy, you may find that you have distrust in the fact that you can attract to you exactly what you need at any moment. Even though again in fourth-dimensional living, what we said to you is that you attract in what you are, either what you love or what you fear, there is a feeling that you are not able to attract in exactly what you want, and that attracting in what you are is not what you want. So let go of that and let whatever—the images or colors or vibrations—just let them come up and continue to do your breathing.

It is a very difficult thing to achieve trust. Trust in the universe and trust in yourself, trust in God, trust in guides and teachers, trust in your fellow man. That is a very difficult thing to achieve because it requires that you believe in the perfection of all things while even as you look around you still see the illusion of imperfection. While you consciously want to move forward and upward, and don't want to learn things the old-fashioned way, you may find that you revert back because there is a lack of trust and a lack of knowing that everything is perfect.

Now it is true that when you are nonphysical it is much easier to know that everything is perfect and that everything indeed has its purpose. But when you are physical, as you well know, it is very difficult to believe that everything around you is happening perfectly when it doesn't seem that you have control over it. But the truth is that you do have control over it, it is just not being done as in the old-fashioned way! You have absolute control when you begin to trust that everything is perfect, even if it feels difficult, and even if it feels as if it is not worthy of the god-goddess energy. And the more that you begin to have trust in the process, the more that you will begin to attract in those things that support that level of trust.

Now, our discussions around the fifth dimension are certainly an area for which you will have to suspend your urge to roll your eyes! For example, in the fifth dimension you can alter time or "bend time within your mind." Believe it or not, you can do these things, even if you are only 10 percent operating in the fifth dimension, even if it is only a small part of what you do. You should still be able to see the results of this. The fifth dimension is the realm of the spiritual healer, and a lot of individuals are having major health issues while being in the fifth dimension or while having moved from one dimension to another. But understand the spiritual healer did not deal with physical wellness directly. A spiritual healer is one who adjusts the synapses of the mind and of the heart so that everything goes into its perfect state. So a spiritual healer is one who heals by seeing the perfection, even if you are feeling the illusion of imperfection. This illusion must be dropped by elevating your level of trust. Are you beginning to see a pattern here?

You may be wondering what the most important thing is that you are learning about the fifth dimension. Well, it is a time when you can attract in the experts that you need to help you deal with the physical wellness issues that you may be experiencing. The relationship issues between patient and doctor can be improved to the point of perfect flow of knowledge and technique for your physical wellness. In addition, you can learn to discern how your interactions with others, and the subsequent exchange of energy, impact your physical body. How does it feel when you are around toxic people, people that don't have very good energy, people that are two—or three-dimensional? As you know, it is very difficult, but it is something that everyone will encounter. And so it is very important that we all learn to discern how we feel in all situations and to trust those feelings.

Another crucial thing to learn in the fifth dimension is how to focus on releasing fear and being centered in your own reality to help release the fears that lead to ill health. As you are centered in your own reality, reassure yourself that you are going to learn your lessons. Again, you are going to move forward while accelerating your vibrational frequency upward. This process is not like a helicopter that takes off directly upward, but it is more like a plane that moves forward and upward on the runway until it is airborne! When we boldly stated before that you will be able to bend time within your mind in the fifth dimension, we meant that you will be able to see the perfection of all things and will live as if there is perfection in the world.

You will see the perfection and not depend on others to be perfect, but instead depend upon your belief system to help you along your journey. Things will actually then begin to get easier; they will begin to be fun for you. You will find that you will not have as many health issues as you have had in the past as those things were due to the fact that your body was trying to do things the old-fashioned way. That is why the body seems to struggle and feels as if it is in need of repair; the old-fashioned way simply will not work in the fifth dimension. Now all of this may sound as if it is something for masters to do. This is true in the respect that if you are to achieve mastery of the physical plane, you must understand the workings of the fifth dimension. You must understand that your soul is connected to the workings of every other soul, and at the same time, your soul is absolutely independent of what other people do around you. Even if it looks like you are connected to the negative activities of others, your outcome is independent of what they are thinking, feeling, and believing.

We would now like you to begin another exercise. Close your eyes and just allow your body to go into a deep state of relaxation. Just let it feel alive, and yet in a bit of a meditative state. Ask your legs what position you should put them in so that they will feel completely relaxed. Ask the same question of your torso, your arms, your hands, your neck, and your backbone, and feel that power coming back to you. That has always been your power; it is not just that you have given it away, but you are still trying to achieve a state of nirvana by learning things the old-fashioned way. Allow yourself to slip into a state of nirvana, again closing your eyes, getting relaxed, asking your body how you can put it in the most relaxed position. And as you do this, you will begin to see beauty whereas before you saw the illusion of imperfection. You will begin to see beautiful, metaphysical sights—some call it the sixth sense, some call it the psychic eye. You will begin to see all of these elements of beauty, and they will very easily come into your energy field. Why? Well, this is because of the new alpha level of consciousness that you have achieved through your journey of moving forward and upward.

It is crucial throughout your journey that you know that your resources are unlimited! They can only be limited by an enclosed belief system. You must believe that you are in this together with your guides and teachers—that you are a work in progress with your guides and teachers! The more that you feel them around you, the more you will receive the intuitive hits, the more that you get what they want you to know. They have a lot of leeway with the universe in terms of what they can tell you. But if you are busy learning things the old-fashioned way, it is impossible for you to hear them.

Are you ready for another exercise? This particular exercise is intended to prove to you that time is nonlinear. So take the next ten minutes to make a mental connection with your fifth body of consciousness. If you say, "Well I can't do that," then you won't be able to! You must allow yourself to just open up and make the connection, let your fifth body of consciousness connect to you. If your inner child says "this feels like too much work," please reassure the inner child that it will only take seconds to make the connection with your fifth body of consciousness. This small amount of time is well worth it, given that this is probably the most valuable resource that you have available. So no excuse, just connect with your fifth body of consciousness.

If you find that you have spent time trying to connect with your fifth body of consciousness and have been unable to, try to imagine the connections. This is going to have the trickle-down effect of your fifth body of consciousness getting more connected with your inner child, who may be bearing an enormous burden at this time. A wonderful byproduct of this process is that it will allow you to get more connected with your physical child. So it is going to be not just you the adult that benefits, but your inner child and physical child are both going to benefit. If you are unable to connect right away with your fifth body of consciousness, do not give up! Continue to practice this exercise with an open mind and an open heart and you will be able to make this connection.

In all of this talk about the fifth dimension, you may be wondering how people can most effectively function in the fifth dimension. Well, self-love is what is necessary. The inner child is always going to need not just self-love, but the assurance that you are wonderful—the assurance that you are a wonderful human, a wonderful individual, a wonderful soul. Often people want to hear that they are an advanced soul. If you are a wonderful, alive, giving, excited soul who has a lot of love to give and a lot of information to share and to serve others, then you are an old soul or an enlightened being. It is very important to the delicate emotional state of your inner child that he or she knows that you are in fact an enlightened being, that you are a wonderful addition to this universe.

Another question that you may have is around how to stay centered in a fifth-dimensional state. In order to do this, you must be tuned into what your heart is telling you. Doing this will allow you to become the observer rather than the participant. You will find that you will become plugged into your heart chakra as you do this, which is strongly connected to your eighth chakra in the fifth dimension. You must listen to your heart, speak with your heart, and follow your heart's path regardless of what those around you are doing or saying. Because many people are still second-, third-, or fourth-dimensional, you will run into people that do not know what a fifth-dimensional experience is all about, let alone living one.

So how do you build up trust within yourself, even when there are others who doubt you? You begin by putting one foot in front of the other as you move forward and upward, and you know that you are doing this consciously. It is not always easy to trust yourself when you do things that you don't trust—in other words, actions that you did without consciousness. But if you are doing things consciously, then it is much easier to build trust within yourself because you know what is right. You focus on doing things that you know in your heart are right, and the more that you do that, the more you develop your soul, and the more you attract that which you want into your life.

So how do you move through those feelings of impatience and frustration? How do you stop putting illusions on others as well as living them yourself? Well, you need to work to ensure that your fifth body of consciousness is an integral part of the family that includes your other bodies of consciousness. We already know that this is very important for the emotional body, but it is really very important for the spiritual and physical bodies as well. The way that you do this is to develop a relationship over time. When your bodies of consciousness develop a level of trust and that lack of frustration with one another, you have a very solid force behind you. You feel integrated, and when you feel integrated internally, then your whole life feels integrated. If you are completely and totally integrated, then it feels as if everything around you is a walk in the park. Because your fifth body of consciousness is so developed, there is a lot of information that he or she has to share with your other bodies of consciousness. And because you did so much for your emotional body of consciousness in the fourth dimension, the emotional body is ready and willing to be integrated as well. The key to remember is that not all of your bodies of consciousness will be fully integrated right away, and that's okay! Remember to ask your guides for their assistance and be patient with yourself and others as this process takes place.

The learning process is not supposed to be challenging, but until you learn things in the "new-fashioned way," it is going to feel challenging. The integration is not supposed to feel challenging, but until you learn to integrate the new-fashioned way it may feel challenging to you. These are not just challenges, they are opportunities. But look what you have right now—you have unlimited resources. While the concept of your choices being unlimited is really a fourth-dimensional one, it is very important that you believe that this is true. Furthermore, your resources are not only unlimited, but they are all within you or what we call the body frame of your consciousness. The body frame is where your guides and teachers come in to help you. It is where your circle of twelve resides although it is really more like an oval table. If you think about it this way, your guides surround the chakras and the body frame.

So that is where your resources are: within you and your guides and teachers. Remember that you have not only major guides, but you have major arcana guides. You have not only single-attribute guides, but you also have teachers. You have not only companion counterparts but you have a twin soul. You have not only a birthright angel, but a cabalistic arcana guide. You have not only fifth-dimensional counselors, but you have lead messengers. You have not only eternal suns, but you have parallel universes. You have a lot of beings that are serving you in one capacity or another, whether or not you know. That is why it is important that you are introspective and allow yourself to feel these resources. Even if you feel limited at times, this introspection will help you to feel connected to your guides and teachers, helping to build your trust again in the limitlessness of your resources. Keep in mind that there are also many resources available to you that exist outside of you and your guides and teachers. Some examples of the resources available on this planet include aromatherapy, flower essences, crystals, and the vortices that surround you.

For a moment, let's think about the concept "less is more." This is a fourth-dimensional concept, and we want you to absorb or to integrate less rather than more. Believe it or not, in doing that you are going to get it more profoundly than you would otherwise. If you take a few concepts and integrate them deeply, then the other ones automatically follow suit, the other ones automatically will increase your joy. You may be thinking, "What! Wait! But I don't understand." Remember, everything is in perfect order in order for you to move forward. When you have said, "But I don't understand!" the truth is that you weren't taking the time to understand. You expected that the lessons were going to show up on your doorstep, and they didn't show up the way that they did in the fourth dimension. Of course they are not going to because you are not in the fourth dimension. You are doing an excellent job on this spiritual journey; do not judge it, and do not put your expectations on it. Trust the journey, allow it to move you upward and forward!

Now for the moment you have been waiting for . . . a repeat summary of the three most important things for you at this time. The first one is to see the perfection where there has been the illusion of imperfection. The second is to accelerate your vibrational frequency so that you are not just moving forward, but you are moving upward simultaneously. The third is to bend time within your mind. So these things are all really the opposite of how things have been. Most individuals say that as their life goes on it speeds up; in other words, a year feels like half a year or a third of the year as you get older, when as a child it might have felt like a decade. But for those that are truly living in the fifth dimension, it feels like time has slowed down. You have bent time in your mind, within your mind. If you do these three things, along with your conscious breathing, being in touch with your fifth body of consciousness, and doing the integration, you will see things around you are going to change in an instant. These things, done in the paradigm of "less is more" (taking a few concepts and learning them very deeply), will allow you to live fifth-dimensionally.

How do you bend time with your mind? Do you feel that things are going by too quickly for you or do you feel as if you are managing time? What do you sense? When you bend time with your mind, within your mind, you will feel as if everything is going in slow motion. You have more than enough time to complete all of your tasks. You have more than enough time for leisure. You have more than enough time for talking with friends and family. You have more than enough time for getting everything done that you want to get done. If feels as if you are in charge of time, that time is no longer linear but is at your command. That is what happens when you bend time within your mind. Believe it or not, once you get it, it almost works too well! It is as if you have too much time on your hands—but it is actually just the right amount!

As you find that you have more time, remember to ensure that your integration includes an inner child that feels safe. If the inner child is not going to be happy through this process, then the learning process is going to take much longer. So think about that when you are putting a lot of pressure on yourself to perform, think about putting the pressure on your inner child and whether it is fair to him or her. Wouldn't it be nice to be living in a world where you do not have to take tests? Wouldn't it be nice to live in a world where everything is going so well that the learning is being compounded exponentially so you don't even have to take tests to see if it is working, you just know that it is working? What a way to live your life! That is in fact what to expect when you take just these three principles, try them, and use that time—the extra time that you now have—to integrate your five bodies of consciousness. Again, take a look at what is working very well, and what is not, in your life and integrate where you need to.

What you will find is that the process will be better than expecting a miracle—you will feel as if you are living the miracle! There is a lot of love and a lot of light out in the world, but none of it is greater than what you have inside of you. And what you want is to attract in what you are. So if what you are is not what you want to be, then you must do this integration of your five bodies of consciousness in order to get to where you want to be, then you will attract that in and you will see it surrounding you, surrounding you, and surrounding you! The only way and the only path to success is when the physical body, the emotional body, the mental body, the spiritual body, and the fifth body of consciousness are all interwoven with you the adult. So get out there and live the miracle and see it alive in all facets of your life: personal, all relationships, and your career or business successes!

* * * * * * * *

And so the growth continued! I took these three simple tools as a personal gift and with my heart and soul resolved to use them!

Ah, the ability to see perfection where formerly I only saw the illusion of imperfection. What does that mean? I consciously focused on how I was thinking, feeling, and acting. I observed myself in my surroundings. I looked around for "clues" to how I fit into the world. I observed and discovered not only my tone or mood in my everyday habits but those around me. Was I contributing to the universe in a positive way? Or perhaps the better question is was I contributing to the universe in the best possible way?

What I found out was that I began to identify the energy all around me. I was developing the gift of discernment! I started observing how I felt when I was surrounded by negative people who spread around their dense energy by doing something as mundane as complaining—complaining of whatever. It did not seem to matter what the complainer was complaining about, but a constant spewing of toxic energy pours forth, polluting the universe. The topic could be the weather, or a disappointment with a sports team, or the bashing or a super athlete who gave a poor performance. The dark cloud even appears as the complainer unloads a more personal opinion of how disgusting they look or feel or perhaps how their friends look, dress, or behave. This unloading is generally an indication of what bad things are going on in their life. If you see the world as negative, just look inside and you will find it resides within! Listening to this barrage gives you a headache! It is time to retreat and to retreat with love. I had to learn that toxic people did not need to affect my life in any way. It is my responsibility to keep my energy field clear and clean. I had to learn to distance myself and not allow any negative energy to come to me. It became very clear to me that with a little adjustment in attitude, the negative energy that spewed forth wouldn't be all that bad. Of course, the goal was not for it to be all that bad, but for it to be all that good. I had read that a thought, any thought form, was energy. So your thought automatically translates into energy that was sent directly into the universe. It was time to send the complainers of the universe positive energy, a little love, and done from a distance.

Our planet is the most negative planet in the universe. And unfortunately the United States is considered the most negative country on the planet and is a haven for negative energy. We are consumed by fear, and fear consumes us, that part of us that is positive and lends itself to serving the world in the best way possible.

Fear is the mother/father of everything negative. How? Why? When someone exhibits fear it is because he or she hasn't awakened to the fact that the love and light of God resides in each of us. It is easier to assume rather that God is separate from our being and that God is that mother/father figure out there somewhere watching down, waiting to punish, judge, and/or condemn all that we are. Each of us may have been taught this, or it may have been part of a belief system that our families believed and it has stayed with us influencing our ultimate value of ourselves in the universe. In reality our God is the love that is within us and surrounds us and is the light that exists in every living thing. So we have a choice: to live from a base of love or to live from a base of fear. Love cannot exist where fear resides, and fear cannot live where love is. We have a choice! I chose love!

I knew that I did not want to be part of the problem. I knew that I wanted to be part of the solution. And I also knew that one person can make a difference. Because the love that one person sends out into the universe is the most powerful energy that exists. I could feel the difference when I felt love and felt loving. My energy was lighter and I could literally feel it flow through me. The reverse is not pleasant. Dense energy is thick, heavy, and lends itself to illness. I wanted no part of that!

I looked at people's faces as I drove to work in the morning. I found the majority of faces were either expressionless, bored, or vacant. I did not see a smile or a relaxed face. That made me sad, very sad.

I then started noticing vanity license plates. Some of the plates were so telling, expressing from either the victim mentality vantage point or emitting a strong, powerful emotion (certainly not a positive one) or a message that shot like an arrow with focused aim at a specific someone. These messages never would have passed the "emissions testing" program. The world was their audience to share in their misery by receiving its message, clearly not one with love at its base and clearly the owner making a statement of how he/she was wrongly used or abused or any other scenario that was expressing hurt, anger, resentment, or bitterness. That got me to thinking. What kind of person would want the world to see how miserable they were? What kind of person sends out a message decidedly negative for others to receive? Doesn't that person realize that the message being sent out is really a thought form or energy? Doesn't that person realize that the message being sent is not making a positive contribution in any way, but quite the opposite? Does that person want to take responsibility for helping the planet to remain negative and its energy field to be dense, filled with displeasure, fear, and everything else negative that you can think of? All because of a message on a license plate! Wow, one simple seemingly harmless little act can affect the universe so adversely.

If your day-to-day and mundane conversations are complaining in nature, are you not sending out negative energy? If you are not happy with who you are, are you not sending out unhappiness into the world? If you grumble or express your displeasure over seemingly unimportant things for all of the world to see—is that who you are? Is that who you want to be? Why would anyone want to be that? And most important—what can be done to change?

I remember reading that all catastrophic events that happen in the universe are magnified by the negative energy being sent out from every level. So let's talk about the hate that led up to the catastrophic events of 9/11. Hate is a very powerful negative energy that manifested an event that was horrific. It is so easy to assign total blame to the terrorists and their activities. Did we ever stop to think that when we have a thought about an event, or a strong negative feeling about a person, or a negative reaction to something, that that energy being released attaches itself to other negative energy in the universe, actually magnifying it? So each one of us is very capable of contributing to negative energy in the universe. Where this energy ultimately ends up, no one knows, but I assure you that it is not in a good way. Now it is very clear how one person can truly make a difference.

Simply identifying a thought or a feeling or an action, acknowledging it and transforming it into something positive is what I needed to practice to begin to send my love into the world. Each one of us has thousands of thoughts during any given day, and we are responsible for all of them! So now it simply was a matter of practice so that choices made in how we think, feel, and act were positive. The energy of love is addicting and sustaining, and that is the feeling that I wanted to have. If it doesn't feel like love, just release it and let it dissipate. You simply can request that the negative energy be released and sent into the universe for transformation. You can give it back to God and let God be God and do with it what is necessary!

I made a simple vow to wake up every morning with a smile on my face. And if it wasn't there at first, I made sure I put one on. If I was going to contribute to the world even in the simplest way, a smile visible to others affects their energy throughout the day. I wanted people to see how easy it was to be happy and to realize that happiness is contagious. I wanted the energy to flow into the world and in my relationship with others in a harmonious way. A friend said to me once that it is just as easy to wake up with a smile on your face in the morning than not. I thought about that and wondered what could possibly happen while sleeping at night to put one in a bad mood or to get up on the wrong side of the bed, grumpy for the world to see?

Was your conscious self being forewarned by your subconscious self that stress was at the end of the rainbow? So when you put your little feet on the floor, ready to start your day, were you already anticipating the traffic, the weather, the work, the wife/the husband, and the kids, all interacting and running in each and every direction? Wow, no wonder why so many people are stressed and not smiling in the morning as they are flying off to work. Of course by thinking of these stressful events and actually anticipating them by reacting to them before they even occur, you are actually creating them! Time to change!

There were days that led into weeks where my workload was unmanageable, dealing with deadlines that were not self-imposed but imposed by others. In my job, if I was not on top of the project, then the project could topple on top of me. If I thought about all that I had to do, it was overwhelming. However, I stopped each night and considered what I needed to get done the next day and how I could get each of the items done in a timely manner. It was how I chose to look at my day, my time, and my accomplishments.

At any given day I could go into work and the race would start where I was off and running and not necessarily in the direction of accomplishing anything. At the end of the day I was tired, spending many hours but not accomplishing what was necessary. The fear of the day took over, and I became nonproductive and felt my time usage unsuccessful.

And then I changed the way I viewed time. My day was there for me to accomplish all that I had on my list, and one by one, seeing myself successful allowed me to become successful. I began to move in with the flow of the energy. If I saw a problem, I moved directly to the solution. The problem no longer existed and the solution led to the conclusion. Wow! What a difference—to learn to become a master of bending time in your mind. What an absolute stress reliever!

Wouldn't it be wonderful if we could teach our children how to bend time in their minds? We would allow them to learn in an environment that produced confident, stress-free children who actually grew up enjoying to learn while developing in a healthy and balanced way. In fact, why are we not teaching our children each of these three simple tools? If our future is in the hands of our children, wouldn't we each want our future safe and secure in a loving, positive environment where we all could share our lives in harmony and be in the flow of each other's loving energy?

CHAPTER XIII

Orion's Techniques

*Let yourself begin a time period in which your life is enriched
and you have opened up to receive the gifts not
that you need but the gifts that you want.*

—Orion

With the new millennium came shifts into energies that are predominately represented by Orion. While you are probably familiar with this name, there is nothing magical about the name itself, but there is a lot that is magical about the energy. So what is this Orion energy? Well, it is what we call a universal principle for unconditional and universal love. Those who are able to experience it begin to experience their world differently, and so their world begins to act in a different way in relation to them. Universal love means that you are not only able to experience your love and the love of another, but that of beings on this planet and beings beyond the planet as well. It is like someone takes the knob and turns it up a notch so that you begin to experience levels of love that are far and beyond what you have experienced on this planet. The source of this unconditional love comes from your guides, teachers, and realms of consciousness that you are not yet conscious of, but you will be!

This Orion energy will allow you to live your life in a way that enables you to see things multidimensionally. We have talked about moving forward and upward, and this energy allows you to do just that! It is a gift, a gift that you chose and one that you in fact have created space for. You have brought it to you not because you need it but because you would like to have it. Like many things from spirit, it is unseen but it is not unfelt. When you accept this gift, you will begin to experience tandem multidimensional experiences in your daily life that bring to you the true essence of love. Not the love that has been in limited form for you in the past, but truly powerful states of love. Your world, your immediate world, will begin to change because you have shifted energy. When your energy shifts automatically, there will be a shift in the energy of that space even if no one else feels it; you will experience it not just in your mind, but circumstances around you will actually change. Now is that cool or what?

With the Orion energy, you will experience what we call a stair-step effect. Let's say that your growth plateaus for a few days or a few weeks or months, and then all of a sudden you have an "aha" experience that bumps you up a level. Following this process, you will find that you quickly and easily move forward and upward. Think of it as the stair steps to heaven! What it really is is the stair step to the experience of heavenly love; it doesn't have some of the games that have been attached to it, it doesn't have some of the pitfalls. It doesn't feel like you are going up and down, but rather like you are going horizontally, and then vertically, like stair steps. It has that type of effect because when you have that "aha" experience—you instantly get it. Your energy shifts dramatically, and you go to what we call the next plane of awareness, beginning to see how to use love to more consciously create what you want in your life.

If you look at manifestation techniques from ancient times, really from before the birth of Christ, they have all been in the pursuit of love. You have probably thought to yourself at times, "Well, I need to do this and that and then I will experience love. I need to achieve this level and then I will experience love." And that is quite true. It did feel as if that eternal carrot was dangling out there. And it was in fact designed so that you would be encouraged to grow—not just to grow spiritually but to evolve physically. So for example, if you did not have the experience of being cold, then there would have been less of a motivation to invent heaters or even to have learned how to create fire. There would not have been the motivation. The same is true in a spiritual sense—that carrot was there, and individuals began to learn some very simple manifestation techniques to help them to get to a place where they could have what they needed to be.

Now we are talking about using Orion's techniques not because you need to get to a certain place, but because you want to. So the collection of techniques that we will be describing has actually been designed by the being known as Orion. If you are not familiar with this divine energy, you will know it personally very soon. As you begin to use these manifestation techniques, you will begin to grow your power. True power is not trying to usurp someone else's power. True power is actually recognizing that you are in a world that is unlimited and that you are not going to benefit at someone else's expense. The six manifestation techniques that we will explore are a gift to you because you wanted to become more conscious. You wanted to expand your energy, and so in the terms of growing your power, these techniques are planting the seeds. And as you deem appropriate, you will practice these techniques and they will become automatic. This power will literally grow through the chakras; it begins in the base and the spleen.

Before we delve into the manifestation techniques, please note that some of them will resonate with you immediately, others may take some time, and even others may not resonate at all. This is okay! None of the techniques is better than the others; just concentrate on doing the techniques that resonate with you, and it will result in materialization. You will have the experience of materializing things in your world, on your planet, sometimes instantaneously. So they are all very different, but equally powerful, based upon the experience of love in order for you to grow your power.

The first technique is very simple. It is called the white light technique, and the white light is symbolic of universal love. You take the white light that you visualize in your mind and you put it right into your body. Feel it as you visualize this white light; sense it as it goes right from your mind into your body. Feel it filling you up until your arms go down due to the fullness. You may be wondering why you should do this. Well, the reason is that you must give to yourself before you can give to others. It is the only way to ensure that your energy is as strong as it can be to benefit others around you. This exercise will help you to grow your power through your chakras. You can do it once a day, or you can do it ten times a day, it doesn't matter. The consistency doesn't matter. All that matters is that it feels like love to you when you are doing it. It is a gift that you give yourself. Do you need it? Well some days you actually do need it. But you do it regardless of whether or not you need it. You give yourself that gift.

Now as you are doing this technique, certain ideas might pop into your mind. That is completely normal and is part of the gift! When you are finished with the exercise, just jot down those ideas for later reference. Because this technique helps to clarify and clear your energy patterns, it allows messages from your guides to be received more clearly. However, don't expect to receive messages every time that you perform this technique. Your guides will never give you filler; they will only communicate with you when there is something important for you to know. So just record the thought and see where it takes you, see what manifests (or doesn't) from these messages.

The second technique is called the earth battery technique. The planet that we live on is constantly changing, always moving into a more advanced state. So you have literally a battery of energy that is inside this planet that is its own life form. You can see a demonstration of it more often than not with earth changes, or perhaps with a vortex such as that in Sedona. This earth battery technique is simply aligning your energy with the planet in order to again grow your power. Now this is an Orion technique because people have, since ancient times, looked to the heavens to help them connect the dots in their own lives (pun intended!). The various constellations weren't a story that they were telling themselves, but rather were a story that they were being told.

Those of you that have lain on the ground and looked up at the stars may have already experienced the connection that it can provide with the earth energy. The energy inside the planet is in fact a condensed or concentrated form of what is out beyond the planet. The same is true with your energy. You are in fact a microcosm of what we are talking about. The energy inside of you is reflected to what is out around you. As within, so without. So if you want to change anything outside of you, change what is happening inside of you. What you have inside of you is either what you love or what you fear. So what you have then as you look to Orion and to the other constellations is a concentrated form inside Mother Earth. It is Mother Earth because it is tremendous feminine energy that works in subtle ways, behind the scenes. And so what you will tap into with this earth battery is the energy that will propel you into these greater states of love. It is all about love and all about being surrounded by love.

In order to perform this earth energy technique, use whatever resonates with you on the planet. For example, some use drumming, others use the bowls for toning, others will use a mantra and they get to that vibratory level in their throat. You will need some type of physical bridge to help you make this connection. Even if you use a mantra, you are being physical when you are using it. So begin by standing and feeling the connection with the planet. Very similar to what happens with the unborn child connecting with the heartbeat of the mother. Once you make this connection with the planet, it is like getting to know someone that you didn't know before. Once you get to know them, then the next time that you need assistance it is easy to call on them. Pretty soon you will just have the thought and the assistance will appear; the process will become automatic.

So what you are doing is simply establishing a relationship with the planet. Your vibration is going to connect with the vibrational level of the planet. The interesting thing is that the vibrational level of the planet is constantly changing, and so is yours. So when you do this, it is like having a guitar whose strings need to be retuned after time. To get it to where the tune is supposed to sound, each note needs to be just right. This is what you are doing with this technique. And it means that more of the earth's resources are available, more from this battery that is constantly being recharged is available to you. All that you have to do is use a vibrational technique to get your energies harmonized with the planet. It is constantly changing, constantly accelerating; that is what happens when you go from one level of understanding to the next, from one level of consciousness to the next. When the energy accelerates, it goes to the chakras, and you will become more and more connected with the planet and its resources.

Technique number three is what we call the purple energy. You may be familiar with the concept of purple energy as a symbol for spiritual progress. If you see purple energy when you are meditating, it means that you are in the presence of what we call your spiritual source, and you might refer to it as your higher self or your oversoul. When you start seeing color, you may see purple or bits and pieces of purple, and if you see a small ball of purple energy, this indicates the presence of your spirit guides that are in your spiritual realm of consciousness. They are the beings who are assisting you with lessons from the arcana and are your nonphysical soulmates, or what we call companion counterparts. These are beings that are helping you with your soul's path and are helping you to remember your connection with what you are trying to do spiritually with your own blueprint.

So this purple energy then has to do with your connecting with a particular guide who is going to help you with the Orion energy. Each of your guides is going to be different. While we will describe the function of the guide, the name of your individual guide is something that will have to come to you, if it has not already. When you see the purple energy in your dreams or meditation, allow the name of the guide to be made known to you. This purple energy technique is so very, very simple! Your job is to simply watch for the purple energy in one form or another. Now remember that what you focus on expands, so now that you are conscious of the purple energy, it will expand for you and you will pay more attention to it. So in a sense this is perhaps the easiest technique because all you have to do is pay attention to what is happening around you either metaphysically or even in the physical realm by seeing bits and pieces of purple energy.

When you see this purple energy, it may also be nice to allow yourself in meditation to see if there is any particular thing that your guide wants to communicate to you. If you see the purple energy in a dream, ask your guide when you awake what it is that they are trying to tell you. If you do not receive the message right away, that is okay! All that you can do is ask. This technique is not about precision, but rather about having the presence of the purple energy be known to you so that you are able to pick it out from all of the activities that you have during the day and night.

When you perform this technique, you will be receiving the universal love that we have spoken about earlier. Your guide that appears is present in the purple energy and is there specifically so that it can make a connection with you and strengthen your link with the universe, thereby allowing you to receive universal love and to receive multidimensionally those things that are coming to you. This technique will widen the path of your soul because the more that energy is coming to you, the more that you are able to feel it, see it, and experience it while going about your daily routine. You are not trying to remove yourself from society but are trying to more fully integrate with the universe.

The fourth technique has to do with adjusting your energy consciously. We all have incredible potential for good in this lifetime. This potential doesn't refer to whether or not you are living up to your blueprint, but is based on who you are and what you have learned in other lifetimes. So there are not any individuals or circumstances that can stop you from moving into your potential. The only thing that can stop you or slow you down from achieving your potential is a collection of beliefs about yourself and the mass consciousness beliefs that you have tapped into. Now if you believe something and in fact you know it to be true, that is not exactly a belief; that is a truth. If you believe something not because you know it to be true but because you haven't seen any evidence to the contrary or because someone else believes it or because mass consciousness tells you that is what it is, well those are the beliefs that we are talking about. They are not truths, and they certainly are not universal truths. They are simply what you have learned up to this point. And if you take the blinders off and allow yourself to really open to new possibilities, you will see that exactly what you believe is in fact what is happening in your life. Now you do not believe in things that are limiting simply because others believe it. But a lot of times unconsciously you accept it because you are not consciously aware that there is a different way to live. There are many things that you just don't attend to because you are not conscious of them.

So how do these beliefs relate to adjusting your energy? Well, you do not need to take out a sword and slay those beliefs that do not serve you, and you certainly don't try to change anyone else's opinion, but what you do is to go within and adjust your energy. Adjusting your energy consciously will actually grow your power. So this involves you just taking a look at things that don't feel like love to you. It is really quite simple. During your day, you know what does not feel like love to you. All you have to do is become conscious of it. When you are not conscious of it, you are unconsciously creating your future without questioning whether or not it serves you. Now that you are looking at it, you are ready to make the shift in energy! You don't have to make dramatic changes in your life in order for this to happen. All you have to do is just tell yourself the truth about what does and does not feel like love in your life. In fact, by doing this, the energy will start to shift for you!

When you raise your consciousness, you adjust your energy consciously. We are not saying you adjust your world, but you adjust the thermostat inside of you by raising your consciousness about what you are feeling. This technique does not just serve you in terms of connecting with Orion, but serves you in your day-to-day life. The beauty of this is that as you adjust your energy consciously, you begin to learn about causality—the truth about cause and effect, what really causes what. So those of you that are mentally inclined, you will enjoy this adventure just from the standpoint of seeing how the bits and pieces of the puzzle fall into place. You will begin to get a sense of how your energy is creating your reality. The really great thing about all of this is that once you change something inside of you, the shifts begin to be made around you even without you raising a finger!

This technique that allows you to move into your potential, rather than a modified version of your potential, is a form of self-love. When you clear out those things in your own energy field that don't feel like love, you will begin to tap into universal love. This particular technique feels a bit like processing, but it is more about truth-telling, allowing yourself to know the truth. The only thing to be afraid of is the not knowing as it creates disharmony in the body. After all, knowledge is power! When you know something, you have the ability to change it, not by trying to manipulate or control it, but by changing those things inside of you that have in fact created it.

The fifth technique is called the arrow technique. Have you ever noticed that when people write notes, they often put an arrow or a star by something that is important? Why do we do that? Well, we highlight the important things so that they are easier to remember. Have you ever drawn an arrow or a star to point to something that you don't understand? Well, the being that is doing this marking is your mental body of consciousness. So who goes back and reads all of your annotations? That is your emotional body of consciousness. He or she doesn't want to miss anything! The emotional body says that it is not the facts but the linkage that is the key. This links to that, and I need to understand the entire context of what is going on. So you have inside of you a scientist and a researcher, and then you have a psychologist who wants to put it all together because they are not discrete points but rather a continuum.

The arrow technique is not something that you need to do daily because it may lose its emphasis if you do. On a day that you choose to do it, start with simply writing down something that you find interesting. Don't worry if it seems to link to anything else or not. There is no need to draw an arrow at this point because you are only writing down things that seem interesting and important to you. What this is really similar to is simply observing that which you find interesting or that which you have learned during a particular day. We call it the arrow technique so as not to confuse you with Orion and the collection of stars. The reason that all of this is connected to Orion is that it shows you the details of your life. Your life is much richer than you ever realized when you were just living it rather than observing it! When you become more conscious of what is going on around you, you more easily see the richness of the universe, the web of how everything connects.

The sixth and final technique from Orion is called the Orion energy technique. How fitting! This technique is not difficult and is available to everyone who chooses to use it. It involves, in a sense, spending the day with Orion. Now who is Orion? As we have said before, Orion comes to teach you about unconditional and universal love. Spending the day with Orion and being in Orion's energy shows you worlds beyond yours, which allows your world to make more sense to you. It is very similar to someone who, when frustrated by a certain task, does a more complicated one in order to make the first task look easier. In a sense it is simplified. That is what Orion will do when he takes you to different parts of the universe.

You may be wondering how you will be able to spend time with Orion. Are you going to do a transmigration, or a teleportation, or are you simply going to have the experience of imagining Orion in your mind to do this? Well, the mechanics are actually simple. You just sit with you feet on your floor. Easy enough, right? Try to have a physical open seat next to you, for example an empty chair or sofa, as if you were inviting someone to sit with you. All that you need to do after providing that space is just ask Orion to come in. Now you do understand on a bigger scale that there is no time and that there is no space. These particulars are paradigms for living on our planet so that you can measure you progress. You do have time and space, you have that continuum on our planet. But you do not have it beyond a physical reality. So what you are going to do is provide a space for a segment of Orion's energy to come in.

Just allow yourself to be in Orion's presence, just as Orion is in yours. Empty your mind and let images come to you. You might see the Taj Mahal, and you might see a spacecraft, or you might see the Nile River. Enfirm all of these images, and as you see them in your mind's eye or in your vitae chakra, let Orion tell you about it and let him give you his wisdom. You will see and you will gain his wisdom, and you will get it in a fifth-dimensional capacity, which means with compassion, understanding through compassion and seeing the big picture. When you do this you will have access to his knowledge, and you will once again get bits and pieces of what universal love is. This is all part of what we are talking about with these *aha* experiences. You will be shown not only what Orion wants to show you, but what your higher self wants you to know.

People have described this connection with Orion as being similar to a close relationship with a grandfather. There certainly are similarities in terms of the way that you will be shown unconditional love and encouraged to develop and move forward and upward. Even beyond this, however, is Orion's ability to teach you what he knows about universal principles, how everything operates, and why it is operating in the time and space that you are seeing it. As we have said before, knowledge is power! Orion will help you to be more knowledgeable and therefore more powerful! This is actually why Orion is often thought of in connection with Atlantis. The beings of Atlantis were extremely mentally advanced and did things that we are not even doing yet on this planet at this time. However, due to the political pursuit of mental power, Atlantis eventually imploded. It did not have the emotional, spiritual balance that was necessary in order for individuals to know their own power. They were going outside of themselves, creating things through their mental expertise, but not balancing it with the other energies inside of them. This is why Atlantis imploded and got so heavy that it could not stay afloat and went underwater. Orion will help you in becoming more fully integrated so that you do not suffer the same fate as Atlantis.

The more you do in order to develop spiritually, the more Orion will be able to show you. With Orion's help, you will be able to move forward and upward in a much more advanced and educated way. As you practice these techniques, you may even be able to see Orion materialize into a very big, broad white energy. This demonstrates to you that you are becoming multidimensional. You may also see Orion during visitations at night in the sleep state. You may detect the presence of what looks like an etheric ball of energy with decidedly white overtones. You will be blessed with this presence as long as you remain open to it and follow the techniques that we have outlined. For everyone that does the Orion techniques, Orion becomes the teacher. Then you become the beneficiary, and then you can distribute it to others. You distribute the universal love by what you say, what you do, and who you have become.

You can watch your dreams to see exactly who shows up, what shows up, and what is being delivered because it is the start of a beautiful adventure for you. It is transformative and will allow shifts of energy in this beautiful process that we call life. Let yourself begin a time period in which your life is enriched and you have opened up to receive the gifts, not that you need, but the gifts that you want!

* * * * * * * *

According to Greek mythology, Orion is the name of the brilliant constellation "The Hunter" and is one of the most beautiful and brightest constellations in the sky. Markas describes his energy as magnificent and extremely divine! Others describe him as supremely divine! It is a huge energy as his constellation illustrates. Many cultures have adapted Orion as their hero and have created different myths about him.

One such myth describes the story of Orion, a masterful hunter who is not only the most handsome man in the universe but the greatest in both strength and physique. He is so tall that he is able to walk in the seas, always keeping "his head above water." (Now you know where that expression came from!) In the sky he is pictured as kneeling with his right hand holding a poised club while his left hand holds his catch, a lion. He is wearing his armor with the famed "Orion's belt" easily displayed by three bright stars, also known as the Magi in honor of the three wise men. His sword hanging off his armor is depicted by two bright stars and the Orion nebula. He is flanked by his two hunting dogs: Canis Major and Canis Minor, oftentimes pictured fighting Taurus, the bull. Located close by is Lepus, the hare.

The story describes our hero, Orion, as searching for the perfect love. His first marriage ends when his wife is banished to the underworld for her arrogance. He meets a second love, only to discover her father is jealous and strikes him blind. Now sightless, he travels the sky and looks to the sunrise each morning for healing. There he finds Aurora, the goddess of the dawn, the mother of the winds and the morning star, who falls in love with him. Orion, finding the power of love within, regains his sight. This love, although very powerful, proves short-lived, and his end comes near as he feels the sting of the scorpion sent to him by yet another love, the goddess of hunting and the moon, who reacts with jealousy and possession and decides since she cannot have him, no one else will. Orion's death banishes him to the underworld. There he heals and develops his power within, continuing to fight, regaining both his life and his sight and once again becoming a brilliant, shining star (or stars) for all to see and recognize with his dog, Sirius, by his side. Many books on the universe have their version of Orion. I particularly enjoyed the version presented to you in this chapter, and this and many other myths of the universe, our star system, and the meaning of our personal constellations can be easily found in Catherine Tennant's *The Box of Stars*.

This wonderful energy has brought to us this chapter on his techniques in developing our power though six different exercises. The importance of developing our power, the power that resides within, is necessary to develop for each one of us to find our center. Armed and centered, we can go out and face any and all challenges. With trust and faith, the sky is the limit or rather limitless with possibilities of happiness and joy.

The suggestion is made to bring into your life and practice from the described group of six techniques that you relate to the most. Your energy and Orion's energy can and will connect with your desire to not only meet him but to have him support your growth on earth. My personal favorites are techniques number one, two, three, four, and six. Perhaps you will relate to several, but I will discuss my experience with the five techniques that I have used.

I believe that the first exercise is the simplest and an easy place to start. It is also a wonderful way to introduce yourself to the white light. When you simply visualize your entire body filling up with white light, you can pour it in through your crown chakra or you can send it in as a whirlwind or as a "white tornado," or you can invent your own visual of sending white light into your body. Whatever makes sense to you and whatever gets the job done is all that is important. However you choose to visualize it is fine, as long as you simply relax and allow yourself to feel the beautiful white light filling your physical structure. This is a great introduction to feeling energy. The fact that it is the energy directed by Orion is wonderful as this energy or white light is hugely felt, just as his presence his hugely felt in the sky. It may also be the first time you have ever felt this gift of Orion, this universal principal for unconditional and universal love.

When I feel this white light in and through my body, I can feel the energy moving through every one of my chakras. I feel the energy come out through me, above me, behind me, and below me. I sense that I am surrounded by this beautiful white light and that my aura is full. I feel complete. This is a memory that I want to hold onto. This is a feeling that I want to repeat again and again. This is a gift that I want to experience and, as Orion has stated, not because I have to but because I want to. I practice this gift of love often as I want to live my life as love and send it out through me into the universe as my gift back to Orion.

The second technique is a technique that can be done during all seasons. However, your climate may determine that the warmer months are more beneficial in connecting to the earth. It is far easier to lie on the ground and simply connect to the earth's energy when the conditions are prime. However, that doesn't mean that you cannot walk in the rain or walk in the snow and still cement your connection with the earth.

I have found when I do the earth battery technique that I love the way my pulse connects with the movement of the earth. I have been able to develop a sensitivity to the earth and can sense a movement or shifting. I never would have understood what that meant if I hadn't experienced it for myself. Lying quiet, relaxing, and allowing your awareness to kick in is a lesson in itself. When your awareness lets you sense the rumblings deep inside, that is not only a reward but helped me to understand the meaning that we are all "one." It is also similar to being in the ocean and allowing the pulse of your heart to meet the great wave of the ocean. Again and again, as you breathe and feel the beat of your heart, a connection is made as you consciously connect to the ocean's wave. How does this make you feel? The connection is vitally strong, and the life of the ocean is the same life energy that is in your heart!

There are many other ways to discover how your vibrational frequency can connect and accelerate as you choose to experience the gifts in nature. I am sure you can ask any child to describe how their body feels when they lie down on the grass and will be delighted with their answers!

The third technique is also a very simple way to see your guides, teachers, or angels. I have always seen color when I close my eyes. Some mornings I wake up and I can see an entire color show. Sometimes I run through all of the colors of the rainbow. The colors are fluid and move slowly to and fro, shifting in and out. Very peaceful! Then there are the moments when I close my eyes, perhaps lying down to nap or sleep, and I see purple. This has been going on for such a long time that when I see the color, it brings a wonderful smile to my face and I feel very much loved deep inside. I often ask the energy if I have a message, and if so I request it to come during my dream sleep, and I try to always request that when I wake I remember it! This technique is again so very simple. A few deep breaths, helping to relax the body and mind, and being aware of what comes in is what it is all about. Notice that when you meet the "purple" energy and you breath in and out, the intensity of the purple changes. You are capable of your own color show, and you can also give your purple energy a name or a nickname that makes sense to you. You may even be able to sense who this guide is for you by the way you feel or what is going on in your life when the energy comes in for you.

The fourth technique is also another technique that is done consciously. I think when you focus on something and/or put your intention out there, you are able to accomplish exactly what you are meant to. I have had to really look at my belief system. Being brought up in a house by a domineering mother, I don't think I owned any thoughts. My thoughts were oftentimes simply a reflection of my mother's beliefs. It took me many years of sifting and shifting to figure out what beliefs made sense to me. Little by little I released some, never to be seen or heard from again, while other beliefs I simply relaxed. Or perhaps I needed to mold a new set around an issue based on personal experience. Shifting, adjusting, and being flexible are fundamental to this experience. If the only constant on our planet is that of change, it made sense to me that not to change a belief simply because it was something that I was brought up with kept me limited, stagnant, and undeveloped. However, when I was able to relax my belief system, I raised my consciousness and actually was able to expand my energy, allowing it to shift and grow with me. I asked the following question about everything: how do I feel about—whatever, or how does—whatever—make me feel? I listened to the answer. I learned what made not only me tick, but how the universe ticked as well. I taught myself by simply being open to shift and change with the universe how to get in the flow of the universe. I became aware of my energy and how it affected not only others but the universe. I watched and experienced how I created my own reality. I not only evolved and expanded who I was but had fun doing it!

The last technique which I have practiced is the sixth one described by Orion. I invited Orion into my life, this beautiful huge energy, and asked him to help me develop spiritually. I oftentimes asked him to accompany me out in the universe. I would fill up my physical body with white light and let it expand and expand and expand, surrounding myself in every direction so that both my physical body and aura were completely filled. I could visualize this beautiful white cloud of light as far away from me as I wanted to. I asked that this white light accompany me traveling from one part of the country to another, from one part of this planet to another planet, and from one part of this universe to another universe. Literally, the sky is the limit! Or rather, a better expression is that "the sky is filled with the *Limitless Possibilities* of unconditional and universal love." They are there for me to experience and discover. I have felt it, and I continue to feel it as part of what I do and part of who I am.

So life with Orion is indeed beautiful. Life as we know it can be expanded and changed into a beautiful adventure. This adventure using the gifts that Orion has given is our opportunity to discover the truly wonderful feelings of unconditional and universal love. They are available to everyone, and my suggestion would be to go for it and allow yourself to develop and feel the unconditional love deep within.

CHAPTER XIV

The Company You Keep

You are the strongest you can be when you believe in something!

—St. Bridget, 2007

Just as your parents probably taught you when you were a child, there is great importance in the company that you keep. As you know, there are seven primary chakras, with those that are spiritually oriented in the healing sense having an eighth chakra. What you may not be aware of, however, is that the intensity with which they spin determines what type of individuals you attract to you. That is why we attract individuals that may be very spiritually motivated, or politically motivated, or mentally motivated, or emotionally motivated. The strength of the chakra attracts to you the type of individuals that you are friends with as well as that you work with. Now, that isn't to say that you will always be in harmony with your coworkers. You may not feel particularly aligned with them, but in knowing that you have attracted them into your life, you will be able to make adjustments so that your energy will spiral upward. The energy of your chakras will help you to do this; they will prevent you from getting hung up on the little problems and dramas of your life. You will no longer feel as if you need to prove that you are right or that you need to defend your ego. Instead you will continue in your quest to move forward and upward.

You may find yourself thinking that there are individuals in your life that you would frankly never consciously choose to be in your life, those that do not feel like love to you. Well, in order to fix this, all that you have to do is adjust your life and continue to see the perfection in all things. When you do this, your chakras will reflect this shift in energy, and you will begin to attract in more of what you say that you actually do want. As we have said before, if you want to change anything outside of yourself, you first have to change what is going on inside of you. This is very powerful because it will allow you to attract what you want into your life, including the company you keep!

The pattern of the energy flows in your chakras can vary. For example, the energy flows in a clockwise direction when you are in the northern hemisphere on your planet and when you are in the upper reaches. Ideally you do want to have your chakras' energy flowing in the clockwise direction. Because the chakra energy is part of your own chi energy, at times the energy field of certain chakras reverse themselves. If you happen to have this occur for more than just a few of your chakras, then you are in what we call reverse polarity. Think of it like an inside-out umbrella. It is not really going to be able to do a very good job of keeping your energy field whole and vibrant. Therefore it is very important to make sure that your chakras' energy is in fact moving in the right direction.

In addition to the importance of your chakras' energy spinning in a clockwise direction is the speed at which it is spinning. For those of you who have studied light body consciousness, you know that it is very helpful to focus on clearing and cleansing the body so that the chakras are not impeded. If they are not impeded, then they are going to spin faster just by virtue of your gaining consciousness. This means that your vibrational frequency will accelerate, and it will help you to evolve to a higher level. This does not mean that you should try to control the speed at which each of your individual chakras spin—i.e., I want my communication chakra to spin faster because I need to give a presentation at work. Instead, you want to reflect and focus on the big picture. You want to concentrate on your own spiritual growth so that all of your chakras' energy flows in the same direction and with a greater vibrational frequency.

Finally, the dynamic between and among your chakras is also very important. There are actually linkages between our chakras, very similar to the ley lines on our planet. Remember that our bodies, our souls, are microcosms for the planet and that the planets are microcosms for universal understanding. So what is happening inside of you is exactly what is happening on the planet on a larger scale. You have ley lines and you have vortices. The vortices are the chakras, and the ley lines are what connect the chakras. So you want to have a good flow not just within the chakras but among the chakras as well. Think of it as keeping the telephone lines clear so that good, quick, effective communication can take place with ease.

Now that we have covered the importance of your chakras' energy in attracting individuals into your life, we now will take a look at how the energies of Atlantis and Lemuria affect this attraction process. You may have done some reading on these energies in the past, but in case you have not or you are looking for a reminder, we will summarize these energies here before we discuss their effect on the world around us.

The Lemurians

Old Lemurians:

If someone is an old Lemurian, they believe that every person operates the way that they do. They are very spiritually based, and they believe that everyone else operates that way as well. Often it is the Old Lemurians that get walked on as they don't feel that they have any right to set their boundaries. Why not? Well, they feel that everyone is going to operate the way that they do, that everyone loves the planet the way that they do, and that there is enough for everyone, so no one would ever need or want to steal from another. Old Lemurians therefore can get very wounded when someone doesn't behave in the same way that they do, when someone doesn't do things their way.

New Lemurians:

A New Lemurian has the energy of understanding that individuals are going to operate in different ways because they have different heritages, different backgrounds, and different blueprints. And so they don't assume that everyone acts the way that they do, nor do they assume that they are supposed to. A New Lemurian therefore has more of a balance emotionally when compared with the clouded vision of the Old Lemurian. Unlike Old Lemurians, New Lemurians allow for the fact that individuals have different agendas and that, on a bigger scale, everything is perfect. They therefore have a greater level of tolerance and understanding, which helps protect them from being wounded when people don't act the way that they do.

Out-of-Control Lemurians:

An out-of-control Lemurian is someone who doesn't want to be on the earth plane at all. They feel too wounded and that it is just too hard to be here. Many of these out-of-control Lemurians are the individuals who use addictive substances as a form of escaping the unhappiness that they feel on the earth plane. They use alcohol or drugs to escape rather than staying conscious and evolving.

Enlightened Lemurians:

To be an Enlightened Lemurian, now this is the quest! This is the holy grail, if you will, for those who are spiritually based in this lifetime. So they are connected universally but from a spiritual perspective. If an individual is a Lemurian, he or she is moving toward enlightenment through an expansion of how he or she connects with their guides and teachers or spiritual beings which are in and around the body frame and that they operate with an imminence within their energy field that looks to be vibrationally pure light.

We will talk about this momentarily, but for now we want to compare these Lemurians to the Atlantian energy.

The Atlantians

Old Atlantians:

An Old Atlantian is someone who views things as black and white. They believe that it is this way or that way only, and they use their successes to define their world. They also put much more stock or value in people who are mentally based rather than spiritually based, and in general, they are set in their ways. If you think about it, the way that we are raised often supports this way of thinking. For example, many of us were told that you have to put your nose to the grindstone and accomplish things in order to be of value in this world. So Old Atlantians are really just doing things the old-fashioned way. When our planet was three-dimensional, this was exactly what needed to be done in order to succeed. You needed to do things trial and error, and you needed to do things one step in front of the other. So there is a good reason why Old Atlantians did very well, and still do very well, on our planet because the planet supported that very mentally based way of behaving. Since the shifting of the planet into the fourth and now the fifth dimensions, however, the energy is no longer here to support the Old Atlantian way of living. Unless these beings can adapt to change, they may be sentenced to living a life of frustration as they will not understand why what used to work no longer does!

New Atlantians:

A New Atlantian is a being who is balanced mentally and emotionally, unlike New Lemurians that are balanced spiritually and emotionally. The Atlantians understand that your emotionality has an intelligence and so you can't understand everything just by looking at the facts; they understand that you can't understand everything just by putting things into categories. The New Atlantians understand that there are things that are unseen that exist and move the world. They don't necessarily pretend to understand spirituality, but they do understand that there is a whole universe, if you will, of other things that they can't see or compute.

Out-of-Control Atlantians:

Out of Control Atlantians are those that make the Lemurians quake in their shoes! Much of this dislike or distrust is from cellular memory of when the Atlantians took control of the Lemurians. In the simplest terms, the Out-of-Control Atlantian is a bully. They will try to get you to do it their way either by manipulation or intimidation or both; for to them it is all about power. So an Out-of-Control Atlantian wants to capture the planet just as the Out-of-Control Lemurian wants to get off of the planet!

Enlightened Atlantians:

An Enlightened Atlantian is someone who is able to see the big picture and is in fact very universally or cosmically connected. As our century progresses, you will be able to see many Enlightened Atlantians as philanthropists or benefactors who are focusing on using the energy of money and other resources for the benefit of the whole. For example, those individuals who would distribute their resources for research for an end to global warming, or spearheading a group that is looking to distribute clean water for the masses, or for research in the area of transportation without having any toxins in the air.

Having reviewed each of these types of individuals, it becomes fairly easy to identify their effect on the world. For example, it probably does not surprise you to hear that it is the Out-of-Control Atlantians who start most of the world's wars because of their constant pursuit of power. When you see a tragic event such as a mass suicide, this has usually been orchestrated by an Out-of-Control Lemurian who believes that the world is too painful to endure. In any event, the energies of both the Lemurians and the Atlantians are very powerful, with the primary difference being that the Atlantian energy is primarily mentally based and the Lemurian energy is spiritually based. So it is not a question of good or bad, it is a question of perspective.

Now, remember that every one of you has had other lifetimes on this planet. Some of you have had a number of them and some just a few, but for all of you the experiences of every lifetime you have had and everything that you have done in between lifetimes are a part of you now. When you decided to have these other lifetime experiences, you spun off and became a separate soul from your higher self, or spiritual self, and began to accumulate experiences. Some of these experiences were delightful, and some of them turned out to be very painful. But when you understood the lesson, you then let go of the pain and it became a blessing in disguise. In any event, you have had experiences on both sides of this Lemurian and Atlantian fence, and all of these experiences have blended for you.

If you have had lifetimes in both Atlantis and Lemuria, the question is not if you are Lemurian or Atlantian, although you do have predominance in one area or another. The question is when you have had these lifetimes, what did you learn and how did you integrate the mental and the spiritual? When you are spirit and before you choose a physical incarnation, you have both the Atlantian and Lemurian energies. That is the exact same thing as saying you have spiritual understanding and you have mental aptitude; you have consciousness. And so the bigger issue then is whether or not you are learning what you need to learn in these lifetimes in order to move you forward in a very powerful way. What we mean by power is not you usurping anyone else's power, but rather going within and finding the energy inside of you that knows how to do all of this already. Whatever you have set out for yourself in this lifetime, you have energy inside of you that knows how to achieve it; you just need to access it. Remember, because ours is a planet of contrast and balance, we need both types of energy; neither is good or bad.

The question now becomes whose company you keep. If you socialize with Atlantians, are they Old, Out-of-Control, New, or Enlightened? What type of Lemurians do you socialize with if that is your preferred energy? Remember that there is no right answer to this question. There is no judgment here as this question is simply meant to help you to understand the framework within which you and others view life so that you can create win-win situations. In other words, answering this question will help you to better comprehend the filters that you and others use to look at the world. As you gain consciousness, you are trying to at first identify your filters, and then you can begin to let them go. As long as you are able to acknowledge your perspective and that of others, you will no longer be looking at the world through a filter but rather at a limitless world without any restrictions.

In order to further step into enlightenment, there are twelve steps that you can follow that will help you to create this win-win situation that we just mentioned. Feel free to practice these exercises in any particular order; simply follow your heart in terms of what feels right to you at the time.

Enlightenment Exercises

1) Allow your heart to reach out to all of those that you don't know. Strive to understand the plight of those less fortunate and envision your heart reaching out to them. There are many individuals who are faceless, nameless, and to heal them in the fifth-dimensional way, you will need to visualize them and to be in the energy field of enlightened compassion.

2) Let yourself receive the wisdom of the ancients! Allow yourself to receive this wisdom nonverbally from the ancient Lemurians and the ancient Atlantians. These are beings who are not physical on the earth plane any longer, but whose wisdom was the hallmark of success in respective societies. Let yourself be open and relax your mind as best you can so that you are open to absolutely anything that they present to you. Doing this will not only move you forward in terms of your enlightenment, but it will also make you feel better physically and emotionally because, after all, this is your heart's desire.

3) Honor the concept of the inner child. You do a lot with your emotional body of consciousness. You become a champion in a sense for the inner child and the emotional body. You cannot move into a state of enlightenment when your inner child has open wounds that have not been healed. Therefore when you become a champion for your inner child, you not only help yourself to move forward into the light, but you will be an example for others to be a champion for their inner children as well.

4) Learn about Atlantian energy through writing and meditation. To understand the power of the Atlantian energy is important as the secrets of the Atlantian civilization and the power of the Atlantian energy is very helpful on our planet today, although not many individuals have researched it.

5) Begin to see your world with new eyes. This is also a fourth-dimensional concept, but it carries very heavily into the fifth dimension. This means that you should question all the mass consciousness filters that you have adopted either consciously or subconsciously. Ask yourself, "Do I really need to believe that anymore?" It doesn't matter if you believed it ten minutes ago, from this moment forward, let it go and look at your world with new eyes. This will give you a chance to see not what mass

consciousness has believed and not what your filter shows you, but you will be able to see the shift in your consciousness which will lead to a shift forward to a much grander state of enlightenment.
6) Focus and feel the energy of enlightenment through the Lemurian energy. The Lemurians did not really care if they become conscious, they just wanted to become enlightened. Just sit by yourself, feel, and visualize yourself bringing in the information and receiving the wisdom of the Lemurian ancients. All you need to do is just be open to receive and to get glimpses of what it feels like to be in a society like Lemuria.
7) Understand aspects of wellness. You have already started doing this by listening to tapes, reading books, and practicing various techniques. Getting in touch with one's own physical energy is the prelude to wellness because each individual entity on this earth plane has a unique or one-of-a-kind energy.
8) Believe in yourself and in the power of your desire to move forward. Every time that you feel a lack of confidence, check in with your bodies of consciousness—your physical, spiritual, emotional, mental, and spiritual healing—and see what you can do to gain more confidence. Once you get in touch with that, ask your guides and teachers to help you. Gaining confidence will help you to gain enlightenment.
9) Bring together the information of body, mind, and spirit to help propel you forward to the next big window of opportunity.
10) Let the aromas for your energy field work individually without the combining of any. We spoke earlier about the synergy of combining aromas, but now you should learn about the attributes of the individual aromas. So experiment with aromas and allow yourself to experience them in a superconscious way. Then write about these experiences so that you can reflect on them in the future.
11) Simplify your life. Don't just simplify your interests, but try to simplify all things in your life so that you can move forward. If you do this, you will find that when your days are not so busy, your energy field and your immediate surroundings will have a feeling of less is more. This is because when you're your life is simplified, you can bring in the wisdom of the ancients and bring up your personal wisdom. This will allow you to take a very big leap on your path toward enlightenment.
12) Allow yourself to defocus and create the opportunity for developing the third eye, the vitae chakra. Make a request for the universe, and while you do this, defocus your eyes so that the third eye has a chance to develop as it is being used. Ask your guides for information to come to you either metaphysically or physically and that this

information will support your own Atlantian experiences. You will feel more centered on the earth plane as you feel those Atlantian lifetimes now work for you. Make the request, let go of the picture of what that will look like, look out into the universe, and defocus your primary eyes to allow for the development of your vitae chakra. After you practice this exercise for about a month, you will see a significant shift forward and upward.

* * * * * * *

When I heard about the categories mentioned in this information about Lemurian and Atlantian energy and its categories, I needed to figure out where I fit into all of this. I had read the histories of both of the civilizations of Lemuria and Atlantis, and I could relate to the information in each group. As I thought about my strengths and weaknesses in this lifetime and how I had lived my life, i.e., my values, my decision-making processes, my preferred thought patterns, my heart's desires, and my emotions, I pretty much concluded that I had developed Atlantian patterns as well as Lemurian patterns.

My heart and my emotions, including the empathy and compassion I bring into my thinking role, help to define me as having Lemurian energy. I do and have always been able to see things from a spiritual bent. My organizational skills, complete with establishing and running a business, help to define me as having Atlantian energy. So I correctly surmised that I was pretty fairly divided, having near equal lifetimes in both of the civilizations. This was confirmed for me in a channeling so that I could understand my strengths and could assimilate both energies so that as I was moving forward, I was also moving upward with the biggest strides possible.

Next I was to decide just what category I am most closely aligned to. As we are growing and evolving and moving forward, it is important to see where you have been, where you are now, and where you are moving to. This was an interesting exercise because of the sense of movement in your development—your energy is constantly changing and expanding. So in an honest assessment, I discovered that during my lifetime I was a combination of New Lemurian and New Atlantian energies currently moving into the enlightened arenas of both.

It is an everyday process of putting one step in front of the other. Throughout these chapters, we describe how each of us creates our own reality. We have learned that we do so by how we think, feel, and act. When we process this, we can clearly see where we stand on all issues, and we can decide if we need to relax our belief system a little more to allow us to move into another arena.

By becoming a fifth-dimensional person, and living in the fifth dimension every day, you can see how you would be moving into the areas of "Enlightenment." It is a process, and it takes time to be able to adopt all of the fifth-dimensional ideals into your life. Staying in the present moment and buying into its power, and living in that power, is what allows you to move into your place of empowerment, your center. And as we will continue to learn, as we change our thinking within, we also should change our life or experience without, so we end up enhancing both areas and not living in two different worlds. In other words, your private self and how you chose for the world to view yourself should not be separate, they should be the same. Being comfortable with self in any surrounding is important as you should be experiencing life the same in all your arenas.

The concept of motion is again an important one as we are always becoming, or at least we should be. Change is not only a constant on Mother Earth, but we should also be in the constant state of change. If we can assume that every living thing on our planet is in a form of change, then we would be able to start viewing change as necessary for growth and development.

Have you ever heard the expression "NO Change is NO Change"? This little phrase is so simple yet says so much. When you think about how a person who experiences "no change" actually exists, it is alarming to think of all of the individuals who actually prefer mere existence over change. It is so easy to be a stagnant human being: no growth, no development, no challenges, comfortable with how things are, and comfortable with self as is! In short, no change means simply existing.

I do not believe that we were made to exist. Being a spiritual being that has come down to Planet Earth to experience a lifetime on a physical plane with a physical body speaks to two important concepts. The first is that a spiritual being is constantly being reawakened to remember how and why spirituality is lived within our soul, being true to our soul's purpose and our heart's desire. Once this thought comes into our consciousness, it is pretty apparent that everything we do needs to be done from a spiritual perspective, looking at things from the bigger perspective and reminding ourselves why we are here and what we are to accomplish while here. Second, didn't we choose to come to Planet Earth? The only constant on Planet Earth is change, so how can we come here to live and experience change and then not change? This makes no sense.

As I was nearing completion of this book, a beautiful ancient energy, four million years old, has come and introduced himself to me, King Mehe Mehe—a king of Lemuria. He is jovial and round, with a crown of flowers around his head, and has longish white hair. He reminds me of a Hawaiian Father Christmas! He is the embodiment of love and joy. I think you get the picture. His purpose in introducing himself to me is to let me know that he has stepped into my auric field and will remain with me throughout the rest of my life. He told me that he is proud of my growth and development and wanted me to know where I stood in the arenas discussed above. He told me that he could feel the love in this book, and that he had witnessed me increasingly writing from a stronger place of love during these last few years. He has watched me evolve, and the more I wrote and the longer I worked on this project, the more love came into my bodies of consciousness. He wanted me to know that all of my five bodies of consciousness have moved totally into the framework of love. I had entered and fully live in the fifth dimension, experiencing all the beauty and possibilities that it has to offer. I was given the gift and I have received it as such. I have honored it and evolved with it and in it. My world has changed, my consciousness has shifted, and I am living totally in this new energy in the new paradigm. As the shift was occurring outside of me, I have consciously evolved so that it was occurring within me. I not only "got it," but I have "made it"—I have arrived!

Oh my, my response was not only evident in the delight that I felt, but I was so proud that my hard work not only was very successful but that I had attracted in this beautiful being. Humbled and honored, I thanked him for coming and told him how much I appreciated his love. I feel his love, and my auric field glows from his love! Life just doesn't get any better than that.

And so as you review the list of descriptions of both the Atlantian and Lemurian types on earth and you begin to identify who you are, remember to be open so that you can see where you are moving toward and be open to receiving the beautiful energies that come your way. And as we have heard a thousand times, it is not the destination but the journey that adds these riches to our life. Receive anything and everything that comes your way with a smile—it doesn't matter whether the smile is on your face or deep inside as long as it is there. If you begin to see the absurdities in life and in what comes your way, pat yourself on the back as the healing effects of laughter will certainly take any sting or tightness away from your heart.

I will mention one little secret to help my Lemurian heart stay full of love and light. When you experience what it is like to have no tightness in your heart, you will be lighthearted. I was given a huge suggestion to simplify my life and to reduce stress. It was suggested to me by one of these beautiful benevolent beings to take anything and everything that is bothering me—it doesn't matter what or who it is about—and simply write it out on a little piece of paper and put it in a little box. Coincidentally, I had purchased some years ago seven teeny little boxes while traveling and brought them home. Not knowing what I was going to do with them, I simply put them in a drawer. When this suggestion was made to me, the seven little boxes came to mind. I wrote my little concerns or issues out and put them in their own little box. Guess what? Seven concerns for seven boxes. Who would have thought? Again, seemingly unrelated acts when brought together create these events which synchronistically all tie together! Imagine that! The bonus, of course, is that your heart is lighter and you can move through life with a lighter load, knowing and trusting that the universe is going to resolve all of your concerns. Yes, you have given them over to God, and again, you choose to let God be God and release them with love and thanks!

CHAPTER XV

Catch The Rainbow

Treat the destiny as a treated friend you have guided with premeditation and wonder and you will be led to places both known and unfamiliar. All places necessary to greet and all dimensions to infinity!

—*Spirit, 2007*

All of us have experienced enough to know that what you focus on expands. That is a miracle in and of itself. If you focus on what you believe, you will achieve it. But what looks like a miracle is usually something that happens instantaneously rather than over a prolonged period of time. For example, imagine that someone is in need of healing for their diabetes. If the Christ energy came and instantaneously healed this person, this would of course be called a miracle. If, however, you were not tuned in to the possibility of miracles and the concept that what you focus on expands, you may be biding your time waiting for the scientific community to discover a cure for diabetes. Those are the two ends of the spectrum. In between you have all of the phenomena for the performance of miracles.

This middle ground, if you will, is the area in which you become consciously involved in the development of your own life. This is an incredibly exciting area because you have the power to manifest what it is that you would like or need in your own life. Don't allow yourself to be overwhelmed with fear of failure or rejection, but instead focus on what it is that you do want in your life and pursue it to the best of your ability. Embrace your inner child as you do this and reassure them that you will be walking hand in hand with them on this life journey, and that together you can accomplish anything.

With you, the adult, helping your inner child, you can move forward; sometimes you move slowly with baby steps, and other times you move with giant strides. Whatever the pace happens to be, this is the process that will allow you to spiral upward. Again, your energy will draw to you those things you love and those things you fear. Therefore as you dissipate the fear, what come to you are those things that you love. Now we are not saying that miracles aren't above and beyond what you would expect to see on this planet. But we are saying the more that you develop in areas on your blueprint, the more you attract into your life those miraculous opportunities that you never felt would come to you.

Now this process of spiraling upward will certainly not be a continuous one. There will be days when you feel you are really moving forward, or upward, and then those days when you feel overcome by your fear. First of all, acknowledge the fear and accept that this is a completely natural part of the process. If you are not conscious of the fear, it will take over your life and dictate the direction that you will take; it will dictate your beliefs about what will be accomplished. When you ignore the fear, it is as though it becomes an invisible veil shielding you from that which you really want in your life.

As long as you recognize the fear, the healing can take place.

So the good news is all you have to do is to identify where the fear is that is holding you back in an area where you want to see success. Now having said that, we are not asking or even implying that you do this alone. You have spirit guides and teachers that are there to help you. You have experts in the nonphysical realm, in the spiritual realm, to help you. You have the angels and the archangels, you have the experience of relatives that have passed over that you are very close to, or even soul mates. You have your spiritual source, which is your spiritual heritage. Yet another level up, you have your birthright angels, and you keep going up level after level until you get to God. With all of these wonderful helpers there for you, you must simply be aware of what it is that is limiting you in order to get in touch with the energy inside of you that needs development.

It is also important to remember that your guides, and teachers, your birthright angel, your spiritual source, all of the different types of beings that are assisting you have a much easier time if your feet are not planted in cement. In other words, if you are moving forward, even taking those baby steps, then your spirit guides and teachers have a greater opportunity to help you because you have initiated the momentum. As we all know, it is much easier to assist something that is fluid, something that is in motion, than something that is stubborn and immobile.

Miracles are developed through manifestation and through materialization. To summarize the difference between these two things, manifestation is something that you do in advance. An example of this is focusing or visualizing something and then having success with it; it might not have happened exactly the way you have visualized it, but it happens just the same. Materialization, on the other hand, is something that all of a sudden is right there in your path and forces you to make the choice of moving into it or retreating from it. So materialization is something that you have unconsciously attracted into your life. It is an opportunity, and you either take advantage of it or you retreat. And the only reason why you would retreat from a positive opportunity is if you have a fear about something. You may tell yourself, "Well I am not qualified or good enough to do this," and you retreat.

So those who want to develop their energies normally feel more comfortable with manifestation techniques. You might say, "Well all right, I want to develop for myself a good career path, so every day before I go into my place of employment I am going to visualize it being a positive experience." That is one way to do it. If you have a very strong connection with the Christ energy, you might instead say, "Well every day before I go into my place of employment I am going to ask for the Christ energy to lead the way to pave the path for me." There are many, many visualization techniques, all of which can be quite successful.

Materialization is not something that you do in advance consciously, but it is something that you bring into your auric sphere. You bring it into your energy as a result of what you have been doing all along, all of your development. So that phrase, "Be careful what you ask for because you may get it" is so very true. If you have been developing certain areas, and then all of a sudden you have this opportunity right in front of you, know that you brought that in by developing your energy moving into expertise, from experience into expertise. You moved into expertise, and again your energy attracts in exactly what you have become.

So let us go back to what all of this has to do with catching the rainbow. A rainbow looks to be a miracle of nature. And a lot of you, when you see a rainbow, automatically think that it is good luck or has a good fortune. The experience of seeing a rainbow can make you feel so in harmony with nature. You feel very privileged, you become very present in the moment, and your inner child is delighted that this gift of love is being presented to you. And it portends the possibility of miracles; you feel that if I see this rainbow, then I just know that everything is going to be all right.

You may feel this same wonderful feeling when you get into your car, turn on the radio, and a song starts that was clearly sent to you from one of your guides. You don't feel alone. You are reconnected to those beings that you love and to the universe itself that you love. To be living in this remarkably wonderful universe is overwhelming. It doesn't matter if you are on Planet Earth or if you get to go to Venus or you go over to the star systems Sirius or Orion. It doesn't matter as it is all extraordinary, it is all unique. So what happens then when you feel connected is that you feel unlimited, even if it is just for a brief moment. You are unlimited. It sets you up in a direction that feels successful.

Now if you see a rainbow and it lasts in the sky for five minutes and then it goes away, you might carry the feeling of that rainbow for another hour or even for another day, but eventually you go on back to whatever it is that you were worrying about before you saw the sign. Once you have an area that needs to be healed, once you have that open wound, it is too late to not have it. You may say to yourself, "All right, I have seen the rainbow and I do not have anymore worries," but the inner child will go back later and say, "I feel vulnerable in this area, I feel very restricted, I feel uncomfortable, I feel like I am a failure." So seeing the rainbow is not going to change what your inner child is thinking if there is an open wound, but it does give you pause for thought. Just for a few moments perhaps or maybe a whole day after such an experience, you feel the synergy of that particular miracle. So little by little it begins to lift you up. It is not a replacement for healing that which needs to be healed, but it gives you a boost; it gives you a head start.

So the idea, the concept, of catching the rainbow refers to allowing the miracles of life to motivate you and to give you the momentum to move forward. If fears come up, you deal with those fears. So to catch the rainbow means that you are allowing yourself to move forward not in the old-fashioned way but by allowing your energy to be affected and to be influenced by these miracles.

Whenever you think about the concept of a rainbow, look to the end of it and visualize what you are looking for, the pot of gold at the end of the rainbow. The pot of gold is the success that comes with the completion of what it is that you are developing, the task at hand, and how you are moving from being experienced to being an expert. So the pot of gold at the end of the rainbow is the success that happens from your accomplishment. Now to catch the rainbow means that you get that energy and all that it entails into your own system, into your own energy field, and then you become again like the little train in *The Little Engine that Could* who says "I think I can," and then "I think I can go up that hill," and then pretty soon says "I know I can." To catch the rainbow is to catch confidence, confidence that the universe is supporting you and that you are plugged into your guides, your teachers, and God and the feeling that the way that this is accomplished is through the feeling of beauty.

Back when the planet was three-dimensional, the only way to succeed was to use your mental skills, and those mental skills were lists of things, and you would get very organized. So it required a lot of mental energy. Now that you are fifth-dimensional, learning things and doing things the old-fashioned way will mean that you will eventually get it accomplished, but you are not getting the support of the planet. Why? Because the planet is fifth-dimensional, the planet supports those who see perfection—to see the rainbow if you will, where there had been the illusion of imperfection. This is what the planet supports. If you do things the new-fashioned way, if you catch the rainbow, you take that energy of beauty, the energy of miracles, the energy of enlightenment, and you begin to associate with that energy. You begin to see yourself in those terms: beauty and enlightenment. Then the development is as joyful as the outcome.

Many times individuals say "I don't want to be involved. I just want the miracle to get here." So if you want to live your life in a joyful way, remember it is the process that you live. The end result is just a fleeting moment. If you want to say "I am only living for the result and I don't care how difficult the process is," then you might as well just do it mentally and it will be a self-fulfilling prophecy for you. You will create a life that is very difficult due to the mental strain that you will have in trying to accomplish the next thing, develop the next skill. And if and when you do get the desired result, it is not going to feel like a miracle because it is not one—the end result is simply a result of your hard work. But if in fact your energy is powerful and you are connected to the universe and you are connected to your guides and teachers, you are not doing it alone but you are doing it the new-fashioned way. You are allowing yourself to be a part of the process and to have confidence in your energy as a way of either creating the miracle through manifestation or attracting the miracle through materialization.

When individuals are faced with situations or events in their life that need healing, it is important to see the solution through the eyes of someone who sees it as a win-win situation rather than a win-lose situation. The power ultimately is inside of you, it is just a question of how conscious you are of it. The power inside of you is not a power that is to usurp anyone else's power or to overtake someone to make them do it your way; it is in fact a very pure, a very clean way of identifying that your development reaps rewards. And the reward that comes from your development is a stronger energy that will bring to you as you clear out your self-imposed limitations. It will bring to you those things that you always said you want to create, and a lot of times those individuals are waiting for someone or something outside of them for that to occur. Not only are you not to wait for it, you are not to expect it as it is not necessary. So a lot of the concepts that all of you learned about fourth-dimensional living: less is more, helping inner children learn to play, keeping things simple, attracting in what you love or what you fear, power is in the present moment, all of these principles that you learned fourth-dimensionally can be put in visual concepts of the fifth dimension, such as the rainbow. When or where you become very present moment, it is very simple: you do play, and you recognize the elements of love that come up from inside of you when you see the rainbow! How long they stay up is a function of what kind of fears you are carrying around you.

Now for a visualization exercise—sit back and relax and take five or six breaths. Visualize a rainbow. Allow the look, the shape, and the intensity of the rainbow to come into your consciousness. Take about thirty to forty seconds to do that. Now when you have that image, play with it. You might put a pot of gold at both ends of the rainbow, you might put a leprechaun standing near the rainbow, you might see the ocean and having a whale leap up and reach for it, you might be looking out of the plane that you are flying in and you see the rainbow out to the horizon, or you might be remembering a time where you were driving and the importance of the rainbow coming to you at that time. Or you might simply play with the colors and you say, "I want to make a pastel rainbow rather than the original colors, or I want to change the form of the rainbow and put it into more of a circle." Create in your mind the picture of a rainbow that brings you delight.

The reason why we are asking you to do this is so that your inner child, your emotional body, can get in touch with the power of this emotional image, the beauty of the rainbow. Recognize that just as when you are changing the look of the rainbow in your mind's eye, your inner child also has quite an influence on how things are going in your life. If he or she is afraid, then they are going to feel a limitation in that area. If he or she is lacking confidence, you will feel the limitation. If he or she is confused or feels unworthy, or doesn't feel as if the wisdom is within, then that will create a limitation in your life, and again that is not a problem unless you do not recognize that it is there. If that is what is stopping you from going where you want to go, the challenge is for you to notice the hesitation of the inner child. That way you can support the inner child so that he or she really can begin to move forward so there is no holding back.

The energy that each of you has inside reacts to the thought "miracle" in a way that is similar to how you react when you are viewing the rainbow. There is a level of excitement, there is a level of anticipation, and the anticipation is half the fun. The anticipation is not trying to predict what is to come but knowing that not only is it in your best interest, but it actually is going to be something that you will enjoy. Remember, as Richard Bach said, we have come to the planet for learning and for fun. What we would tell you is that the learning and the fun need to be combined. There is no law—there is no spiritual law, there is no incarnation law—that says that you must experience pain in order to understand joy. It is like saying that the only way you recognize light is to be in the dark. It is simply not true. You can recognize light just as it is.

So those that can anticipate what is to come and be excited about it will find that your energy is affected as well. As it affects your energy, so then you attract in something that matches your positive anticipation. The performance of miracles is ultimately done as a combination of your energy as part of the bigger picture. Think about how all of you are part of the oneness and that each of you has a unique role—it is like a body has a unique role for the successful utilization for the body. And so your energy is imperative in order to have miracles either created for you or attracted to you. But you never do anything alone because you are interconnected with others in the universe as you are all part of God, of the god—goddess energy. So what this means specifically is that the performance of miracles is a cooperative effort that easily takes place in your life.

A particular miracle will only happen in your life when you have the level of expertise or mastery for it to come your way. This is why the development that we spoke of earlier is necessary. And as you develop, everyone around you benefits. The wiser you get, the more wisdom will be available to those with whom you are interconnected. The more that you anticipate that wonderful things will happen and you heal those fears and those limitations that are inside of you, the more everyone benefits. Those who were in the eighteenth or even the nineteenth century used the practice of magical arts to create what they wanted; that was effective, but remember that was a three-dimensional reality. You could take that route, and you could do that today, but it would be more difficult because you are out of sync if you do that with the way in which the earth is developing or has developed. So what you want then, without having a fear about it, is you want to attract or again to create miracles or attract miracles in your life with the realization that this is a co-creation.

Take a look at your life and see the areas of your life that don't seem to give you a lot of problems, where you have seen miracles and you have been delighted by what has transpired. Then allow yourself to know the truth about the area of your life that feels the most out of control for you, the area of your life that feels as if you cannot successfully influence it, that you cannot have the direct impact on that which you would like to. And then recognize that you just need to become an expert; you need to move from someone who is experiencing something and into a state of knowingness as you allow those fears to dissipate. It will then become an area that you are knowledgeable about, and you will be able to step into the creation or the attraction of miracles for yourself personally. But it will not happen if you are a novice or just someone who is experiencing certain things in that area; you must go at least into the area of expertise.

When the Christ energy came to the planet for purposes of salvation, he also came to demonstrate that if you have a firm faith in what you are able to do, then you simply do it. He knew that he could heal individuals, and he showed different techniques for doing it. For some he would get clay and spit into it and make a type of material and put it onto the eyes, for others he simply would command them to rise up, for others he would do it remotely and say when you go home your child will be well. For still others he would do a laying on of hands. He used all of those techniques to show that in this area of spiritual healer, the energy coming to him would come from a multitude of sources. And in creating the miracle of healing he was showing his level of confidence, his level of faith; he never questioned if he could do it or not.

It is like someone who is a top ten tennis player who gets into "the zone" and doesn't miss a shot. It feels as if they are living the extraordinary life. And in fact they are. So when you get into expertise, you may want to move into mastery, such as what the Christ energy had, but you don't have to. If it is an area that has been difficult for you but it is not really an area of interest, just become the expert rather than the master in that area. Then move back then into the other areas of life knowing that this area is handled. Remember that you always do it the fifth-dimensional way; you don't sit there and think about how you are going to set it up, you just allow the energy to flow through you. You consciously allow yourself to become an expert in a certain area, the fear dissipates, and you begin to have the energy, the miraculous energy, coming into your sphere, your particular surroundings, your etheric circle of energy that is around you.

The more that it happens, the more you will find that you do it not for the effect of showing others, although as you become an expert in a certain area you can help others, but you can be a silent guide for them. You can do it through the spiritual laws rather than the physical laws. You can help others and give assistance to others without them ever knowing it. The reason for this is because you came to the planet with an agenda, whether you realize it or not! Everyone came with a blueprint; there were certain things that you wanted to accomplish, to understand, and to appreciate. So it is not just the accomplishment that is significant, but the whole process. The things that can and will be accomplished through your attraction of miracles into your life will bring you joy, and they will also be a source of learning. Again, you came to the planet for learning and for fun!

Learning does not have to be difficult. This of course probably flies in the face of what you were taught as a three-dimensional individual. You most likely learned that things were not open-ended, that you could only win if someone else lost. Those are mental concepts that have no place in fifth-dimensional reality. Your efforts and your accomplishments are not taking away from anyone else; they are not restricting anyone else. You are simply improving and heightening your energy, and everyone benefits either directly or indirectly from it. As each link in the chain gets stronger, the entire multidimensional chain of universal energies gets stronger. This chain includes energies that flow all through the universe, those parts of the universe that you can see and those parts of the greater number of sub-universes that you cannot see. You know they are there, you have an awareness of them, but they are not in your line of vision. You came to the planet not to explore that you which you cannot see in other parts of the universe, you came with an agenda to experience love and remember that self-love is the prelude to universal love. And what better way to express love to yourself than to heal those areas where you feel fearful, where you feel wounded, and to develop an area of expertise? Living on the planet will continue to have surprises for you, but they will most often be surprises that make you feel uplifted, not ones that blindside you.

While you do come to this planet for learning and fun, you will still encounter challenges. You will still find yourself in situations that you have no interest in or would prefer not to be a part of, areas that you would prefer not to be an expert in. So why, you may ask, would you need to partake in anything that is not fun? Well, the answer is that there are certain things that you do because you do it for more than just yourself, you do it for the god-goddess energy that is in everything, for the bigger picture. Understand that there is a reason why you are going through the process even though it is in an area that you are not interested in.

Most likely if you have had difficulty, it is an area that you have a fear about. Certainly, from the individual standpoint, you have to handle the fear right away because it is an open wound that you are carrying around with you. Everything is perfect, and there is a reason why in this particular area you need to become an expert; part of it is for yourself, and part of it is for the greater workings of the universe. Furthermore, becoming an expert doesn't require a great amount of time, it only requires a motivation, a commitment to learning, and a willingness to become an expert. Now if you really enjoy that area, then go forward and become a master! But for the performance of miracles, you only need become an expert, not of the whole area, just of the area that is having an influence on you, a negative effect on you.

And do you want to be a part of that movement going forward, or do you want to be caught in old belief systems that no longer serve you? This is important, and you will understand why when you face the first challenge. Undertake to do so joyfully, and you will find time and interest are actually on your side. It is not like you are being told to sit there with a book on chemistry and you are being forced to read it. You will find a level of excitement, and the developing level of expertise, simply by saying "let's give this a try" or "let me do some exploration in this area." Once you are no longer afraid to step into that area, and again you need to help your inner child to recognize this, and once you do step into this, then everything flows with your energy and not counter to your energy. You are no longer fighting the process, but you are embracing not just the possibilities now but the probabilities as well!

Finally, remember that everyone has a filter with which they see life. Sometimes the filter is one of love, and you see everyone around you as part of this big cushion of love. Some have a filter of hate, so that they distrust their neighbor, or they distrust their coworker. Others have a filter of quest where they feel that they have never arrived and they are still on the quest to get to that place where they can sit down and say finally I am where I am supposed to be. So then we all must accept that we do in fact have a filter. You don't have to change it or even try to remove it, just recognize that is where you are coming from and that is how you view things.

Then ask yourself if the filter is limiting you. Is it holding you back? Is your filter something that keeps you from having the greater bounty? If it is, the solution is quite simple. Just ask the nonphysical being that you feel closest to to pave the way for you. So if you feel closest to your spiritual source, you ask this being to help you. If you feel closest to your twin soul, you ask that being to help you. If you feel closest to Archangel Michael, then ask him to help you. If you feel closest to the Christ energy, then ask him to help. When you do this, what you will find is that the filter will not interfere with the process. Your filter is not bad and should not be judged as it is assisting you in creating direction in your life. You can improve your filter, however, by dealing with your inner child and dealing with those open wounds.

* * * * * * * *

It was New Year's Day, January 1, 2007, and I was in South Florida over the Christmas holidays. My son, his wife, and I were leaving the movie theatre around 8 p.m. I looked up to the nighttime sky and there was a full moon, and the full moon was totally surrounded by a rainbow! A miracle of miracles! I had never seen a rainbow in a dark sky, much less one that was in a full and complete circle. The aura of the full moon was bright and golden and the rainbow was clearly visible. It was as if the aura was a backdrop for the rainbow. Was this a sign? Was this a miracle? What was its meaning?

This beautiful once-in-a-lifetime event was witnessed by many people in many parts of the country. Days later, people were asking one another, "Did you see the rainbow around the moon on New Year's Day evening"? People were talking about it all over town. Its appearance created excitement way beyond simple interest. The combination of the rainbow with the full moon was an experience that perhaps no one had ever seen before. The energy surrounding this event was electrical. It had sparked a lot of attention and on many levels meanings could be derived. Yes, it certainly was a sign and it certainly was a miracle. Could it be on a universal level we were given a beautiful gift of faith and trust? Our new year was beginning with this treasure chest, a treasure chest that included not only faith and trust but also hope and love. On a personal level, the meaning was unique to each one of us, and we were each given an opportunity to receive an answer to a question that arose from within. Was it a personal assurance that everything on your mind was going to work out just fine? Or did you receive an inner knowing that a specific issue would turn out fine? A miracle is a miracle, no matter what you choose to derive from it. The miracle has meaning for you in the way that it makes sense to you, in a way that you want it to.

I have been given so many beautiful blessings in my life. I am rich with the love of people and the love of beautiful events. I am grateful and every day I thank my "lucky stars." How scientists and astronomers may have explained this event didn't really interest or affect me for I understand the meaning of miracles and the meaning of faith. I do not need an explanation from the community of "logical thinking" to explain something so that I may believe it on that level. Rather I choose to understand and accept that logical thinking has really no place on the level that I chose to receive this event. I know that this event simply was a gift, a gift to all of us on Planet Earth. This was one of those events which further add to the richness of our lives. How you choose to accept and receive the gift is going to determine the richness and the depth that you receive the miracle!

To me the meaning of the rainbow that is enclosing a full moon out in the nighttime sky, on New Year's Day evening, speaks volumes. The idea of a rainbow in a complete circle speaks volumes. Perhaps it is that the rainbow is part of the continuing motion of miracles and luck. This continuing motion in the form of a circle is cyclical. Intuitively I could understand the meaning of this event as it related to me. The miracles in my life would continue, they would continually be presented to me throughout my life. I glowed with happiness!

I wonder how many individuals who saw this event were looking for the answer in a strictly linear way. Perhaps it is time to explore the difference between viewing things in a linear way as compared to viewing things in a nonlinear way. Our ancient elders on the planet as well as the Native American nations have been a wonderful example of cyclical teachings and cyclical thinking. Each of us can recite an example of how this way of thinking has in fact impacted our life. Looking to the heavens, wisdom was spoken to earth's early inhabitants. How was the ancient wisdom from the skies received by our forefathers? How many miracles in nature had they received and revered? What have we learned or adopted from this way of thinking?

Currently each of us through our own experiences and issues can look to this rainbow and full moon event and extract from it the meaning that needs to come in, the meaning that needs to be honored. Our unique ability to look at the same event and see things differently is part of our growth and learning on this planet. I really do not want to have the same feelings or experiences that anyone else may have. I want to honor my differences and my uniqueness. No one can duplicate who I am, not on the physical level, not on the soul level. I want to have the totality of my experiences which will affect me in the way that I want them to, and that my guides want them to, and not to be either influenced or perhaps even limited by anyone else's experiences and thinking.

This event in my life allowed me to validate my faith and trust that everything would be fine in the upcoming year. I simply knew that my experiences that year would expand into beautiful experiences. I looked up into that nighttime sky and saw such perfection! What a way to start a new year; the message was received by me loud and clear.

We giggled at its beauty, and we were amazed that the rainbow had taken the shape of a circle completely encasing the golden full moon. It was indeed a circle of love. It was heavenly!

Each of us drew a different meaning into our lives. But the excitement that we shared that evening was truly felt by the three of us and others that shared in this miraculous event. Each time we think back to that evening and we mention the rainbow and the moon the electrical energy returns. When you simply bring the visual backup into consciousness, you help that energy return. Reenacting an energy in one's body is a great way to prevent your energy from ever feeling stuck. As we know, stuck energy is immobilizing and prevents us from moving forward and/or moving in the flow of the universal energy.

During the original event, a feeling of confidence fell over me, a knowingness. I was so tickled to have witnessed this beauty, and I knew not only that it was to make me feel great but to help me to understand that we were all seeing and sharing in this event. It was another example of how we are all connected—how we are all one. All participating in a moment together, I not only felt this connection but fell in silent thanks to the wondrous creator who had bestowed to each of us on earth this gift. I was seeing this event from a new paradigm, shifting into the non-linear and seeing the perfection, honoring the moment and opening up to the myriad of possibilities that this event held for each of us.

CHAPTER XVI

Magic!

*The world is full of magical things patiently
waiting for our wits to grow sharper.*

—Bertrand Russell

Magic is a subject with which you are probably familiar at some level. But did you know that you can use the elements of magic to enhance your wellbeing and to redirect your luck? Well that is just what we are going to learn! We define luck as simply energy that is waiting to be directed to move in your favor. Have you ever had the feeling before that everything was going your way? Well, allow yourself to feel that feeling right now. As you do this mental processing, try to become aware of how many times you have stopped yourself from going with this feeling that things are going in your favor. You stop yourself because there is an element inside of each of us that believes that things are a system of checks and balances: if I have a lot of good luck, then it will have to be balanced with some not-so-good luck. That is a belief, it is not reality. The universe continues to expand; it does not expand and contract, despite the belief of mass consciousness. So don't allow yourself to fall for the myth that your luck is limited! This is something you have to train yourself to remember; it will be an effortful process to become magical. After all, becoming a magician who touches something and transforms it into something that will be in your favor is no small task.

To begin this magical process, the first key player that you will be introduced to is your major arcana guide. The major arcana guide sits in the spiritual realm of consciousness and is your guide for magic. You will need to say a prayer, blessing, or mantra to this guide because these beings come from the spiritual realm of consciousness. When you recite a prayer for your major arcana guide, or the magician, and ask them to come to you, they will respond. We all usually have between eighty to ninety guides, with twelve in our auric field at any one time. So when you invite one in, they are seated at the seat of honor and will be with you for the entire day and sometimes even the next day as well. You are building energy as you build your connection with the magician.

As you know, when you perform feats of magic, what you are doing is materializing something from what seems to be nothing. So is magic the same as manifestation? In short, no, they are not the same. Manifestation techniques are used to create your future consciously. Although manifestation is connected with magic, the manifestation techniques you will use are actually designed to help to awaken your emotional body of consciousness, and for your mental body of consciousness to see things in a new light. You do not have to use manifestation techniques in magic—you simply have to focus on the energy of magic in order to feel magical. Magic is also something that is much more playful than most manifestation techniques, which your inner child will be quite happy to hear!

Symbolism is a very important part of the magical arts. When you think of magic, one of the first things that come to mind is probably the many symbols of magic. While these magic symbols are probably very familiar to you, the meaning behind them may not be. For example, the black hat energy means to blend in, to stretch, to go beyond, to know your power and that less is more. The wand represents that you are given a blessing and power. The wand involves consciously looking at your physical reality and seeing opportunities. If you have ever had a magic wand, you know that the more that you play with it, the more magical it becomes. That is because you are giving it the properties that are inside of you.

Another symbol of magic is the most famous magician of all: Merlin. Merlin wore purple to represent that he was mysterious and of a celestial nature. Perhaps most importantly, Merlin taught us that we can and should make our life playful and entertaining. Merlin encourages us to enjoy our environment without abusing it. He used celestial and universal wisdom and information to create magically. He taught how to use the power from within, to believe in possibilities, and how to be a true leader. Merlin came as a teacher to Arthur, who was then able to teach others by Merlin's example. In the same way, you too have a magical teacher, the major arcana guide.

There are aspects of magic that are such a big part of our everyday life that you may not have even thought of them as magic. For example, have you ever heard the expression the gift of gab? Well, did you know that that is actually a magical gift? When individuals are able to heighten their level of consciousness by creating a phrase or a song lyric, they are in fact bringing magic into your life. When you listen to a lecture, read a book, or watch a performance that touches your heart in a truly profound way, that is in fact a magical experience. If you look for these things, they will help you to understand magic as it pertains to your life.

Stardust is a particularly magical concept, but is probably quite different than the connotations that you learned with it as a child. What stardust represents is that you are what we call a "travelist," an individual who travels the universe constantly, sometimes in sleep state and sometimes through teleportation or astral travel. Stardust refers to individuals who do remote viewing, where your mind goes to a particular location and you are able to see it and report on what you have seen. Remote viewing is available to everyone, and like so many things in life, the more that you practice it, the better that you will get at it. In order to do remote viewing, you must go into a relaxed deep conscious state and choose a location that you are comfortable with and one that you have access to so that you can get confirmation that you are in fact remote viewing. You look through your physical eyes even though your body is not in that location and bring the etheric energy of those eyes to that location using the third eye or vitae chakra. This is a very good tool for practicing the prelude to teleportation. The power of it speaks for itself, and it feels doable for individuals who want to consciously go farther than they have been told that their physical bodies are capable of. Astral travel is usually unconscious, but remote viewing is quite conscious.

The power of touch is a very powerful tool of manifestation. What you are going to do to create magic in this instance is create a dry elixir. Think of a few things that are of value to you—souvenirs from a wonderful trip, a gift from a beloved relative—and place them together in a certain area. This area will be your magician's corner or magician's circle, whatever you want to call it. In order to bring more favor into your life, touch these favorite items with your fingers. If you touch a favorite picture of a loved one with whom you want to stay connected to, you will not be influencing their free choice, but rather strengthening the connection. If you want to be in touch with someone with whom the connection would be negative to you, you will find that the connection for which you are longing will be met in a different way. For example, if you touch a picture of your sister with whom you long to stay connected but who has a lot of negative emotional baggage, your connection with her will probably not be strengthened, but people will come into your life that are sisterly influences. In any event, what you are doing is creating magic and connecting the elements. When you perform magic, remember that you are not doing so because you are deprived of something in your life, but because you are going to use it for greater and grander things.

If a certain symbol or technique does not resonate with you, do not use it in your circle of magic. Instead, find one that does. Variation is a key in making your experience with magic fun and playful, as it should be. For example, if using a photo of a loved one does not work for you, play with touching apple seeds, which represent growth, fertility, and abundance. If you are trying to manifest more financial prosperity, you may include a special coin. Or your spirit may resonate with water, the most magical substance on earth! You can also light a candle in your corner if that feels magical to you. While you should feel free to put any favorite thing in your circle, it is recommended that you only include one of each type of item. If you include too many items, you may crowd the energy and imply that you are not good enough to manifest magic without these things. Remember, less is more!

When you practice these techniques, you will find that the teachings will appear. In fact, we strongly recommend that you keep a small notebook in which you record everything magical that happens in your life. This should not be a laborious task—just jot down a sentence about the experience and the date. You will find that you will quickly be filling your book because you are consciously recognizing what you are in fact materializing. You will be able to see the expansiveness of the magical materializations, how far they go. The whole materialization process itself is not meant to be effortful but should begin to flow automatically in direct response to the energy vibration that you put out. This is similar to the concept that what you focus on expands, except that you are actually creating these moments of magic in such a way that the materialization happens upon you. Materializations by definition are nonlinear, but they will continue to multiply even if it is in a nonlinear way. Just allow yourself to be in love with the process, and the results will speak for themselves. Magic is intended to enrich your life, and those who are lucky enough to be drawn into your magical circle, or your energy field, and will benefit as well. You cannot create a circle of magic for anyone else, but you can help them by placing them in your circle.

Moving away from the concept of manifestation, let's talk about the magical act of sitting. What, sitting? Yes, that's right! Now don't just sit in any chair or sofa in your home, but find one that feels magical to you. It might be magical because it is an antique or because it was a gift given to you by someone special. It may have cushions or not. Find the one chair that is magical to you. When you find this special seat, put your feet on the ground, just slightly spread, and allow the energies to flow in and out of the earth. If you have a chair where your feet do not touch the ground, find a way for your feet to get connected to the floor. What you are going to do is to bring forth the energy of nature, the fairies, the gnomes, and the elves. This energy is going to literally come up through your feet and into your base chakra. Once it gets there, lay your hands with the palm up on either leg or the arms of the chair and feel the power of the earth's energy. Feel it because now it is inside of you.

You will soon feel as if you can't contain it all in your base chakra, and it is going to go to the spleen chakra, and if you listen very closely and you are able to relax your mind, you will hear the angels, the fairies, the elves, and the gnomes giggle. You will hear them giggle because it is not often that they see humans do this, but they are familiar with it themselves. Once you feel as if your spleen chakra is reaching the saturation point, imagine it going all the way up to the crown chakra, and then all the way back down through the other chakras to the base chakra. Then just say out loud or to yourself, "I am complete." Relax in the chair and resume a normal position for your legs; just let them be dangling or lying gently on the ground. This connection with the earth's energy is equivalent to taking a twenty-mile walk in nature. What you focus on expands! Now you will not see the results of what you have just done that day or the next day, or maybe even the day after that. But you will see that as you do this over time, all of the nature's energy will begin to accumulate and accelerate right in that area. You are magically tapping into physical mastery on the earth plane.

Although magic is independent of space and time, it will appear in a certain time on a certain plane in order for us to experience it on this planet. In fact, the timing of magical events or experiences is quite important because if it is even off slightly, it may lose some of its spark or excitement. You came to this planet in order to be delighted and entertained spiritually and magically. You want to be able to create these things in your life so that you feel good, so that things go in your favor. Your guides are working for you and helping you to be aware of the fact that you can actually create magic in your own life.

Magic is such an ingrained part of our lives that even your first name has magical significance. So what is significant about your first name? Well, begin with looking up the meaning of your name. What is the magic in the meaning?

When you determine that you were given your name for a reason, then you will see that magic exists. Not only will it adjust your view of reality, but it will adjust your entire energy field. Does your name pertain to the adult version of you, or your spiritual, emotional, mental, or physical inner child? Or does it pertain to a combination of all of them? The cultural heritage of your name can have a magical meaning as well. For example, if you have a name such as Kathleen that has a Celtic energy, the Celtic energy rises up for you in symbolism and psychic attunement. By consciously attending to what your name is, you can direct that energy, and it is quite magical. Spend some time in front of the mirror saying your name aloud and listening to how the intonation shifts as you come more into your power and into the magic of your name. Concentrate on your first name as it is or what you are most often called. What do you hear, feel, see when you recite your name?

Do you have a middle name? Would it bother you if you didn't have one? For most people, they like their middle name. Your middle name is a way of connecting and a way of defining you. Everyone wants to be recognized as a powerful, positive, and completely accepted unique entity. Often if you don't have a middle name, the inner child gets very upset about that because they stand out as being unusual. However, in many cases, individuals that don't have middle names go on to be quite powerful, not because they are trying to make up for what is not there but because they get to fill in their destiny! They do not have their destiny defined for them, so they are able to create their own destiny. They do not see themselves through the eyes of a family member or a family connection. This is not necessarily a good or a bad thing; it is just different than it is for most individuals.

When you play with magic, you are playing in the big leagues! Be conscious of the fact that the energy of magic will effect change in your life. With practice, you will become more and more effective at materializing that which you want into your life. You will become conscious of the fact that magic is everywhere; you will begin to see the different ways in which you are materializing. So get out there and have fun playing with magic.

* * * * * * * *

I have a cat named Claude. He is black and white, long-haired, and very elegant, with an extremely powerful presence. Some may refer to it as arrogance, but I would rather not so that I can stay on his good side! Let me tell you how he found his way to me.

Limitless Possibilities

I had been living without a pet for a period of time but now felt I was ready to explore the possibility of bringing a loving responsibility into my life and began to familiarize myself with different breeds of cats. I was attracted to a breed that was termed a "ragamuffin." I had heard that these cats were extremely lovable and extremely affectionate. I put out the word that I was looking for a kitten or kittens, and very soon after, I received a call from someone who had a litter of "ragamuffin" kittens that needed good homes. Imagine that! I visited the home and was very impressed with the mother cat, father cat, and the other animals on the premises. They were affectionate, calm, and their home was spotless! I fell in love with a male and a female, both having the colors of buff, beige, and chocolate brown. I put down a deposit and went home to prepare their space. Soon it was time for me to go and pick up my two kittens.

On that particular day I had made an earlier appointment with a local psychic as she was helping me expand my resources of knowledge. As I was leaving, she mentioned that she could "see" that I was going to pick up my "three" kittens that day. I quickly corrected her, explaining that I had put down a deposit on two of the kittens in the litter and that there were no more kittens available. I further explained that it was impossible for me to be getting "three" kittens. She simply looked at me and said, "Well you are going to be surprised because a little black and white one is waiting for you too!" I decided it was pointless to argue with her so I simply said, "Well, we shall see!"

I drove to the country to pick up my little ones. I walked into the "nursery" and immediately sat on the floor as a flurry of small soft creatures quickly came to me. The first was a small black-and-white. He was so friendly and very sweet. I was told that he was supposed to go to North Carolina the next day, but the new owners called the night before to say they needed to decline taking him as the husband had been transferred and a kitten simply would not fit in with their upcoming move. So this little one became available! Without a moment's thought I said, "I don't think he is available because he is coming home with me!" Enter Claude.

It turned out that Claude is the alpha cat of the three. Anyone who has come to my home has been met, checked out, and given the okay to enter by Claude. He then telepathically sends the message to the other two that they may approach. Etienne and Giselle appear out of nowhere to introduce themselves to my visitor and to review the situation.

As they grew and as I grew spiritually and began to learn more about the *Limitless Possibilities* that expand our world, I started noticing that Claude always seemed to be at the right place at the right time. Too many coincidences and too many sightings made me realize that he was purposely putting himself in situations to aid or to magically help to create what was going on.

As I mentioned earlier, I belong to this small planet healing group. We meet once a month in my dining room and create a healing environment of fifth-dimensional energy which we in turn send out to the planet for its healing. Every month I write a prayer incorporating our guides, nature, and the planets, tapping into all of that energy and sending it out to the universe with a specific focus. We were advised by our guides and mentors that we could ask for healings for friends or families or situations close to us in return for our work for the planet. The energy that we manifest each month is very distinct—soft, electrical, taffylike, liquid, or hard—teaching us the many different forms that fifth-dimensional energy can manifest on our planet.

We noticed that Claude would enter and take center stage. He would pick a choice seat and wait for the "action." Depending on the energy that we created and who our guests were for the evening, Claude would direct Etienne and Giselle. There were times when he would bring each cat in and they would sit in a circle.

Sometimes our group would do a physical healing on a friend, five Reiki masters doing their thing, creating a healing environment to bring a friend into the state of wellness. We worked on several cancer victims, having them lie on the massage table which we placed on a ley line which ran through my front hall. We noted that Claude placed his two siblings so that each cat sat at two points of a pyramid while he walked the path from point to point to point, the point under the massage table on the ley line being his primary point. Claude, my beautiful black-and-white cat, got sacred geometry! How is that possible?

One of the women in my healing group is an expert animal communicator. Diane would talk to Claude and ask him what he was doing and why. Claude in an ever-so-solicitous attitude would simply reply that he was creating an energy grid to keep the energy as strong as he could while walking the shape of the pyramid, tapping into its healing properties! He walked from point A to point B to point C again and again while the healings would take place, oftentimes for over forty-five minutes to an hour.

Well, after that we never questioned Claude or his motives but often asked that he explain to us (mere humans) so that we would understand better how our energy works. Claude's role to this day to our healing group is certainly not one of mascot but one of mentor. His knowledge and his response to situations not only exhibits his utter knowledge of what we are doing but his total understanding of our language and our goals. His brother and sister play the parts that Claude lays out for them and as a group have performed as master healers, helping the healing energy stay strong, directed, and powerful. I then saw the living proof that cats (as well as many other animals) are certainly a higher-dimensional being than most human beings—in fact, all human beings! Yes, animals vibrate higher and have a purer consciousness than humans.

So of course, I had to ask, remembering back to the day that I went to pick up my two kittens, why did I get to bring Claude home? I was told that the universe saw the direction that I was heading in my growth and that Claude could be far more helpful to me in my efforts to heal the planet and could help me open up to the magnificent workings of animal energy in the universe for the universe!

Is it any surprise that my black-and-white cat's energy came from that place in history, that point in time that Merlin left his magical mark on our planet? So as it turns out Claude is truly a magical cat and one that as a student of Merlin is here to spread his knowledge and make our world just a little bit better! Wow! And to think I actually argued with the psychic that I was getting three cats instead of two! Yes, the informational highway was sending the message, and I just needed to accept it as it was manifesting itself all by itself!

I have had other experiences at home with Claude that have taught me about manifesting and the magical properties in our universe. I have learned how to work with my major arcana guide. I knew I needed to sell my house, which of course was a conscious decision, so I needed to manifest a buyer. I said a prayer and requested help every night, and then the information came through with my guide's name. He came and identified himself, giving me instructions on what to do. I am to say my prayer or mantra, call my guide's name three times, and he will come.

You may create your own personal mantra. A simple rhyme is sufficient. Your guide knows what you are doing so he or she will respond to your creation. Here is a suggestion:

"I am ready to receive whatever you wish to come to me!"

After saying my personal mantra, Claude would arrive and jump on the bed and be right there, swinging his black tail back and forth. Initially I thought his actions were cute, but then I realized that he appeared every time I would say the mantra, inviting my guide in to help with my house sale (whether I said it aloud or silently). This was no coincidence—this was a way that Claude was assisting in this magical moment, helping the energy to expand and flow in this direction!

One day I felt a strong urge to stop at my local crystal shop. I wasn't sure why I was there or what I was to look at until I saw the clear crystal wands. They were being housed in a display case opposite from the store's entrance. I worked my way back to them and then needed to decide which ones were for me to take home. By now I clearly knew I was to present a crystal wand to each person in my planet healing group. I knew that crystals found their way to their owner, so I wasn't sure how to go about the selection. Then it came to me: I called out one of the girl's names and simply ran my hand two to four inches above each crystal. The crystal's response could be felt by the heat that I felt in my hand. Five planet-healing members and five crystals selected and purchased. I came home and put each member's name on paper with the selected crystal. I then took my pendulum and verified that the crystal selected was in fact for the person I bought it for. The next planet healing, I presented each person with their crystal. Subsequent channelings brought in for each member their personal mantras and the names of their magic guides.

It is recommended that you let your crystal get to know you and you get to know it. You can see the beautiful markings within; ours had rainbow specks and many varied occlusions. As your relationship grows and changes with your crystal wand, its appearance changes as well. The more you use the crystal, the more it enhances your magic, and it is special to be able to see and witness the changes within—there is magic in that alone!

I was also told to buy a pyramid and place the request in its healing spot inside! The healing spot is typically the little shelf inside the pyramid. The request is heard by the universe, and the energy in the healing spot can help manifest and expand the energy to accomplish your requests. Typically my requests are for healings for others who are ill or who need help healing a difficult situation for themselves or others. I often request prosperity or abundance in my healings as life is so much more complete when you are given the gift of prosperity in your life: an abundance of love, an abundance of friends, an abundance of activities, etc. The pyramid can sit in a special place in your home (preferably in the north) that is truly a sacred place, and at the same time every night you request the healings out loud as you turn the pyramid clockwise three times facing the north.

The request for a healing must come from a pure heart and be for your highest good if the healing requested for is personal. If you are asking for a healing for another or a situation that needs to be healed, this too must come from a pure heart and be for the highest good of all concerned. A miracle cannot ever hurt another human being or bring additional pain into the universe. This must be remembered when determining what you want to manifest for yourself. This is also why it is really important to have no expectations or a set way that a miracle can happen. The universe knows the big picture and we don't, so how it chooses and when it chooses to answer the request determines the result, and the answer comes from a place of universal knowing and not from our place of limited knowing! This is why it is important to always remember that little phrase: be careful what you ask for! Are you prepared to deal with the answers to your wishes or the gifts that you are receiving based on your request?

In an earlier chapter I discussed that I was also taught to "sit in the silence," giving myself the gift of ten minutes by sitting quietly with no distractions. I loved doing this little exercise as I could clearly identify the benefits that came to me: quieting my mind, relaxing my body, and refreshing my spirit. I was very careful to choose a time when the house was quiet, with no TV, no music, nor cell phones or other distractions. Typically I would sit for a thirty-day period and take a break for a couple of months and then sit for another thirty-day period. As the benefits were becoming more and more apparent, I decided to alternate months—one on and one off. During one of these thirty-day sessions, I saw a deer. That's right, I saw a deer—right there in my bedroom! The deer was sitting above my bed, simply watching me with those beautiful eyes, loving and soft. My first reaction to the unusual or strange is typically one of questioning my sanity: am I really seeing a deer? And then upon quiet reflection, I received the information that the deer would be my totem for the next six months. I was instructed to read up on the meaning of the deer in one of the Native American medicine guides that teaches about the energy of animals, insects, and birds. The totem brings you his energy to perhaps help you learn a lesson or guide you through the meaning of an event that has occurred for you. You simply thank the totem for his presence, his knowledge, and the gifts that he is bestowing on you. And you thank the universe for allowing you to have this magical experience. Again you are in awe of the universe and its magic as it continues to teach and guide you.

Message from Lancelot
Focus: Personal and Planetary Healing—after 9/11/01

Channeled September 2001

This is your time on the planet. It is an opportunity and it is a gift to step well into wisdom. These moments of conflict will shift into many more moments of togetherness. The shields that have been protecting you will turn as you heal the world because you are the center of your reality, and that is where your power lies. If you take these moments of wisdom, wisdom that is coming to you in an unlimited form, and you allow those moments to be your present-moment consciousness, then you will heal the current conflict, you will heal diseases, you will heal rips and separations, you will heal planetary occurrences, and you will heal your environment. The wisdom is there. You access it simply by being open to it. Let your energy focus not on a solution but on opening to receive the wisdom—opening to receive the wisdom. If you receive it in meditation, then that is a good route for you; if you receive it in the pews of a church, then that is the appropriate route for you; if you see it by walking through nature, then choose that route. Whatever your route—or you might have several routes—let yourself be open to the wisdom and your present-moment consciousness will do the transformation.

You are not living in a world of contrast. You are not living in a world defeated. You are living in a world that is waiting to be healed, and personal healing is the same thing as planetary healing. There is no difference just as your world is my world—there is no difference. Remember that individuals on your planet pass over every day, every moment of every day. Some are starving, some have diseases, some are killed through abuse, accidents, or murder; these souls are passing over all of the time. It needs to change. We (we being spirit) want your planet to come into its power where you pass over consciously because you want to be there, not because you don't want to be in your world. And that you pass over consciously and without any harm to the physical body. You don't have to go into trauma in order to see the light. That has been a very big issue for those who take a lifetime on the physical plane—that you must have trauma in order to get your reward. If you heal the world by healing yourself, then you will find that all of this makes sense. It just makes sense—you don't have to figure out what is going on. When you heal the world by healing yourself, then everything makes sense—past, present, and future!

I want you to know that your planet is in a better place environmentally than it was a few years ago, not because of the actions of the occupants of the planet but because the planet ridded itself of its toxins—not all of them, but a lot of them. If the planet has the consciousness and has the capability of doing this, do not each of you have the capability of ridding yourself of toxins, be they physical, emotional, mental, or spiritual? Heal the world by healing your life. It is time for you to enjoy the fruits of the world. It is time for you to have that peace. It is time for you to do something other than worry. If you didn't worry, you would really see your world with new eyes. During the time of Camelot, it was a time of seeing the world as it "could be" and as it "should be." Some of you are ready to start at the beginning, a wiser soul, and the wisest soul knows that you don't have any of the information yet to change your world, but you will have it when you are ready, when you want to know you will lay down your shields and your preconceived notions and let yourself be open to the wisdom.

To live on your planet is a privilege. Every moment well lived ensures your future happiness. All of you have wanted to gain consciousness, and Markas has helped you with that and all of your guides, teachers, and counselors have helped you. I want you to gain wisdom. All you must do is be open to the wisdom. Be open, be receiving. You came here for the same reason that I speak to you at this time. You came to help your planet, and you do that by learning about love. I come to your planet with many others, and we form a blanket around your planet, just as a mother will take the newborn child and wrap the child in blankets. When we who come to help with the healing of the planet do that—when we act as a blanket over the planet—we do it because we see what your planet has to offer and we want all of you to see it. Markas has said that you heal the planet by healing what is inside of you. And I agree. But you can do things simultaneously. You can be focusing on loving the planet and sending love to the planet while you are simultaneously ridding yourself of your toxins. It is all about love, and anything that doesn't feel like love inside of you is not serving you in the way that you want to go.

I will be happy if just one of you falls in love with the planet. I will come to you as your teacher or as a fifth-dimensional counselor, and I know that there are many of you that are very, very close. Just take that additional step and take the risk of being in love with your planet. It is like stepping off into the void, but it is not a void. You can't really see the beauty of the planet until you fall in love with it.

I will depart as I leave you in love.

—Lancelot

CHAPTER XVII

Healing the World

Be the change you wish to see in the world.

—Gandhi

When we think of great American tragedies, most of us immediately think of September 11, 2001. This event was caused completely by free will. Individuals made a series of choices to make a violent statement and to have a profound impact, figuratively as well as literally, on America. These types of events can be so difficult to rectify in our minds. Do these individuals that carry out such hateful acts have guides and teachers that are trying to get through to them? If individuals invoke their free will and in the process they impact on my reality, how can it be that everything is perfect? The questions that arise after a tragedy such as this are numerous, and they are often not quickly answered.

First let us say that no one exits the earth plane until they say that they are ready to go. They might not say it consciously, but they do so by agreement between their soul and their spiritual source, the oversoul or the higher self. Each soul has the ability to choose when they are going to go and the statement that they are going to make when they do. So what you have is every opportunity for you to make your statement about how you are going to consciously create your reality. Are you going to do it in an arena of fear? Are you going to do it surrounded by anger? Are you going to make a statement that says that we win as a team and we lose as a team? Or are you going to say that both the souls that departed innocently and the souls that created the devastation are all part of the oneness? As difficult as it is to believe, they are.

Remember that the links in a chain determine how strong the chain is. While you cannot control anyone else's free will, you can strengthen your life and your surroundings by strengthening what is happening inside of you. The concept of winning as a team and losing as a team includes all of us, including even terrorists. As we have mentioned before, the fifth dimension is the realm of the spiritual healer, and all of us are going to be playing a role in terms of creating a healed world. The good news is you don't have to control anyone else's activities in order to step into healing. Instead, you simply decide to continue to move upward and forward, despite what is happening around you. You decide to stop all judgment. You no longer look at a certain country or government and think to yourself, "Well, a terrorist act was bound to happen there," or, "That country seems only capable of producing terrorists." You must stop that line of thinking because that kind of energy will keep you going in a circle instead of going upward in a spiral. Those who choose to practice their spirituality and take complete responsibility for their actions and choose them wisely will go into a state of a healed world. As you do your part in this process, the chain will grow stronger.

As a fifth-dimensional being, you feel a tremendous amount of compassion and love for those individuals who left this world in innocence, the victims of someone else's hatred. However you must also feel the compassion for the individuals on your planet who don't know what love is yet. Because that is what this is all about. You come to this planet to learn about love and how you are going to demonstrate love, and every time you judge someone you are not in a state of love. Now that doesn't mean that you must approve of behaviors that the terrorists did or even the people that they are; you have every right to be angry when you see grave injustices. You have every right to say, "That is not my reality; that does not happen in my world. Just as I love my country and as I love my family, I love my world." You have every right to those emotions. But when you begin to judge the individuals that carry out these atrocities, you perpetuate the isolation that created the entire thing in the first place.

Do you think that the individuals that planned the September 11 attack and those that sacrificed their own physical lives, do you really think that they did this because they felt love? No, they were isolated. Mind control works. You isolate, you create a fear that it is either us or them. Again, that doesn't mean that you don't have every right to be angry, but you must claim ownership of your feelings rather than acting on them, a spiritual lesson that the terrorists have yet to learn. You must ensure that you have everything to do with the power of spirituality and nothing to do with the separation, the isolation. In fact out of these horribly trying events, so often good arises. We realize that we must reach out in love to take care of one another, that all the technology and infrastructure in the world is only fleeting, that it is one another and the natural bounty of the planet that are more than enough.

The way that you stop terrorism in the long run is to simply choose peace. When you begin to understand those cultures and what is important to them with an open mind and open heart, you will remove the veil of separation, the illusion of imperfection. That is not to say by any means that the hatred that the terrorists feel will immediately dissipate, as we all know that this is unrealistic. However, to begin a dialogue with an open, peace-loving heart is certainly the correct place to begin in rebuilding international relationships and healing the pain that has been felt by multitudes of people. We all have an opportunity to choose peace. When you do in fact choose peace, you change not only your own life but the lives of those around you. Remember that you will not be alone on this journey toward peace as your guides and teachers will be with you, as will those whose souls have passed on. Believe it or not, it will not only be those who gave their lives as victims of terrorism who will work toward peace, but also those who committed those hateful acts and have now seen the light who will help to build bridges of peace and love. Let the process begin with you, and accept help from wherever or whomever it is offered.

Enlightenment is something that happens upon you as a result of you doing what you do on a daily basis. As you work daily to heal your own inner world and feel that enlightenment, the external world will begin to be healed as well. When you do this, you will be laying down the thoughts that are really weapons in your life. We all have hurtful, dangerous thoughts at times. For example, you may think, "I don't like this person," or, "That person hurt me," or, "I can't handle that relationship." When you take responsibility and you lay down your arms internally, then you create a healed world. Think about it for a minute. You have your energy that is already going out in all directions. Now if it goes out and you are not healed, what signal are you sending to someone? You are making it all right for them to be in an unhealed state. Well, the same is true on a global level. Energy is very powerful stuff, and you must be a good steward of that energy and share only that which will help heal this planet of ours.

As human beings, we have the tendency to try to think our way through every situation. Well, my friends, the intellect will not aid us in healing the planet. If you try to figure out the mindset of terrorists, you will be unsuccessful. You will not be able to fully understand their perspective no matter how hard you try. So rather than focusing on why something happened or where we go from here strategically or militarily, concentrate on your own spiritual energy. Do what you do best as a spiritual healer in your fifth body of consciousness—bring forward the energy of healing. If you try to figure out all of the other things that are not in your realm of understanding, you are wasting your energy. Feel the anger, feel your fear, feel your frustration, and have your opinions, but *do not* judge others! When you have the cessation of "againstness," you are able to turn your energies in a direction that serves everyone. Again, you win as a team and you lose as a team. So ask your guides for assistance and then trust that they will help you in your quest for healing. Know that you are not sitting idle on your hands and that you are not denying your feelings. What you are doing is so much more active, so much more fruitful than any military or intellectual activity in terms of bringing healing to our world.

These violent days on our planet are actually an opportunity, a gift to step well into wisdom. These moments of conflict will shift into many more moments of togetherness. The shields that have been protecting you will turn; you will heal your environment. The wisdom is there. You access it simply by being open to it. Let your energy focus not on a solution but on opening to receive the wisdom. If you receive it in meditation, then that is a good route for you. If you receive it in the pews of a church, then that is the appropriate route for you. If you see it walking through nature, then choose that route. Whatever your route or routes are, just be open to the wisdom, and your present-moment consciousness will do the transformation. You are not living in a world of contrast, you are not living in a world defeated, you are living in a world that is waiting to be healed. And personal healing is the same thing as planetary healing; there is no difference.

Remember that individuals on our planet pass over every day, and every moment of every day. Some pass away due to starvation, others due to disease, still others through violence or accidents. Individuals pass over at every moment, and many do so unconsciously. This needs to change. The goal is for your spirit to come into its power where you pass over consciously and without harm to your physical body because you want to be there, not because you don't want to be in the world that you are in now. You don't have to go into trauma in order to see the light. Instead you must heal yourself in order to heal the world; this is how you will truly be enlightened. When you heal the world by healing yourself, everything will make sense, past, present, and future. Each of us has not only the capability but the responsibility to rid ourselves of toxins, whether they be physical, emotional, mental, or spiritual. It is time for you to enjoy the fruits of the world. It is time for you to have that peace. It is time for you to do something other than worry. If you didn't worry, you would really see your world with new eyes.

Lancelot's messages are worth repeating on these pages as the wisdom is timeless. Some of you are ready to start at the beginning a wiser soul, and the wisest soul knows that you don't have any of the information yet to change your world, but you will have it when you are ready, when you want to know you will lay down your shields and your preconceived notions and let yourself be open to the wisdom. To live on our planet is a privilege; every moment well lived ensures your future happiness. All of you have wanted to gain consciousness, and all of your guides and counselors have helped you. In order to gain further wisdom, you must simply be open to the wisdom, be open and be receiving. Every one of us came to the planet for the same reason, to learn about love. But you can do things simultaneously: you can be focusing on loving the planet, sending love to the planet, while you are simultaneously ridding yourself of your toxins. It is all about love, and anything that doesn't feel like love inside of you is not serving you in the way that you want to go.

To begin this healing process, examine inside of you what does and what does not feel like love. Examine what does not feel healed. If you want to change anything in the macrocosm, you must begin by focusing on your inner energy—what is happening and what is not happening with that energy. As you begin to do this, you will see the very separation that you see reflected around you. Go into this separation in detail in order to heal it. What you have is the experience and the opportunity to go within and change, to heal, if you will, all of those things inside of you that don't feel like love. Take a look at all of your thoughts and those things that you keep going back to as those are the areas in which you are making someone else wrong in order for you to feel right. Now it is not a question if they are actually wrong or are they not wrong, that is not even the issue. The issue is the impact that it has on you.

If you are genuinely spending all of your time looking at why it is that their approach is wrong, whether or not it is, then again you are going in a circle: around and around. If you do this, you are not taking advantage of the limitless opportunities on our planet, of the gift that you were given of spending time on this physical plane. As you examine these issues, in some cases you can simply drop the curtain. That is to say, you can simply put an end to the feelings of discord and start in a new direction. With other issues, as you know from fourth-dimensional processing, you need to bring them forward and to converse with your inner child in order to resolve them. Sometimes you actually need to talk with someone else about it and to come to an understanding of how to release these feelings. And in the end, this is exactly what the goal is, to release them. Why? Because they don't feel like love, and they are at cross purposes with what you want to have on this planet. Often these feelings that you are harboring are actually from long ago, something that happened with a parent or something that happened with a sibling, and it has carried forward all of these years.

When we talk about healing the past experiences or things where you are in conflict, who is in conflict? Well, it is one or more of your bodies of consciousness. So you might have been hurt emotionally and that keeps you hooked looking at things a certain way. You might have had a physical interaction, and that keeps you looking at things a certain way. It might have been mental or some combination of the two. It is your job, your opportunity, to ensure that all of your bodies of consciousness are in harmony. If you do this, you will no longer feel the need to try to make someone else wrong because you are simply trying to make yourself feel better. And the truth is everyone around you is doing the same thing. You must not expect or wait for others to change, but instead make changes that you desire to see internally. So if you really want to take charge of your life in a positive way, realize that you get to dictate the terms of your own life. You do in fact have absolute control over what is happening inside of you. You do not, however, have any right to control others or to judge them. After all, every relationship has three components: you, the other person, and the exchange or dynamic interplay of the relationship. The only one that you can control is you.

It is true that the more that you heal within, the more you will see the healing outside of you. If you want good health in your life, then shower yourself in experiences of wellness. If you want to have prosperity, then be abundance. If you want to have high-quality relationships in your life, then be love. Focus on the love and remember that if you want to see harmony in your world, have harmony inside of you. When you have achieved this harmony, you walk with grace, you walk with purpose and on purpose. When you change and you choose love and when you choose wellness, not only does your energy shift, but the energy that is part of the interaction with others shifts as well. It evolves. So you do have an impact on the other person, but not because you are telling them how they should live their life. Instead they will see you changing your own life and moving upward and forward, and they may learn from your example. If this individual is meant to be in your life, then they will in fact learn and grow with you. Remember that anyone can be in a relationship, but to create and maintain a healthy interdependent relationship requires two healed individuals. Just the same is true with your bodies of consciousness: if they are not healed, they cannot be in a healthy relationship with one another, and you will feel the effects of this.

You have two very helpful chakras that will help with the purposes of healing yourself and healing the world. Those two chakras are the solar plexus and the heart chakra. Now you might think that it would be your eighth chakra because that effects the fifth-dimensional healing, but the two primary ones are the heart and the solar plexus, and actually in that order. You know the phrase "as within, so without," well, it is applicable here. Your solar plexus is where you store all of your experiences that have emotions attached to them, and so all of your memories are stored in this solar plexus area. Therefore a lot of what motivates you subconsciously are these repressed emotions or these unhealed emotions that are derived from an earlier time period. And as you know through your processing, the way that you help to release them is to get them up to the surface into consciousness so they come right up into the heart chakra region. Once they are there, you do not just feel the repressed emotion, but you are bringing it up to the surface. You allow yourself to bring it up to the present time, and you allow yourself to feel it, to love it, because it is your creation. Once you actually love it, then you are able to release it and send it home to God.

You send it home to the universe, and then the universe takes that energy and creates something more useable, something of value for you and your world. So every time you go through a healing process, you are helping your world because you are getting rid of toxins. Every illness, whether it be physical or mental, stems from an emotional imbalance of sorts. So if you want to heal the world, then take a look at the microcosm and then just allow these things to come up. You repressed them for some reason or another because they did not feel like love to you. It can of course be frightening sometimes for the inner child to bring these things up because in the process you must tell yourself the truth. You must acknowledge that something or someone hurt you, that you are still not over it, and that kind of honest acknowledgement can frankly be so challenging for the emotional body of consciousness that it sometimes chooses that it is much easier to sweep it under the rug and not acknowledge it. So give yourself permission to bring it up to the surface into present-moment consciousness and then just release it. Once you have owned it, then you can release it.

When you bring your personal experiences from the solar plexus chakra that stores your own personal experiences into the heart chakra to be released, you broaden the heart chakra itself. This allows you to more easily bring in those things that you are drawn to. As you think about this, do not forget about the power of energy. Remember that when two or more are gathered in love, what you have is more powerful than any terrorist attack. When you are able to come together with other individuals and choose love, your power is limitless! You send out a message to the universe that says that you are ready for the next step of growth. You are saying that you are ready to continue going up the spiral. You are saying that you are ready for a teacher, for a major arcana guide. You are saying that you are ready to be shown either what you can do or what you will be doing. You send a signal of love to those who are grieving their loss, not just those in your own country, but individuals from all over the world whose families are grieving their losses. So by coming into this state of awareness, you are giving them the very best of what you have to give, which is the whole that is greater than the sum of the parts. What you are doing is consciously choosing love while allowing yourself the freedom of emotional expression. Again, if you cease to judge others and you focus on being as pure an energy as you can, you will heal the world! It can't be any other way.

* * * * * * * *

I have learned many interesting little phrases from Markas as I have attended these seminars. Some of these phrases you have read throughout these chapters. I have found that focusing on the phrase and the meaning of the phrase and then how it relates to me is one way that I have been able to shift my attitude, my thinking, and ultimately, my energy. I have also discovered that these little phrases carry huge amounts of wisdom!

Let's examine the phrase: "A chain is only as strong as its weakest link." When I think about the meaning of this phrase, I first think about it on the literal level. But in order for me to grow or evolve, I must now take the next step. I now need to see how the chain and its links can be a metaphor for me and those five adorable bodies of consciousness! I think about how this relates to me and what kind of a person I am. I can make a very long list of all of my weaknesses, and unfortunately, I can make a much shorter list of all of my strengths! But by looking at these two lists, I see where I stand with myself. I know what needs work, and I know what parts of me I am proud of, and then I have that talk with myself and the work continues! I have figured out that I must start with myself before I can even think about how I relate Markas's phrase to the world.

After a time I took another next step: after reviewing my two lists of strengths and weaknesses, I saw some shifting. The long list of weaknesses was getting shorter, and the short list of strengths began to lengthen. I was able to measure growth, internal growth, from simply being introspective. With a huge dose of honesty and awareness, I could evaluate myself. What kind of person am I? Who do I want to be? What does that feel like? How do I get there? Being consciously aware of what needs to change is a vital step. Focusing and discipline are the tools that helped me to keep that hard work in the forefront of my mind. Being able to feel and being able to identify those feelings are key because as you shift and change your thinking and actions, you need to know which parts of you feel like love and which parts don't. Then the housecleaning starts—anything that doesn't feel like love has got to go, and anything that does feel like love may stay and can find room to expand. A form of decluttering! Toxins are toxic—it is as simple as that! So each of those five bodies of consciousness needed to step up to the plate and come forward ready to turn over everything that did not feel like love. Now if you are a detail person like I am, this can be a very long list!

Now that I am cleansed and cleared, my strengths are stronger and more apparent. I can actually use them! The weaknesses must be dealt with on a daily basis. But it is at this point that I really took a look at myself, and after acknowledging growth and change, I could see exactly what links were keeping that chain weak. What those links represented needed continuing work. It was only after I reached this point that I really took a good strong look around at my world and decided what needed to be changed there. How did I fit in? It certainly was not surprising that my weaknesses within myself needed to be made stronger so that I could make a stronger impact in my world.

It was time to ask the bigger questions: How can I make the world a better place? What did I need to do to make the world a better place? What changes do I need to make? How do I make these changes? Of course I could have continued to ask question after question, but I did want to accomplish something, so I chose not to get caught up in the evaluation of the problem process but moved right into the solution to the problem process. That meant action!

I took a baby step, and then more baby steps. The changes came. Initially I made sure that all of my five bodies of consciousness were onboard. I needed their cooperation and their enthusiasm, all the while making sure that each felt that they would be loved and respected through the process. I started working on the very smallest of changes, and I asked them to provide assistance to me so that we could travel this new road together. We decided to begin with kindness. Did you know that it takes no effort to be kind? There is no excuse not to be kind, and the rewards are great. The more that you are, the more you feel like love inside. Attention—I started paying extra attention to those people that I interact with and that are in my daily world. Caring—I had and showed concern to the people that I interact with. Listening—not something to take for granted. If you really listen, you can really hear! What I did hear spoke volumes about the people in my life. Generous—I became more generous in all ways—in time and money and effort. And the list goes on and on.

All these steps and many, many more led me one way: down the feel-good path. The process was transforming. I now knew that I was affecting the world one baby step at a time and it felt great! My chain became stronger and stronger, and if a weak link popped up, I have only me to blame. And I only have me to figure out how to fix it. Did I lose my focus or my discipline? If I slid backward, all I need do is pick up where I left off, loving me all along the process. I learned how important it was not to have judgment, either of myself or others around me. Judgment doesn't feel like love. In fact when what you do, think, and feel—all that feels like love, and you fall into the bad habit of judgment, your internal dynamics change and it certainly doesn't feel like love. It smacks you in the face and it reminds you of something that is abhorrent. This is simply an opportunity to remember and then to get stronger.

The next phrase, "the microcosm is simply a reflection of the macrocosm," really plays off the first one. I certainly was able to understand this phrase after I had been introspective and performed all of the self-growth necessary to strengthen those links in my chain. Because now I had a clear picture of what my microcosm was all about. I have seen how my microcosm has affected my world, and now I needed to expand that vision and look toward the planet.

I took my original list, with all of its weaknesses described, and saw that everything I had written was magnified by all its inhabitants contributed to the overpowering negative energy of the planet. I did not like that energy. I did not want to be a part of it. I really started to personalize my role on the planet and made me look beyond the obvious. I started to dissect the negativity on the planet and looked to see if I contributed to any of it. If I did, then I still had work to do, which meant that I had better just work harder because I did not like to see the direction the planet was heading. I needed to take responsibility for what I saw and then look within to see what I was thinking, how I was feeling, and how I was acting.

Which brought me to the next phrase, "what you send out you attract in." You may have also heard of the other popular varieties: "what you sow, you reap" and "what you send out comes right back to you." These are descriptions of the law of attraction, which is one of the universal laws that our universe operates under. By what we do, think, or act, we actually create karma for ourselves. I had a choice: did I want to be in the credit column or the debit column on the karmic balance sheet? Knowing that all debts from other lifetimes would be paid off in subsequent lifetimes oftentimes takes the responsibility and pressure off from doing the right thing in this, the current lifetime. Fortunately or unfortunately, depending on your view, I now learned that the karma each of us is creating currently is an instantaneous one. Debit need not carry over hundreds of years, but you pay up right in the here and now. Yes, the universe was tired of the old way of doing the checks and balances, and so to help us become more responsible, we suddenly need to be very aware of the present moment. Is it going to be a good moment or not? This change is good to know and more important to keep in mind as we go forward in this fifth dimension!

This brings us to the phrase "if it doesn't feel like love to you, simply release it and let it go." And when you do release and let go anything that doesn't feel like love and it is transformed and sent into the earth for healing, the world becomes a better place and so "as within, so without."

And of course our last phrase is "let go and let God be God." And it is here that our faith shines and the power of love is sent out to the world. This phrase is the perfect lead in to the most perfect bumper sticker in the world: "When the power of love overcomes the love of power, the world will know peace."

CHAPTER XVIII

Healing Eyes of Atlantis

Look up to the blue sky to keep your purity of thought!

—Tecumseh, 2007

As we have stated before, in the fifth dimension, the spiritual healer heals by seeing perfection where there has been the illusion of imperfection. This is how the Christ energy heals as well as how Archangel Rafael and many of the other well-known healers heal as well. They heal by *seeing* the perfection before experiencing the perfection of being in wellness. The Atlantians actually used their third eyes to affect change as well. Because there was such a strong mental state of being in Atlantis, it was of course second nature for those that were advanced mentally to use their third eye, which is also referred to as the vitae chakra or the psychic eye. Psychic development comes through in the vitae chakra, which is the primary source of communication with spirit guides as well as of teleportation and transmigration. Each of these techniques has to do with the psychic eye and were developed by those who were masters in Atlantian ways and Atlantian wisdom.

Whether or not you are a Lemurian or an Atlantian, you will have the ability to use the energy developed in Atlantian lifetimes to have that flow into your physical eye's sockets to see life with fifth-dimensional patterns. In order to experience this for yourself, allow yourself to feel the energy that comes from the psychic eye. Imagine that chakra as you relax and visualize the energy that floats very naturally into what we call your two birthright eyes, one on either side of the psychic eye. If you have Lemurian energy, don't worry! You too can tap into the wisdom that was gained by the Atlantians and have that chi-like energy flow. So relax your psychic eye, allow the energy flow into your two birthright eyes. This is easier if you keep your eyes closed because you will not be distracted and you will more easily be able to feel the energy.

As you relax your eyes, you will probably be able to see certain patterns and colors begin to form. Patterns are very important because it is through them that you are able to create fifth-dimensional consciousness in your lifetime. It is very much like the artist who says, "I have a vision and now I am going to draw that vision." The same is true of the fifth-dimensional healers and those with fifth-dimensional eyesight. At first what you see may not seem like anything much, but keep it as raw data and let the patterns begin to form. You will find that over a period of a few months, different patterns for your life, for your consciousness, for the lives of your children and your significant others will appear. This is not something for you to give much thought to, but rather something to let take its form from your guides and teachers.

There will be seven guides that will help you in this process. Each one represents a different color and will help you to open up your psychic eyes. Now when your guides get you to think in terms of color, it bypasses the consciousness. The reason for this is so that your guides can work with you with fewer filters. As we discussed previously, the fewer the filters, the more profound the information! If your guides speak to you and you hear it through color rather than a statement of words, then you are getting the information in its purest form possible. As with all of the information that you receive from your guides, remember that you cannot force or lead what you will receive. The information that is supposed to be revealed to you will be revealed to you.

You may be wondering what all of this has to do with healing. Well, the tone of colors and the feeling that you have with those tones affects what kind of healing you do. It is therefore very important that you experiment with color and find out how different colors make you feel. What does red do for you? What does green do for you? What does magenta do for you? For this exercise, you will have to go less on the mental interpretation of the color and more on how your body reacts to the color. Why do you think that you are given eyesight on the planet? You were given eyesight so that you can drink in the beauty of the planet through color. So use the beauty of color and the way that various colors make you feel to heal yourself and others! Let the colors dance in your third eye right now, and know that anytime the colors dance, they can also come together to form yet another nuance of color.

Just imagine how delightful it would be to live in Atlantis and play with the colors all day. Well, you can experience some of this delight by taking out some crayons and doing automatic coloring. Now it doesn't sound as sophisticated as automatic writing, but it will enable you to bypass your conscious desire to pigeonhole everything. When Jane Roberts did automatic writing for the philosopher William James, he correctly identified that scientists, in their desire to create order, accumulated facts and lost knowledge. Many of us feel the most comfortable in the area of facts and figures because we were trained in a three-dimensional arena.

So you couldn't just take someone from the third dimension and throw them into the formlessness of colors. You had to give them some order. And now you are going from the fourth to the fifth dimension where you think less and feel more. So how do the colors feel to you? As you go through the day, be conscious of how various colors feel to you. Let the information reveal itself to you rather than trying to figure it out logically. In other words, enjoy the colors without trying to assign an order to them. All colors are for healing, all colors create blessings, and all colors give you benefits. There are not good and bad colors, right and wrong colors. You have to see what appeals to you, what has a healing effect on you. Simply let yourself bathe in the colors. That is the first thing that individuals do when they go to a place that is very Atlantian—the Bahamas, for example. They like to look at the different colors of blue—the sky and the water. When you go to a place that is Lemurian, you bathe in different colors of white and yellow. However, that does not mean that you can't enjoy all of the colors of the universe in any location. Remember, this is a joyous process of appreciation for the various colors that you are fortunate enough to see, of allowing the patterns to come to you and receiving the information that your guides would like you to have.

* * * * * * *

Our physical eyes perceive only 2 percent of all that is out there, which means that a whopping 98 percent of what is out there is not perceived! Wow! Let us see if we can perceive more of what we are not perceiving by understanding how to work through this limitation.

Let's begin by working with how this wonderful slant on color and pattern really helps us to stretch beyond our usual into the unusual, to stretch beyond our limitations into the world of no limitations. One of the most wonderful experiences that I have had to help me see beyond the world of "me" is to play with my developing third eye. The new psychic knowledge that I have obtained has certainly helped me to "see" things in a new way, a different way, a more advanced and fun way of seeing all of the possibilities that life holds for each of us.

I remember the first exercise of relaxing my eyes and simply waiting to see what would appear. In a few minutes, I saw very clearly little lemon-yellow-colored teardrop shapes all lined up in straight little rows. (Now what do you think that says about me?) Actually, I was surprised at how precise both the pattern and the color were. I remember thinking that my "vision" must reflect very organized thoughts! I don't know why I thought that, but I did. It was another example of linear thinking, I am afraid! Actually perhaps I was falling into the mode of "thinking" and trying to pigeonhole what I was seeing instead of simply allowing myself to "feel" the colors and getting comfortable with that experience.

Another exercise I learned helped me to see or discover something that wasn't really there! Simply cup your hands around your eyes, keeping out any distractions or other colors while staring down at a plain piece of white paper. You do not allow your eyes to see anything outside of this piece of white paper. After a few minutes of staring, what do you see? What takes shape? What are the colors you see? Perhaps you may need to try this for a couple of times before anything appears for you. But don't give up as being able to "see" something that is not apparent on a plain white sheet of paper is an interesting phenomenon; to look beyond the real, to see beyond the obvious is another way of looking at our world. It is a discovery all by itself!

Keeping track of the colors you see will be helpful as you are developing your color story. You may see the color over and over again, or you may close your eyes, defocus, and you see a very fluid color flowing in and through your consciousness. When you get comfortable seeing color, please pay attention to the intensity and its hue. If you see green, is it a bright green and deep similar to an emerald? Or is the green a neon green—that is, a bright lime green? Or do you see a very cool green, an aqua green, like the green in the ocean? These colors not only define your color story but define your guides that are coming to you as well. As you become comfortable identifying the colors, try to identify the feeling associated with each color.

Keep a record of your colors until you have seven colors, each representing a guide. If you are doing this exercise with someone else, do not compare your colors to theirs. Remember, each color is a different vibration, and no one color is better than another. Each color is simply different. You also should not look to see what colors you do not have. Simply pay attention to the colors that you were given and that came to you. These colors are your gift and should be treated accordingly. Each color is unique to you and is a specific pattern helping to define a unique you and no one else. Each color is also an expression of beauty, and each color represents love. All of them have been given to you for purposes of healing.

Pulling crayons or colored pencils of the seven colors you have chosen is the next step in working with the colors or working with your guides. Simply play or scribble—it doesn't really matter. How do these colors feel to you? As long as you can in meditation or as you are going through your day, just stay with your colors. Let the information reveal itself to you rather than your trying to figure it out. Again there is no point in trying to train yourself to be a fifth-dimensional healer because you were never trained to be a fifth-dimensional healer in a three-dimensional world. Forego all mental activity and allow this activity to become a feeling activity.

Every time I close my eyes to simply rest for a moment, I see a purple that is very fluid and a yellow that seems to come in and through and around the purple. I have identified this energy as a guide of mine that actually is in my circle of twelve. He takes center stage and is literally right in front of me, so it makes sense that when I close my eyes he is right there. There have been times when I was looking for an answer or searching for clarity, and who pops up? Yes, the strength of the purple and yellow energy. This energy has helped me to develop so much strength around my heart chakra. I know that the purple and the yellow simply represent an energy, and no matter what colors I see, all of the colors come from a place of love. It is so comforting to know that I am constantly being guided and loved by this guide and that he is always here for me!

These colors can help to define colors that may be needed to be drawn to you in your life. Each color has a purpose, and you simply let yourself be surrounded in the colors and allow the healing to occur. So if lavender is one color that you see, perhaps you should invest in a lavender candle. To bring in more of the energy and to add to the healing energy, lavender aromatherapy would be a great idea to incorporate in your home. This can be said for other color tones as well: eucalyptus, citrus scents, or sandalwood are wonderful additions as color may be incorporated in the healing energy of aromatherapy.

Each color you identify is a wonderful gift to you and helps you to bring the guide that the color represents into your life in a more important way. This may be the beginning of a really "colorful" relationship with your guides as your inner child begins to heal. When you are nonphysical, your angelic influences are simply love, and you cannot say that one guide loves you more than another guide or that one guide loves you less than someone else he is attending to. You can say that each guide's way of loving you is unique as each color they represent is unique. Why? Because in your relationship with your guide, there is you, there is the guide, and there is the exchange of love. Nothing can be more unique than that relationship! So enjoy and allow yourself to be awash with colors and bask in the healing they bring to you!

As you get comfortable with the notion of using your physical eyes to help you develop your third eye, you can continue to practice different exercises to increase your development. I practice one of my favorite exercises just before I fall to sleep. The bedroom is dark and your eyes are closed and you are quietly lying there, and if you are patient you see a beautiful black sky and many stars, and you realize that as you fall asleep you are one with the universe.

CHAPTER XIX

Dolphins in the Fifth Dimension

It is interesting to note that while some dolphins are reported to have learned English—up to fifty words used in correct context—no human being has been reported to have learned dolphinese.

—Dr. Carl Sagan

Welcome again to the world of the fifth dimension! Our planet actually evolved to the fifth dimension initially through the ocean, and then to land. Therefore one could easily theorize that dolphins were living in the fifth dimension even before humans, and in certain parts of the world that is true. The really great news though is that dolphins, and all other marine mammals, will assist individuals based upon where that individual is in their spiritual development. So if the individual needs fourth-dimensional assistance in the realm of emotionality, the dolphins and whales are going to assist them in that capacity. If they need assistance with the fifth-dimensional energy, they will assist the individual with that. So what we are talking about is really the continuation of fourth-dimensional assistance as well as the fifth-dimensional interplay between you, the individual, and marine mammals.

The dolphins will assist individuals in the fifth dimension by teaching us about respect. It is of course crucial that fifth-dimensional individuals honor the planet and have respect and reverence for all things that occupy it. The dolphins and the whales are going to step up to this opportunity and help individuals to learn how to apply the concepts of respect and reverence. What you will find when you follow these concepts and incorporate them into your life is that you will become more Christlike and more like those energies that have purified energy forms. As you understand mutual respect and having a reverence for all living things, it is as if you are holding the world in very gentle and very compassionate hands. You will not see a separation between you and any other person, animal, planet, or circumstance because there is no separation. So how will the dolphins teach these important lessons? They are going to teach through their activity or inactivity; through their presence or their absence.

The marine mammals will teach you this respect and reverence through your encounters with them either physically in water or in dreamstate. If a marine mammal comes to you in a dreamstate, be sure to check with a resource such as medicine cards that will tell you what their appearance symbolizes. If they do come in sleep state it is usually a precursor to having an interaction in the physical realm in one form or another. It might even be as simple as a spontaneous trip to an aquarium or oceanarium where you encounter some marine mammals and it brings your dream into your consciousness. They will teach you to think with your heart, to ask yourself how you would like to be treated and how you would like to be honored and appreciated. It is certainly true that the more that you ask these questions to plants, animals, and minerals, the more that your own energy field will be purified. You can very easily and very gently be guided by the marine mammals in order to purify your energy field. This is actually not just emotionally, spiritually, or even mentally, but it is also physically.

The marine mammals will help you to be constantly reminded of our connection, our oneness, with all things. So what would it feel like to feel as if everyone and everything is part of your extended family? What would it be like to feel that there is no conflict, harshness, or animosity? Try to get a sense of what it would feel like to have that level of respect for everything in the universe. And as you are getting a sense of it, understand that this is very much in accordance with living on the planet in a fifth-dimensional way. Of course you can and should still speak your truth, but you will do so in a very respectful way.

Because you are a fifth-dimensional being in what is now a fifth-dimensional planet, you have the opportunity to create a winning situation for all living things. While this is a beautiful way to live your life, there will always be those that will rebel against this idea. They will think, "I can't treat others with respect if they are three-dimensional. I can't be reverent to beings that don't appreciate what I know spiritually or what I am learning or practicing spiritually." But those who are truly wise recognize that you cannot touch heaven if you are not heaven. If you have not purified your energy field, then you will always be out of sorts, feeling left behind. If you are a being left behind, remember that it is because you have created that scenario. So don't let yourself get caught in that rut of judging others; instead continue to practice love. When you practice love, you will reap so very many rewards, not the least of which is more finely tuned interactions with marine mammals.

Do you remember that we said earlier that the fifth dimension is the realm of the spiritual healer? The spiritual healer sees perfection where there has been an illusion of imperfection. The dolphins are going to teach individuals about environmental responsibility. You may think that you are already environmentally responsible. You recycle, you do not litter, you respect animals, so why do you need this lesson? Well, what is the state of your own personal environment, the energy field surrounding your physical body? The dolphins will teach you how to have respect and reverence for your own body, how to clean your own energy field so that there is a great improvement in the environment. This can happen because if each of us walked around with minimal toxins in our bodies we would feel happier, more alive and have more energy. This of course would then translate into a much happier, much more positive environment for all of us. Just as the dolphins take care of their physical body through activity and healthy eating, you too must nurture your temple through health and wellness.

In this quest for healthy living, you do not need to give up every naughty indulgence. For example, you can still have chocolate, caffeine, refined sugar, or alcohol from time to time, but what you don't want is to continue in a pattern of this behavior. For example, imagine that you start every morning with a big jelly roll and a cup of coffee. You eat healthfully the rest of the day, but you begin it habitually with these toxins of refined sugar and caffeine. Well, that is simply a pattern that you have to break. You have created this pattern most likely for emotional reasons, but it is now having a physiological impact on you. You might even have a bit of an addiction to it.

What you need to do in order to break this pattern is reorient yourself so that you have variety in your life.

Even if you are a vegan who eats rice and vegetables every day, guess what? That is a pattern, and patterns don't serve you. You are only getting the same nutrients over and over and in the same way. It may be from several different sources, but if you are only using the same sources, your body registers that. Believe it or not, dolphins are going to be teaching you about breaking patterns. And when you have broken these patterns, you will be able to enjoy what it is that you crave occasionally. It will not be a big deal if you want to have a big cup of caffeinated coffee as long as this is not your regular routine.

When you break these patterns, you will see that eating is simply a part of the process of maintaining and expanding energy for your physical body. It is nothing more. It is not shameful; it is not a Band-Aid for any unresolved emotional issues. When you listen to what your body really craves and honor those cravings with variety in healthy foods, you will be continuing the process of creating a win-win situation for you and for others. When you eat in a way that feels like love, you will feel better because you will be trusting yourself, which will in turn make those that are around you feel better as well. If you want the world around you to change, then modify, redirect, restructure what is inside of you, and begin right now!

Another thing that the dolphins and whales come to teach is spirit communication. You may be wondering how in the world marine mammals are going to teach you to communicate with spirit. Well, these beings have heightened sensory applications for telepathy, teleportation, and, yes, for transmigration. They will use these gifts to enhance your connection with spirit. They will aid in your communication with your guides and teachers as well as with nature divas, including flower essences, for example. They will help to soften and dispense your filter so that you are able to see things as they really are and more easily communicate with spirit clearly and articulately. This is quite a gift that the dolphins are offering for anyone who wants to be an intuitive or wants to be more psychically attuned, or just wants answers to the many questions that they have.

The marine mammals are also coming to your rescue in order to help you to create the best world possible. We are not talking here about the environment as a whole but about following what is on your blueprint to create the very best for yourself. You may be wondering, "How do the dolphins and the whales know about my blueprint?" They don't. They have much too much to do and other interests, so when they scan you they are not going to read your blueprint. They are going to help you to create the best world possible by bringing forward a level of passion in you. They will not allow you to procrastinate on items that really should be done today in order to better your personal development.

In the fourth dimension when individuals were focusing on passion through the help of the dolphins, it was solely from an emotional state. This is wonderful as you know the emotions are the keys to the kingdom, they really are. But what we are talking about now is passion the fifth-dimensional way, a passion for spirituality! That doesn't mean that you don't have emotions in the fifth dimension, you absolutely do. But the dolphins are going to be helping you as a spiritual healer. Now as we have said, spiritual healing is seeing perfection where you formerly saw the illusion of imperfection. But what else is spiritual healing? It is what we call the Law of Natural Flow; it is what we call spiritual mastery. But how does this relate to passion? Well, fifth-dimensional healers have a passion for spirituality. They have a passion for being unlimited. As part of this passion, dolphins will also help to show you just how blessed you are to be in a human form on this planet. You have so very many, many options available to you. If you want to read a book, you can. If you want to go for a walk or a swim, you can. If you want to travel, or meditate, you can. They will help you to have this expanded perspective, to appreciate the many blessings that you have been given.

Practice connecting with the dolphin energy by doing some conscious breathing techniques. Picture the dolphins swimming through the water. Visualize the jumping and flipping in the ocean. Let yourself be open to receive their wisdom primarily through the heart chakra. Just lay your hand right in the middle of your chest to activate your heart chakra. You may be wondering what would happen if you were to encounter an eighth-dimensional dolphin. Well, you will not be getting eight-dimensional information. Why? Because you don't speak the language! But what you are able to understand, the dolphin will transmit so that there will be a blossoming, an opening and an expansion to your life. In order to receive this gift, you must keep your heart chakra open. When you do this, you will find that their insights, gifts, and wisdom will come to you and help you to realize that you are in fact unlimited.

* * * * * * * *

In an earlier chapter, we spoke about the ancient civilizations of Lemuria and Atlantis. Both of these civilizations represented people that were polar opposites. The first group is the group from the area known as Lemuria. Today this area is in and around the Pacific Ocean, and its energies exist primarily in Hawaii, Japan, New Zealand, Australia, the Easter Islands, the Philippines, and other closely aligned countries. The energy was primarily a very spiritual energy, and the people were kind, loving, and compassionate.

The Atlantian energy was its opposite. This society was very advanced and had technical capabilities that we are just now being retaught or are being reintroduced into our society. This Atlantian energy was primarily in the Atlantic Ocean area stretching from one continent to the next and was not only technically advanced but also produced aggressive thinkers. This group decided it was time to determine the "superiority" between the two civilizations, so they decided to go to war with the Lemurians.

Is it any surprise that the Lemurians lost? They simply were no match for the highly developed and technically superior Atlantians. Lemuria disappeared, eaten up by its aggressor. So it was decided by the powers that be to gift the planet with the Lemurian energy, and the energy has remained in some of its original land and also in the form of the dolphin. This mammal entered into our world spreading the energy of joy and love throughout the waters, helping to heal the physical world. However, being spiritually advanced, the dolphin is a great help for anyone who wishes to heal their spiritual world. The Atlantian energy is still very much part of the second—and third-dimensional world and is primarily represented by people on the planet who are aggressive, very mental, and extremely competitive. The Lemurian energy is also representative of the feminine energy while the Atlantian energy is considered to be the masculine energy. (Please do not confuse the use of the terms *feminine* and *masculine* with the gender of female and male).

The Native Americans believe that the dolphin is the totem for the breath of life. This represents the very life force that exists within each of us and of course is a requirement for all humans if they are to exist on this planet. The dolphin teaches us that by changing our breath, we can reach other levels or planes of existence. We can travel to other dimensions. To enhance our spiritual growth, the dolphin helps us to remember to connect with spirit through our breath. (My favorite totem reference books are Nicki Scully's *Power Animal Meditations* and Sam's and Carson's *Medicine Cards* for meaning to many of the totems that we come into contact with.) The use of many sources can expand the totem's meaning, and if some parts don't relate to you, others will. You will judge which parts resonate deep within your heart.

How can we hope to grow and develop spiritually if we do not learn to relax, get centered, sit in the silence, and tap into our higher self? The dolphin will help us to do all these things as well as enter our dream state to teach us and help us to explore these higher planes. When we are able to maximize the breath, we are able to connect. When we are able to connect, we are able to feel the life force within us. When we feel the life force within us, we know we are one and are more easily able to connect with every other living element on the planet.

When we think of the place that the dolphin holds in our oceans, we know that this energy has been sent to rescue not only those who are at risk in the oceans but those who are at risk spiritually. The dolphin, with the feminine energy, nurtures those that need help and continually breathes life and connection into the human form. This is yet another example of how this marine mammal is aiding us in our search for the divine.

The research that has been done in working with the dolphins has shown that not only are they an extremely intelligent mammal, but their demeanor and mannerisms create playfulness and joy. What are they teaching us by example? To not only enjoy our life but to learn to work toward expanding out joy through loving and respecting ourselves and teaching others to love and respect themselves. We can be a great example of these qualities when we get in touch with our own inner joy. Individuals will naturally gravitate toward those that have accomplished joy and the expression of it in their lives as well as being able to attract in like individuals and helping the energy of family and friends that are close to your auric field.

Anyone who has swum with the dolphins will tell you that their energy is amazing. My friends recently went to Miami and swam with the dolphins and shared with me their insights of their experiences. Each described the dolphin energy as fun, playful, full of life and love but also extremely peaceful, just as you would picture them. They also felt that while they were in the presence of the dolphins, they felt a total calm sweep over them. Experiencing no fear allowed them to totally trust the dolphins and fully experience their loving presence. In describing the way others interacted with the dolphins, they saw that everyone felt alive and happy, that the dolphin energy was contagious and that everyone experienced this carefree energy.

The healing energy of the dolphin is powerful and strong, and any emotional or physical problem that may have existed is minimized just by their very presence. Dolphins have a very strong spiritual presence. It is not unusual while in the presence of the dolphins for the first time that individuals may experience tears of joy. The energy of the dolphin is so pure and so joyful that being in its presence becomes an emotional experience. Typically a very strong connection occurs between the dolphins and their trainers, each nurturing the other. Recognizing the connection as beautiful, it is obvious an exchange of love is being transmitted and received from both sides.

It is also known that the dolphins have the natural ability to heal themselves. If a dolphin has a scratched nose or back, the next day there may be no visible sign of any injury. Their communication skills are superior as well as they are able to communicate with other dolphins miles apart through vibrations and tones. Is it any wonder that we are to learn from them?

In an earlier chapter, I mentioned that one of the members of my planet healing group is a master animal communicator. Diane has developed her gift to such a masterful level that she easily is able to communicate with dolphins and marine mammals. Coincidentally, she just happens to have an ongoing relationship with dolphins as the dolphin is one of her totems. I asked her to connect her energy with the dolphin energy to see if they had a message that they wanted sent out to the world. The following is a summary of the conversation between Diane and the dolphins. The dolphins expressed deep concern about the condition of the oceans. They feel that we are losing the battle with creating clean waters and currently go to the masters who are on the planet for assistance. However as the planet is transitioning into the 2012 energy, the dolphins are concerned that they will not have anyone to go to for help as the masters will be leaving the planet in 2011. Diane assured them that masters are evolving every day on the planet as they are learning and evolving into the fifth-dimensional energy and are using the spiritual healing energy to help heal the planet. (Our planet healing group had previously been told that the responsibility of our world, the health of our natural resources, and the health and wellbeing of our animal kingdom and ultimately the entire planet will rest solely on our shoulders. We have been given this fifth-dimensional energy as the means or healing tool to help every area of life on Planet Earth to grow and evolve into a state of wellness. We each as members of our planet must accept responsibility for our environment; the more committed you become as a fifth-dimensional healer, the better healing you will send out into the world.)

The dolphins are peace. The dolphins are saying to us: "We do not fight unless made to, and then we go right back to peace, immediately. Peace is part of who we are. Please use our peace to find yours. We are all interconnected. Tap into us and you will see the way. We are superior beings, and our success for our mission on earth is tied to you. If you succeed then we succeed. We have been helping you for thousands of years, but the more technology you discover, the less you listen. This is not good. There are so many of you, your number far exceeds ours, yet you need us. Glide through your existence and don't make waves. This is the way to true peace. We will not give in like some species have. We are committed to our mission and to Planet Earth. We were one of the first to volunteer to be a guiding force, and we will not leave you. If our physical presence is compromised, we will be with you in spirit as we are dedicated to your success."

The dolphin energy further encourages a commitment to spirituality and its development. The dolphin becomes a part of your everyday existence by giving you its energy and thereby it becomes part of who you are. Its essence and your essence become one. As you grow spiritually, this energy is given right back to the planet and felt by others.

As the dolphin has gained his reputation for being the spiritual leader in the ocean, we too can take this lesson and become our own spiritual leader. We need to be as enthusiastic as the dolphin, we need to be able to rescue ourselves and our planet as the dolphin shows us by his example. We need to be able to communicate with all people by using a common language, the language of love as the dolphin has demonstrated by his language. We need to be able to heal ourselves first and then others as the dolphin does, by learning how to live from the heart.

So the next time you see a dolphin in the ocean, or perhaps a picture of one, ask yourself, "What does this energy mean to me?" And as you are answering, smile in the knowingness that the dolphin energy is here for us to totally enjoy the energy, the spirit, and the love that the dolphin has come to teach us. Feel that love and that joy and allow it to permeate your being. And as the world expands and evolves, don't be surprised when you are in the company of your children or grandchildren and they exclaim, "I can talk to the dolphins and this is what they are telling me . . . !" or, "Last night when I was sleeping, the dolphin came to me and told me this . . . !" Just smile in the wonder of it all. Of course, if your grandchild has just shapeshifted into a dolphin, you will know that your grandchild is well along on his or her evolvement—and perhaps has been shifting in and out of future dimensions!

What a world we are evolving to!

Message from Mother Earth

How much angrier do I have to get to wake this world up? This is your world we have given to you. You have become a nation of convenience, and the planet is paying for it, as are all of your resources. Each one of you worries about terrorists; however, you have become your own terrorist to your planet with a lack of respect to the whole human race and all of mankind.

All earth changes come from the water on earth. All mammals have the highest sensitivity and have been giving you messages. The dolphins and the whales have been speaking to you that the gift of water is on shaky ground. The waters need healing, but it goes much deeper than that. The mammals wish to be listened to and respected so that in turn the planet may be respected, which it hasn't in a very long time. Listen to their purity and their energy.

You will see creatures both in the waters and on the land that are acting in very strange ways. They are drawing attention to themselves, a cry for help, so that they draw attention to the problems on the planet. Look at the clues as they are the signs that nature is giving to you.

When it rains, before the first drop hits the earth, ask for the rain to come in its purest form so that it heals the earth. This intention is very powerful and it has the power to remove all toxins from the rainwater. How can rain that is laden with toxins heal the earth? Teach the children the power of this prayer.

I send love to all of you for the work that you are doing to raise your consciousness. With your knowledge and awareness comes a great responsibility. Healing starts with what you are doing in your own home and then it moves outward. Each of you please accept the gift of awareness. I will also send each of you love and healing as each of you can make a difference. With that I will take leave.

Channeled 2006

Planet Healing

CHAPTER XX

Feng Shui

Everything should be made as simple as possible, but not simpler!

—Einstein

Welcome to what is often called Feng Shui! We call it the art of geomancy, which is divination by intuition and design. Feng shui is yet another gift given to us to help us combine the outer and the inner worlds to create not just your own element of perfection but perfection for what is to come. You create your future right now, and what you focus on right now is what will come to be in one form or another. As you focus on both the elements and the fundamentals, the outcome is assured but not predictable in terms of design of what is to be for your life. You create your future literally on your next breath. The more conscious you are that the energy flows within and without, the more you will create a future that is harmonious for your present and your future. You may not even know what you want in the future, and that is all right. Being conscious of the flow of energy is really the most important step in creating perfection in your life.

The most important element is, obviously enough, is your element, which is one of the five possibilities. (These elements will be described toward the end of this chapter.) This is the most important element for you, and as you begin to identify the different aspects of yourself, you add the layers to this element. Layers are simply more information that you determine about yourself, that create a more complete story for you about you. An example would be to identify yourself not only as "fire," but fire born in the year of the snake or ox, or whatever year you may have been born. All of these things are revealing different aspects of your potential. If you needed to know them earlier, then you would have known them.

As you move forward, it is important for you to understand that the best is yet to be. The best is yet to be because as you continue your spiritual growth, you will feel more connected with your own flow of energy. Your chi energy, as it goes up through your chakras, will cause you to feel connected to the chakras on the planet. You become aware of this energy flow, all flowing in a continual pattern, and feel the connection of oneness.

If you think about your planet at large, identify the energy flow as it relates to the chakras on your body. The geographical areas are: the base chakra is the Egyptian pyramid region; the area known as Sedona is the area known as the spleen chakra; the solar plexus chakra is centered in Tahiti and its islands and the archipelago (but not the atolls); the heart chakra covers most of the islands of Hawaii and is centered on Oahu and all of the way down to the northern tip of the big island; the communication chakra is in the area of Mt. Shasta; the vitae chakra (the third eye) is in the region of Glastonbury and it fans out from there; and the crown chakra is in the region of Tibet. These chakras correspond to the flow of energy on the planet. Similarly to you rediscovering elements about yourself that allow your energy to flow harmoniously within yourself, the planet too must have points where the energy flows to bring it also into harmony. Remember that we are a microcosm for the macrocosm and there are many vortices that are open to the flow of energy around the planet. You do not have to visit Hawaii to bring your heart chakra into the flow, but you do need to identify the vortices that contribute to this particular flow of energy. This activity does not happen in a linear way, it happens in a nonlinear way.

For your own body it is important to understand that body weight has an impact on your feng shui abilities and opportunities. It is important to understand that this has little to do with weight in terms of what you want to be aesthetically, but it has a lot to do with your energy. In ayurvedic terms, this is the *vata*, *pitta*, and *kapha*. Your energy begins to match your physical weight so that the energy within you begins to flow more easily and your body has a positive feng shui experience and will then experience the ultimate geomancy within it!

You can determine easily if you are dominant for vata, pitta, or kapha energies. In Deepak Chopra's book, *Perfect Health*, there is a questionnaire that will help you identify your energy type. One easy way to identify your energy is to get a sense of how your energy moves. If you move very slowly in the morning and it is difficult to get your day started, then you have a dominant kapha energy. If you are someone who likes to get up very early, with the sunrise for example, and begin the day accomplishing many items on your list with lots of energy, then you are vata energy. If you are someone who gets started in the middle of the morning, say seven to eight o'clock, with a set and organized agenda, your energy is the pitta energy.

How then do you match your energy type to your body weight? If you have the dominate vata energy, you should be lighter and slighter in your frame. If you have kapha energy, it is a bit like carrying the energy of the world on your shoulders and you should have a more solid weight. That being said, it is important that your muscular structure be toned so that you can carry this heavier weight. If you are predominately kapha but you are slight, it doesn't mean that you need to gain a lot of weight, but you need to bulk up in key areas. Many times those that are predominantly kapha will do weightlifting in order to build up the muscular elements inside your physical body. If you are pitta, you are in between those two extremes of vata and kapha. So if you are vata and you have a lot of weight, then it is in fact important that you should do body sculpting. You will be very aware of the weight as it isn't comfortable and it doesn't feel like love to you. If you are predominately pitta, you would have an average-size frame but you would do more exercise to keep yourself in shape so that you would feel comfortable. As you determine how you fit into these three types of energies, you should feel that your body sculpture fits the energy that you came into this lifetime with. You will also feel comfortable as now you are able to feel that you are a match with yourself.

Once you have determined your body type, the next thing you need to do is to take a look at your body. If you can imagine yourself as a turtle (with your head being in the same place as a turtle's head) and you lie with your stomach down on top of the *bagua*, then you have in your own body identified the different sectors on the bagua. The bagua is a chart in the shape of an octagon that is used in feng shui that helps to teach how and where the different areas of your life are so that you can use the information to help bring you and your life into perfect energy flow. (You can pick up a bagua at any bookstore for your own reference and learning or go online and print one out.) Your head should be placed on the career area of the chart. If you follow down your life side and look to your left shoulder, that would be the area of benefactors and the expression "angel on your shoulder" is truly applicable. The left shoulder area also includes the relatives who are important to your development, the relatives that you know that have passed over and/or relatives that are with you right now and are physical.

If you look to the right shoulder, this is where knowledge and wisdom come in. Many times you will hear whispering in the right ear and this is where not only spiritual knowledge comes in but universal knowledge as well. So many times your teachers will sit off to your right side. Yes, they are your benefactors, but they are also here to teach you. Your birthright angel also sits off to this side as you have both spiritual and universal teachings. If you go down this arm along the side of the body, it represents family. If you have any holding back emotionally with the family and are feeling out of sorts, sometimes you will have pain or chronic pain that runs down through this side. This is a feeling that the body sends you signaling that something is not right with your family or with your extended family or even with your circle of friends.

If you continue down to the right leg and to the right foot, you are going to your prosperity. If you have some discomfort or injury in this area, your body is sending you a signal that you are not receiving wealth the way you want to. Now the most important thing to remember with the body is that it is signaling you through the signs of comfort or discomfort, and it is a reflection of what you are or are not attending to that is important. If you go into the genital area, this is your fame and reputation area. So if you have heard the phrase "sleeping their way to the top," that is exactly why sexuality gets intertwined with how individuals want to achieve a level of fame. But what does it really affect? Well, their reputation of course. Now when you go to the left leg, this is the area of partnerships, relationships, and marriage. So if you feel some kind of discomfort or a stiffness in this area, that is indicating that there is something that is not right in that sector of your life.

As you go up this side of the body and this arm, this is your area of creativity. This is why individuals say if they are right-brained, then they are left-handed and left-handed individuals tend to be the more creative as that is where all of the creativity energy is flowing. So if you feel something that is not quite right here, it means that you are resisting your own creative opportunities. You are telling yourself a story about why you are not creating things in a successful way for yourself, you are arguing for your limitations. Think about yourself as this turtle and how it relates to the same area on the bagua, and you can identify where you have discomfort and that will signal you that something is out of kilter in that segment of your life.

The solar plexus chakra is right in the center, both of your body and on the chart, and this is the area the yin-yang symbol relates to. Everything springs from this emotional base of your solar plexus chakra, awareness or illness. Everything comes from how you relate to things emotionally, and this energy is constantly flowing back and forth. When individuals say I want to do better in certain areas but I am afraid, they feel it right in the solar plexus. If they say I want to do better in certain areas but I don't have a great track record, it is felt right in the solar plexus as that is where you store all of your memories.

When you bring these thoughts, ideas, or concerns up to consciousness, what you are doing is bringing the memories up to the heart chakra. If you are concerned but do not want to deal with those memories or if you are afraid that it is too late, you are already feeling them. But what happens is that you push them back down and then your energy flow gets constricted. You end up with a physical illness or a physical discomfort that is manifested as a broken arm or a twisted leg or may even materialize as a migraine headache.

Remember when something shows up as a symptom in your body, it is too late for it to not be there! When it comes up, it comes up for a very good reason because it is time for you to clear that part of yourself that has been in limitation. It is time for the issue to come to the surface so that you may look at it, claim it as it is part of your creation, and love yourself for taking the risk of being human and coming into a world that doesn't know what love is yet, and then you transform it and you send it home to God where it is transformed. You do not need to figure it all out and send it up to your vitae chakra.

When you do acknowledge the issue and embrace it with love and send it off with more love, then you begin to feel that all of these signals of discomfort dissipate, and what you are left with is a body that has less to do with aging and more to do with self-acknowledgement. It is a body that has less to do with limitations and more to do with self-love. It is a body that does not feel restricted even though you are in the physical realm. It is a body that says, "I am now ready to see beyond this line of vision and do all of this processing." It is a body that acknowledges the work that you have put in to your spiritual development and realizes that you have gotten to the point where you have cleared out the spiritual toxins, a body that truly feels God. Is this as good as it gets, or is it in fact just the beginning? In fact it is just the beginning of what is to be and what is to come. So it is a body that begins to live even if you are surrounded by individuals that still aren't living their own lives. You begin to make choices that don't feel risky to you any longer. You begin to make choices that reinforce these many layers that you are but that you are just beginning to find out about. You discover, "I am this element, I am this astrological sign, or I am compatible in this region of the country, or that my numerology number is this number." All of these things become realized as different expressions of self, and you begin to look forward to the next enlightening moment rather than feeling either overwhelmed or restricted. You begin to move and live in the flow of your energy. Furthermore, concentrating on your solar plexus area helps you to see the value in learning about feng shui.

Every once in awhile you may step back, look around, and deduce that for every ten people that are out there, at least nine of them are not doing this work and their lives look okay. You may wonder, "Do I just have a lot further to go or why am I doing this when it doesn't seem that anyone else is?" Well, what happens is that if they are on their blueprint, then you do not need to understand what they are thinking or what they are processing. If they are off of their blueprint, the body will signal this to them as described above. If they do not get the first signal, then they will get a stronger one and a stronger one, etc, until they get it. It is very human to compare your situation to others, but you cannot and should not do it. You are unique and your situation is unlike any other situation. You do not know what anyone else's blueprint looks like or what their agenda was for their previous lifetimes or for this current one. And if you spend your time looking outside rather than inside, then you reinforce the feeling that whatever you are is not enough. All that you need to do is raise your consciousness, and as you feel the urge to compare yourself to others, turn up your love for yourself. Remember, "Let God be God," and let go of everything else.

Now think about this in relation to your body as the bagua. If the element of water has been defined for you as your personal element, that means that up in your head region you do a lot of thinking and a lot of planning to the different possibilities in your life—your personal journey, including career and successful business. If your personal element is the earth, then you may be sensitive in the stomach and spleen areas, and your main concern is for your health and wellbeing. If your personal element is wood, then you relate to the sector that is family, which is about growth and movement. Simply let yourself feel the energy in your feet, throat, and buttocks regions. If your element is fire, ask yourself what is the energy that is flowing in your heart and think about it in terms of energy and not as an either-or situation. Fire also relates to your eyes. Simply feel this energy. When you do, you will begin to feel moments of bliss. If your personal element is metal, your mouth, head, and lungs are the area that is affected. This energy is feminine energy and concerns itself with children and has to do with creativity. The energies will appear because as you are developing, all of a sudden your intuition kicks in and the energy just flows. Simply stay focused on this raw energy and don't worry too much about where it is going. Now if the body signals you, you must attend to that area because the body is telling you that something is not right. Everything that you want to change around you is most easily done by changing or transforming things within you that don't feel like love to you.

Now in terms of the ancients, if you look at the Atlantians, they tell you that "knowledge is power." You have all of this knowledge in the cellular structure of your body. You have all of the answers. If you look at the wisdom of the ancients from Lemuria, a very spiritual civilization, they tell you that "love is everything." So you have all of this knowledge, and the easiest way to get to it is the key which is love. What you want to do is to combine the best of what you are and don't be afraid to get in there and let yourself know how you are truly feeling from moment to moment. For example, "I'm not feeling good this morning," or "I am stressed." If you alter the stress level within the body consciously and attend to those things that don't feel like love to you, you will begin to see the energy flow very easily around you and you will naturally go to those locations that are the most supportive of your energy. Now what we are talking about is this automatic process. You move from it being effortful to being automatic. You move from the situation of the little train that says "I think I can" to the little train that just flows, saying "I know I can, I know I can because I am doing it, I am doing it, I am doing it!"

As you look at these designs for the body, the designs for the home, and the designs for the environment, the more that you play with the possibilities, the more you will be able to have great thoughts, to expand your consciousness, and to have greater levels of spirit communication because you are not worrying about handling each of the details. Now if you want a feng shui guide to consult with, this guide is found in the physical realm and is a single-attribute guide for a location. The reason why the term "location" is used is that everything is a location within and around your body as well as in your immediate location and your immediate surroundings. Location guides may also tell you where the best place is for you to live and to work or to set up a business. They will help you to understand energy flow. You may ask yourself the question, "Is this a good location for me, based upon my own personal element, for me to live or for me to open up my business?" Your location guide will give you your answer based upon these layers and layers of unique qualities that all come together to form individuals unlike any other.

As you become more versed in geomancy, your location guide is able to help you with the bigger issues. You will begin to understand how guides operate, and you are able to get a lot of information intuitively and then you ask for clarification and help with seeing the bigger picture. So whether you choose to call this being your single-attribute guide of location or your feng shui guide or your single attribute guide of geomancy, this guide is here to you maximize your energy flow in and around not only your body but your personal and professional environments and the world at large.

* * * * * * * *

As we begin to understand and embrace the meaning of feng shui, we become aware of how important the flow of energy is in all areas of our life: the body, our personal spaces, our professional environment, and into the world beyond. We also have learned when our body is not in the state of wellness, the lack of good feng shui contributes to our general state of health and wellbeing. The work of Simon Brown entitled *The Feng Shui Bible* is a wonderful overview of the meaning of feng shui and all of its applications in our world. This book further describes the optimum situations as well as remedies or cures to bring yourself into an optimum situation should your environment be lacking. The more you become a student of feng shui, the more you will be able to see how you are able to not only enhance your life but add to the value and meaning of your life by living in the flow of the chi energy. There are many other manuals and guides that will help describe ways to evaluate your environment which I encourage you to read.

ANIMALS

I will concentrate on Markas's words and a few additional thoughts that he has for our consideration and awareness. I would like to begin talking about animals as they are in a class by themselves and really can and do impact our lives in all of the physical areas of our life: our body, our home, our work environment, and the world beyond! Animals of every energy have been given to the planet as gifts; we learn from each of them as we walk and share our earth, and they learn from us. We need to remember that having pets is not only a very healthy extension of ourselves into our world, but what we receive in terms of benefits from our animal friends is unmatched. Our love is of course returned by them unconditionally. They have been given to us as the perfect example of unconditional love. Not only do we benefit from them directly, but the energy that flows from them to us is also greatly enhanced as they come with benefactors. These benefits just by virtue of having pets can be described as "unseen but certainly not unfelt" and greatly add to our experiences here on earth, bringing us joy and laughter and companionship at every level. We then benefit on every level.

It is not unusual for an animal energy to return to us during different lifetimes—both ours and theirs! We may have had a dog in a previous lifetime or lifetimes, and this energy returns during this current incarnation on earth. He or she just seems to find its way back into our lives! A contract may exist between both parties (the animal party and the human party) that may need completion, or perhaps there is a continuation of lessons that may need to be learned. The animals even come in as expert or master healers. Perhaps you have contracted to have a physical ailment and the animal energy comes in to help you through the experience. It is not unusual to see an animal friend lie next to us, their paw touching our body, allowing the transfer of a healing flow of energy. Occasionally, you will hear that someone contracts cancer, and their pet of twelve years passes away shortly thereafter while the human patient may journey to remission. The gift that the animal was giving to his owner/patient was indeed priceless! The connection is strong as it is obvious—as mentioned earlier, animals are a gift to us as the perfect example of unconditional love!

Animals do vibrate at a higher energy frequency than we do and are more highly evolved than we are. Their understanding of our language is remarkable and complete. They have feelings and emotions and can express them in both positive and negative ways: the use of body language may exhibit depression, physical ailments, or mental ailments, etc. In short, we have been given a beautiful gift, and our furry friends should be honored and loved and respected. It is a very common occurrence to see a cat or dog focus or stare up to the ceiling or corner of a room. They are able to see our angelic influences or unseen benefactors as they are vibrating at an energy level that allows them to see far more than we are able! These beautiful teachers are here because we have much to learn from them, and as such, we have much to be thankful for and give them back the unconditional love they extend to us.

THE BODY

Let's first look at how we can relate feng shui to our physical bodies and see what changes may need to occur to achieve the desired outcome of ease and wellness. Is your body in balance with the kapha, pitta, and vata energy? This is our beginning point. So the first thing you need to do is to make the determination—which of the three energies are you dominant in? Remember you can be a combination of all three energies, but your dominant energy needs to be determined so that you can determine if you are living in the flow of the energy that is dominant. If in fact you do have all three energies in your physical body, then a dominance could be as little as 36 percent of the energy while the remaining two energies could be 34 percent and 30 percent. After the determination of which energy is your dominant energy, then you can assess your body's weight and shape and decide what work needs to be done so that you body is functioning with its maximum flow of energy. I believe Markas suggested Deepok Chopra's *Perfect Health* as a good resource for helping to identify your energy.

While learning the concepts of feng shui (as we suggested earlier, using either the *Perfect Health* or any other guide), you will be able to identify your element and your personal number. This information becomes part of you, and you feel comfortable with where you are compatible and where you are not, then you begin to get the next layer of information. You will be able to get this intuitively, and then you will be able to design your environment that will begin to foster this feeling of wellness in the body. One of the most important steps would be to remember if you are creating your future on your next breath, it is important for you that your next breath is the most important thing going on for you at that moment. It is more important than anything you may have been thinking about, any concerns, worries, or the stress in your life—none of this matters as much as to be conscious of your next breath. Soon you will increase your level of consciousness, and then your energy will begin to flow and you return to an energy flow that works for you.

THE HOME

As we look throughout our home, first look at the level of clutter and then the number of incomplete projects you have. Now the fun begins! Let's each determine our state of feng shui! On a scale of one to ten, with one being *not* very good feng shui and ten being *very* good feng shui, how would you rate yourself? So take a walk and look around. Do you see simplicity, and more importantly, do you feel a nice flow of energy? As you answer the questions and you do look around, check out and review your selections of meaningful objects that you wish to display to surround you and to contribute to your energy flow. You can take a "bagua" and place it in your home and review the areas of your home that are "congested." Since your home symbolizes your life in general, you can probably identify for yourself the areas that may need some work and then ask yourself what would be the appropriate objects to use in this sector.

Okay, let's go to the ever-important marriage corner! Remembering the rule that "less is more," what few objects can you choose that feel like love to you? Choose them carefully as they represent you and what you would like to have in your life. Next, let us look at the prosperity corner. Everyone wants to experience prosperity! What objects feel like abundance to you? Again choose wisely. Why the rule "less is more"? Understand that "less is more" helps you to send a signal to the universe that says I have room now to make my next advancement. So when you do this you will find that you will become the recipient of wonderful experiences that you cannot anticipate but that are life-enhancing and rich in value as well as a lot of fun!

So now let's look at the incomplete projects and piles of items waiting to get sorted to help us to understand the concept of stuck and stagnant energy! Every home has just such areas, and when you walk into the area you can feel that the energy is not flowing! Perhaps that is why we walk right out of the area and never get to our projects and piles—we can't stand being in that energy! So we become breeders of dead energy! Our home should only have completed projects so that we may feel nurtured and supported. However when there are incomplete projects, the fact that they exist weighs on the mind, which creates a heaviness as well as limitations. In addition, as we complete projects, we make space so that more things make their way to us and our home feels lighter and lighter. So by completing projects and simplifying our personal spaces by decluttering, it gives ample breathing space to the objects in our rooms. We not only feel lighter, but with the lightness we are able to work with the energy as we see it flowing unencumbered throughout our home. So choose a few objects that have meaning and give them ample space for display, and as we do that, we begin to understand the art of placement. We all need to understand the concept that "less is more" so that the flow of energy supports and sustains us, allowing the environment to be alive with the flow of energy and allowing us to connect our energy to this flow as well. By doing this we are increasing the energy as it relates to our family and friends as their energy is affected directly by ours.

However and wherever you chose to live, we all encounter those beings that by virtue of a shared wall in a condominium or townhouse are not part of our energy, nor should we share in their energy. How do we keep our energy clear of any negative influences? The Native Americans smudge or cleanse by using a sage wand or perhaps a couple of incense sticks of sage and cedar. You light the herb, and starting in a clockwise manner, you smudge each floor room by room. You may crack open the front door as well as a rear door so that the negative energy may exit your space. It is recommended that you smudge every four to six weeks the entire home as well as the shared walls between condominiums or townhouses. This redirects your energy back to you and lets go of any other energy. Simply by stating your intention you can create a living space with beautiful energy, free and clear of any negative energy. What is truly important is to cleanse each opening, doors and windows, from the inside of the house in a clockwise manner. When the inside is complete, you can cleanse the exterior of your home in the same manner. Using aromatherapy and placing lavender throughout your home is also an excellent cure and helps to freshen and heal the space.

THE WORK ENVIRONMENT

It is important to set up your work environment that does not include or encourage competition. It is more difficult in a work environment to create your space free from any negative energies as oftentimes your office area is in close proximity to others. Placing crystals on or in your desk as well as lavender or a lavender candle in your area will help you define your energy and keep it clear. You may also wear a lavender scent, which will help keep your energy connected to you. The same rules of decluttering and incomplete projects apply to your workspace as they did in your home. As you travel on your journey and develop and grow, you are aware that you are not like your peers. The fact is that each of us was never really like our peers, but the age-old ritual of peer approval and peer acceptance seems to keep cropping up. Intellectually we know we are all individuals and have learned that our paths are unique to each of us. We may see ourselves as being "out there" while the rest of the individuals are all "over there." It is important to understand that you may not be like how the majority is operating and to realize that that is not only okay but is a goal! It is important to get comfortable with that and that the way in which you must operate within this optimum flow of energy is going to improve your life. The rewards may be that you are going to feel your physical health improve as well as both your personal and professional lives. You may be afraid and think you are too far out there that you may be losing touch with reality. Feng shui is designed to improve the energy flow around you and not to separate you from the planet. It will only separate you from those systems that don't serve you. If you look at it this way, you will see that others will come at their own pace and that others will come to join you just the same.

Don't worry about the destination, but always make sure you are moving in the correct direction. As you take each step, you begin to feel as if you are in charge of your reality. Everyone feels that way, but occasionally you may slip into the pattern of thinking that you are a victim of your circumstances. It is all right to feel that way if it is a step that helps you to get back into your power. As you are taking these small steps, the universal energy of your guides can come in and help you and again "the whole is greater than the sum of its parts." Baby steps and the winds of change will come and propel you forward. When you feel that things are outside of your control, then recognize that your inner child of your emotional body is right there in the solar plexus, and you turn up your love for yourself and things will make themselves known to you. You go within and be the best friend to your inner child or take the role of the supportive parent, the one that loves unconditionally, and as that fearful energy gets transformed, you may release it and send it home to God. You will become very present moment, and as you do that, things begin to shift around you.

Sometimes you will see your results the very next day, and sometimes you will see it two weeks down the road, but if you know that everything is happening when you focus on what doesn't feel like love inside of you, then it doesn't matter to you when it happens because you know that you are back on your path and you know that you are moving forward in a way that really and honestly serves you—you are telling yourself the truth. Your body will begin to let go of all of the perimeters outside of it that says: success, failure, doing enough, not doing enough, need to hang on or not, and then you begin to feel the results as they will happen upon you. All that is required is becoming conscious of the ways that you have created stress in your body based upon your belief systems and memories. It is very hard to believe that you can focus on restoring and expanding the love within you and that it is going to have all of these effects outside of you. But you know that when you have tried it the other way by looking outside of yourself and trying to fix it, eventually it will get done—but at what price to the body?

THE WORLD BEYOND

There are simple cures that we can do to help the energy flow around our property, and there are ways to increase the energy and its sources around our property as well. Let us look to another gift given to our planet that not only enhances our life aesthetically but also the quality of energy that we surround ourselves with.

To amplify your feng shui flow of energy, it is wonderful to be able to choose a location in which the front yard is either parallel to the front door of the home or if the yard slopes down. However, if neither of the above is your situation, or even if it is, you can always improve your location by planting flowers. The beauty of the flowers is wonderful as you receive this added benefit by inviting the energy of the elementals in. The elementals will bring their wonderful chi energy and will be grateful that you planted flowers as that makes their job easier and they don't have to work as hard! Consider planting lavender outside as it brings with it a very healing energy and creates a wonderful energy that flows to all that pass by.

The elementals are very spiritual and bring with them a lot of spiritual energy, but they are in the physical realm, and they don't have the power that they would if you were living in a nonphysical reality. So when you put in the treatments, you are actually helping them complete their purpose which is doing what they love by working and helping with the flow of the energy.

It is wonderful that the front door of your home be gracious and inviting and so it is beneficial to have a small fountain or a pond located there. It is important, however, that if you do, you send the right message. As you look out the front door of the home, it is good to have water on the left-hand side, but not on the right-hand side. The reason is very simple: water is the universal symbol of sexuality, and it will draw to you what you desire! If water is on the right-hand side, it will draw in a situation with more than one lover! When water is on the left-hand side, it is symbolic of the rings on the left hand and is further symbolic of monogamous relationships that have traditionally been valued in our society! So my advice to the happy homeowner would be to be conscious of where the other half wants to see water as they enter the home. Perhaps this will uncover a hidden desire or fantasy that you never knew your spouse or significant other had!

CHAPTER XXI

More Messages from Markas and Friends

Hope flows the passion of the gentle searching steps into the worlds and thoughts of the unknown. But the steps lead you onto the road that you have imagined as a directed force of destiny.

—*Spirit, 2007*

As you continue your journey, you are beginning to discover things that have always been there but had not attracted your interest until now. That is because of your own growth and evolution and because you are beginning to perceive things in a fifth-dimensional way. This is not just about the things that are on your planet, but things that are in your universe, things that are in the cosmic arena—at least that part that is in your awareness.

So why is it that we are living on such a relatively small planet when it is such a big universe? Why are we living in a microcosm when you could be, in a nonlinear and nonphysical way, part of the macrocosm of the universe? The reason is that most of us have come to this planet to experience not just a three-dimensional life, but the experience of going into the fourth and fifth dimensions of consciousness. You chose this not only to experience it for yourself, but for what the impact will be on your physical plane of awareness. What you are probably finding as part of this journey is that it often feels like you are taking one step forward and two steps backward. This is all part of what some would call trial and error but what we call mastertakes. Mastertakes are things that are not really mistakes because they are not made over and over, but they are made once in order for individuals to learn. When you make an error and you "get it" the first time, this is a mastertake.

Quite often the reason why you are here eludes you. You think to yourself that there must be some great meaning to your existence. Perhaps you came in order to promote world peace. Perhaps you came because you had a karmic interest in a certain philosophy or a doctrine. Perhaps you came because you needed to learn what love is. Now while love is always on the agenda in one form or another, most of us came to experience stepping into the new fifth-dimensional reality.

Some of you came, as you know, to be spiritual healers and to experience it that way. Others came to experience the highs and lows of living on this earth plane. Some individuals even came to this planet in order to achieve mastery in a certain part of fifth-dimensional reality. Now that doesn't mean that they have more enlightenment, it just means that it is their path compared to your path. It is not better or worse as everyone comes into various lifetimes for various reasons; some individuals may have come into what would turn into a fifth-dimensional planet in order to achieve mastery of something fifth-dimensional that perhaps had eluded them in previous lives or to address an issue that they had not dealt with before.

As we have stated before, fifth-dimensional living is about seeing the perfection where there is the illusion of imperfection. So if you want to achieve mastery in one or two aspects of the fifth dimension, then you will experience this even while you are living the illusion of imperfection. Even while you are living something that feels imperfect, something that most of us can relate to, you know that this is all an illusion and that everything is in fact just as it should be, everything is perfect. Once you let this belief shape your thoughts, you will find that all of these illusions of imperfection will begin to dissipate because they no longer are the center of your reality.

How many of you have been looking at the illusion of imperfection and wishing for something else? This is normal and is to be expected. Your spirit is having a human experience, a human incarnation, so of course you do not have available to you the bigger picture at all times. Sometimes you never see the bigger picture. So of course you are going to be wishing for the perfection while very much experiencing imperfection. But again, when you get into the knowingness, the beingness, or the perfection of what you are living, the illusions will begin to dissipate because you no longer are focusing on them as the center of your reality. When you have let go of your fear and anxiety, you become the center of your reality. When you are the center of your reality, you are all-powerful, and that is when you have your strongest connection to the god/goddess energy.

This is often referred to as "waking up," and to a certain extent that is what it is. It is becoming aware that you are the center of your reality and you are aware only of the present moment. You can focus on not using your power to create what you want but being in your power. Whenever you focus on using your powers to create what you want, you are outside of yourself. But when you focus on being the power, you are in your beingness. Then those other things that used to occupy your time do not have importance to you. Growing and evolving and becoming the soul that you hope to be is how you get the illusions of imperfection to vanish. You are not trying to get rid of them consciously, but instead you have just moved on to the truth of your reality. The truth is that you are the center of your reality.

As you allow yourself to stand in your own power, you will be open to the realization that less is in fact more as it relates to your emotional body of consciousness, your inner child. Now how is it that your inner child is going to appreciate the concept of less is more? On the surface you might say that it would be very difficult because the inner child wants what he or she wants and usually thinks that more is more! But the truth is that it is just the opposite. This concept relates directly to the inner child because less is more means that there is less effort in order to achieve more of what you want: less effort, more production; and less pain, more enlightenment.

Ask your inner child right now what it is that he or she wants to more easily embrace in your lifetime. Is the inner child getting to the point that he or she is not having any fun? Is the inner child getting to the point where he or she is not doing what it is you love to do? Have a conversation with your inner child to see how he or she is feeling about the decisions that you are making in your life. Let the inner child tell you in his or her own words what it is that they would like out of life; let each speak not as an adult but with the innocence of youth. Your inner child may be angry, but the more that you consciously connect with him or her, the more of a loving experience these conversations will become.

When you are receptive to what it is that your inner child has to say, you will find that what it is that your inner child longs for in your life will become more of your reality. This is not just because you have been involved in conversations with your inner child, but because you have made a movement from conditional into unconditional love. Not only will your inner child be grateful for this, but your other bodies of consciousness will feel this immersion, this profound immersion of love into your life.

As you work with your inner child to bring more of what you love into your life, you may find that one of the things that your inner child is craving is more travel. When you think about travel, ordinarily you think about traveling somewhere on our planet, perhaps to a place that you have been before and enjoyed or to a place that you have always wanted to visit. Now expand that concept and imagine that you could travel anywhere in the known universe. Where would you like to go? Would you like to stay within our solar system, perhaps traveling to Pluto or to Venus or to Mercury? Would you like to travel to another constellation, like the Scorpio constellation or Gemini? Would you like to travel to different places in the Milky Way?

Just for a moment let yourself imagine traveling intergalactically. You have not heard about places outside of our solar system in the same way that you do on our planet. You have heard a lot about Australia, or perhaps you have heard a lot about France or you know certain things about China. The reason that you have not heard more about travel outside of our planet is because most individuals have not done this kind of travel, not consciously, that is. Sleep state allows for this kind of travel, or even travel between lifetimes, but it is not something that many individuals can recall consciously.

So get a sense of what it would be like to travel to them and say, "Well next year, I am going to Venus," or, "In seven months time I am going to Jupiter, or I might be interested in Saturn or I might be interested in one of the stars of Orion's belt. I might really want to see that Gemini constellation or a certain part of it," and just let yourself be open to that and see what happens in your dream state. You will see that certain types of information that you didn't know that you even had access to will make itself known to you, and it will increase your understanding of what happens when you give yourself the opportunity for astral travel. It could be a teleportation or a transmigration, or it could be something as simple as astral travel, which virtually everyone does. So open up to that possibility and see what types of information and, more importantly, what insights come to you during your sleep state.

In spite of the fact that we are inside a physical body, it is not often that we allow ourselves to feel physical. This is one of the reasons why there is a need for sexual encounters on our planet—because it gets us to feel physical. Those that want to be more physical will often undertake what will be a more risky endeavor so that they can feel physically alive. However, you do not have to do certain things in order to feel alive, you simply need to redirect your focus to your physical body. For example, individuals who are depressed really need to get outside in nature. Allow yourself to breathe in the healing powers that are all around you but that you do not get when you stay inside your home. Those individuals that are experiencing chronic pain need to surround themselves with trees or a water environment such as the ocean. When you begin to think in these terms, then you begin to envision yourself in natural states of being, involving nature and you.

You must allow yourself to be in nature and encourage this to happen in a spontaneous way. If you feel like taking a walk one day, do it. If you feel the need to drive to a nearby lake, pond, or ocean tomorrow, do it. Remember that there is no substitute for the connection that nature allows you to feel with all other living beings. Just as taking a multivitamin is quite different from eating a healthy meal of fruits and vegetables, there is no shortcut to achieving the natural state of being.

One of nature's most powerful gifts to us is water. Water of course sustains all life forms on our planet, but it does so very much more than that. Water is what we call an imminent power, meaning that at any point it can spring into action! Water can be a truly magical property, but the same water will not have the same effect on every individual. For instance, there is some very magical water from Marantha Springs, where Mother Mary often visits. It is a very holy sight and it is a very strong vortex, but it will not work for everyone. The water will never hurt, but it may not help either. It depends upon what you are working on and what you are focusing on and what you are open to at that particular time. You can ask your guides what water source they recommend for you and then be open to their answer and trust your intuition!

In speaking of the healing, magical properties of water, you may wonder why then water can cause so much destruction as with the incredibly deadly tsunami a few years ago. Unfortunately it often takes tragic events, such as the tsunami or even 9/11, to bring human beings together. The tsunami came to create new ley lines for the fifth dimension, and however difficult it is to accept, the passing of those many individuals was necessary to get the world's attention. As a result of this tragedy, many of the world's inhabitants reached out in love, and in generosity, and helped to usher in the fifth dimension on this planet.

As we have discussed, being in nature is one of many powerful healing techniques. There is another group of healing techniques that are both fourth—and fifth-dimensional called complementary techniques. These include techniques that we discussed earlier such as crystal work, visualization, and aromatherapy. Using these techniques together does not cause one to interfere with the other, but rather produces a synergistic effect.

Now as we talk about complementary techniques, you may be wondering how it relates to your first major guide, your complenary guide. For those of you who have studied the guides, you know that complenary guide is a combination of the words *complete* and *plenary*. *Plenary* means having to do with a group of people, and *complete* of course being the totality. Therefore your complenary guide is your major overseer in your physical realm. So think about complementary techniques and your complenary guide. This guide oversees complementary guides, which include the timing guide, the physic guide, the blueprint guide, and the sunshine guide. Remember that your complenary guide is the overseer for your physical lifetime, so that direct board includes the other six major guides. But you have a lot of guides in the physical realm. You have, for example, your base chakra assistant, your physical attribute guide, your lifetime processing assistant, and others. Even though you have an immediate board of directors, the direct board consists of your major guides, and your complenary guide presides over them.

The complenary guide has jurisdiction over all of the guides in your physical realm of consciousness, and all of those guides provide complementary information, insight, wisdom, and guidance. That is a lot of input; it is no wonder that you are not aware of it consciously. If you were, you would spend all of your time outside of your physical reality. But know that they are there and that they provide complementary wisdom, data, and guidance. They provide that and there is no conflict between them or between them and you. They are there to help you just as in other lifetime scenarios you have been there as a guide to help them.

Isn't it a wonderful thing to know that all of these wonderful guides want to help you in this life journey? Are you ready for another wonderful thought? What if we told you that you have *no* more important decisions to make? It does not sound possible, does it? Well, my friends, it is absolutely true! You have no more important decisions to make because, as fifth-dimensional beings, you have already done your work. You have done your development, you have gained your consciousness, you have reached out to others. You have tried to see and to embrace the unseen. It doesn't mean that the rest of your life will not involve any learning. It just means that the decisions are no longer difficult.

You step out of thinking and into knowing, you step out of believing and into knowing, you step out of wishing and into knowing. Now that is not the same thing as beingness. But again these steps become clearer as you have become a clear vessel for such wisdom, for such understanding, and you get help from so many sources. You know this, you get help from guides, you get help from teachers, you get help from your chakra assistants, and you get help from the angelic influences and the eternal suns.

That being said, if your feet have been stuck in the cement, it is very hard even with the most persistent wind to push you forward. Don't allow yourself to get stuck, but continue your evolvement upward. Are you familiar with the song "Up, Up and Away" by the Fifth Dimension? In the song, they talked about going up in a beautiful balloon, and that is what we are talking about—you are going forward as well as going upward. You are here and you continue to make decisions, but they are not going to be difficult because you have that level of knowingness, you have done your homework so that the decisions that you make are good, better, best, and beyond. You know what feels right to you and you know which way to go.

The challenge that you may have in believing is that when you look around the world, you may feel as if you are alone on this spiritual journey. That gives you pause for thought, absolutely. It makes you wonder if perhaps there is a different way to go, and then you start to get confused in your processing, and analyzing the data becomes more important than trusting your gut feeling. But the more that you listen to your inner voice, the more that you open up your communication with your guides and teachers, the more that you allow yourself to live in the light and those decisions do not then become difficult decisions. They are just the next step on your path. And so what if you chose a "good" best choice when perhaps later there would have been a "best" choice, you can re-evaluate. You can take your next step, and it might be like a jigsaw puzzle, with no decision set in stone. You are going "Up, Up and Away" in that balloon, and at the same time you can adjust the direction!

* * * * * * *

When I was learning about different ways to expand my consciousness and move along into the fifth dimension, my first requirement was to have an open mind and an open heart. By being simply open, I was able to remove any feeling of limitation or restriction that I have been living under.

I started to read about astral travel, teleportation, and transmigration. Each of these forms of movement are very different, and I wanted to clarify what each meant so that I was clear on how or why they might be beneficial in my life.

First, why would anyone want to learn more about movement of energy and more particularly the movement of their personal energy? My reason was very simple. I wanted to push through the limitations of my thinking that I had grown up under. Assumptions that what the imagination may conjure up or a vision that one might have can in fact be dismissed. I knew that those individuals that were willing to stretch the limits of learning by expanding their experiences and consciousness could really create anything that they wanted to. I also was aware that we use a very small portion of our brain, and that some types of travel actually can use and expand into those areas formerly unused. I knew that the mind was/is one of the most powerful gifts that we have been given—but who uses it to its fullest capacity? My dad was a thinker, an inventor, an engineer, and he worked and worked on projects until he solved the problems that prevented them from existing. I would watch him for years have an idea and then little by little bring that idea into a reality. He always said that to not try something was to admit defeat. So my dad worked and worked until he defeated the limitation that something could not exist.

I was not aware of it at the time, but I was learning valuable concepts by watching my father. I was learning that he challenged his sources of knowledge and that he allowed himself to move beyond his limitations by solving problems in ways that stretched boundaries. Every night on his bed table he would have a stack of legal pads, drawing and colored pencils, and, of course, many sharpened number 2 pencils! On the top line of the page he would write an equation or equations. In the morning the pad was full as on page after page were written the solutions to the equation, answering his questions. A man with limited formal education, he had learned to tap into the unseen, and during his REM sleep, my father allowed himself to be open to channel in the answers. During the course of this book, I had a wonderful visit by Einstein who told me that he had channeled my dad for over fifty years. He would come and help him solve problems that were preventing him from completing many of his inventions. My dad contributed many solutions to our planet that were intended to help our environment become healthier. I was not aware that this behavior was unusual. I thought everyone's dad went to bed armed with paper and pencils, ready to receive information while they slept at night!

I also clearly remember being a little girl and flying! I guess flying is as good a word as any because it does indicate that I moved from one location to another.

I typically would wake up extra early on a Saturday morning or a summer day when I did not have to leave for school. After my father left for work, I got out of bed and went to my favorite quite little spot, which was in one corner of the living room that was not visible from the traffic flow. Feeling very safe and secure that no one would see me, I would curl in a little ball in front of the heater and simply relax. I remember that I always began by picturing myself on a little Oriental rug that I knew would fly through the sky! (I remember seeing a commercial on TV of a little genie who flew on a flying carpet.) I simply closed my eyes, jumped on my flying carpet, and saw myself flying around the world. Sometimes I would be gone an hour or two. I would come back and awake in my special spot in the living room having visions of where I had been and what I had done, so alive and real in my head. This was such a favorite thing for me to do. I looked forward to being able to experience the intrigue, the exotic lands, and the beautiful scenery as I flew around. I remember doing this for years. One day I simply stopped. Something deep inside of me knew that I was more alive when I was flying than at any other time of my life. This was indeed a special feeling for me and one which I am happy that my memory has kept alive for me. To this day, I can remember bits and pieces of where I had been, but more importantly I remember the feeling that what I was doing was something very special.

There are several forms of travel which may have been described earlier in other chapters but are again relative to this one. I feel that they should be repeated, and I will summarize these experiences for you.

Astral travel is the movement of energy in the dream state that allows the soul to grow by experiencing learning and knowledge out of the body. Oftentimes your guides accompany your soul on a nighttime journey to visit a special place, a learning center, or meet other souls as a way of introducing your soul to learning or knowledge by experiencing something firsthand. Perhaps it is necessary to experience an energy that you may need to know about sometime in the future. Your guides may take you to another planet to re-introduce it to you firsthand. Or perhaps they may take you to a learning center of light for a project that your soul may be working on. There are many learning centers throughout our planet. Each center may impart special knowledge to souls by their renowned teachers or visiting teachers or ascended masters. There are many such centers located in and around the United States: Arizona, California, Colorado, Montana, Wyoming, Missouri, New Jersey, Massachusettes, and Hawaii are areas that many homes for ascended masters exist in.

Everybody has had the experience that when you wake up from a very deep sleep, it may feel as if your arms and limbs are numb. You fall back to sleep because you simply cannot wake yourself up. A little while later you wake again and this time you stay awake, but it does take some effort to be able to move your arms and legs. Why? You were out of your body and when it was time you did return, but sometimes it takes awhile for you to adjust back into your body, and so your arms and limbs feel numb and prickly until you are fully back in. After a few moments they feel alive and you feel full in your body again. Each trip out of your body is different. If you haven't had the experience mentioned above, you may still be astral traveling, but your soul returns when your body is still sleeping and there is no awareness or disturbance that might call attention to your return. It has been written that we leave our bodies every evening, if only for a short while, as the knowledge we are gaining cannot be learned any other way.

I have been told that I am often taken by my guides to the Pleiades. I have learned that I have a parallel life there and that sometimes that part of my soul comes to this body and vice versa. The knowledge that my soul is gaining through my experiences on this earth is simply transferred to my soul fragment that is living on the Pleiades. I have many more opportunities here to learn many varied lessons, so this part of my soul is much stronger than the part of my soul that lives on the star group. My strengths may then be transferred to the parallel life. The strengths that my Pleiades life is gaining may also be transferred to me on earth, and so my soul is learning its many lessons from two lifetimes in two very different realities.

About five years ago, I took a class on teleportation. I knew something about it as the trance channel for Markas, Dr. Gwen Tatterdale, had written a book with Dr. Jessica Severn entitled *Teleportation, A Practical Guide for the Metaphysical Traveler*. I knew that she teleported and my teacher had been her student. I read the book to increase my knowledge and to answer any questions that I might have about this form of movement of energy and then promptly signed up for the class!

Each of us was given a special teleportation guide. This guide is simply here to accompany you to and from your destination as you are moving through dimensions. Typically, this guide has a nickname that tickles you in a special way that makes sense only to you! It may be that the nickname is the name of something you love, or a name that is similar to a pet or is something that you relate to. This makes the connection between your guide and you not only special but strong as the elements of trust and faith are very important to perform this movement of energy. My teleportation guide's name was a combination of two things that I truly love: Chocolate and Cats! (The exact name I will reserve from making known publicly—but that doesn't mean that you can't take a few guesses to try to figure out what it might be!)

You must begin with practice. It is suggested that you pick a very quiet time to practice, preferably the same time every evening. The energies are quieter in the evening, so it is easier to teleport at this time. You lie or relax in a chair with the back of your head facing east. You call your teleportation guide by name and ask that he accompany you to your destination. You are very specific with your destination, providing street address, city, state, and country. As you breathe and relax into the space, you say your mantra. (It is important that you are dressed—because you do arrive exactly as you leave, and you would certainly not want to shock someone by arriving naked!)

This is a mental activity, so you must see yourself already at your destination, releasing yourself from your body and traveling to your destination. Upon landing (yes, it is teleportation only when your feet touch the ground), you allow yourself to take in as much of your surroundings as you can. The smells, the sounds, the temperature, the feel of the sand or pavement under your feet—whatever it is that you feel surrounds you helps to make your experience complete. The details fill in your mind, and your vision of where you wanted to go is realized.

Initially, you may only be successful in having a limb or part of your body arrive at your destination. Practice makes it easier as well as three drops of an herbal supplement called bladderwrack. This product is a special seaweed derived from the ocean that simply allows your spirit to slide easier out of your body. It tastes as bad as it sounds, but the traveling experience far outweighs the wretched taste! (I learned to disguise it in a strawberry, and so it was palatable!)

Each evening I created a time and space that I set aside to practice my teleportation and to hopefully gain some skills. It is about a ten to twenty-minute practice session. I would lie down on the floor with a pillow under my head, the back of which faced east, call in my guide, and say my mantra out loud. I would see myself at my destination, a friend's house about three miles away. I would envision myself sitting at their kitchen table. I knew if they walked into the room and I had been successful and they saw me at their table they might faint, so I warned them that I might "drop in," but I don't think they believed me!

I guess initially I was only doing flybys because I never landed in their kitchen with my feet touching their kitchen floor. One evening I was very close as I literally was face-to-face with their kitchen clock on their range! Another night I smelled bacon that was served for breakfast. I knew I was getting closer and closer to success. Our practice was to be every evening for thirty days, and then a couple of group dry runs.

The synergy of the group makes it easier to teleport. Energy working together is very strong and very powerful, so it is easier to accomplish any task when like minds are all working together for a common goal.

We were women on a mission, trying to see if we could leave our bodies and arrive at our destination! What a class! Our destination was the Casa, in Brazil. The Casa is a renowned healing center run by a very special man who you may have heard of referred to as John of God. Our mission was to arrive at the Casa and to meet at the entrance sign and then to meet John of God himself on the premises. Each person was to bring a petition to him for a special healing. And so the journey began.

Lying on my bedroom floor with my head facing the east and the petition in my hand, I called in my guides and requested their assistance as I began my mantra. Eyes closed I envisioned the Casa and the entrance sign (I had seen pictures so I could visualize correctly). I then actually saw a hand reach down to me through my third eye. I reached out (in the nonphysical sense) and felt connected to my guide, and I was off!

Walking on the cool tile floor of the chapel, I made my way to a statue that was off to the side. I walked over and knelt down, saying my prayer and requesting that my petition be answered. I rose and walked out of the chapel, walking down the hall toward the main part of the building. Walking toward me was a very kind-looking man, with warm and wonderful eyes. I looked at him and continued to move toward him. He saw that I was a "visitor" and our eyes locked. I knelt in front of him, handing him my petition, and drawing his hand to me, I kissed it. I stood up and looked him again right into the eyes and smiled and nodded. Tears streamed down my face as I acknowledged this loving man filled with humility and depth of soul. I was awestruck.

Continuing my journey, I managed to walk to the entrance sign outside by the gate, and there I was met by my mentor, Dr. Totterdale, and my teacher, Theresa. We were instructed to describe what we saw them wearing upon our return. I e-mailed their clothing descriptions the next morning and received a return e-mail that I had successfully described their clothes. I had passed my test with flying colors: I had teleported down to Brazil!

Coming home was another story. I opened my eyes and saw that I had returned to the floor of my bedroom. There on my bed all lined up and looking down at me were all three of my cats. One by one I looked at them, and wide-eyed they stared at me. I got up and looked at the clock and a full hour had passed. I knew I had been successful, and amazingly enough the cats with the look in their eyes had confirmed for me that I indeed had been successful!

I had taken a step toward stretching my experiences, but even more than that I had pushed my limitations out of that box and accomplished something that in the past I would have only read about. But now with my newfound confidence and my desire to feel the power of my mind, and then to express that power, I had successfully reached a new dimension. I had moved beyond my normal brain usage and used parts of my brain that were untouched. This exploration touched me as I truly began to feel different, in a wonderful and unique way. I had expanded my mind and my consciousness and was just beginning to discover more of the *Limitless Possibilities* that lay ahead not only for me but for all of us!

CHAPTER XXII

Journey into Wellness

Health is a state of complete harmony of the body, mind, and spirit.
When one is free from physical disabilities and mental distractions,
the gates of the soul open.

—B. K. S. Iyengar

As we move deeper into the twenty-first century, we become increasingly aware of the chaotic events that are transforming life as we know it on Planet Earth! These events are happening in all levels of society and are making us take a step back to review, reflect, restructure, and reorganize our lives so that we keep what is meaningful. These events have caused our Planet Earth to expose her darkest moments created by the darkest qualities that exist in humanity: greed, power, selfishness, irresponsibility, deception, and dishonesty. We are now cleansing and purging. We are resetting ourselves to come to a new place, to experience a fresh start, and to try again, but this time our value will be to return to a simpler life steeped with traditional values at its foundation. This time we will be coming from a higher place, a place of spirituality. We are examining all of our motives, looking for the best, finding the best, and giving the best of ourselves to ourselves. We are creating a world that is sharing in the best part of who we are and who we want to become. We are working together to find solutions to problems that we have created. It is time to stand up and question the wisdom of inventions of convenience in all areas of our lives. What are we achieving? How are we selling ourselves short? On one hand, our egos tell us we are creating a civilized society which is greatly intelligent, employing the newest and highest degrees of technology, while on the other hand, we wonder why environmental cancers have increased dramatically. Is there a correlation? No doubt. It is time to go all out and look to heal all situations that simply are not healthy. Where do we start? It is a huge housecleaning. Some of the solutions to our problems must stem from a place of originality, imagination, and creativity while coming from a place of love and compassion. We are being shown that it is time to transcend from a time of materiality to a time of spirituality. We are being shown the golden age of the twenty-first century.

The following topics briefly described in this chapter are in fact the additional layers that are available for us to help us develop a more complete look at who we are. You have all done the work, and now this should be the icing on the cake! Each of the topics summarized finds its base in ancient knowledge and wisdom: numerology, colors and crystals, and how energy within and without ourselves tells its story through our chakras and our auras, and information on the body, mind, and spirit that will be a steppingstone to further learning and development. The more information you bring into your development, the more you become and have a greater sense of who you are and who you are meant to be. You are able to color in the pictures, to help write more detailed chapters about yourself and the more interesting living your story is.

You may innately know some of the following information as you play into that part of you that has awakened, and that memory may help you to recognize those things that you resonate to. Perhaps many Atlantian lifetimes have provided you with a fascination for stones and crystals. If you have a strong connection to Mother Earth, you will understand how totems can add an additional layer to your story. Whatever your inclination, simply go with it and enjoy the experience. Following is a simple summary of the topics. There are many fine guides and books on each individual subject to satisfy your fascination. I have included some of them in the Recommended Reading and Bibliography section at the end of this book.

Animal Totems

Our ancient elders believed that animals, birds, and insects were gifts to us to be used as instruments of learning. Indigenous tribes living off the land observed and witnessed the universe's way of helping man grow and develop. The meaning of each appearance—whether it is a sighting of an animal, bird, or an insect—has been passed down over the centuries to help individuals on the planet. It was believed that the animals appearing in either dream state or in real life brought the lesson or lessons that we needed to be acknowledged to help us on our journey. These animals were representatives of the higher realms and were sent by our great creator to help man continue on his earthly journey. These lessons were to be taken as gifts from above and were taken seriously by the native or person it appeared to. Many lessons could be interpreted from the presence, and it was up to the native and his/her tribe to garner as much learning as possible from the experience. It is important to not only acknowledge the visitor but also encourage the visitations so that the receiver could carry the wisdom or power of the animal. It is for this reason that animals are used as totems in our lives. The power or wisdom we garner from them are not only timely but help us stay connected with earth, and it is through this connection that the life force of the animal is brought to us and if allowed can be felt very strongly by each of us.

It is very powerful to maintain this connection with animals, birds, and insects. Oftentimes we see the extraordinary and we know that this totem has been brought to us for consideration and learning. So when the extraordinary enters your life in an extraordinary way, or even an ordinary way, it is time to take notice and ask yourself the big questions: Why has the totem come? What is the specific meaning of the totem? What lessons can be learned from the visit?

Observing the body language of the totem and the details surrounding its appearance is important as the more detailed a picture you can paint, the more you will be able to discern the meaning. You will begin to discern the difference between an animal that you may see on a daily basis and a totem being sent to you. Follow that instinct and keep it alive as you develop your awareness! There are many wonderful books or Websites which describe the meaning of totems so that your interpretation of the event or visitation is accurate.

Each of us have several totems that stay with us every day of our lives, but there are times during our lives that new totems come and go, bringing us lessons or helping us with the meaning of events occurring in our lives. Perhaps we need to learn to focus, or to reduce the clutter in our life, so that we can focus and not miss this opportunity for learning.

Have you ever seen the same picture repeatedly or perhaps a picture in silhouette, or in dream state, that identifies an animal, bird, or insect that catches your attention? You may be driving down the street and a truck passes with an eagle as part of its logo, you stop at the doctor's office and see a picture of an eagle on the wall, driving home minutes later you see an eagle soaring overhead—you wonder if there is a connection. During the course of the next week, the image or silhouette of an eagle is brought to your attention again and again. You need to determine why the creatures are appearing, paying attention to the timing and then the message. What is going on in my life that warrants an eagle visitation? The experiences go on and on. This is yet another gift that the universe is bestowing to help you as you travel along on your personal journey. The knowledge and the meaning is yet another layer that adds to the richness of life. This gift from the universe is not to be missed but should be cherished as the layers add upon each other, adding many more pieces to your puzzle, helping you to "get it."

Remember my earlier "hawk" experience described in the introduction? I discovered that this hawk is one of my totems because I carry the hawk energy. It seems that during a lifetime as a shaman in the Mohave Desert, I saved a hawk that was dying and the energy has been forever grateful. They continue to assist me in my lives on earth and present themselves in many ways, all received by me as ways that the universe is trying to confirm or validate an experience for me. I simply "know" why they come, and that message is received by me loud and clear. While the hawk visitations continue, I now am being gifted with the white dove and have recently had an eagle visitation! Each new bird's meaning made such perfect sense to me and concurred with events happening in my life.

We all know many young children that are fascinated with a certain animal—or a totem—and we have no logical explanation for the why or the how. Have you ever witnessed little ones that from a very early age have loved and collected frogs, or turtles, or bunnies? (I, of course, am not saying their collections are alive—they may be in the form of stuffed animals, or ceramic animals—but this little animal treasure chest is a symbol that carries with it the energy of the actual animal.) Since each and every animal energy carries with it its own message or meaning, each child is simply tapping into their innate knowledge of what their special totem is. Every household should consider having a "totem bible" to help identify the meaning so that the experience is richer with its knowledge for the whole family. To love one of God's little creatures is very wonderful, but to be able to discern its meaning and then to identify the "whys" adds to the enrichment of life, and the experience becomes a validation for the truths to be realized or anticipated. We also again can stand in awe as we realize the oneness of this vast universe and feel a deeper connection with "all that is."

Numerology, Colors, and Crystals/Stones

Looking at who you are and who you want to become is the motivation to review and see all of the gifts that the universe has provided for you. This will shed some light and give us additional information to play with as we continue doing our work and assimilating knowledge. We can enrich our life and move with the flow of the energies presented to us if we identify what day it is for us according to numerology, incorporating the color that relates to that day as well as understanding the energy of the complementary crystal that enhances both the day and color. The following list incorporates all three energies as they work together. As we tap into the theme of our personal day, the theme of our personal month, or the theme of our personal year, we gain a greater understanding of why the universe is bringing us these lessons. It doesn't really matter whether the lessons are learned by challenging or happy events, it is the knowledge that expands our life and at the same time may relieve our stress in the not knowing. Remember, knowledge is power and awareness is key!

In the list below, the number indicated in the first column is the number that you use in learning about your personal day, personal month, and personal year. As you read across you will see which color is associated with the number and the theme that relates to both. The subsequent crystal/stone is the energy that can be used that day which complements the energies of the number, the color, and the theme.

The chart below has been updated to include the new master number 33/6. The entire chart is presented in full in case you are not familiar with the meanings of numbers, colors, theme, crystals, and stones. There are many wonderful sources to expand on the knowledge of these topics. For example, the class that I took used information in Louise L. Hay's book *Colors and Numbers* for its foundation. It was validated by Markas that the information is accurate and should be repeated in this book so that everyone is working off the same foundation. This information has been updated with the new 33/6 information. I have written this information in chart form as I think it is easy to remember when presented this way.

CHART:

Number	Color	Theme	Crystals/Stones
#1	Red	New Beginnings	Ruby
#2	Orange	Cooperation	Moonstone
#3	Yellow	Enjoyment	Topaz/Citrine
#4	Green	Practical	Emerald/Jade
#5	Blue	Change	Turquoise/Aquamarine
#6	Indigo	Responsibility	Lapis/Pearl
#7	Purple	Faith	Amethyst
#8	Beige/Brown/Pink	Successful Business	Diamonds
#9	Pastels	Completion	Opals/Gold

Master Days:

#11/2	Black/White/Gray	Intuition	Silver
#22/4	Coral/Greatness	Coral/Copper	Russet
#33/6	Gold	Change/Balance/Harmony/Karmic	Gold

On the calendar (which is discussed in the next section) that you are going to create for yourself, when you have a one day, it is advised that you wear the color red as red represents the energy of new beginnings. If you would like to continue the theme, you may enhance the day and tap further into the energies by wearing a ruby stone. The above chart may be applied to your personal day, your personal month, or your personal year. Intuitively, you may also listen to what makes the most sense to you and choose the color that you know will enhance the energy you need to draw to you. So if you are in a personal month that is a #5—blue for change—but your personal day is a #8, which means successful business, and that energy doesn't apply, you may decide to opt for #5 blue day. Remember all energies are wonderful. There isn't one color or energy that is better than any other. Each has its own qualities and attributes, and each can be drawn to you when you need to use it. Let your intuition guide you and have fun with the colors and their meanings. You can also incorporate two colors or more if you feel that you need to have change in order to have a new beginning. So perhaps you wear more red than blue, but you use both. The whole idea of this chart is simply to add another layer to your life, enhancing it and using some of these ancient gifts that have been given to us in a way that will bring beautiful energies to you. This will help you to move within the flow of what the universe is providing, thus making your life richer and the experience of life deeper.

NUMEROLOGY

How to Determine your Personal Year, Personal Month, and Personal Day!

A wonderful tool to help you use the energies being sent to you personally every day of every month of every year is to make your own calendar with all of your personal information in it. You can purchase a readymade calendar; one that is in the form of a journal is ideal. This format allows you to add your numerology to the calendar, keeping a running record of the energies coming to you so that you can use them for maximum effect. As you begin to journal your dreams and note the experiences that occur during your meditations or while sitting in the silence as well as any other unusual events (totem sightings) that come into your awareness, the observed information starts telling a story or drawing a picture for you, helping you to draw conclusions. When you have added them to your personal calendar, this journal gives you not only instant recall but helps you to see an expanded picture of how you are flowing with the universal energies.

Determining your Personal Year

Let's begin by looking at the numerology of your personal year. It is important to calculate the number of your personal year so that you understand the overall theme of the year. This knowledge will help you see the direction your year will take. To arrive at your personal year, simply add your birth month to your birth day and the current year as the example below illustrates and you will arrive at your personal year.

Using the following formula: Birthdate plus Universal Year equals Personal Year.

Example #1: February 14, 2009

So if you were born on February 14, and it currently is the year 2009 your Personal Year is the number 9. Simply: 02 plus 14, plus 11 equals 27. (The 11 is arrived at by taking the year 2009 and adding its digits 2 + 0 + 0 + 9.) Then 2 plus 7 equals 9. See below. This number 11 represents the universal year.

February 14, 2009
02 + 14 + 11
Added together equals: 02 + 14 + 11 = 27
27 is 2 + 7 = 9 or P.Y. 9 (Personal Year 9)

Some birthdays, when added as in the above example, will have 11 as a total. The number eleven is considered a master number and cannot be broken down any further than an eleven. So for those individuals, please see the following example:

Example # 2: (using the master number 11)

If you were born on March 15, and it currently is the year 2009, your personal year is the number 11. Simply: 03 plus 15, plus 11 equals 29. Then 2 plus 9 equals 11*

March 15, 2009
03 + 15 + 2009
Added together equals: 03 + 15 + 11 = 29

29 is 2 + 9 which equals 11* (Personal Year 11)

The number 11* is considered a Master Number and cannot be broken down. This holds true for the numbers 22, and 33 as well. So when you encounter these numbers there is a special master meaning associated with them which needs to be brought into the meaning of the year. (11, 22, and 33 will always remain as they are; they can never be a 2, or 4, or 6).

Every other number may simply be added together or broken down to a single digit.

The above chart shows the number, and the color associated with that number, the meaning of the number (theme), and the crystal or stones whose energy enhances the number. So after you determine your personal year, you simply go to the above chart and see what the theme of the year will be. If we continue to use the March 15, 2009 example, then the personal year is an 11. This is a master number and so the personal year will be a master year. The meaning of the master numbers will be discussed in detail after the personal month and personal day explanations are presented.

Determining your Personal Month!

Let's now figure out the numerology of your personal month! Using the same birthday as we did in the above example #1, February 14, 2009, we can do the following calculations. We know that February 14, 2009 represents the personal year #9. We add the number 1 to your Personal Year #9 and we arrive at the number 10. By breaking down the number 10 we arrive at # 1.

So January would be your Personal Month # 1.

Here is the simple formula:
P.Y. + 1 = P.M.
9 + 1 = 10
10 is 1 + 0 = 1 which is your P.M.

Take the 9 of the personal year and add the number 1 to it and you get 10 or, as it breaks down to its lowest point, a 1.

Determining your Personal Day!

Your personal day is determined by taking your personal month number and adding the number 1 to it.

Since we determined above that January would be your Personal Month #1, then if we add one to that number, the first personal day of the new year would be the #2.

Here is the simple formula: P.M. = 1 = P.D.

Now let us put this information to use and add it to your purchased calendar. Here is an easy way to begin.

Calendar: Creating your Personal Calendar!

Take your purchased calendar and turn the page to the first month. At the top of the calendar, write the universal year (let us assume we are using 2009, so we would write the number 11 at top).

Write U.R. = 11

At the top of the month of January, you now can write your personal month, the number 1 in this example.

Write P.Y. = 1

Starting with day one in January, mark your personal day. Write the number 2 on the first box (January 1).

Write P.D. = 2 (write on January 1st.)

Continue the month of January, writing the number 3 (on January 2), the number 4 (on January 3), the number 5 (on January 4), the number 6 (on January 5), the number 7 (on January 6), the number 8 (on January 7), and the number 9 (on January 8), and then 10 when broken down becomes the number 1, so continuing you would put number 1 (on January 9), the number 11/2 (on January 10), the number 3 (on January 11), the number 4 (on January 12), the number 5 (on January 13), the number 6 (on January 14), the number 7 (on January 15), the number 8 (on January 16), the number 9 (on January 17), the number 1 (on January 18), the number 2 (January 19), the number 3 (on January 20), the number 22/4 (on January 21), the number 5 (on January 22), the number 6 (on January 23), the number 7 (on January 24), the number 8 (on January 25), the number 9 (on January 26), the number 1 (on January 27), the number 2 (on January 28), the number 3 (on January 29), the number 4 (on January 30), and lastly, the number 5 (on January 31).

Please note the following master numbers and how they fit into the month:

When you are counting consecutively and come to the number 2, it can either be written as a 2 or an 11. You determine which number "fits" by simply adding the day to the personal month number. So January 10 becomes a 11/2 day because 10 plus P.M. 1 equals 11. And January 21 is a 22/4 day because 21 plus P.M. 1 equals 22. There happens to be no 33/6 day in the month of January following the above numbers. But when you continue to carry through the subsequent months and days, you will eventually happen upon one.

As you continue, you will record that February is a P.M. 2, March is a P.M. 3, etc. Following January 31, which is a five day, February first is a #3 day, etc.

Meaning of Master Numbers 11, 22, and 33 and How to Work with this Special Energy!

Master Number 11: This master number eleven means that there will be energies available to you that will help you to effect changes in your relationships. They will affect how you relate to others and how others relate to you in the physical world. Specifically, this master eleven energy involves intuition and vision.

When you work on the high side of this energy, you will be able to transform your relationships by using the gift of intuition and/or vision. Your intuition will be right on, and if you are open to listening and to receiving information, you will be able to make a huge impact on your life and the relationships in it. As with all periods of introspection, it is important that you spend time reflecting, investigating, and dissecting the meaning of close personal relationships, family/friends, and employee/employer relationships. Not only is it an opportunity to open up to new approaches and new pathways that will take the relationship to a different level, you may receive insight on any past life relationship issues that may remain either within you or the other party/parties.

Your intuition and vision will certainly be able to shed some light on any area of a relationship that needs to be healed. It is important, therefore, to meditate or simply sit in the silence and allow any and all thoughts to come to you. I would ask your guides for help in bringing this information as well as help in receiving it. This will help you to develop that part of you that is referred to as your "sixth sense." The messages that you may receive may involve a part of you or an event that has been carried over and that karmic obligation needs to be settled. Can you ask what specifically the obligation is, and with whom? Do you have a sense when you are with someone that there is an irritation or wound that needs some attention even though no event in this lifetime has occurred to warrant this feeling? Have you ever met someone and felt that they "rub you the wrong way"? Or perhaps the opposite is true? Someone is really kind to you, going out of their way, and you cannot figure out why. Or perhaps it is you who meet someone and you go out of your way to be really kind to them and you wonder why. When you investigate this feeling deeper, you see that perhaps this kindness is being extended by you to someone who perhaps you hurt in the past! Using your intuition to help resolve issues, either yours or someone else's, is a beautiful way for you to add credit to your karmic tally sheet.

Of course you know that we must do things from our hearts, with pure intent. Otherwise, if we expect something in return, we are actually taking away from the purity of the act. Your soul and the goodness of your being certainly doesn't benefit in this situation. And you most likely would not receive the eleven energy as your action would not warrant it. It is likely then that you would be reduced to working with the two energy, which is the energy of cooperation and relationships but in a less spiritual way. This is why you often see the energy written as 11/2. How you use the energy and your intention helps to determine if you are using the high side (11) or its lower counterpart (2). All energy is a gift and has a valuable place in helping us to achieve what it is we need to achieve. So the two should be honored as the prelude to the eleven, but both are to be honored as they are gifts from God to help us achieve our highest potential.

Master Number 22: This master number twenty-two means there will be energies available to you to help you align your energies spiritually so that you may advance in your spiritual development. This would be the appropriate time to partake in the use of metaphysical tools: manifestation, visualization, tarot, meditation, etc. Specifically this twenty-two energy involves greatness and control.

When you work on the high side of the twenty-two energy, you are able to regulate your energies by controlling or being ultimately in command of them.

This potential enables you to regain your power as you center yourself, unifying the energies so that they enable you when you put them in practice to have the greatest impact. The use of the twenty-two energy is life transforming and powerful. As the energy relates to greatness, it is achieving a very high place of power within yourself, not in an egotistical way but in spiritual way. It is the ability to use all of your energies aligned and controlled, creating the impetus for greatness within.

Allowing yourself to be centered through meditation is exercising discipline, and its reward is the control and power of the energies when used. When this state is achieved, the use of power in the right circumstances for the right reasons will achieve ultimate success. As you continue to develop and fine tune this technique, you will continue to achieve higher levels of success. Again, success is only achieved when you have done the work. Being centered and disciplined is but one step in the process; having goals and a clear vision of what is to be accomplished is necessary so when the energy is received it is able to manifest what is desired. This master number 22 is received by a person who is spiritually directed. The description of the use and its ultimate success may appeal to someone less spiritual and more worldly. It is the ego that ultimately must not be involved so that this master number can bring you to a level of greatness. How are you working with the energy? Is your intention pure? Are you able to corral all of the beautiful energies, focusing on aligning them so that they have power? The practice of discipline and focus is greatly enhanced by meditation or by simply sitting in the silence to help formulate your plan or goals. Are you able to remove yourself from the ins and outs of daily life and dedicate some time to the art of meditation or any of the metaphysical tools that you feel comfortable with? As you become more and more introspective, removing the layers one by one, replacing them with petals of love, you feel the difference in your being. The totality of who you are has become enlightened, and you begin to ascend the spiral, moving forward and upward. Once you are aware of upward growth, you will never want to fall off the ladder and revisit the person you used to be.

If you are unable to use the master number 22 on the high side, the four means that you will receive energy to help you focus on your techniques of meditation through discipline, ultimately creating foundations and principles. This four energy then may be thought of as a forerunner to the twenty-two. It is also a valuable energy because what it helps to create is of the greatest worth to the soul.

Master Number 33: This master number thirty-three means that there are energies for you to tap into that will help you develop and understand universal awareness and universal understanding. This knowledge will help you during your lifetime on this planet as you apply the cosmic concepts and use the cosmic energies. This energy may also help you to be aware of any karmic lessons that you may need to revisit or have an opportunity to correct by responding differently, hence, balancing your karma.

The number 33 represents an energy that has returned to Planet Earth in 2009. This energy has not been on the planet since before the year 2000. It is indeed a master energy as its respectful use can and will create beautiful miracles in your life. In order to work with this energy, it is important that ground rules must be followed so that you can assure a beautiful outcome.

The number 33 represents the energy of the solidification of success. This energy will help you work with your creation and help you attain the goals that you have set out to achieve. It represents the culmination of your heart's desire and helps you to reach a position that is secure and desirable. It represents the completion of many sought-after goals on many levels. In the spiritual level, this goal is the awakening of the higher self, working with the highest levels of energies to develop a consciousness into all things on every level of being. It represents the power to be successful in all achievements and highest ambitions.

The groundwork that is necessary in order to work with the thirty-three energy must be a deliberate and conscious act of preparation and planning with prior intent in order to make a clear and concise outline of what is desired to be accomplished. This step is mandatory and is to be accomplished through meditation the morning of your thirty-three day and the evening of your thirty-three day. It is a time of reflection, pure intent, request, gratitude, and thankfulness that must be spoken from the heart. This energy force has to be understood and must be used exactly as it was intended as misuse of the thirty-three energy destroys the roots and the foundations. The net effect of the misuse means that all possibilities of what might have been can no longer be attained. Great powers on earth have been eliminated through the abuse of power, and any misuse will have similar serious consequences. This energy, as with all other energies, must be respected and used in the highest level as it was intended.

As with many of the gifts that have been given to us in our universe, it is important to remember that the universe gives us the gift that we most need at the time we most need it. That being said, our life on earth consists of receiving and sending out these beautiful energies. We trust in the divine that we are given what we need. We thank the divine for sending us love in the form of these energies and helping us to get in the flow of the universe so that we can experience all of the perfection it provides. We therefore should not think that the eleven energy is better than the two, or the twenty-two energy is better than the four, or the thirty-three energy is better than the six. We simply need to appreciate each of the energies for what they can provide us with and receive each of the energies as a gift that our being needs in order to grow and evolve.

COLORS

Every color imaginable has its own vibration. How we feel is enhanced by the colors that we choose to not only wear but to surround ourselves in our home and work environments. It is important that as you begin to get into the flow of energy, you allow yourself to experience it and just "be" in it. Eventually you will learn to identify the energy that the color represents. As you become more and more in touch and aware of your needs and your feelings, you will intuitively understand what energy you need, so you know what color to pull in around you. Some people have an affinity for one color or another, and it is interesting to understand why. A little introspection can perhaps introduce you to your favorite color or colors and will help you immerse yourself in their energy, balancing your feelings and thus your wellbeing and bringing you into a state of harmony. Ultimately, this state of harmony and wellbeing is our goal in all areas of our life, and the use of color is easily accessible to everyone.

There have been many studies done on the relationship of color to harmony. Since each color represents a different energy and thus a unique vibration, is it any wonder that we intuitively know which energy our physical body can rest in, which energy is stimulating, and which energy is creative? As we learn to live and work with color, our natural inclination should be to allow the energy of the color to be felt and then to determine how we feel about it or rather how we feel in it. Our mental health is also either calmed or can be revved up, depending on the stimulation surrounding us. A calm and neutralizing environment would be one primarily in blues and greens. Individuals who experience depression may not want an entirely blue environment as they are already feeling blue. Blue may work for them, but only if offset with yellow or red. Orange is a color that while stimulating, perhaps is too stimulating to be used alone, and so blue or purple or green may need to cut the energy, allowing the space to be vivid and lively. Not everyone could live in that environment so another option would be to cut the orange with an earth tone such as taupe or khaki, presenting a more sophisticated and stimulating look but taken down a notch or two to create a more livable environment. When you think yellow you think happy, but alone it grates on the nerves and can be very irritating. So blue or red or green may serve to help balance the effect on the nerves. The earth tones are calm and regenerating and allow for a quieter environment while connecting us to our planet.

Reds and oranges are far too stimulating and do not allow for rest to occur if used in a child's sleeping area (or anybody's for that matter). These two colors also do not work for a playroom as children and their guests cannot play but rather "bounce off the walls." Your intuitive sense along with your common sense should be consulted to determine colors to live and grow by and help achieve harmony in the home. It is really important that we realize that all of our bodies of consciousness need to feel safe and secure in order to be centered and that color can greatly impact our sense of security and create a nurturing environment. Looking to the bigger picture, the light and the climate of the geographical area you have chosen to live in also should be considered when choosing colors that are the most comfortable and support your wellbeing.

Colors and Chakras

We have previously discussed our physical body and the chi energy that flows within. We have many energy centers throughout our body that this subtle energy from the etheric plane flows through. There are seven main chakras that are located from the base of the spine continuing up through the center of our being to the top of our head. The chakras exist in what is referred to as our etheric body. This etheric body exists right outside of our physical body. It cannot be seen, nor can it be touched. Also, the chakras are not physical in the sense that you can touch them or see them as you can other parts of the physical body. But these chakras are vitally important to the health and wellbeing of our physical body. A chakra that is open allows the flow of energy to move unencumbered from one chakra to the next. A chakra that is closed actually allows no energy to either come into or flow from it. In this situation an individual can feel a heaviness or tightness in the chakra area that is closed or perhaps an overall lack of energy. You may feel that this malaise is physical when in fact it is coming from a lack in the nonphysical or etheric body. The way we process how we feel and the way we process our thoughts can also help to determine whether our chakras our open or closed. Narrow and rigid thinking does not allow for an open environment, and so it is not unusual in those individuals that their chakras if tested would be closed.

It is easy to find someone to test your chakras; any Reiki master or other alternative healer can test and help open your chakras or direct you to someone who can. If you are comfortable using a pendulum, you can test your chakras yourself. As you may have previously learned, each chakra consists of a different energy and thus is represented by a different color. You can visualize each of the seven areas as a ball, a wheel, or a disc, and when the energy is moving freely through them, you can see the chakra spinning and actually feel the energy swirling through the chakra. The faster the chakras spin, the higher the vibration and vice versa. The chakras as they appear consecutively are each assigned a color that are the very same colors as the rainbow. Imagine that: the beauty of the divine giving us yet another gift of how our microcosm (our body) relates to the macrocosm (our world)! Learning the meaning of the chakras and how they affect our wellbeing is yet another barometer to judge our wellness.

Red is the color of chakra number seven, which is the chakra at the base of the spine. It may also be called the root chakra. This chakra represents our security and our basic survival and how we connect to our environment in nature. Moving up the spine about two inches below the navel is the sacral chakra, which is the color orange and represents sexuality, pleasure and our well being. This sixth chakra is constantly challenged living in our society as the sexual norms of the world have become progressive, which may or may not align with our belief system, creating an imbalance. The next chakra is the fifth one and is located two inches above the navel. It is the color yellow. This chakra is called the solar plexus chakra and represents our emotional body of consciousness. All of our inner child issues of our emotional body of consciousness arise from this location, such as issues of self-worth or self-esteem. Every human being on earth has a delicate relationship with this chakra as we have each come in with low self-esteem or self-love issues. As this area represents our emotional health, it thus affects our physical health. A healthy solar plexus chakra helps us keep illness and diseases at bay. Our fourth chakra is the heart chakra and is the color green. The heart chakra represents love and the loving relationships you have with your family and friends. The love sent out into the world returns to you in the form of joy and bliss. For some individuals, the heart chakra may relate to the color pink (the color of unconditional love). The third chakra is the throat chakra and is blue in color. This chakra helps you to speak your truth. The second chakra is located between your eyebrows and is called the third eye chakra or may also be referred to as the vitae chakra and is the color indigo. This chakra represents our psychic self and allows us to see or visualize. This chakra when open allows the flow of creative energy through our intuitive self, through the use of our imagination and through our thoughts and ideas. We also note how we relate to our world and are open to the other world receiving psychic energy through this chakra. The first chakra is located at the top of the head and is referred to as the crown chakra and is represented by the color purple or violet. This area is the same area that we refer to as the "soft spot" at the top of a baby's head. The crown chakra is the opening that allows us to be connected to the divine, and the flow of our spiritual source comes through this chakra. The bottom three, the red, orange, and yellow have to do with our lower body and how it functions on earth while the top four have to do with our higher or more spiritual self. There is an eighth chakra that resides outside of our body, located about eighteen inches above the crown and is our fifth body of consciousness or our spiritual healing body of consciousness. The color of this energy is magenta. This is the energy of the fifth dimension that arrived to our planet on April 21, 2001. This is the energy of miracles and mastery and instantaneous healing. This fifth dimension is the dimension that we are currently navigating through. When all of these eight chakras are open and the energy is flowing freely and easily, chakras spinning at a good pace, we feel healthy and alive. This is our primary goal, to keep these energy centers open so that we can allow good health to be part of who we are. There are many experts who have written self-help books to help you identify and work with your chakras. And then there are many self-help books to help you once the chakras are open to keep them open and uncongested by helping you be aware of your attitude and your thinking! An open mind and open heart are key to all that is healthy and, once mastered, continually present unlimited gifts to the body, mind, and spirit from the universe, showering us all in the divine.

As we begin to heal, it is useful when we meditate to wrap ourselves in different colors or to observe what colors wrap around us. We may draw to us what we need, which would be not only easy but convenient. Simple doesn't always work as we may need the energy from a color that repels us. Why? When we draw to us what we need, our emotional body is suggesting to us that we could use the energy of the color as it may make us feel how we need to feel. So if we are sad, and we have a choice between wearing a yellow shirt or a gray shirt, intuitively, which is the better choice? However if we dig a little deeper, perhaps we really despise the color gray. We need to find out why. Does the gray energy represent an issue that occurred long ago that was never healed? If so, we need to use the gray energy to help bring up that issue into our consciousness so that we can work out the issue and heal that part of us. Either way, all colors provide all energies that have the potential to heal all parts of ourselves at the time that we need it. Remember no one color is better than any other color. Each color stands alone and has a meaning and purpose in each of our lives. You can also request your guides to help direct you to the colors you need and then pay attention to what colors repeatedly come into your vision. Soon you intuitively will be able to pull what you need inside of you during a meditation or centering time to help that chakra area.

As I have worked with my chakras, I have become so in tune with them that I can feel the flow of energy. I know when they are spinning at their maximum and I can feel the difference when they are sluggish. Immediately, you can open your chakra/chakras by doing a healing on yourself (as learned in Reiki) or have a healing done on you. Once open it is easy to examine what is going on that would have shut them down and then to make a physical, mental, or emotional attitude adjustment. Usually the energy in the form of fear or any other negative emotion arises from the emotional body of consciousness or solar plexus area and congests or may shut down a chakra. As discussed in previous chapters, as we practice the healing techniques described and work with our inner child, he/she comes back to center and the balance and harmony returns to our body, once again allowing us to experience wellness. We learn to take charge and regain control of our health!

Colors and Aura

Each one of us has a field of energy that surrounds our physical body. This energy comes from our etheric body and is called an aura. Our aura is unique to each of us in size, color, and intensity. It identifies our general state of affairs: it indicates our physical, emotional, mental, and spiritual wellbeing. It can tell the reader a whole "color" story about where we have been, where we are headed, and what is currently going on in our life.

Throughout history we have witnessed paintings in museums and have seen how the great masters have depicted auras. Many portraits clearly show a "halo" around the head area or even around the whole body. The artist was simply finding a way to describe to the viewer the beautiful energy coming off the body of the person depicted. One such painting recently in the limelight is *The Last Supper* by Da Vinci which clearly illustrates Jesus's aura in the painting.

Two Russian scientists believed that the human body consisted of energy and vibration and set out to prove it. In 1903 Semyon and Valentina Kirlian invented a camera which would photograph the energy encompassing the body. This camera was called an aura camera, and the success of this camera gave scientific belief the documentation necessary to take seriously the study of energy as it relates to man. This invention changed the mass consciousness belief and opened the field for speculation, controversy, and new ways to think about man.

My spiritual development teacher, Theresa, is a master aura photographer and reader. She has taken my aura picture many times and is able to describe my growth, my experiences, and my health! Being a novice, I needed an expert to explain not only the meaning of the colors, but was very impressed to hear her describe with great accuracy events occurring in my life. She is also incredibly accurate and has remained so throughout subsequent aura picture sessions. She describes aura photography in these words: "When taking a picture a sensor device will measure vibrations of energy emitted from the different zones of your hand. This information is transferred from the sensor electrodes and displays the colors of your aura which are currently around the body. The colors or the aura are a reflection of what is happening internally on many different levels, and it is interpreted accordingly."

Continuing, Theresa states that "since the beginning of the new millennium, I have witnessed a wider spectrum of colors. I feel that the range has doubled, most likely due to increased energy fields and expansion of intergalactic phenomena. Everyone looks for different things in a photo. A child's photo is not read as an adult's, but this is where I first noticed the change in children and their energy fields. Suddenly children started showing different growth levels. I noticed as soon as emerald green showed up on a child's left hand, they were ready to learn to read and I started teaching them. It helped tremendously with age appropriate activities. In adults, I use the colors to find spirit energy (specifically relatives who had passed) and was almost always accurate to the person and sex. Illness is also very obvious and also most accurate. Severe and life-threatening illnesses such as cancer are evident as is depression and all general states of mental health."

A good reader should be able to help you discern and recognize your general states of wellbeing and discern ill health while also interpreting the colors to help you paint your story. Being forewarned is being forearmed. You can make intelligent choices to do and see things differently, and each subsequent picture will recognize that change and is simply telling another chapter in the story you are writing for yourself.

For example, if you are a loving person, it is not unusual for you to see pink around your heart chakra and for others who can see auras to see a pink glow around you. If you are a healer, a doctor, or a nurse, or in the medical profession in some capacity, it is noticed that the professional healer has a green aura, and when working on their heart chakra you can see the color green.

Since our lives are filled with events and experiences that are contributing "issues" or "baggage" to our lives, the areas in between the chakras appear to be gray in tone. So the colors we are emitting from our body are not simply a purified rainbow as we typically would picture it because these gray areas are indeed blocking the light! The actual colors of our chakras cannot be seen clearly as we would like; sometimes they a muddied version of what we are trying to attain. As the cleansing and clearing process begins and as you do the work, the colors get brighter and brighter and clearer and clearer. As issues get handled and the negative effects dissipate from our lives, that muddied area dissipates as well.

As the aura identifies our general state of health and wellbeing, a healthy and well-balanced person gives off a "glow" and is observed as a beautiful "presence." Others are able to pick up and feel the beautiful energy that is flowing in and through and around, allowing the aura to be clear, bright, and large. We are attracted to those individuals whose auras are colorful, full of life, and emit a positive energy, and conversely, we are dispelled by those whose auras are dark and murky. Many individuals can see and learn to read auras. There are many guides to teach you if you desire. Perhaps as you develop your psychic gifts, seeing color or auras will draw you in and help you help yourself and others by learning to see and interpret color.

If you have an opportunity to have an aura photograph taken, it is a wonderful visual to help you see your energy and what colors/energy you are sending out into the universe. Understanding your aura is yet another tool given to us to help us to understand our general state of being. Colors do not lie, and since each color has a meaning and a vibration, a hue and an intensity, all of the variations of life can be observed and then detailed by an expert aura photographer and reader. Once you have had your aura picture taken and energy read, it is time to take stock of yourself and begin to continue to purify the body.

CRYSTALS/STONES/METALS

The last column of the chart at the beginning of this chapter indicates which crystal or stone should be used on a particular day. Its use coordinates with the color and theme. I was amazed to discover that all crystals and all stones are alive and thus each emit a different energy. This energy is electromagnetic, and each stone is able to absorb energy as well as transmit energy. The appropriate crystal or semiprecious or precious stone may be used for many different distresses: health issues, clearing and cleansing energy from a space, protection, to alleviate addictions, depression, and many other illnesses known to man! Nature has provided a beautiful healing mechanism by gifting the earth with not only the beauty of crystals but their healing properties. It may take some time, but it is a good developing exercise to hold a crystal or stone in one hand and simply let it be. When your awareness becomes sensitive to the feeling, it is fun to see how acutely aware of energy you become. You can hold two different clear quartz crystals in each hand, and after a few minutes can identify an energy from each. You will note that each energy is different. And size doesn't matter! The smallest crystal may be a power stone while a large crystal may vibrate less frequently and less intensely. So pick up a crystal, let it be, and tune into its vibration: does it pulsate, make your hand feel warm or hot, vibrate softly, or vibrate more intensely?

In ancient times, crystals were used for many different kinds of healings. During this century, with the arrival of the fifth-dimensional energies, we have seen a reawakening of the use of crystals in healings and in energy work. The ancients were able to identify what crystals were to be used to aid different parts of the body. Many fine crystal "bibles" or "encyclopedias" are available for reference and provide picture identification of stones and their healing properties. Both the civilizations of Atlantis and Lemuria used crystals in their highly advanced healing technology. Crystals with their healing energies and crystal formations are able to respond vibrationally if you sit silently and remain open to the energy they will transmit to you. Talking to your crystal or crystals allows the crystal to become your friend, and you can actually witness changes within the structure over a period of time. If you receive a crystal as a gift, it is the universe's way of sending you an energy that will enhance you life. Every crystal can tell a story, and future generations will be able to read that story and imprint their lives within it.

If you are renewing an interest in stones or simply beginning a relationship with them, a good place to start is to select a quartz crystal. In the book *Love is in the Earth—A Kaleidoscope of Crystals*, the author, Melody, describes quartz as having the ability "to bring energy of the stars into the soul." Traditionally, the natural quartz crystal was said to both harmonize and align human energies (thoughts, consciousness, and emotions) with the energies of the universe and to make these greater energies available to humanity. The natural tendency of quartz is for harmony, and it is recognized as a "stone of power." Practically, quartz is one stone that has been a major participant in the industrial revolution, a great stone for its innate properties that have been put to use in developing technology over the years. We have used quartz crystals everywhere from being able to transmit and receive radio waves, the quartz watch, to the home environment where most recently quartz crystals have made their debut in such decorative and practical uses as the application in countertops and floor tiles.

Gemstones have been used as birthstones for eons, each a different color and each with a different meaning or vibration that relates to the energy of the birth month. People were so connected to the earth and knew the power of using crystals, stones, and metals in their everyday life. We are returning to the time when we looked to our earth for these gifts and as a source of knowledge. These beautiful traditions, although once lost, are becoming more popular as we are connecting more with each other and the planet we live on. The more we become one and live our lives honoring that belief, the more pleasure, beauty, and wellness may be drawn from our earthly experiences.

Since the crystals and stones both emit and absorb energy, it is important to keep your stones cleansed and blessed. One simple way is to put them in a china or glass bowl outside and let the rainwater wash them and then allow them to dry in the sun. The sun reenergizes and restores the energy of the crystals and brings each back into its maximum power state. You may also smudge each crystal with sage, cedar and sage, or any other incense stick with protective and cleansing qualities, or you may simply bless them with holy water. After every healing or handling by others, crystals must always be cleared and cleansed.

Crystals and stones have a way of finding their owner, and you never know where you will be when you will be drawn to a stone. Its color, its beauty, or its shape, it really doesn't matter, the crystal's energy knows where it is to go and to whom it is to belong to. A metaphysical or spiritually based person understands this and will be happy to pass the crystal along to the person it is meant to be with. It is similar to a true gardener who is always willing to thin their garden by sharing a cutting, a bush, or a shrub to someone who admires it, helping to pass along its energy in someone else's yard, the beauty of which is forever giving. It is a selfless act, forever blessed and forever honored.

GOLD, COPPER, AND SILVER

Gold, copper, and silver have been used by our ancients as healing elements for thousands of years. Society has appreciated each as overt signs of wealth, fashioning the metals in jewelry, silver flatware, goblets, and chalices. Churches throughout the world accumulated and wealthy landowners bartered and baited their offspring to marriage, each using the possession of such elements as an extension of their material wealth. Since their discovery, gold, copper, and silver were believed to not only have medicinal powers but were used metaphysically and spiritually. Each of these elements or metals relate to our master numbers 11/2, 22/4 and 33/6 as previously discussed.

Gold is an element that has long been desired and coveted by all people throughout all times. It is considered a precious metal and as such maintains a very high value. Both its beauty and color have been revered and has decorated royalty and the wealthy since its discovery. Gold has been called the elixir of life and has been given the highest place of honor throughout the ages and has been used by the ancients medicinally, metaphysically, and spiritually.

Gold has not lost its appeal nor its demand as we still value what it represents. In our daily life, gold represents success, the ultimate, the best. We give a gold wedding band to our one true love, we see gold chalices and gold tabernacles honoring our God in our churches, we see gold framing masterpieces in our museums as well as gold statues being rewarded to those who have achieved the highest honors, the ultimate success. Many countries value gold so highly it is used as a standard for monetary exchange—so gold coins and jewelry through the ages have set a very high standard. Gold to this day has not only maintained its interest, it is actively sought after.

Gold has been used as a healing agent for centuries, and currently gold "flakes" in creams and lotions are being marketed as extra-luxurious. Other forms of gold are used in treating many diseases, including cancer. Many of us enjoy gold fillings in our teeth. Is it any wonder that this beautiful metal is the metal assigned to our 33/6 master number? This master number represents the ultimate success and miracle of a sought-after desire, and gold symbolizes the attainment of that desire.

Copper has been used by ancient healers in both powder and piece forms to cure open wounds of all types. A piece of copper metal was applied directly to the afflicted area to heal and to kill germs. Today we toss a copper penny into a vase of fresh flowers with the expectation that the flowers will live longer or have a greater staying power by simply eliminating bacteria in the water. In the latter half of the twentieth century, the copper bracelet became the rage. "Miracle cure" was advertised, and hundreds of thousands of people sought relief from wearing a simple copper band around the wrist. Males and females alike continue to wear the bracelet with the hopes that pain from arthritis will disappear or at the very least become more bearable. Copper is extended into our everyday world as we use copper in our kitchens as cooking with copper or copper-lined pots and pans has proved to be a quick and excellent conductor of heat while providing a natural barrier to germs and bacteria. Copper certainly has found its place in our homes, in exterior usage as decorative roofing over bay windows, copper gutters, and copper firepots and vanes are all the rage while deep inside the interiors, copper piping remains the most expensive of pipes, transporting water to and fro, purifying as it is transported. Society has and is used to copper in its environment. Every day we come into contact with copper as we go about our daily life, never thinking, never questioning, simply accepting its place and value in our homes and in our life.

Copper is assigned to our master number 22/4. This master number is for "greatness" and "control." It also means that you have the ability to realign your energies so that they can be used for spiritual development and growth. The element of copper when experiencing the 22/4 day when used is life enhancing and spiritually directs all energies toward a desired outcome.

Silver is an element that we have valued and desired since ancient times. Silver appeals to the eye as its shiny color, its smooth texture, and intricate engravings have added to its elegance. Silver today is just as beautiful as in the past and has become a major fashion statement as its elegance in jewelry can be worn by all. Its popularity may have increased its demand since its ability to capture many of the same qualities of gold but its monetary value remains lower. Silversmiths throughout the United Kingdom and continental Europe created beautiful items that were used by royalty and the wealthy throughout the world. Sterling flatware, silver trays, silver goblets, silver tea sets, and a myriad of serving pieces were elegant accessories decorating country manors and city estates. The use of silver objects has become a mainstay of good taste and good upbringing. The silver cup was created to be given as a gift in honor of someone's first prize. Today this tradition is still in use.

Silver was used for medicinal purposes to prevent infections, as an antimicrobial, an antibacterial, and as an antibiotic. Today silver has reappeared as there is a renewed use to help prevent infections in wounds caused from specialized situations.

As with our other metals, silver has maintained its appeal. Spiritually and metaphysically, silver relates to our master number 11/2, the master number of intuition and vision. As you look into a piece of silver, you can see yourself, a reflection of who you are. When you look deeper, you can intuit who you are. This introspection allows you to get to that place deep within you, and when you do tap into that place, you intuitively know you are there, listening to your inner voice, allowing what you want to create to be created. Is my vision to create a masterpiece of my life? Silver is that element that surrounds you and supports you and allows your intuition to develop so that you may clearly see those around you and develop your world in a meaningful way, complete with loving relationships adding value and meaning to your life.

OUR PHYSICAL BODY

Our physical body has been described as 99 percent energy and 1 percent matter. We are simply energy and vibration. When the body is in perfect condition, every atom and every molecule perform as they were meant to. Our bodies have often been compared to automobiles. I am sure you have heard the expression that we should take care of our body as if it were a well-oiled machine. The automobile with all of its parts in perfect working condition should be able to run smoothly for thousands of miles. Expensive cars that demand high test gasoline to run to their maximum ability often sputter and choke when given a lower grade, or the lowest grade. Similarly, our bodies are the same. When the body is not in perfect condition, the result is that it doesn't function as it was meant to, opening the door to disease and illness. As previously explained, our physical illnesses stem from the solar plexus chakra, so it is important to make sure that this chakra is open and that the energy is flowing freely through it. It is really much more than that as the solar plexus chakra is tied to our emotional body of consciousness. When each of us arrived on Planet Earth, we each came with varying amounts of self-esteem or self-worth issues that ultimately affect how we love ourselves. As discussed in earlier chapters, this lack within is oftentimes how we can explain "dis-ease" in our body or the lack of ease in our body. This concept is well worth repeating.

We have learned earlier that the fourth dimension brought in the realm of emotionality. And we have described that during this time period, during the latter half of the twentieth century, we acknowledged that we all had emotions. Emotions came out of the closet! We actually talked about them in social situations, produced movies and TV shows that had emotional themes, and created an entire record/music industry as we sang about them. The music industry was overflowing with songs about making up, breaking up, hooking up, as well as speaking up and speaking out against or for peace, war, and poverty. Listening to Billy Joel's song "We Didn't Start the Fire" is an amazing recant of current events from this era of emotionality. Every possible emotion has been sent out into the open, from dying to loving, praying to hating, politics, government, religion, family, friends, and even the establishment! No one part of our life was left untouched and unsung. This era of the fourth dimension was a major turning point and opened the doors for healing in all areas of our emotional selves.

We have also learned that what we think, feel, and how we act creates our reality. So it is important to acknowledge that what and who we are contributes to our general health. We can create a perfect physical body, it is in our control. You may ask, "Well what if someone is absolutely perfect and has contracted a debilitating disease, how can that be?" One explanation is that the person has on his/her blueprint that he/she is to suffer from a chronic disease so that the lesson of suffering is understood. The soul decides to come to Planet Earth as this planet is the only one where the soul can reside in a physical body and may also experience emotionality. So a contract is drawn up, and the soul and its guides agree to allow many experiences that lead to ill health so that the soul can understand and learn its lessons at the very core of its being. As the life is led, and the ill health is experienced, if the lesson is learned easily and quickly, then that item on the blueprint may complete. This part of the blueprint being fulfilled, the soul and its guides may decide that the physical body may now enjoy good health and no longer needs to draw ill health to it, and so the contract being complete, the body may move back into a state of wellness. Of course, it is really important to remember that the soul may also have a contract with another soul or souls and that it was previously decided that this experience would help those souls experience compassion and unselfishness as those items were on their blueprint. Lessons are to be learned and experienced from many different perspectives.

So it is impossible for us to be able to determine exactly what each situation and each lesson is to be learned by the souls that we come into contact with. For this reason, it seems to make the most sense that if we keep the idea that Planet Earth is a school of learning and the student that learns the quickest and grasps the lessons is able to move off the lesson quickly and thus the experience. If you choose not to look at life and its experiences as lessons and allow the experiences to overwhelm you or you get swallowed up inside of them, then experiences will continually present themselves to you until you "get it." The choice is up to you. What everyone can do regardless of what lessons we have chosen to learn while in this physical body is to simply learn to be the purest you can be and to enjoy the most perfect good health that you can. Each of us is in control of our own destiny!

Mother Earth has reminded us that we need to reexamine our life of convenience. Are we leaving a legacy of a beautiful world, or are we selling ourselves short or perhaps even selling ourselves out? Here is just one example of how we have settled for convenience in exchange for common sense and good health. We teach our young pregnant mothers to refrain from alcohol and drugs and smoking to be able to give birth to the purest and healthiest baby possible. For nine months, the birth mother works diligently to provide the most nutritious environment to create the healthiest baby. Labor day arrives, and the happy moment is about to be experienced by new mothers and new fathers throughout the globe. Some of these babies will arrive to a stark reality in a hospital delivery room, a sterile environment complete with fluorescent light bulbs and LED equipment! Have we determined just how unhealthy this is? Not only is that an awakening, but again in the name of convenience the very first diaper applied to the baby's beautiful and pure skin is a "a throw away" diaper. Have we explored how toxic these diapers are? We put this baby in its new bassinette or new crib with new sheets, assuming that our baby is in a healthy environment. But is he or she? We need to ask ourselves a few very pointed questions; there are countless others that we should have answers to. Are we choosing convenience over health? What are we teaching our children? What health issues are being uncovered in the above scenario?

Yes, each of us *is* in control of our own destiny. Certainly on one level this is true as we look to see how we can control our own destiny. How? Have you ever heard the expression "you are what you eat"? If you think more than a second about what that means, it really will gross you out! So how do we remove the toxins from our bodies? Let us start with what we drink. It has been said that water is the single most perfect element from God. Water is naturally pure and naturally purifies. Drinking adequate water allows us to flush out our kidneys, removing all of the accumulated toxins from food and drink and medicines that we consume. The recommended amount of water to drink is sixty-four ounces per day. The benefits are long-lasting and span more than the obvious of keeping our bodies hydrated. For example, it prevents our skin from drying out, and we have less wrinkles when we have a purer body. So we look better, younger, and that helps us to feel great and act great! Drinking adequate water also keeps weight off. Of course, this gift is in jeopardy now as we reexamine how we have treated our natural water supplies and compromised their purity and their sources. We must work fast if we are going to save our world's water supply. Life cannot exist without water, for we and our food sources depend on it. This focus must be our number one priority.

As the world further realigns itself, it is time for the consumer to demand that our food is purified, removing the toxins that have been snuck in little by little. The rapid growth among the populace of an intolerance to gluten is an indication that food that is meant to nourish and sustain is tainted and toxic. Our corporations have been concerned with their bottom lines and have substituted the cheapest glutens possible. By doing so the focus is no longer on nutritious and healthy foods. Rather we are being sold processed food that has little or no nutritional value. When we give the body little or no nutrition, there is nothing for the body to process, and the body simply demands "more." So our bodies tell us to eat more, and we ultimately eat more toxins. We as a society have been an obese nation of undernourished beings, laden down with toxic food. Our bodies are reacting and exploding, sending a very strong message to its owner. "I cannot take this anymore!" The gluten-free movement is now moving into mainstream

America. What are we going to do about it? How are we going to send the message to these corporate giants that we are not paying for toxic food? As more and more children are being diagnosed with gluten intolerance, there are more and more gluten-free products appearing on the grocery shelves. This intolerance if not controlled leads to celiac disease. These little bodies are pure, and when eating means we are poisoning these little bodies, the body simply wants no part of it and sends a strong message that impurities and toxins will not and cannot be tolerated!

As more and more people are purifying their physical bodies, we are experiencing the resurgence of organic food. Organic has gone mainstream as noted by one of the largest warehouse superstores selling organic items as the movement is successfully reaching many peoples in all walks of life. Organic is no longer a specialty food for the wealthy as many more people are able to purchase and experience food with no chemicals. Organic should not be a buzzword or a fashionable trend. Consumers should demand its availability, and as organic food becomes more readily available, prices should become far more competitive. What are we going to demand? Good food? Healthy food? It is up to us.

We are returning to the time when communities will take care of each other. Food gardens, vegetable gardens reminiscent of victory gardens, are cropping up all across the world. Small communities and villages are beginning to see and feel the need to help each other. We are even beginning to barter so that a community sees value in all of its residents and places a value on what you are able to give. People of all ages will begin or continue to contribute to the quality of life that will be felt and experienced by all. Although not all gardens will be organic as our soils are already tainted with chemicals and poisons, people working together will create new ways to grow healthy vegetables. We will find new ways to cleanse our fruits and vegetables and go back to the time when fertilizer was natural and not chemical.

Eating what has been kissed by the sun or eating foods directly from the earth which have been given by God is a far healthier way to live than consuming processed or fast foods. Doesn't it make sense that eating an orange or an apple off a tree is far healthier than eating something processed that uses the word *orange* or *apple* in its name? Fruits and nuts eaten raw and vegetables freshly washed and either eaten raw or steamed are healthier than processed foods or overcooked vegetables. We can eat a very balanced meal while enjoying foods that perhaps we would not consider to be a meal in the traditional sense. We can achieve a healthy balance by eating all foods of all colors. A plate consisting of fruit or vegetables, rice, and nuts affords a nutritious meal. Meatless meals will be commonplace, and for those who will consume meat, a lesser quantity or perhaps less frequently during the week will be the trend. As we clean up our diet and eat less toxic food, we will also clean up our inners. It has been determined that many foods undigested remain inside our bodies as a decaying residue for many, many years. How gross is that?

The value of colonics and colon therapy speaks for itself when the patient experiences a body regenerated and refreshed, enhanced food absorption, increased energy levels, and improved digestion. This practice is becoming increasingly popular as we focus on how important cleansing is to wellness. These clinics cleanse and clear the body of debris and of all of the toxic chemicals we consume through food and from pharmaceuticals. Many years ago, my cousin had established in Sarasota with her husband the finest colon therapy clinic in South Florida. Currently a second location has been opened in Asheville, North Carolina. Being forerunners and experts in this area, they developed the "Gentle Menard-Technique," which is a comfortable slow inflow of water into the colon, gently cleansing the colon. Subsequent visits "afford the body the time necessary to release toxins from successive organs until the whole system has been cleansed." As the debilitating effects of all toxins are removed from the body, the rehabilitating effects are discovered. Alain and Marsha through their dedication and commitment to patient care, patient health, and patient wellbeing have successfully brought this medical treatment to a whole new level. Patients with many chronic diseases and conditions after completion of a series of treatments report such a positive change and for the first time can experience a quality of wellness that had previously not existed. Miracles are being created every day in their clinics! Our bodies were not made to store toxins. Our bodies were made to perform as exquisitely sculpted machines, all in perfect harmony. Holistic and alternative medical practitioners have always known the intrinsic value of colon care, but recently there has been a resurgence. We have that ability now to reach a state of perfect harmony and wellbeing; it is ours for the asking as the concept of colon therapy is being talked about out in the open, offering the public a means to excellent health as affordable clinics are beginning to open up throughout the world.

So as we think about how we choose to live in the fifth dimension, it is clear that for us to heal, we must first begin to heal ourselves. As we begin to heal our physical body, by drinking right, eating right, and cleansing right, we are able to move from a state of existence and begin the journey into a state of wellness. As we reach this point, we are creating a condition which helps to enhance the healing of our other four bodies of consciousness, all working together creating a life that honors our highest self, the best that we were meant to be and living in the best possible way so that we may experience the harmony, balancing our body, mind, and spirit while tapping into the perfection of the "all that is."

CHAPTER XXIII

Beauty in the New World

I am alone but not afraid. I am within the masses, but I am not afraid. I am without voice, but I speak with my heart. I am followed and lead, but I am not afraid. The only fear in my mind could be the absence of spirit from my world.

—Spirit, 2007

THE NEW BABIES

As our planet shifts into this new ever-evolving world, so too have our babies shifted. The consciousness of the babies being born today is very evolved and will be able to not only exist but to thrive beautifully within this new paradigm on earth. These beautiful pure and innocent babies are much more in touch with their higher self than we are! We, as human beings, were born in another time in another consciousness and can certainly be in touch with our higher self, but it comes with study, due diligence, and a lot of old-fashioned hard work. The new children being born in this century will not have to do that. These children will already be in touch with their higher selves and will be living lives that demand more truth and more honesty. These children will indeed help shape this twenty-first century and create the environment which brings the old-fashioned values to light. (No pun intended!) The children will help raise our planet's consciousness. Our planet will see its glory days once again, and these children will teach us how to reconnect with our true selves, our higher selves. We will all learn and shift together, creating the energy necessary to create a consciousness that has the ability to continually expand to a higher level, and then higher again, and then to the next higher level in future years. Why is this necessary? Let's review our past and then look to our future to see where our Planet Earth is headed.

Historically, let's look back to the earlier part of the twentieth century and remember the consciousness that existed during the years of our great-grandparents and grandparents. We can recollect through family stories, movies, or books to see how those earlier generations lived: what was important to them, how they survived and created a life for themselves and their families. As we move forward and think about each subsequent generation, we can ask ourselves how does each generation differ? What events transpired to move the consciousness off of one pattern shifting to another?

We see that the generation born before 1945 has a very different consciousness than the generation born directly after World War II. The war and the holocaust were the main contributors to the shift post-world war. This group became known as the baby boomer generation, which notably spanned the greatest number of years, nineteen to be exact, of any generation in the twentieth century. And as this generation grew, it defined itself as the greatest period of rebellion and change. Moving in the direction of our current transition, this generation's consciousness had to be changed to help us adapt as we are learning to reset ourselves and to help our planet survive. So experiencing and working through all of the upheavals was a necessary step for this generation, and in order to progress to reach this point in time, they needed to continue to move toward an evolving consciousness.

Is it any surprise that the sixties generation raised independent children? Children of the sixties were allowed to ask questions, but we the baby boomers were not allowed to ask questions. We did what we were told to do, we did not question the hierarchy or authority, and we were expected to accept everything because that was the way it was. This may have been okay in the past, but the children of the sixties were not at home with this attitude as they came in with a different energy, questioning things and experiencing their life by becoming free-loving and high evolving, all in the name of love, with the intention of love. They looked for love in whatever way they could, and in so doing they found their answers through music. Enter the fourth dimension, the dimension of emotionality, and the world continued to evolve.

And then the indigo children evolved from the children of the sixties as we continued this forward movement toward the fifth dimension. Today children are being born who are compassionate and loving. They still will have their own roadblocks and their own sandpaper issues to march up against to experience and learn from. They will still have to work at life. But while we struggle for our spirituality, they get it! Each generation has had their own problems to deal with. If we go back to the sixties and look to our parents' generation, which was called the "greatest generation" ever, there was another generation or consciousness. It was the generation between the indigos and the sixties children, and it was called the yuppie generation. A lot of those individuals born during the yuppie generation have generated some of the issues that are going on here on earth today: greed and narcissistic behavior. There existed a different thought process among them. The spirituality was there for some, but for the majority, their egos and greed took control of who they became. This generation was greatly disappointing, and that is why in 1987, the masters came to earth to help make the change and to help make this shift.

Now with this change in consciousness, each person on earth is going to have to work to reach his or her mastery. Spirit will be leaving earth in 2011, so each of us needs to start integrating with spirit so that spirit will be so much a part of you the god/goddess energy doesn't have to come to you, you will have it right within. You may have had to work very hard in the past to connect directly with spirit because you lacked the faith and the trust necessary for this connection. But now the answer is here, right in front of you. You have learned that when you surrender to the truth, spirit is going to be right with you and you will be able to achieve mastery and be able to be right with spirit when spirit is on the other side!

The energies of our children being born shifted again toward the end of the twentieth century with the arrival of the crystal children. This very sensitive and intuitive type of child is making a huge impact on the planet. Primarily, the crystal child is a very old, old soul that has come with his or her wisdom to meld with the energies of earth. The crystal children, simply by "being," are contributing this ancient wisdom to the planet. The children are typically very sweet and loving and can be described as "wise beyond their years." They arrived in the planet with a pure energy. They are very organized, and they are very clear with how they want to live and to do things both at home and at school. Many of the crystal children prefer an all-vegetarian diet, to the amazement of their siblings and parents. These children are spiritually advanced and are helping earth to raise its vibrations during this transitional time. They work very well with the other energies coming into the earth plane at this time as the crystal children are the ultimate peacemakers, spreading love and peace wherever they go and to whomever they encounter.

The planet continues to transition as another group of new young children, the rainbow children, are now being born to indigo parents as they have come to reactivate our moral code. We will be re-experiencing and doing things the "new-fashioned way" as truth, honesty, and integrity become the new mainstays of our new foundation. Each of us will be able to witness steps and glimpses of this change, but the transition will not happen overnight, it will take eight, ten, or twelve years to grow into it. These younger children will demand a change in attitude, a shift in values, and a behavior that is respectful and loving. The rainbow energy is arriving as more and more children are being born on the planet, bringing with them the energy of balance and moderation to put our planet back in gear. We are already feeling and seeing this shift. You may not understand what is happening on one level, but on another, individuals are waking up noting changes on the planet: the planet is moving at a much faster pace and seems to be moving faster and faster. We are in the process of resetting our political, business, economic, and social structures as we watch them tumble one after another, at the same time welcoming the arrival of a rebirth of spirituality.

The guides that will be coming in to work directly with these children will be helping them to achieve this balance by increasing their gifts to a much higher level than what they will be coming in with. They will be learning differently and will be developing a much higher sensitivity and will be able to achieve a much higher level of consciousness. They will not have to learn things the hard way as past generations have had to do, and they will be calmer and practice nonviolence as they are coming in with fifth-dimensional energy. Since the consciousness of these babies is all fifth-dimensional, their guides will be fifth-dimensional as well. These children will not be aspiring to reach the fifth dimension as they will have that consciousness already, but they will be aspiring to the higher dimensions of the sixth, seventh, and eighth. They are our future on this planet.

Many indigo children are born of the parents from the sixties, and they are especially put into those families who mainly have had heavy karmic lessons. It was a good place for them to grow as the environment is structured where they are able to more easily learn their lessons. Indigo children are highly sensitive, and so they have come in to learn, to observe, and to view the pain. Many of the indigos if you watch them are simply numb. Some of the indigos also seem as if they have almost no personality and don't express their emotions because they are coming in with their past life memory where they have witnessed so, so very much. Those who are working currently in the fifth dimension are really working on understanding and becoming conscious of how to work this dimension into their daily life. One day we will simply wake up and will realize how and why to do this and we will just "get it." So the "aha" moment is in front of us, and we can get it and simply know that that is what it is. You are not to worry or contemplate on it or to have any heavy thoughts about it. It is just a moment to understand that you will understand your today by knowing where you were yesterday and the opportunity for all of us in the fifth dimension is to open up and then to understand it!

My son's energy is clearly a very early indigo child. He was born in the early 1970s and as such is one of the forerunners of the indigo children whose purpose was to prepare the planet by bringing in the indigo energy. He has always been described to me by his teachers as having a sensitivity unlike any sensitivity seen before. As a student he was strong-willed and really only loved to work on subjects that he loved, all too often making up his mind that he wasn't going to learn about other subjects that held no interest for him. Only recently did I discover that he has the most amazing gift which was demonstrated in his strong love for the military. He told me that when reading military history, he could envision the entire battle in his head. Alive with movement, it was as if he was there, on the battlefield, knowing where every officer stood and what was about to happen. He clearly envisioned it all. Since indigos bring in their karmic lives and the memory of them, it is not at all unusual to understand how and why he was able to do this. I have also been told by his guides and teachers from the other side that he had been a general in at least five of his past lives, so those memories of those battles are very much alive within him.

The indigos that arrived later in the twentieth century arrived to help transition this planet to bring in the energies that paved the way for the fifth dimension. As children born of children of the sixties, they arrived in groups, their souls purposely kept together to be more effective as synergistically their energy is stronger and more powerful. Those children of the sixties that didn't get it and missed the revolution of consciousness have probably missed participating in this process. But those who experienced the shift in some form or another gave way to the future of the indigo children. They themselves gave birth to the indigo children, and the indigo children have been able to bring in the rainbow children, the new generation of children on our planet.

The indigo children, the crystal children, and the rainbow children are now here, and these children are most fascinating for us to watch and observe as they live and teach and experience earth fifth-dimensionally. Parents of these children need to provide boundaries in an environment where the expectation is appropriate behavior. Consequences of inappropriate behavior are encouraged to teach and learn. It is this new old-fashioned way that will provide a healthy balance to our children—all given with love. Some beautiful souls chose to come in with autism to help our planet through this planetary shift as they are wired to assist in bringing in the new energy associated with this electromagnetic shift. Other souls have chosen to come in with a predominant energy to help bring in that energy's purpose, i.e., a child who is coming in with primarily green energy is coming in to help save our planet. Each of the souls and their unique presence is indeed providing a new world with expanded growth and purpose in all areas of life on earth. While alternative medicine is becoming mainstream, many of these children are coming in with an altered DNA, different from our DNA. It will take some time as our pediatricians and medical establishments will need to adapt formerly successful medical treatments for these new children. Some of the medicines simply will not work on them. Research and medical advancement will need to be the focus of traditional medicine so that our new babies are able to be treated with protocols that are successful in bringing these children into a state of wellness.

As pregnant mothers carry these new little souls, nourishing them to bring them into this world, the babies respond in the womb to the gentle, loving feeling of calm. When the mother is stressed or concerned, these feelings pass on to the baby in the womb, and the baby not only feels the energy of the mother but it affects the baby adversely by becoming fearful. So the mother must learn to surrender to the feeling of providing a loving environment, allowing the baby to grow and develop in a beautiful place so that the baby incorporates this feeling of love and security in his very being, thus maximizing the spirit of love and minimizing fear. These parents must also remember to make choices so as to keep the energy field as pure and as calm as possible since it is what it is in their energy field that affects the baby as well. This is the time for the baby to feel nourished and to feel the sun of his angels and the warmth of not only their spirit and their presence but their love. In more recent years, the new babies bringing in this new energy are observed to continually watch, and see, and are very sensitive to their environments. Music is important for them to listen to as it is relaxing and calming. Spending time in the nourishing and healing environment of nature is another avenue for them to develop this overwhelming feeling of warmth and security, peace and calm.

One great and simple thing for a pregnant mother to do is to get energy boosts from the planet. As Orion describes, it is these boosts that bring balance to you and help you to provide a beautiful environment for nurturing a baby in utero. Think of the sky and remember the words "as above, so below." So by spending time outside and learning to relax within nature, Mother Earth will send her healing energies into you. Your connection with the land and your contact with the land enables you to connect with the pulse of the earth. So if you are in a warm environment, lying down on the earth is a wonderful way to bring yourself into balance. For those of you that are in a colder environment, you can still lie down in the warmth of your home and still benefit from the connection with Mother Earth. So no matter where you live, by focusing on the earth energy and making it a mental energy, you are allowing the bigness of this energy to focus on the baby inside of you. During labor the mother may also try to get comfortable by focusing on the earth energy and the heartbeat of Mother Earth. As you focus on the heartbeat of Mother Earth, your child connects to your heartbeat; it is just a continuation of the circle of love. So if you connect with the wave and the ocean, you can let Mother Earth rock you and cradle you and that will help the baby tremendously. Visualize where you are the happiest, and lying on the ground, feel the warmth of the sand in between your toes and the sun and lull your baby into perfect contentment. Mother Earth hopes that you use her love to help you nourish and love your baby as she continually nourishes and loves you.

THE NEW DISCOVERIES

The ancients taught us many things, and we are returning to that wisdom. Our world is by nature one of duality. This duality keeps life on Planet Earth interesting and challenging and provides the playground for life's lessons. During the last several years there have been hundreds of new discoveries throughout the planet. We are newly discovering the old, across the oceans, the mountains, and our lands. Our Planet Earth is giving us gifts in the form of new ways to look at what had come before. Discoveries when uncovered teach us how the ancients lived so we can experience their world from their eyes so that we can better understand and experience our world, helping us to answer the big questions.

Have you noticed the increased headlines as scientific discoveries are heralded, scientific mysteries are related, and scientific oddities have become curiosities of wonder? We live in a time of great change, a time of upheaval, and a time of great growth. The new energies are indeed chaotic and challenging. As our planet evolves, we can choose to look at things the same way, or we can approach these events from a new angle, a new perspective. Einstein taught us that you cannot solve a problem from the same dimension that it was created in. We must change to a new perspective, a new vantage point, and solve the problems from another realm. We must be open to this wisdom for to succeed and to evolve depends upon it. It is up to us.

In recent months, TV news headlines, magazines, newspapers, and the Internet have all had many articles describing the most recent ancient-world discoveries: antiquities of all kinds giving us clues of how the ancients viewed their family, their cultural traditions, and their work ethic. A few highlights of discoveries showing us glimpses of city life, social life, cultural life, and personal life, including tools, coins, and jewelry, all painting new details on an already painted canvas, the most poignant of which describe family life and how families not only prayed together but were buried together. Why are these discoveries happening currently across the planet? Why are we receiving these gifts from the past? What does this mean for you and me?

Lost cities and civilizations have been discovered under the existing cities of Rome, the country of Peru, and the Guatemalan jungle, to name a few. These very similar events have occurred across the world during the same time period on our planet. Coincidences? Hardly! What knowledge is here for us to uncover? How are we to relate these civilizations and their findings to our lives? What are we to learn?

Sculptures and other smaller carvings have been discovered illustrating the beauty and grace of the figure as well as spiritual and political visuals. The carvings were a beautiful example of an evolved culture and its intrinsic artistic abilities from a time centuries past. Magnificent jewelry, necklaces and earrings, fabricated from gold and enhanced with beautiful gems and pearls, have been unearthed while coins, hundreds of gold coins, have been discovered across the planet. These may be considered small treasures but are certainly not insignificant. Are we amazed at the quality, fineness, and artistry of the engravings that these finds display? Are we able to learn more about the culture of the artisans? Have we shown our gratitude to the ancients for paving the way for artistic expression? Again why are we finding these treasures now?

All of these discoveries throughout the planet are offering insight into the lives and lifestyles of our ancient residents. You can "google" ancient discoveries and see a picture gallery of many, many discoveries. Again why are these discoveries about our ancient world happening now, touching our lives in all parts of our world? What are we to learn from them? Asking these and many other questions and looking for the answers will lead us to where we are headed. Figuring out where we will be able to find these answers and what to do with this knowledge once we have the answers is a task, but we are in a beautiful position as those whose love is all about these discoveries are here to lead the way.

Alive, preserved, or dead, creatures large and small are showing up throughout the planet. Remember the huge squid that came to the surface of the ocean off the coast of Japan? Other ancient wildlife, or tiny insects and unusual animals, have all been recently spotted in jungles, rainforests, and in the oceans. These seemingly "one of a kinds" are here existing in the twenty-first century. A recent fossil, a female named Ida, has been discovered as a perfect primate specimen, offering clues to her life forty-seven million years ago. How have these creatures survived on our planet with its deteriorating natural resources? What is driving these formerly hidden creatures out into the open? For what purpose? What are we to learn from them? We continue to seek answers and pose more questions as more and more of these animals present themselves and more and more mysteries are uncovered for us to solve. And it is not just the animal kingdom that is showing itself as the plant kingdom is coming forth with newly discovered flowers or plants that haven't been ever seen or identified as recently happened in China.

In addition, many wonderful scientific mysteries are being identified. On a weekly basis, a new discovery is announced, citing new facts that shed new light on beliefs once held about a certain planet, star group, or a comet. Astronomers are gleaning new information as advanced scientific telescopes and other technology are allowing them to answer the mysteries of the universe. We are reading about black holes, supernovas, exploding stars, and afterglows. We are learning about many different kinds of energy. As advancements are being made and new technology is being developed, it is being developed worldwide. Have you ever wondered how someone in Tel Aviv can make a scientific breakthrough while simultaneous advancements are announced in Germany and Brazil? We are being gifted with new information constantly which is deliberately being sent to us uniformly throughout our world, allowing us to expand our knowledge and to dismiss limitations about the universe while eliciting new speculation and new beliefs. The more open we are to receiving information, the more information we will continue to receive. Our beliefs are being tested, and as we have glimpses of new scientific breakthroughs, we venture into new ways of thinking, into new paradigms. We are expanding our knowledge base, and as some mysteries become clearer, other mysteries appear, making us continue to strive for new solutions to age-old questions. Why is this new information about our universe being discovered today? What are we learning about our universe in our Milky Way galaxy and other universes in other galaxies?

And then there are the oddities, many unusual events happening both externally and internally that are occurring to make us stop and think and to help us to grow by challenging our belief system. One such example of a recent external event is the birth of a baby girl who was born in Asia with two heads. The birth was described far and wide. She will be a prophet and a visionary, seeing what others cannot. The masses will have difficulty accepting her because they will not be able to see beyond her deformity. What is the significance of this event? What is this event going to teach us? What is this special child going to teach us? How would you react to seeing this baby ten years ago? How would you react by seeing this baby tomorrow?

Have you noticed anything going on different in your space, your own personal space, that seems unusual? We have all noticed how time seems to have speeded up. Look beyond that and perhaps there is something that you can't quite put your finger on, but for a second you have a passing thought that made you take note of it being unusual, or you may have felt that something was odd or weird! Have you taken note of your dreams? If you journal them it is now easy to see patterns or hidden messages that your guides are giving you to help you make sense of your past events or past relationships. You may be receiving the messages in the form of a riddle as your guides want you to have fun as you try to figure things out. Dreaming now is extremely active, and the messages are clear. Since we currently are in a master year, an eleven year, our dreams are indeed cleansing as we are clearing out old events. Perhaps your dreams are revisiting your karmic lessons or karmic events in your life, allowing you to learn from a new perspective or a new vantage point. Are your dreams helping you to let go of past events? Do you have a greater understanding of previous events in your life as these events are revisited in your dreams? Have you been able to identify and learn the lessons? The lesson being learned, life may move forward.

You may also notice that you think that you are dreaming, but in reality you are simply participating from another state of being. One evening I was dreaming that three deer were walking down my driveway. The dream was very lifelike and very real. I awoke and couldn't shake the visual that I had in my dream as it was so real that I actually got up and looked out my bedroom window, only to see three deer walking down my driveway! This is the fun part: pay attention to these details in your dreams as they are allowing you to experience and participate in life in an expanded way as you bleed into not only your reality but perhaps another's.

The next family birthday party or gathering of your loved ones, take pictures, many pictures, and see what you see. The photographs of today are showing you energies of every shape and size and color in the form of orbs! Actually, when you take a photo, look closely in the background or above someone's head or even in the corner of the room. And there you will see the orbs, the energies that are from your deceased loved ones or spirit guides. If you look very closely, it is not unusual for you to see a face in the orb, or perhaps bits of different colored energies in different orbs. Some orbs may have green energy inside while others have blue, and still others may have all of the colors of the rainbow. The veil between realms as we have mentioned earlier has indeed thinned, and the spirit energy is allowing itself to be photographed. Taking pictures outside on a wintry night with the wind and snow blowing is a wonderful way to see how the energy comes in. An electrical storm provides another great photo opportunity! Photography may be the simplest way for you to tap into the unseen as well as validate energy and its existence on the planet. It also makes for a great conversation piece as the family wonders just which grandparent had visited the birthday party of his/her grandson or granddaughter!

As we expose ourselves to these events and begin to answer the questions, we begin to expand our knowledge base, our feeling base, and our base of awareness. We are being asked to challenge what we have been taught—not to discard it, but to use it as a jumping block for diving into the unknown to explore and to get comfortable with our place in this ever-changing and challenging world. We get comfortable by being uncomfortable. We are asked to make changes so that we can create change. We not only reach out of the box, but we must now jump out of the box, stretching to question to get to a place of expansion.

SOUL—HERE, THERE, AND EVERYWHERE!

Let us talk a little about our soul so that each of us can have a clearer picture of how the soul works and how our life on earth affects our soul both here and there!

Here refers to our soul in this physical body and *there* refers to our soul in another physical body, another reality, or even another parallel universe. This book primarily has dealt with bringing you up to speed so that your life is ready and equipped to deal and live beautifully in the fifth dimension on the physical plane. There have been many chapters, each taking a different approach and working from a different angle on how to help you heal yourself so that your reality is the beautiful reality of your choosing. The group has explained again and again the importance of choosing your thoughts, words, and actions so that the reality that you do create is exactly the reality that you want. Following the guidelines set forth throughout the book should enlighten the reader and help the reader's vibrations evolve to a higher and higher level as the exercises are practiced and the work is begun. But how does all of this affect our soul, that part of us that is here, there, and everywhere?

Our soul that is in our physical body on this planet in this lifetime is simply a segment, if you will, of the soul that exists on the other side, oftentimes referred to as your oversoul or your higher self. This soul segment may exist on Planet Earth and be incarnated at the same time in another physical body or bodies as other of your soul segments choose to experience life on earth as well, thus experiencing simultaneous lives. Upon death all of the soul segments that have been living in their physical bodies on Planet Earth transition home. They return and join their higher self. There the experiences gained by their lessons here on earth are melded into their higher self. The higher self then becomes the sum total of all experiences—in all incarnations on Planet Earth. But there is more.

Another one or several or, for that matter, many of your soul segments may choose to learn their lessons on another planet, existing in the nonphysical state during the same time period that a lifetime on Planet Earth is existing in the physical state. This is an example of a parallel life living in a parallel reality. Your world expands from here, your parallel realities expand as your soul experiences different lessons through different realities. Ultimately, each segment comes together and the experiences from the parallel reality all become part of your higher self. Your soul then has many different ways to learn, places to go, and other soul segments to see, but all of these experiences ultimately come back to their higher self.

So knowing that there are other soul segments, it makes sense that the soul or soul segments learning lessons can affect their other soul segments and their experiences. So if a soul segment is in the light and learning its lessons, but another segment of its soul is continually making bad choices and perhaps not on its path, how does one affect the other? The soul can feel and access the information from another segment of its soul and its feelings and then may express this knowledge of its soul's counterpart by feeling emotions that seem unexplainable, such as sadness or confusion. And so it is for this reason that we always want to make the best decisions that honor our higher self. We offer no judgment but wish to experience only the unconditional love of self so that we can continue to learn and experience and honor our higher self.

We can learn about our simultaneous lives, a life that is ongoing currently in another body in another place on earth, or about our parallel lives as we venture out into the universe. One of these lives may or may not be aware of your existence; are you aware of its existence or their existence? The more you expand your understanding of your body, soul, and the power of your mind, the more you will realize. Your life on earth, whether or not you are aware of simultaneous or parallel experiences, will certainly transcend as you consider the existence of these parallel realities. As you begin to understand all that is unseen, you can comprehend your expanding horizons when you both recognize yourself as multidimensional and you develop into a multidimensional being. Then you will be able to experience other realities at the same time. It is very similar to watching a televised show—and the knowledge that at any minute you can see several shows at the same time. As you develop this feeling and bring this knowledge into your awareness, you may experience bleed-throughs, realizing that you are meeting at an intersection out in the pathways, or in dreamstate experiencing the movement to other planets. Can you remember an incident where one minute you were here but the next instant you actually had a very real feeling that you were there? Yes, here, there and everywhere—it is all possible!

Our world on Planet Earth is but a small part of the reality of the world beyond. As we have learned to work in the light, our light shines brighter as we experience life's lessons working from a place of love. We can never really comprehend the number of lessons here for us to learn as they are infinite. Infinite experiences accompany these lessons as our world continues to grow and expand. But have you thought about how your heart expands? The heart becomes so big as it continues to learn and experience and grow and evolve—it too becomes infinite. So is it any wonder that as we grow and expand infinitely, our universe also expands infinitely? Of course it makes perfect sense that our parallel lives be infinite as well.

These parallel lives live in parallel realities in parallel universes, and it goes on and on and on. As our universe expands, this means the consciousness within it expands and so our lives expand. This is the world of *Limitless Possibilities*. This is the world we live in!

THE NEW WORLD

As you know, we expand in many ways. For example, we may be emotionally drawn to a story that elicits compassion from our heart. As we are transitioning, we are becoming more sensitive, and that is a good thing. Tears come easier as our hearts are touched by human tragedies, human accomplishments, and other human events. Tears help us to wash away the conscious boundaries we have established within and help us to move into new territory, allowing insights to be born. Every new experience is a new way to open the soul. As we heal and expand, this energy transcends into our communities and into our world. The consciousness shifts, and many more lightworkers are reawakened, actively pursuing change and transformation. We discover that just "one" of us can make a difference! We feel it and the world feels it and receives it. New heroes are being born every day!

Throughout our world, young and old are being drawn to develop new ways to contribute to our world, our planet. These men and women are patriots for the world, reaching out far and wide so that no one is too removed to receive the love and healing being sent their way. Young people are participating in countless numbers to help solve our world's problems. Have you ever seen an awards list of our dedicated young people recognizing their inventions, ideas, and/or volunteer work that they have masterminded, creating solutions to problems existing in our society, thus contributing to our world in amazing ways? You would be proud and amazed at the level of problem solving. Yes, our youth are indeed not only stretching their boundaries but living outside of them. Organizations are being founded to help people understand how to survive during these times by helping them use resources that are available, making their life easier, safer, and more secure. These organizations help with food and water, natural resources, housing, healthcare, energy conservation, and natural conservation, to name a few. If you can think of a need, you can be sure that somewhere someone is out there thinking, working, and helping others create a plan to help alleviate that need. On the international level, microcredit organizations are cropping up in underdeveloped areas, helping people to create businesses and jobs to generate income while upholding the fair trade business practices, including safe and healthy workplaces, paying fair prices, laborers receiving fair wages, all the while expanding the market base for many, many products and services. It cannot be any other way, and we should not accept any less. We need to raise the bar, not lower it. Subsequent generations will learn by example and witness firsthand basic business principles to survive off the land, meshing their needs with the needs of the land and honoring both. Hand in hand, new partners are being born, working toward common goals. The Internet is filled with newsletters reporting on their organizations' responses and successes in answering the needs of humanity. Beautiful human beings working hand in hand with other humans in the name of peace and love.

It is not enough to simply go "green." We must now explore and use every energy of every color until we achieve the rainbow and can experience total wellness and balance in all areas of our lives. Going green is the beginning to healing our physical environment. Every household in the world must stand up and take responsibility for the planet's condition. It is time to change our habits so that healing may happen. Recycling begins with recycling our thoughts and our actions. The majority of consumers are conscientious and wish to reduce waste, reduce energy consumption, and reduce water usage while not sacrificing health and safety concerns. This majority wishes to support all sustainable efforts on our planet. It simply is a way to contribute that costs absolutely nothing, no time and very little energy. It is the new way, the only way to coexist in a selfless way on our planet. Countless manuals, brochures, and Websites are available to help describe all of the ways each of us can and should contribute to our planet. Your children or perhaps neighborhood children are a great resource as young teachers. They are learning the new way, a better way to help the community help the planet. These children are a great resource for any of us who need to be brought up to speed!

Why have the ancients allowed us to rediscover the ruins from centuries past, the prehistoric creatures that still inhabit the ocean depths, and a host of other scientific breakthroughs in the universe? By allowing the wisdom to be extracted from these past experiences, we can prepare and come from a better place when learning how to experience the new. It is very clear that we have the power within ourselves to heal ourselves, and it is very clear that on our earth, Mother Earth is again gifting us with extraordinary healing tools. We need only to rediscover these and then process how the ancients capitalized on their hidden strength and be open to receive the magic and the miracles as their mysteries are revealed.

One of our planet-healing mentors has come forward with just such an example. Edgar Cayce has been called the Crystal Genius, and in his role as healer he wishes to tell us about new crystals that are arriving on earth. Edgar wants us to know that we can and will all be experiencing the healing ability of crystals. "Crystals never before seen on your planet will be discovered. These new crystals are coming to you via meteorites as more and more will be hitting the earth, distributing the crystals throughout the world. Out of the depths of the ocean floor, as the land is shifting, the ocean floor is moving, thus exposing more healing crystals. This is not an accident but is part of the divine plan. These crystals will provide a benefit that is very similar to the Atlantean and Lemurian stones that were brought to your planet centuries ago. Those crystals carried messages in them and so will these. As always, crystals will find their way to their new owner and new friend. You will also notice that these crystals will be coming in the new energy colors—stones of such colorful beauty that you have never seen before! The colors are vibrant, exciting, and are presented with a luminescent wash through them. Please watch for them as these gifts are arriving!

"Healing with crystals will become more and more popular. Please remember the crystals that you shy away from are the ones that your body needs the most. You have blocked in your memory cells issues that you have never dealt with. These issues are associated with the colors that you shy away from. When you buried the issue, you have buried the color with it. We encourage you to seek out the color and the issue and begin the work. This is an ideal opportunity to bring things up to the surface, deal with the issue, heal it to move forward. Again these gifts are coming for you to help you move forward and upward, healing past wounds, thus enjoying a newfound lighter energy. Call upon me, Edgar, and I will guide you to the appropriate crystal."

In the very near future, Markas has stated that we will find our cure for breast cancer! This is one cancer that we will be able to wipe out. There will be no more breast cancer on our earth—it will take the same path as polio. We are very close, but a combination of a blockade coming from the beloved bureaucracy sector and the approaching discovery of a new natural cure are holding us back. We are almost but not quite there. There exists a natural remedy deep down within the depths of the ocean—a combination of crystals and marine minerals or vegetation. This discovery is very close at hand. Ultimately fear will no longer exist about this cancer. We are almost there! But it will take strength and integrity to allow this cure to come forward and reach the public consciousness. Sometimes our humanness gets in the way of doing good for humanity.

We have all learned about the power of our intention. We can manifest in an instant that which we set our intention on. But what about something seemingly insignificant and unintentional? Let me give you an example. Have you read that if you write beautiful loving words on a glass of water, the molecules in the water actually react to that message and become absolutely individually unique elements of beauty? Well, if that is true, then isn't the reverse true as well? Let's say you write something not so nice on a water glass, trying to be funny or sarcastic or whatever; you can imagine what those molecules look like as they react to the message. Any of Dr. Emoto's books (*The Hidden Messages in Water*) will illustrate how easy dysfunction appears. So does the same hold true when we are running or walking for a cure and all wear a T-shift with the disease plainly displayed on our chests for all to see. Thought forms are energy, and think about the energy in each of the words that represent disease or a lack of wellness within the body. Since we so easily can manifest what we either love or fear, how many people love breast cancer? How many fear it? Perhaps we should rethink this approach and opt for a life-affirming message instead—something to think about!

Our vantage point has indeed changed. We need to remember that to reach this vantage point we must approach it from a place of love. We cannot and should not approach this new world from a place of fear. Another of my guides who has come forward in the role of taskmaster to help assist me not only with the message of the book but to help finish this project is an ancient energy named

Kirunda. This energy exists today in Australia, and there exists a river named after him. The pronunciation is different, but the energy is the same. Kirunda works with Markas and was his guide in many of his past lives. Kirunda has come with his prescription for a beautiful life amidst the changes, amidst the uncertainties, amidst the shift. "I am Kirunda! I am a master of God. I have come to help guide your way. Please take the following five points to heart:

1. More laughter. Laughter is necessary to not only increase your light but the light on the planet. Please remember to approach even the most serious of topics with the lightest heart. A balance should be maintained between seriousness and lightheartedness!
2. More discipline. During your transition phases to reach the fifth-dimensional energy, discipline and focus are the tools to help you to evolve, grow, and ultimately ascend.
3. More simplicity. Look inward to your thoughts, to how you choose to live, and to your surroundings—it is the simplicity that allows you to strengthen the value you have placed on the basics.
4. More purity. Your bodies will not fail you if you help to purify them. Water is the gift and is the purist element on the earth and as such has miraculous healing properties. Water should be honored and consumed with gratitude and thanks.
5. More of the elements. More enjoyment of them. Enjoy the earth, air, water, fire, wood, and metal. These six elements should be loved and respected so that that energy along with power of love is sent to the planet and received as healing.

"It is time that you need to understand the sun, and the moon, and we want you to play with these and to move into their energy. We want you to look into the sun, the moon, and the stars and to use the energy that is given before it is gone. You haven't begun to understand but you think you know. What sounds like a riddle is actually very basic. Basic as the four corners of the pyramid with one pointing to the stars—the point of the pyramid. Enjoy this journey, play with it, have fun with it and stop making it difficult.

"Know the following: soul has to be pure, and the body has to be pure. Your guides are expecting you to do a self-examination. Pure body and pure soul will have a wonderful longevity.

"Happiness comes not only with the knowledge of your heart's desire but how to integrate all of the above preparations. Working on yourself with your guides is the first step. A self-examination will allow you to evaluate your current state and how you need to get to your desired state. Being and becoming. The power of the mind should not be overlooked as a simple request or thought before bed can create the perfect reality that you wish to experience. If you desire rich foods in your life, simply think about them before bed, and upon rising you will desire them less and less. As your mind, body, and soul becomes purified, then and only then will you be able to connect to your higher self. As this occurs, your higher self with be able to give you messages and direct you to help you create the very best reality. Listen and listen and listen! Be open to all possibilities so that you will experience your heart's desire in perfect time. Whatever needs adjusting or change, remember to always love yourself so that you are not only pleased with who you are but happy with yourself so that you and your higher self can be One. Love yourself, and you will experience the expression "Heaven on Earth."

These loving energies have come and brought us these beautiful messages. Their intention is pure and simple and of course comes from a place of love. Their love for us is obvious as they deliver their wisdom and knowledge so that we can live the best possible life on our planet, staying above the chaotic energies while moving into the flow of the fifth-dimensional energy. How are each of us receiving these messages? Are we receiving them while in a state of love? We are constantly being given beautiful gifts. These gifts when we receive them with the purest intention take us to the next level, bringing us closer to our higher self, allowing us to experience this connection of oneness.

As each of these beings has come forward, each has brought with them many, many gifts. With an open mind and an open heart, we can receive their love, witness their faith, and trust in their knowledge. Their wisdom is obvious, and now we must apply it to our world, this new world, and to be able to see the beauty within it. New leaders have stepped forward, and it is very easy for us to recognize who they are as we witness the beautiful and dedicated individuals who are transforming this world into a better place. Recognizing the power of faith and love in these individuals and observing what is really going on in one level is what allows us to know at a deeper level that our world is truly in good hands.

The time is here for us to share in a new vision, a vision that is shared by many throughout our world, allowing the tipping point of human consciousness to shift. We experience the shift, the movement of the energy, and we align ourselves so we move in its flow. We become the change that the world needs us to become. We share the vision, we share this new world. We journey together, arriving at a new world of shared enlightenment. We become the light that the world needs us to shine, and we shine this light, allowing our love to heal the world!

With each person waking up individually throughout the universe, it is thought that millions upon millions of individuals now "get it." Each of us might think that we are standing alone in our newly awakened state. However as each of us walks and works on this earth, we need to know and feel that we are part of a much larger group, part of the whole. Feel the shift and feel the change. Can you discern those that have shifted and are part of this larger movement? Can you also feel that cohesiveness that binds us together? This movement is unlike anything that any of us has ever experienced, and so it is a beautiful opportunity for us to show our faith, our love, and our trust, as we each are walking our talk. This open expression of who we are will be noticed, acknowledged, and received by others. Their connection with us will get stronger and the movement will gain more energy. We will also be an example for those fence-sitters that may need to see in order to feel—and may that feeling be a nudge in the direction of selfless love for others.

The beautiful masters who are on earth that have moved into leadership roles, positioning themselves to help us move forward, are helping by developing this new awareness. All of these leaders in their many, many fields have come during this time in expanded roles, helping to guide and assimilate and direct this new mass consciousness. These leaders are from every field imaginable and represent and speak to all on earth that hold this new vision. They are transformative in their approach as they enlighten the world. Alive with enthusiasm, challenged by creating an unknown path, these masters are leading with their hearts first while the body, mind, and soul are all integrated under love. It is a beautiful scene to find the masters of religion, science, psychology, philosophy, sociology, human development, education, spirituality, traditional medicine, alternative healing, and many, many other related and interrelated fields all integrating their thoughts and conscious minds toward the celebration of our oneness on this planet! With interplay and a marriage of language, emotions, and ideals, this new mass consciousness is evolving. Our new age is becoming! Our new age is expanding its consciousness! Our vision is its new potential and is successfully coming of age as the golden age! And golden it is as the alchemy of all of life on the planet as we know it is transformed and melted and stirred and becomes altered into this higher state of consciousness with purity and wisdom. We have reached the golden age and we have come in love. Our planet may now be secure in the knowledge that we will proceed into the sixth, seventh, and eighth dimensions.

We can be proud to be alive during this time on this planet. Each of us agreed to be here to help transition this planet into the fifth dimension. Some of us arrived to lead, some to play a supporting role, some to provide the energy, some to move the energy about, and some to just "be," all playing parts to help this transformation occur. Our guides have worked very hard in assisting us, and by assisting us they too have assisted with this transformation. Yes, we can now see the perfection where we formerly saw the illusion of imperfection. The "butterfly effect" is alive and well. One thought, one action, or one feeling can occur in one place and is being felt around the earth. Of course, our butterfly as the symbol of transformation knows exactly how this transformation is taking place—as he exists as part of the "one."

To experience beauty in the new world, we all must be able to see our world with new eyes, Atlantian eyes, and a new heart, a Lemurian heart. The beauty comes as we learn to live in the fifth dimension where each experience is seen as a life lesson and that experience is viewed as perfection where we formerly saw the illusion of imperfection. This new vantage point takes us beyond the physical into new realms as we remain open to receiving all of life's *Limitless Possibilities*. Our history forever changed, we will now bring new experiences to our planet, new ways of thinking, new ways of doing, new ways of feeling—all the while entrenched in faith, trust, and love. What better way to walk through life—on the most beautiful path of our choosing, experiencing life with a softened heart, touching the world as it evolves into the love and peace that resides deep within each of us. Each of us living his or her story as "one" and as one of the Greatest Stories ever told!

EPILOGUE

And so here we have it. We have come full circle. And I hope that this circle has become a circle of love for you as it has been for me. I thank you if you have made it through the book. Thank you for absorbing, thinking, reflecting, processing, all contributing to the end result of a new you, a healthier and more balanced you. Doing the work is not easy, but it is necessary if you are to live a life of beauty in this new fifth-dimensional world.

The good news is that you have learned that you don't have to do it alone! There are so many unseen benefactors and angelic influences that when invited into your life help make the journey fun. Knowing that help is truly here in your corner, just for you, makes the hard work seem easier. Someone is always here for you, to put their hand on your shoulder, to comfort you and support you, all the time showing you love and respect. These guides are truly your most sincere friends. And to think you have upward of ninety such friends is not only amazing but remarkable!

Opening up to a new way to see yourself and others, and opening up to a new way to do things, is the greatest avenue for advancement. It is this advancement that leads you to learn to do the dance, that forward and upward movement that we discussed again and again. We could call the dance the "spiral" as we ascend moving higher and higher, feeling lighter and lighter, our energy vibrating faster and faster as we reach for the stars.

And as we reach for the stars, where are you? Well, you are standing tall, becoming one with the universe, seeing how we are all part of the collective whole. No problem is too large that once we take it outside we see it from a different perspective. And that is just what we need to do to keep our problems in perspective—to keep them outside of ourselves, so that we do not become our problems or internalize our emotions. We learn that by standing tall we can come from a place that is centered and whole, creating balance and harmony in our small world. As I am writing this, I remember that I was given a guide whose name is Standing Tall, and now I know why—not only why I was I was given him but why he wanted me to know to call him Standing Tall. See, this is how it works—another piece of the puzzle to help you arrive to that "aha" moment!

Our small world gets bigger and bigger as we venture out into the world, but its values do not change. We take our heart with us wherever we go, helping each other to get to that next step. What we reflect in this small world becomes reflected in the world at large. We can make a difference! We do make a difference! This knowledge is the catalyst that we need to spur us on to bigger and to brighter things. We become the world that we want to be, and our world is one of light. We shine our light in all that we do and to all that we meet, and as we do, our soul gets brighter and brighter, affecting the light in others.

We have witnessed the impetus of our youth, our new entrepreneurs, our new mentors working in areas around the world, as if they were working right next door. Compassion and kindness are standing side by side with hard work, dedication, and commitment. The focus is on change and helping our neighbor to help himself. The goal is making the world a better place, a place to live the best quality of life—not settling and all the while raising the bar to a new standard.

What am I doing? What is my next step? To continue to learn by observing how the world is changing. I want to be right there—right in the action. And as I stand here from my new vantage point, one truth that is constantly being demonstrated is that the earth is in a constant state of flux. That is the one thing we can always count on on this Planet Earth—change. So I will keep up, speed up, or slow down, whatever is required. I will look to the sky and ask for help to be adaptable and flexible so that I am not left in the dust. Whether I am out there or in here, I am moving in the flow of the energy of the universe. As it rises and vibrates higher, I want to participate.

As a lightworker, I have learned that oftentimes we simply need to just "be" and let our light shine wherever we go. This is effortless. But sometimes we are called upon to do more. We are called upon to participate in other ways. Let me give you an example. Have I mentioned that I lived in a home whose front door and front hall was located on a ley line? (A ley line, according to the Oxford Dictionary, is "a supposed straight line connecting three or more ancient sites, sometimes regarded as the line of a former track and associated by some with lines of energy and other paranormal phenomena.") Because the energy comes through stronger, it is easier to transmit and receive energy. Occasionally I would walk by my front door and I would intuit a word or a feeling. One evening I was having a Christmas party, and one of my guests mentioned that she had "heard" one word as she was walking by my front door—it was a proper noun! A couple of months later, a gentleman walking through my front hall mentioned the same last name and began to talk about a shipwreck that sported this name. After discussing the incident, he stated, "I have no idea why I just told you this story!" Well, I certainly did! Were these events coincidences? Of course not! There are *no* coincidences! What was "heard" by these two individuals were validations for me that we were all receiving or picking up the same thing! Buy why? I decided that I needed to work on the why and investigate what was really going on here. I didn't know where this was going to lead me, but I definitely knew that I needed to be doing something as the nudge I felt deep inside just wouldn't give up!

I went online (I thank God for the Internet) and did research on the incident and printed out everything that I could learn about the event. I read the official accident report that was filed and any and all documentation, looking for clues. I asked my guides for assistance and asked that they provide me with information in my dream state. Little by little when I awoke, I had clearer feelings and more information of what I was to do. I was approaching the "aha" moment! And then one morning I figured it out—we were nearing the anniversary of the shipwreck, and I "knew" that I was to have a memorial celebration for those that had died. Somehow I "knew" that all of the crew members had not crossed over—I "knew" that some who had died were trapped at the bottom of the lake in the very vessel that they loved. I knew that this memorial celebration would be the event that would rescue those that were trapped and help them to transition to the other side.

I began making my preparations. Who was I to invite to help me take these earthbound souls to the other side? How was I to hold a memorial? Decisions and ideas simply fell into place. I learned that Archangel Gabriel is the archangel in charge of all of the bodies of water on the planet Earth, so I invited her to be the honorary chairperson of the event! I also included several friends to join me. Each guest was an intuitive, a medium, an empath, and all sensitive to the seen and unseen. One guest was a medium that channeled the angelic realm and was also a beautiful artist, another was a medium that channeled those from the other side, another a gifted astrologer who happened to work for the company that had built the ship, another a loving and compassionate healer, and another a very psychic and highly empathetic young friend who I felt would add to the mix. Individually these women are fantastic, together as a group they are magnificent and the combined energy invincible!

The evening came. I began with a reading celebrating the anniversary of the shipwreck and a prayer as I explained what I was going to do and requesting assistance from God the father, the Son, and the Holy Spirit as well as the archangels and saints and any other of the higher-ups that were in a position to help. With a copy of the ship's manifest I had access to the entire crew. I rang a bell and called out each name one by one, beginning with the captain. When the captain appeared, he thanked us each for coming and said he was honored that we had come together this evening to help his entire crew go into the light. He said he was sad that all of the crew members had not reached the light but did not know how they could help from the other side. As I called each name one by one, the energy came and I checked them off the roster, lighting a white candle and a green candle in each's honor. (White to honor their soul and green to honor Archangel Gabriel.) Down the list I called off each name, requesting each man to come forward until I reached the steward. The steward came forward and requested that I complete the roster and call his name last as that is how he would have done it on the ship. This moment touched me as I realized the enormity of what was happening.

The energies of the crew were all loving and very concerned that some of their crew members did not come forward. Six men on the roster did not come forward when called. Aware that these six had not gone to the light, I requested Archangel Gabriel as well as the entire crew to help find the trapped souls. Everyone stood ready as we called each missing name again, and again the sound of the bell rang out into the quiet of the dark night air. Little by little we aroused the souls, and each came one at a time. We explained to each soul to not be afraid and asked them to listen as we explained the shipwreck to them so that they could understand what had happened and then why we had come to assist them in going to the light. Each of the missing six had a different take on what had happened as well as a different reason for not ascending. Once they understood the actual event, and trusting in the presence of their captain and their crew members, they were able to understand their state. Some souls were easier to take to the light, very willing to ascend, while others held back as fear is paralyzing. One by one we were able to reach each soul, and each came and stood with their crewmembers until they were all reunited.

One of my guests had been receiving the name Tommy the day or two before the event, and she felt strongly that Tommy was down in the deep water, waiting to transition as well. I called his name, and he arrived! He had drowned in a fishing accident in 1945 and had been down in the bottom of the water and did not know how to move into the light. We asked the captain if he would include Tommy with his crew and escort him to the light. The response was beautiful as the captain replied that it was with great honor that the entire crew of the *Edmund Fitzgerald* would take Tommy to the other side. Tears streaming down our faces, seven men transitioned one by one to the other side, where members of their spiritual families and members of their physical families from their many lifetimes on earth were waiting. The Archangel Gabriel came with St. Germaine (St. Germaine is an ascended master and is the keeper of the violet-flame. He is considered to be the lightworker of all lightworkers as he keeps the highest energies to direct freedom, love, and brotherhood throughout our planet.) to thank each of us and brought many thanks from the heavens above as choirs of angels, and all of the spiritual and deceased family members, came in a united display, thanking us for helping one of their own to transition to the light where they finally would be able to find peace and love. What a celebration!

It was the most beautiful evening as each of us realized the depth of love that existed on both sides. Now the souls could process and rest within the love of their families and friends. I not only was amazed at how approachable all of the higher-ups were and how they assisted, but I learned a little more about how the universe functions and how easy it is for us to ask for assistance and to be open to receive it.

I also felt so proud and honored to have participated in helping the souls to transition. I was amazed that I put the evening together—that I listened and acknowledged all of the little nudges and thoughts that popped into my head. Doing the research was easy, and it proved to be a very necessary part of the plan as the success of this mission required me to have the details of the crewmembers' names and their jobs onboard. It had taken some time for me to figure it all out, but as I acknowledged the validations that I received, it helped me to get the confidence necessary to move forward with my plan. But what I really understood was the role of me as lightworker—the ever-expanding role of the lightworker on this planet, always being in service to others, participating in ways that I didn't know were possible. I received many congratulations and blessings from the other side, and later my guides told me that my first "mission" as a lightworker had been very successful and to be ready for my next assignment!

I learned another lesson. I learned that my reality can be created and defined by what is unseen but certainly not unfelt. I was able to expand my role as a lightworker and actually worked on a committee where I was the only being that existed wholly in the physical world. The fact that the rest of the committee members were beings that resided above and below—so to speak—did not for a second negatively impact the success of my mission! My intention was to take the beings to the other side, pure and simple. I did, and my world grew in the knowledge that nothing is impossible and that the possibilities are endless.

My second mission? I do know what it is, and I intend to complete it as soon as I can. It takes place in a country far from here—the rewards for the planet are great—as I begin the research about a horrific event or events that took place in the first century AD, leaving behind dark and destructive energy. (Again I thank God for the Internet!) It seems that a lightworker's work is never done as a major cleansing and clearing of this energy is required to bring this area back into the flow of beautiful energy! I can't wait to begin—to shine my light so that others may live in a purer energy field. Yes, one person does make a difference!

And so there it is—my story until we meet again. Perhaps I will see you out there somewhere and we will share our adventures. You can tell me yours, and I will tell you mine, all the while keeping the lessons in mind as we share in this new knowledge, hoping to gain some wisdom from our experiences. I will always include you in my circle—my circle of love. So remember to honor who you are and to learn to live from the heart, being the best that you can be in all that you do. As you live from this place of love, enjoy the expansion, enjoy the transformation, and enjoy the ascension. I will always be close by in my thoughts and in my love as will your ever-faithful guides, assisting you in every way as we explore these *Limitless Possibilities* together.

And we will be meeting again as I already know that there is another story that must be told.

As we bring this story to a close, I thank you for your time, effort, and attention. It has been a journey of sorts, hasn't it? As we part, I ask you to simply "be" love and "be" light and to know that you can walk with strength as your light shines brightly in every direction. In the words of Markas, Lancelot, Orion, and all of our special guests:

We leave you in love!

EXERCISES

Breathing Exercise to Calm and Relax:

A form of breathing which relaxes your entire body. It should particularly be practiced for those suffering from nervousness, insomnia, or anxiety or for calming in general. This breathing exercise is also particularly effective for those individuals suffering from inflammation, high blood pressure, dysfunctional heart, and/or generic aches and pains.

Sit in a comfortable position with your back straight against the chair and your feet flat on the floor. Close your eyes. Put your right hand on your nose and close your right nostril with the tip of your right thumb. Breathe in and out using a regular rhythm through your left nostril. Do this for at least five minutes.

Sitting in the Silence:

Sitting in the silence is a great help as it is a way for you to get connected to your inner self. It is also a great little exercise to help you learn to become present, and so it is a prelude to helping you live in the present moment by developing a present-moment consciousness.

It is time to turn off all music, television, cell phones, and hang the "do not disturb" sign so you can take ten minutes to begin to learn to center yourself in the silence. It is best to pick a special quiet space and to sit in the silence at the same time every day or evening. When you work this gift into your day, it is amazing to see how much you will begin to enjoy your time with yourself and how much you look forward to it.

Sit in a comfortable position with your back straight against the chair and your feet flat on the floor. Invite one or two guides to come with you and stay with you during the period. Simply sit and get comfortable with yourself. You do not need to journey anywhere or think about anything at all. If thoughts come into your consciousness, simply ask your guides to take them away or you simply send them on their way! This exercise becomes easier and easier as you do it over time.

When your ten minutes are up, simply thank your guides for being and working with you. If you can sit in the silence for a thirty-day period, you will be amazed at how relaxed and how calm you become. You will connect with parts of yourself that you didn't know about and you will observe subtle changes in your being. Enjoy this gift and use it often!

Connecting to your Higher Self:

This meditation is very simple and is very freeing! Its purpose is not only to help you release any and all issues that are currently weighing you down by helping you to connect to your higher self, but also looking for answers to questions you pose as well as direction. Upon releasing any issues, your heart softens and lightens, and you are able to open to receive information from your super consciousness.

Sit in a comfortable chair, with your back against the seat back and your feet flat against the floor. Relax your body, starting with your head, shoulders, torso, arms, and legs. Begin to release any issues that are on your mind. Simply ask that they be turned over to God for transmutation and transformation.

Breathe in through the nose and out through the mouth three times. Use slow, deliberate, clearing breaths. Allow any lingering issues or concerns to be released. You will feel lighter and more relaxed.

Say the words: Superconsciousness, superconsciousness, superconsciousness.

(You may invite a particular guide to join you to assist you with helping you to connect with your higher self.)

As you are sitting quietly, be mindful of how you feel. Do you notice a shifting of any energy? As you practice this exercise, be mindful of any subtle shift with each session. It may take some practice to feel any changes, and it may take some time to open to allow you to access your superconsciousness.

Ask any questions that you would like an answer to. You may receive the answer in your dream state, or in the morning upon rising, or the answer may just pop into your head!

This meditation as stated earlier is very freeing. The effect on the body, mind, and soul is amazing, and it just takes a few minutes each day to do.

Charging a Stone or Crystal—30 Breaths

The meditation allows you to activate your crystals or stones. You may activate one or more crystals in each of your hands. Once this is done, you will be able to keep the stone or crystal near you, and you may intuit what and how to use the stone for healing. In this meditation we will take you on a journey so that you may learn to use the technique of visualization. Please note that in the visualization exercise you are picking up one stone or crystal, but in reality you may have several with you that you are activating.

Sit quietly in a chair, feet flat on the floor and with your back against the chair. Relax your body, starting with your head, your shoulders, your torso, your arms, and your legs.

Quietly close your eyes and begin to visualize a beautiful scene in Hawaii. Find a lush path and walk slowly toward a waterfall. As you are walking along the path, gaze into foliage and become aware of the beauty of their colors, notice the leaves and the shades of greenery that appear to be everywhere. The colors of the flowers close by and at a distance are all full of life as you notice they are the colors of the rainbow. Continue walking along the path and allow your eyes to gently look down to where your feet are stepping. Begin to look for a wonderful small stone to pick up and accompany you to the waterfall. You look in front of you, and then to the left, and right and there you see it, a small white stone that appeals to you as you see its light shining as the rays of the sun touch it. You bend down and pick it up, carrying it in your right hand. You notice the warmth of the stone and its smooth surface. You continue on your journey, and you begin to hear the water falling—small drops at first, but as you get closer you begin to hear more water dripping down and splashing off the green leaves and rocks and dripping down to the pool at the bottom of the falls. You love the sound of the water as it relaxes you. It makes you smile. You find a comfortable spot on a rock to sit, and with your face up to the sky soaking in the warmth of the sun, and with both of your hands open—your right hand still has the rock that you found in it—you begin to breathe quietly and slowly until you have slowed your breath down.

While quietly breathing, you begin to relax into your scene, absorbing the warmth of the sun, basking in the beauty of the colors, and hearing the trickle of the water slowly and quietly falling down into the pool of water. You relax your head, your shoulders, your torso, your arms, and your feet.

Breathe (counting one to ten) in through the nose and out through the mouth, slowly and deliberately at a comfortable pace.

Breathe (counting eleven to twenty) and as you do so, begin to focus on pulling the beautiful white light up through your feet. Allow the white light to swirl ever so gently as it fills your physical structure. Feel this white light flowing up through your feet into your limbs, into your torso, and through you chakras—the root, the spleen, the sacral, and into and throughout the heart chakra, up through your neck and throat area, your third eye, and into your crown.

Breathe (counting twenty-one to thirty) and as you do so, begin to visualize a beautiful magenta color swirling above your crown chakra. Allow this color to come through your crown and travel downward, mixing with the beautiful white energy as they swirl together from the crown through the upper body, through the shoulders, the arms, wrists, hands, and fingers.

As the swirling white and magenta energy reaches the fingertips, you feel your stone or crystal (whether you have one or several in one or both hands) become alive with energy. You are activating the healing power of your crystals.

Sit for a few minutes and allow the crystal to absorb the beautiful energy. Thank your guides or teachers for the experience and for allowing you to receive the wonderful energy from which your crystals or stones may be energized.

(Remember to keep your stones and crystals energized, cleansed, and cleared. Simply let the stones sit in a china dish or bowl out in the rain and allow them to dry in the sun. As they do so, nature is cleaning and clearing them and the sun is reenergizing them. If you use your stones to heal someone other than yourself, remember to cleanse and clear your stones after each use.)

Kirunda: Energy Balancing during Transition to Ascension

Have you noticed a lightheadedness or dizziness? If so, when you notice these symptoms coming, doing the following exercise will balance you immediately.

Place your left hand in front of your head, right hand in back of your head, and leave for thirty seconds. Then switch hands for balance, for another thirty seconds.

If you feel any symptoms coming in your back:

Place your left hand in front of your stomach and the right hand on your back, leave for thirty seconds. Then switch hands for balance, for another thirty seconds.

Please note: please validate to yourself that you are having these experiences so that you acknowledge the transitioning within yourself.

GLOSSARY

Acupuncture—a form of alternative medicine where special needles are inserted along points or meridians of energy in the body for treatment/pain relief.

Alchemy—the ability to transform substances into gold, or to alter one substance into another. Wizards or magicians were known to be alchemists throughout the ages.

Alternative Medicine—referring to any complementary or alternative medical practices from the traditional forms practiced in the West. It has been stated that Western medicine treats the symptoms while the Eastern counterpart treats the root causes of disease.

Ancestral Benefactors—our ancestral benefactors refer to those beings who were family members throughout the ages or past lifetimes that have come to us with assistance.

Angelic Energy—this energy is the energy from the angelic realm/realms which are said to be seventh—and eighth-dimensional.

Archangels—the highest legend of angelic beings in the higher realms.

Aromatherapy—the use of aromatic plant extracts and/or essential oils, either alone or in combination, for healing.

Astral Travel—an experience where the soul leaves the body. This may be done consciously or unconsciously as in dream sleep.

Atlantis—an ancient civilization known for its highly evolved and developed technological society.

Ayurvedic—an ancient science of health and medicine originating from the Hindu tradition being practiced today.

Aura—a field of energy surrounding the body of every living creature.

Aura Photography—highly specialized photography that captures not only the image of the person but also the entire field of energy filled with the colors of the aura.

Auric Field—that part of our energy field that surrounds our physical body.

Bagua—a tool used to help describe the elements and their placement in locations to create balance and harmony both in and around the body.

Bilocation—to be in two places simultaneously.

Birthright Angel Group—this group represents the essence of the soul with similar souls of like essence from the universal realm. The birthright angel is the overseer of this group of souls of like essence.

Bliss—a state of perfect happiness.

Cabalistic Arcana Guide—guide from the universal realm who assists with your belief system.

Chakra—an energy point within the body that allows energy to flow. There are seven main chakra points and many lesser ones in the body.

Channeling Process—is the experience of being in such a relaxed state that you are able to receive information from the higher realms.

Cherubim—a legend of angelic beings that we typically picture as chubby, childlike or babylike angels.

Chi Energy—the energy that is considered the life force within the body.

Clairaudience—an enhanced faculty of hearing; a metaphysical gift that allows the recipient to hear what typically cannot be heard.

Clairsentience—an enhanced faculty of smelling; a metaphysical gift that allows the recipient to smell what is not present.

Clairvoyance—an enhanced faculty of seeing; a metaphysical gift that allows the recipient to see or can refer to someone having the gift of sight into seeing or perceiving what is not physical.

Color Harmonics—a healing modality that incorporates the use of light rays which when shined on various centers of the body create balance or wellness and is used to treat different illnesses or conditions.

Communication Chakra—another term for the throat chakra.

Cosmic Consciousness—the energy or thoughts as perceived from the mind of the universe and not from the earth plane.

Cosmic influence—our world beyond, the galaxy, and/or all areas of our universe that influences our daily life.

Crown Chakra—the chakra that is at the top of the head.

Dominion—a legend of angelic beings in the higher realms whose job is to praise God.

Drumming—beating an instrument which actually tunes you into the pulse of the universe.

Elation—the feeling that sweeps through your body validating that a miracle has occurred.

Enlightenment—a state of growth referred to in metaphysical and spiritual circles as having reached the state of a higher awareness or of spiritual insight.

Eternal Suns—guides in the universal realm that are either from the physical or etheric realms.

Etheric Field—is the matrix of the physical, emotional, and mental bodies as exists in the higher realms. The etheric body consists of these energies that immediately surround our physical body.

Etheric Weaver—a healing tool that is a combination of crystal, metal, and magnets from the earth to assist with self-healing and meditation.

Euphoric feelings—the feelings associated with joy and bliss which accompany a heightened spiritual state.

Feng Shui—the art of achieving balance and harmony by being aware of the meaning of the placement of objects within the body and the environment.

Fifth Body of Consciousness—the body of consciousness that represents the spiritual healing body. This is the eighth chakra and exists outside of the body eighteen inches above the head.

Fifth Dimension—the dimension that is currently transitioning to Planet Earth whose energy is representative of the higher realms.

Fifth-dimensional Healing Energy—the energy that is currently on Planet Earth and has arrived as the planet has transitioned into the fifth dimension. This healing energy is represented by the color magenta and comes from above the physical body, from the spiritual source, and brings with it the miraculous healing energy.

Fourth Dimension—a dimension of the 80s that represents the emotional realm of consciousness—emotionality.

Geomancy—a term which refers to the feng shui or the placement of objects to achieve harmony and balance.

Heart Chakra—the fourth chakra, represented by either the color pink or green.

I-Ching—translates as "The Book of Change," which is consulted as a practical guide to the wisdom of the ancients. It is over three thousand years old and contains the ancient philosophy of Confucius.

Inner Child—is that part of our emotional body of consciousness that resides in each one of us that is representative of our emotional selves that is typically between the ages of three to five.

Interplanetary exchange program—the movement of souls in between planets for the purpose of learning and knowledge.

Joy—the feeling of great pleasure and happiness.

Kabbalah—an ancient Jewish version of the Bible.

Lead Messengers—guides in the universal realm in the emotional, mental, or spiritual areas.

Lemuria—a civilization that existed thousands upon thousands of years ago which was known for its spirituality and love.

Ley Lines—are meridians on the planet where energy easily flows to and from other realms.

Lightbody of Consciousness—that body of consciousness that applies to the higher energies.

Lightworkers—a name that applies to humans who have come to Earth to increase the light or vibrations on the planet.

Manifestation—a process by which one can create what one desires.

Metaphysical—beyond the physical, coming from a higher source.

Microcosm—a small part of a much larger whole.

Miracle—an extraordinary event that cannot be explained by a logical mind but rather comes from the creative source.

Magic—the power of creating events by using energy from the universe.

Natural Channel—a natural channel is a human being who has received the gift of prophecy and is able to receive messages with no formal training.

Numerology—the ancient study of numbers that have meanings other than the obvious.

Orion Energy—the energy of Orion, The Hunter, is a cosmic energy as he is part of the Canis Major constellation.

Oversoul—another term for our higher self that exists in the higher realms.

Parallel Universes—other universes that exist in other realities that are parallel to ours.

Pendulum—this divination tool is any object that hangs on a chain or string that an energy can communicate through.

Physical Incarnation—is the soul coming to earth in a physical body to experience a lifetime here.

Planetary Shift—the transitioning from one energy level to another—as from the fourth dimension into the fifth dimension. As the transitioning occurs, the planet shifts its consciousness to a higher consciousness.

Pleiades—the group of stars known as the Seven Sisters.

Primordial Sound—a form of meditation which relaxes to the state of calm.

Principalities—a legend of angels that exists in the higher realms.

Reflexology—an alternative form of medicine that studies massage of the feet, hands, and head to ultimately release stress, pain, and/or illness within the body.

Reiki—a healing technique from Japan based on the principle that the healer channels energy into the patient by means of touch which activates healing in the body.

Sacred Geometry—the ancient use of geometry in a universal sense whose meaning connects the spiritual with the mathematical, i.e., the pyramid.

Seraphim—A legend of angelic beings that exist in the highest realms.

Sixth Sense—that part that is strongly intuitive, going beyond the five senses to the sixth, which is unseen.

Smudge—the act of clearing and cleansing energy from a space or from an object.

Solar Plexus—the third chakra, represented by the color yellow and housing the emotional body of consciousness.

Space Continuum—the area as it exists on the other side where there is no spatial confinement.

Spiritual Healing Body—this body is the fifth body of consciousness which exists outside of the body and is defined by being in the fifth dimension.

Spleen Chakra—this chakra is the sixth chakra of the body and is represented by the color orange.

Superconsciousness—the state of consciousness that reaches the highest realms, the higher self.

Synchronicity—a set of seemingly unrelated events that come together, all contributing to a future event.

Synergy—the thought that when two or more techniques or people are combined, that combination produces an effect greater than the sum of their parts.

Tarot—a deck of cards, each representing a message or thought, that spirit communicates through.

Third Eye—the third eye is located between your eyebrows and represents the area on your physical body that you can connect to your psychic guides. This is the sixth chakra on the body and is also called your vitae chakra.

Time Travel—to be able to move forward in time into the future or the past.

Telepathy—the communication of thoughts by means other than by the known senses.

Teleportation—the dematerialization of the body and the rematerialization of the body in another location instantly.

Third Dimension—a dimension of consciousness on Planet Earth that existed primarily pre-1984. It is the consciousness that consists primarily of matter in the physical world.

Third-dimensional Planet—the consciousness that exists on the planet, a consciousness of matter.

Totem—an animal, bird, insect, or natural object whose meaning is used to expand the meaning of events or situations in one's life.

Trance Channel—a trance channel is a person who typically leaves their physical body so that another energy can take over and present information coming in from another realm.

Transmigration—the passing of the soul immediately into a different body after death.

Vibrational Frequency—a frequency which measures the level of energy. If the vibrational frequency is high, the energy is fast and the sound or vibration transmitted is very high, and if the frequency or energy is slow, the sound or vibration transmitted is a lower frequency or dull.

Vitae Chakra—this is your sixth chakra and is also called your third eye. With an open third-eye chakra, you can easily receive guidance from spirit guides.

Vortex—an opening in the physical realm where energies are able to move in and through as they travel in between realms.

BIBLIOGRAPHY & RECOMMENDED FURTHER READING

Alder, Vera Stanley. *Finding of the Third Eye.* San Francisco: Weiser Books, 1980.

Alexander, Jane. *The Smudging and Blessings Book: Inspirational Rituals to Cleanse and Heal.* New York: Sterling, 1999.

Allen, Edward Frank. *The Complete Dream Book: The Classic Guide to the Mysterious World of Dreams.* New York: Grand Central Publishing, 1985.

Amber, Reuben. *Color Therapy: Healing With Color.* New York: Aurora Press, 1983.

Amorok, Tina, Marilyn Mandala Schlitz, and Cassandra Vieten. *Living Deeply: The Art and Science of Transformation in Everyday Life (IONS/New Harbinger).* Oakland: Noetic Book/New Harbinger Publications, 2008.

Anderson, George, and Andrew Barone. *Walking in the Garden of Souls.* Calgary: Berkley Trade, 2002.

Anderson, George. *George Anderson's Lessons from the Light: Extraordinary Messages of Comfort and Hope from the Other Side.* Calgary: Berkley Trade, 2000.

Anderson, Greg. *The 22 Non-Negotiable Laws of Wellness*. New York: Harperone, 1996.

Andrews, Colin, and Synthia Andrews. *The Complete Idiot's Guide to 2012 An Ancient Look at a Critical Time*. New York: Alpha, 2008.

Andrews, Lynn. *Spirit Woman: The Teachings of the Shields*. New York: Tarcher, 2002.

Andrews, Shirley. *Atlantis: Insights from a Lost Civilization*. St. Paul: Llewellyn Worldwide Ltd, 1997.

Andrews, Ted. *Animal Speak: The Spiritual & Magical Powers of Creatures Great & Small*. St.Paul: Llewellyn Publications, 1996.

Andrews, Ted. *Animal-Wise: The Spirit Language and Signs of Nature*. Jackson: Dragonhawk Publishing, 1999.

Andrews, Ted. *How to Heal with Color*. St. Paul: Llewellyn Publications, 2005.

Ardagh, Arjuna. *Awakening Into Oneness*. Boulder: Sounds True, 2007.

Atwater, P. M. H. *Beyond the Indigo Children: The New Children and the Coming of the Fifth World*. New York: Bear & Company, 2005.

Bach, Richard. *Illusions The Adventures of a Reluctant Messiah*. New York: Delacorte, 1977.

Bach, Richard. *One*. New York: Dell, 1988.

Bach, Richard. *Out of My Mind*. New York: Dell, 1999.

Baldwin, Christina. *The Seven Whispers: Listening to the Voice of Spirit*. Novato: New World Library, 2002.

Barnard, George Mathieu. *The Search for 11:11*. Portland: 11.11 Publishers Pty Limited, 2005.

Benish, Gloria D. *Go Within or Go Without: A Hands-On Guide to Healing Body, Mind and Spirit*. New York: Citadel Press, 1996.

Berger, Joseph, and Frank Caprio. *Healing Yourself with Self-Hypnosis.* New York: Prentice Hall Press, 1998.

Berger, Merrill, and Stephen Segaller. *The Wisdom Of the Dream: The World of C. G. Jung.* New York: TV Books, 2000.

Bernhardt, Michele. *Colorstrology: What Your Birthday Color Says About You.* Philadelphia: Quirk Books, 2005.

Best-Jackson, Alice, and Dennis Jackson. *Together Again—Twin Souls Reunite in Love and Life.* Markham: Denalilove Publications, 1999.

Bien, Julianne. *Color: Awakening the Child Within.* Toronto: Spectrahue Light & Sound Inc., 2006.

Bien, Julianne. *Golden Light: A Journey With Advanced Colorworks.* Toronto: Spectrahue Light & Sound Inc., 2004.

Bishop, Karen. *Remembering Your Soul Purpose.* New York: iUniverse, 2006.

Bishop, Karen. *The Ascension Companion: A Book of Comfort for Challenging Times.* Bangor: Booklocker.Com Inc., 2006.

Bishop, Karen. *The Ascension Primer.* Bangor: Booklocker.Com Inc., 2006.

Bloom, William. *Working With Angels, Fairies, and Nature Spirits.* New York: Piatkus Books, 2003.

Bopp, Judie, Michael Bopp, Lee Brown, and Phil Lane. *The Sacred Tree.* Twin Lakes: Lotus Press, 1984.

Borax, Mark. *2012: Crossing the Bridge to the Future.* Berkeley: Frog Books, 2008.

Bornstein, David. *How to Change the World: Social Entrepreneurs and the Power of New Ideas.* New York: Oxford University Press, 2007.

Borysenko, Joan, and Miroslav Borysenko. *The Power of the Mind to Heal.* Carlsbad: Hay House, 1995.

Braden, Gregg. *The Mystery of 2012: Predictions, Prophecies and Possibilities.* Louisville: Sounds True Inc., 2009.

Bragdon, Emma. *Spiritual Alliances: Discovering the Roots of Health at the Casa de Dom Inacio.* Woodstock: Lightening Up Press, 2002.

Brennan, Barbara. *Hands of Light: A Guide to Healing Through the Human Energy Field.* New York: Bantam, 1988.

Bro, Harmon H. *Edgar Cayce on Dreams.* New York: Warner Books, 1968.

Brown, Byron. *Soul Without Shame: A Guide to Liberating Yourself from the Judge Within.* Boston: Shambhala Publications, 1999.

Brown, Simon G. *The Feng Shui Bible: The Definitive Guide to Improving Your Life, Home, Health, and Finances.* New York: Sterling, 2005.

Brown, Sylvia, and Lindsey Harrison. *Insight: Case Files From the Psychic World (LARGE PRINT).* New York: Doubleday, 2006.

Browne, Sylvia, and Antoinette May. *Adventures of a Psychic: A Fascinating and Inspiring True-Life Story of One of America's Most Successful Clairvoyants.* Carlsbad: Hay House, 1998.

Browne, Sylvia, and Lindsay Harrison. *Life on the Other Side: A Psychic's Tour of the Afterlife.* New York: NAL Trade, 2002.

Browne, Sylvia, and Lindsay Harrison. *Past Lives, Future Healing: A Psychic Reveals the Secrets to Good Health and Great Relationships.* New York: NAL Trade, 2002.

Browne, Sylvia, and Lindsay Harrison. *Prophecy: What The Future Holds For You.* New York: Dutton, A Division Of Penguin, 2005.

Browne, Sylvia, and Lindsay Harrison. *The Other Side and Back.* New York: NAL Trade, 2002.

Browne, Sylvia. *God, Creation, and Tools for Life.* Carlsbad: Hay House, 2000.

Browne, Sylvia. *Meditations.* Carlsbad: Hay House, 2000.

Browne, Sylvia. *Soul's Perfection.* Carlsbad: Hay House, 2000.

Browne, Sylvia. *Sylvia Browne's Book of Angels*. Carlsbad: Hay House, 2004.

Browne, Sylvia. *The Mystical Life of Jesus: An Uncommon Perspective on the Life of Christ*. New York: NAL Trade, 2007.

Buckland, Raymond. *Gypsy Dream Dictionary*. St. Paul: Llewellyn Publications, 1999.

Buckland, Raymond. *The Spirit Book*. Detroit: Visible Ink Press, 2005.

Buscaglia, Leo. *Living, Loving & Learning*. New York: Fawcett Columbine, 1982.

Butler, W.E. *How to Read the Aura*. York Beach: Samuel Weiser Inc, 1976.

Butterworth, Eric. *Discover the Power Within You*. New York: Harper & Row, Publishers, 1968.

Byrne, Rhonda. *The Secret*. New York: Atria, 2008.

Calabrese, Adrian. *Sacred Signs: Hear, See & Believe Messages from the Universe*. St. Paul: Llewellyn Publications, 2006.

Campbell, Don. *The Mozart Effect: Tapping the Power of Music to Heal the Body, Strengthen the Mind, and Unlock the Creative Spirit*. Brattleboro: Harper Paperbacks, 2001.

Campbell, Joseph. *Myths of Light: Eastern Metaphors of the Eternal (Collected Work of Joseph Campbell Series)*. Novato, CA: New World Library, 2003.

Campbell, Joseph. *The Inner Reaches of Outer Space: Metaphor as Myth and as Religion*. Novato: New World Library, 2002.

Carroll, Lee. *Kryon 2000 Passing the Marker: Understanding the New Millennium Energy Book VIII*. Del Mar: Kryon Writings, 2000.

Carroll, Lee. *Kryon: Alchemy of the Human Spirit*. Del Mar: Kryon Writings, 1995.

Carroll, Lee. *Kryon: The New Beginning (2002 and Beyond) Book Nine*. Del Mar: Kryon Writings, 2002.

Carroll, Lee. *Letters From Home*. Del Mar: The Kryon Writings Inc., 2003.

Carroll, Lee. *The Journey Home: A Kryon Parable, The Story of Michael Thomas and the Seven Angels*. Carlsbad: Hay House, 1998.

Carroll, Lee. *The Parables of Kryon*. Carlsbad: Hay House, 2000.

Carson, David, and Jamie Sams. *Medicine Cards*. New York: St. Martin's Press, 1999.

Cayce, Edgar Evans, and Henry Reed. *Edgar Cayce on the Power of Color, Stones, and Crystals*. New York: Grand Central Publishing, 1989.

Chadwick, Gloria. *Discovering Your Past Lives*. New York: McGraw-Hill, 1988.

Chasse, Betsy. *The Little Book of Bleeps: Quotations from the Movie . . . What the Bleep Do We Know?*. US: Captured Light Distribution, 2005.

Chia, Mantak. *Taoist Ways to Transform Stress into Vitality: The Inner Smile, Six Healing Sounds*. Louisville: Healing Tao Books, 1985.

Chopra, Deepak, and David Simon. *The Chopra Center Herbal Handbook: Forty Natural Prescriptions for Perfect Health*. New York: Three Rivers Press, 2000.

Chopra, Deepak, and David Simon. *Grow Younger, Live Longer: Ten Steps to Reverse Aging*. New York: Three Rivers Press, 2002.

Chopra, Deepak. *Ageless Body, Timeless Mind: The Quantum Alternative to Growing Old*. London: Harmony, 1994.

Chopra, Deepak. *Everyday Immortality: A Concise Course in Spiritual Transformation*. New York: Gramercy, 2003.

Chopra, Deepak. *How to Know God: The Soul's Journey into the Mystery of Mysteries*. New York: Rider & Co, 2000.

Chopra, Deepak. *Peace Is the Way: Bringing War and Violence to an End*. New York: Three Rivers Press, 2005.

Chopra, Deepak. *Perfect Health: The Complete Mind/Body Guide, Revised and Updated Edition.* London: Harmony, 2001.

Chopra, Deepak. *The Seven Spiritual Laws Of Success—A Practical Guide To The Fulfillment Of Your Dreams.* Novato: Amber Allen/New World, 1994.

Chopra, Deepak. *The Soul in Love: Classic Poems of Ecstasy and Exaltation.* London: Harmony, 2001.

Chopra, Deepak. *The Spontaneous Fulfillment of Desire: Harnessing the Infinite Power of Coincidence.* New York: Three Rivers Press, 2004.

Clark, Hulda Regehr. *Cure for All Diseases.* NYC: Motilal Banarsidass, India, 2002.

Cleary, Thomas. *I Ching: The Book of Change.* Boston & London: Shambhala, 2006.

Cloud, Dr. Henry. *The Secret Things of God: Unlocking the Treasures Reserved for You.* West Monroe: Howard Books, 2009.

Clow, Barbara Hand. *The Pleiadian Agenda: A New Cosmology for the Age of Light.* New York: Bear & Company, 1995.

Cohen, Andrew. *Living Enlightenment: A Call for Evolution Beyond Ego.* Lenox: Moksha Press, 2002.

Cohen, Kenneth. *Honoring the Medicine: The Essential Guide to Native American Healing.* Chicago: Ballantine Books, 2006.

Condron, Barbara. *How to Raise an Indigo Child: 10 Keys for Cultivating a Child's Natural Brilliance.* Cambridge: Som Publishing, 2002.

Conway, D.J. *Flying Without A Broom: Astral Projection and the Astral World.* St. Paul: Llewellyn Publications, 2002.

Cox, Terah. *Birth Angels: Fulfilling Your Life Purpose and Potential with the 72 Angels of the Tree of Life.* Kansas City: Andrews McMeel Publishing, 2004.

Crabtree, Maril. *Sacred Feathers: The Power of One Feather to Change Your Life*. Avon: Media Corporation, 2002.

Crary, Robert Wall. *The Still Small Voice*. Marina del Ray: Devorss & Company, 1987.

Crary, Robert Wall. *The Voice From Within*. Cleveland: Rishis Institute of Metaphysics, 1996.

Crary, Robert Wall. *The Way to Spiritual Mastery*. Cleveland: Rishis Institute of Metaphysics Inc., 1991.

Creeger, Catherine E., and Rudolf Steiner. *An Outline of Esoteric Science*. Berlin: Steiner Books, 1997.

Crosweller, David. *Buddhist Wisdom: Daily Reflections*. North Clarendon: Tuttle Publishing, 2003.

Cumming, Heather, and Karen Leffler. *John of God: The Brazilian Healer Who's Touched the Lives of Millions*. New York: Atria Books, 2007.

Cunningham, Scott. *Cunningham's Encyclopedia of Crystal, Gem & Metal Magic*. St. Paul: Llewellyn Publications, 2002.

Cuthrell, Jack. *Letters of the Soul from the Silence of the Mind*. New York: Spiritual Quest, 1995.

Daniel, Alma, Timothy Wyllie, and Andrew Ramer. *Ask Your Angels*. New York: Ballantine Wellspring, 1992.

Day, Laura. *Practical Intuition in Love: Let Your Intuition Guide You to the Love of Your Life*. Brattleboro: Harper Paperbacks, 2000.

Day, Laura. *The Circle: How the Power of a Single Wish Can Change Your Life*. New York: Atria, 2009.

DeLong, Douglas. *Ancient Teachings for Beginners*. St. Paul: Llewellyn Publications, 2000.

Deger, Steve, and Leslie Ann Gibson. *The Little Book of Positive Quotations*. Minneapolis, MN: Fairview Press, 2006.

Denning, Melita. *Practical Guide to Astral Projection: The Out of Body Experience.* St. Paul: Llewellyn Worldwide Ltd, 1979.

Diamond, John. *Holism and Beyond: The Essence of Holistic Medicine.* Bloomingdale: Enhancement Books, 2001.

Diamond, John. *Life Energy: Using the Meridians to Unlock the Hidden Power of Your Emotions.* Milwaukee: Continuum International Publishing, 1990.

Diamond, John. *The Healer: Heart and Hearth.* Bloomingdale: Enhancement Books, 2000.

Diamond, John. *The Veneration of Life: Through the Disease to the Soul and the Creative Imperative.* Bloomingdale: Enhancement Books, 1999.

Diamond, John. *The Way of the Pulse: Drumming With Spirit.* Bloomingdale: Enhancement Books, 1999.

Diamond, John. *Your Body Doesn't Lie.* New York: Grand Central Publishing, 1989.

Dixon-Kennedy, Mike. *A Companion to Arthurian & Celtic Myths & Legends.* Seattle: The History Press, 2006.

Dosick, Ellen Kaufman, and Wayne D. Dosick. *Spiritually Healing the Indigo Children (and Adult Indigos, Too!): The Practical Guide and Handbook.* San Diego: Jodere Group, 2004.

Dreamer, Oriah Mountain. *The Dance: Moving to the Rhythms of Your True Self.* New York: Harper, San Francisco, 2001.

Dreamer, Oriah Mountain. *The Invitation.* New York: Harperone, 2006.

Druhan, Marlene M. *Naked Soul: Astral Travel & Cosmic Relationships.* St. Paul: Llewellyn Publications, 1998.

Dyer, Wayne W. *Inspiration: Your Ultimate Calling.* Carlsbad: Hay House, 2007.

Dyer, Wayne W. *The Power of Intention.* Carlsbad: Hay House, 2005.

Dyer, Wayne W. *There's a Spiritual Solution to Every Problem.* Brattleboro: Harper Paperbacks, 2003.

Eadie, Betty J. *Embraced by the Light.* New York: Bantam, 2002.

Eadie, Betty J. *The Awakening Heart: My Continuing Journey to Love.* New York: Pocket Books, 1996.

Eagle, Brooke Medicine. *Buffalo Woman Comes Singing.* Chicago: Ballantine Books, 1991.

Eason, Cassandra. *The Modern-Day Druidess.* New York: Citadel, 2004.

Edward, John. *One Last Time A Psychic Medium Speaks to Those We Have Loved and Lost.* New York: Berkley Books, 1999.

Ellis, Peter Berresford. *A Brief History of the Druids.* New York City: Carroll & Graf, 2002.

Elsbeth, Marguerite. *Crystal Medicine.* St. Paul: Llewellyn Publications, 1997.

Emoto, Masaru Dr. *The Hidden Messages in Water.* Hillsborough: Beyond Worlds Publishing, 2004.

Fazel, Christopher, and Mark Thurston. *The Edgar Cayce Handbook for Creating Your Future.* Chicago: Ballantine Books, 1992.

Feathers, Margaret. *Journey of a Soul.* US: Jamar, 2001.

Ferguson, Anna-Marie. *A Keeper of Words: Legend The Arthurian Tarot.* St. Paul: Llewellyn, 1995.

Ferguson, Gail. *Cracking the Intuition Code: Understanding and Mastering Your Intuitive Power.* New York: McGraw-Hill, 2000.

Ferguson, Marilyn. *Aquarius Now: Radical Common Sense and Reclaiming Our Personal Sovereignty.* San Francisco: Weiser Books, 2005.

Field, Ann, and Gretchen Scoble. *The Meaning of Herbs: Myth, Language & Lore.* San Francisco: Chronicle Books, 2001.

Fiest, Bill. *Halo Repair—a nudge toward wholeness*. Alexandria: B3 Publishing, 2005.

Flem-Ath, Rand, and Colin Wilson. *The Atlantis Blueprint: Unlocking the Ancient Mysteries of a Long-Lost Civilization*. New York: Delta, 2002.

Ford, Debbie. *The Dark Side of the Light Chasers*. Boston: Riverhead Trade, 1999.

Ford, Debbie. *The Secret of the Shadow: The Power of Owning Your Story*. New York: Harperone, 2002.

Fox, Matthew. *Creativity: Where the Divine and the Human Meet*. New York: Tarcher Putnam, 2002.

Fox, Sabrina. *Loved by Angels: Angels Are Right Beside Us-Even If We Don't Yet See Them*. Berkeley: Amber Lotus, 1998.

Frankl, Viktor E. *Man's Search for Ultimate Meaning*. New York: Basic Books, 2000.

Frankl, Viktor E. *Man's Searching For Meaning*. New York: Pocket Book, 1963.

Gammill, William. *The Gathering: Meetings in Higher Space*. Charlottesville: Hampton Roads Publishing, 2001.

Gawain, Shakti. *Creative Visualization: Use the Power of Your Imagination to Create What You Want in Your Life*. Novato: New World Library, 2002.

Gawain, Shakti. *Developing Intuition: Practical Guidance for Daily Life*. Novato: New World Library, 2001.

Gerard, Lynne. *Expect Good Things*. Norwalk: C.R. Gibson Company, 1993.

Germain, St. *Twin Souls & Soulmates: The I Am Presence of St. Germain Channelled Through Azena Ramanda and Claire Heartsong*. Cairns: Triad Publishers, 1994.

Geryl, Patrick. *How To Survive 2012*. Kempton: Adventures Unlimited Press, 2007.

Gienger, Michael. *Crystal Power, Crystal Healing: The Complete Handbook*. New York: Sterling, 1998.

Gilbert, Elizabeth. *Eat, Pray, Love: One Woman's Search for Everything Across Italy, India and Indonesia*. Boston: Penguin (Non-Classics), 2007.

Goldberg, Bruce. *Astral Voyages*. St. Paul: Llewellyn Publications, 1999.

Grabhorn, Lynn. *Excuse Me, Your Life Is Waiting: The Astonishing Power of Feelings*. Charlottesville: Hampton Roads Publishing Company, 2003.

Graff, Dale E. *Tracks in the Psychic Wilderness*. Rockport: Element Books Ltd, 2000.

Grant, Robert J. *Are We Listening to the Angels?: The Next Step in Understanding the Angels in Our Lives*. Totoras: A.R.E. Press (Association Of Research & Enlig, 1994.

Green, Roger. *I Ching Workbook*. San Francisco: Main Street Books, 1979.

Greystone, Alex, and Mary Summer Rain. *Mary Summer Rain's Guide to Dream Symbols*. Charlottesville: Hampton Roads Publishing Company, 1996.

Hagan, Kay Leigh. *Vow: The Way of the Milagro*. Beltsville: Council Oak Books, 2001.

Haldane, Albert, Simha Seraya, and Barbara Lagowski. *Angel Signs: A Celestial Guide to the Powers of Your Own Guardian Angel*. New York: Harperone, 2002.

Hall, Manly P. *The Secret Teachings of All Ages*. Boston: Wilder Publications, 2007.

Hanut, Eryk. *Blessings of Guadalupe*. Beltsville: Council Oak Books, 2002.

Harris, Barbara. *Conversations with Mary*. Osprey: Heron House Publishers, 1999.

Harvey, Andrew. *Essential Mystics: The Soul's Journey Into Truth*. New York: HarperCollins, 1996.

Hauck, Dennis William. *The Complete Idiot's Guide to Alchemy (Complete Idiot's Guide to)*. New York: Alpha, 2008.

Hay, Louise L. *You Can Heal Your Life*. Santa Monica: Hay House, 1984.

Hay, Louise. *Colors & Numbers: Your Personal Guide to Positive Vibrations in Daily Life*. Carlsbad California: Hay House Inc., 1999.

Hay, Louise. *The Power Is Within You*. Carlsbad: Hay House, 1991.

Head, Joseph, and S. L. Cranston. *Reincarnation*. New York: Causeway Books, 1967.

Heinemann, Klaus, and Miceal Ledwith. *The Orb Project*. New York: Atria Books/Beyond Words, 2007.

Hoffer, Abram. *Healing Children's Attention & Behavior Disorders: Complementary Nutritional & Psychological Treatments*. Toronto: CCNM Press, 2004.

Hollihan, Tony. *Great Chiefs: Volume III*. Edmonton: Folk Lore, 2002.

Hopcke, Robert H. *There Are No Accidents: Synchronicity and the Stories of Our Lives*. Boston: Riverhead Trade, 1998.

Hoskins, Susan M. *Dancing With Angels: The Journey Home*. Westerville: Integrity Press, 1998.

Howard, Jane M. *Commune With the Angels: A Heavenly Handbook*. Totoras: A.R.E. Press (Association Of Research & Enlig, 1992.

Howell, Francesca Ciancimino. *Making Magic with Gaia: Practices to Heal Ourselves and Our Planet*. York Beach: Red Wheel, 2002.

Huber, Cheri. *Be the Person You Want to Find: Relationship and Self-Discovery*. Murphys: Keep It Simple Books, 1997.

Huffines, LaUna. *Healing Yourself with Light: How to Connect with the Angelic Healers*. Tiburon: Hj Kramer Inc., 1994.

I-Ming, Lui. *The Taoist I Ching (Shambhala Classics)*. Boston: Shambhala, 2005.

Jahnke, Roger. *The Healer Within: Using Traditional Chinese Techniques To Release Your Body's Own Medicine *Movement *Massage *Meditation *Breathing*. New York: Harperone, 1999.

Javane, Faith, and Dusty Bunker. *Numerology and the Divine Triangle*. West Chester: Para Research, 1987.

Jenkins, Philip. *Dream Catchers: How Mainstream America Discovered Native Spirituality*. New York: Oxford University Press, USA, 2005.

Jones, Marie D. *2013: The End of Days or a New Beginning: Envisioning the World After the Events of 2012*. Franklin Lakes: New Page Books, 2008.

Joudry, Patricia, and Maurie D. Pressman. *Twin Souls: Finding Your True Spiritual Partner*. Center City: Hazelden, 2000.

Kardec, Allan. *The Spirits' Book*. Las Vegas: Brotherhood of Life, 1989.

Keyes, Jr., Ken. *The Power of Unconditional Love: 21 Guidelines for Beginning, Improving, and Changing Your Most Meaningful Relationships*. Wausau: Love Line Books, 1990.

Keyes, Ken. *Handbook to Higher Consciousness*. Coos Bay: Love Line Books, 1997.

Kidd, Sue Monk. *All Things Are Possible*. Norwalk: C.R. Gibson Company, 1979.

King, Godfre R. *The Magic Presence*. Schaumburg: St Germain Press, 1999.

King, Godfre Ray. *Unveiled Mysteries (Original)*. Schaumburg: Saint Germain Press, 1982.

Kingston, Karen. *Clear Your Clutter With Feng Shui*. New York City: Broadway, 1999.

Kipfer, Barbara Ann. *8,789 Words of Wisdom*. Chicago: Workman Publishing Company, 2001.

Kirmond, Patricia. *Messages From Heaven: Amazing Insights On Life After Death, Life's Purpose And Earth's Future*. Corwin Springs: Summit University Press, 1999.

Kunz, Dora. *The Personal Aura*. Wheaton: Quest Books, 1991.

Lama, Dalai, and Howard C. Cutler. *The Art of Happiness (A Handbook for Living)*. New York: Griffin Press, 1998.

Lama, The Dalai, and Nicholas Vreeland. *An Open Heart: Practicing Compassion in Everyday Life*. New York: Back Bay Books, 2002.

Lawson, David. *How to Develop Your Sixth Sense: A Practical Guide to Developing Your Own Extraordinary Powers*. London: Thorsons, 2001.

Lesser, Elizabeth. *Broken Open: How Difficult Times Can Help Us Grow*. New York: Villard, 2005.

Lewis, Laura, Jamie C. Miller, and Jennifer B. Sander. *Heavenly Miracles*. New York: HarperCollins Publishers, Inc., 2000.

Lightman, Alan. *Einstein's Dreams*. New York: Vintage, 2004.

Linn, Denise. *Past Lives, Present Dreams*. New York: Wellspring/Ballantine, 1997.

Livingston, Gordon. *Too Soon Old, Too Late Smart: Thirty True Things You Need to Know Now*. Cambridge: Da Capo Lifelong Books, 2008.

Long, Max Freedom. *The Secret Science Behind Miracles*. Marina Del Rey: DeVorss, 2002.

Lorr, Regina Eveley, and Robert Wall Crary. *The Path of Light*. Marina del Ray: Devorss & Company, 1983.

Luk, A. D. K. *Law of Life, Book I*. Pueblo: A. D. K. Luk Pub., 1988.

Luk, A. D. K. *Law of Life, Book II*. Pueblo: A. D. K. Luk Pub., 1983.

Macfarlane, Muriel. *Heal Your Aura: Finding True Love by Generating a Positive Energy Field*. New York: Citadel, 2000.

Machale, Des. *Wit*. Kansas City: Andrews McMeel Publishing, 2003.

Manne, Joy. *Soul Therapy*. Berkeley: North Atlantic Books, 1997.

Marciniak, Barbara. *Bringers of the Dawn: Teachings from the Pleiadians*. Rochester: Bear & Company, 1992.

Marciniak, Barbara. *Earth: Pleiadian Keys to the Living Library*. Rochester: Bear & Co., 1995.

Marciniak, Barbara. *Family of Light*. Rochester: Bear & Company, 1998.

Marciniak, Barbara. *Path of Empowerment: New Pleiadian Wisdom for a World in Chaos*. Novato: New World Library, 2004.

Markale, Jean. *The Druids: Celtic Priests of Nature*. New York: Inner Traditions, 1999.

Marlow, Mary Elizabeth, and Joseph Rael. *Being and Vibration*. Beltsville: Council Oak Books, 2002.

Marshall III, Joseph M. *The Lakota Way: Stories and Lessons for Living*. Boston: Penguin, 2002.

Martin, Barbara Y., and Dimitri Moraitis. *Change Your Aura, Change Your Life: A Step-By-Step Guide to Unfolding Your Spiritual Power*. Sunland: WisdomLight Books, 2003.

Matthews, Boris, and Ashok Bedi. *Retire Your Family Karma: Decode Your Family Pattern and Find Your Soul Path*. Berwick: Nicolas-Hays, 2003.

McAfee, John. *Into the Heart of Truth: The Spirit of Relational Yoga*. Woodland Park: Woodland Publications, 2001.

McAfee, John. *The Fabric Of Self: Meditations on Vanity and Love*. Woodland Park: Woodland Publications, 2001.

Mccune, Shirley D., and Norma J. Milanovich. *The Light Shall Set You Free*. San Diego: Athena Publishing, 1996.

Mello, Anthony de. *The Heart of the Enlightened*. New York: Image Books Doubleday, 1991.

Melody. *Love Is in the Earth: A Kaleidoscope of Crystals (Love is in the Earth) (Love is in the Earth)*. Wheat Ridge: Earth Love Pub House, 1995.

Melville, Francis. *The Book of Angels*. Hauppauge: Barron's, 2001.

Michael, Todd. *The Twelve Conditions of a Miracle: The Miracle Worker's Handbook*. New York: Tarcher, 2008.

Mickaharic, Draja. *Spiritual Cleansing: Handbook of Psychic Protection*. San Francisco: Weiser Books, 2003.

Miller-Russo, Linda, and Peter Miller-Russo. *Angelic Enlightenment: A Personal Process*. St. Paul: Llewellyn Publications, 1999.

Mills, Janet, and Don Miguel Ruiz. *The Four Agreements Companion Book: Using the Four Agreements to Master the Dream of Your Life*. San Rafael: Amber-Allen Publishing, 2000.

Mills, Janet, and Don Miguel Ruiz. *The Voice of Knowledge: A Practical Guide to Inner Peace*. San Rafael: Amber-Allen Publishing, 2004.

Moolenburgh, H. C. *Meetings With Angels*. New York: Barnes & Noble, 1995.

Moore, Thomas. *Soul Mates: Honoring the Mysteries of Love and Relationship*. New York: Harper Collins, 1994.

Moran, Victoria. *Lit from Within*. New York: Harperone, 2004.

Morwyn. *The Complete Book of Psychic Arts: Divination Practices From Around the World*. St. Paul: Llewellyn Publications, 1999.

Moss, Robert. *Dreaming True: How to Dream Your Future and Change Your Life for the Better*. New York: Pocket, 2000.

Murphy, Joseph. *How to Use the Laws of the Mind*. Camarillo: Devorss & Company, 1981.

Murphy, Joseph. *Miracle of Mind Dynamics*. New York: Prentice Hall Press, 1972.

Murphy, Joseph. *Your Infinite Power to be Rich: Use the Power of Your Subconscious Mind to Obtain the Prosperity You Deserve*. New York: Prentice Hall Press, 1986.

Myss, Caroline. *Sacred Contracts: Awakening Your Divine Potential*. New York: Three Rivers Press, 2003.

Myss, Caroline. *Why People Don't Heal and How They Can*. New York: Three Rivers Press, 1998.

Nichols, Ross. *The Book of Druidry*. Edison: Castle Books, 2009.

Occhiogrosso, Peter, and Ron Roth. *Holy Spirit: The Boundless Energy of God*. Carlsbad: Hay House, 2000.

Ophiel. *Art & Practice of Creative Visualization*. San Francisco: Weiser Books, 1997.

Orion, Sareya, and Lauren Thyme. *The Lemurian Way: Remembering Your Essential Nature*. Lakeville: Galde Press, Inc., 2000.

Oslie, Pamala. *Life Colors: What the Colors in Your Aura Reveal*. Novato, CA: New World Library, 2000.

Packer, Duane, and Sanaya Roman. *Opening to Channel: How to Connect with Your Guide (Roman, Sanaya)*. San Fransico: Hj Kramer, 1993.

Padgett, James E., and Daniel G. Samuels. *Celestial Messages: A Chronicle of the Progression and Transformation of the Soul*. West Palm Beach: New Heart Productions, 1999.

Page, Christine R. *2012 and the Galactic Center: The Return of the Great Mother*. New York: Bear & Company, 2008.

Parker, Dorothye. *Color Decoder: Unlock Your Physical, Spiritual, and Emotional Potential*. Hauppauge: Barron's Educational Series, 2001.

Pearl, Eric. *The Reconnection*. Carlsbad: Hay House, 2003.

Peirce, Penney. *Dreams for Dummies*. Philadelphia: Running Press Miniature Editions, 2001.

Pellegrino-Estrich, Robert. *The Miracle Man. The Life Story of Joao de Deus*. Cairns: Triad, 2001.

Peniel, Jon. *The Lost Teachings of Atlantis*. Alamosa: Network, 1997.

Petrak, Joyce. *Angels Guides & Other Spirits*. Loudon: Curry-Peterson Press, 1996.

Phillips, and Denning. *Practical Guide To Psychic Self-Defense: Strengthen Your Aura*. St. Paul: Llewellyn Publications, 2002.

Pinchbeck, Daniel. *2012: The Return of Quetzalcoatl*. New York: Tarcher, 2007.

Ping, A. C. *Be*. New York: Marlowe & Company, 2004.

Ponder, Catherine. *Dynamic Laws of Healing*. New York: Parker Publishing Company, 1972.

Praagh, James Van. *Reaching to Heaven*. New York: Signet, 2000.

Prevost, Ninon, and Marie Lise Labonte. *Wings of Light: The Art of Angelic Healing*. San Diego: Blue Pearl Press, 1998.

Price, John Randolph. *Angels Within Us: A Spiritual Guide to the Twenty-Two Angels That Govern Our Lives*. Chicago: Ballantine Books, 1993.

Price, John Randolph. *The Alchemist's Handbook*. Carlsbad: Hay House, 2000.

Prince, Gail, and Basha Kaplan. *Soul Dating to Soul Mating*. Chicago: Perigee Trade, 1999.

Pritzker, Barry M. *A Native American Encyclopedia: History, Culture, and Peoples*. New York: Oxford University Press, 2000.

Prophet, Elizabeth Clare. *Creative Abundance: Keys to Spiritual and Material Prosperity*. Corwin Springs: Summit University Press, 1998.

Prophet, Elizabeth Clare. *How To Work With Angels (Pocket Guide to Practical Spirituality)*. Corwin Springs: Summit University Press, 1998.

Prophet, Elizabeth Clare. *Karma and Reincarnation: Transcending Your Past, Transforming Your Future*. Corwin Springs: Summit University Press, 2001.

Prophet, Elizabeth Clare. *Soul Mates & Twin Flames: The Spiritual Dimension of Love & Relationships*. Corwin Springs: Summit University Press, 1999.

Prophet, Elizabeth Clare. *Violet Flame To Heal Body, Mind And Soul (Pocket Guide to Practical Spirituality)*. Corwin Springs: Summit University Press, 1998.

Prophet, Elizabeth Clare. *Your Seven Energy Centers: A Holistic Approach To Physical, Emotional And Spiritual Vitality.* Corwin Springs: Summit University Press, 2000.

Prophet, Mark L., and Elizabeth Clare Prophet. *Keys to the Kingdom: And New Dimensions of Being.* Corwin Springs: Summit University Press, 2003.

Prophet, Mark L. *The Masters And Their Retreats.* Corwin Springs: Summit University Press, 2003.

Quinn, Gary. *May the Angels Be With You: Access Your Spirit Guides and Create the Life You Want.* New York: Harmony Books, 2003.

Radhoff, Sandra. *The Kyrian Letters: Transformative Messages for Higher Vision.* Virginia Beach: Heritage Publications, 1992.

Rain, Mary Summer. *Trined in Twilight.* Charlottesville: Hampton Roads Publishing, 2000.

Ratisseau, Elizabeth. *Guardian Angels.* Seattle: Laughin Elephant, 1999.

RavenWolf, Silver. *Angels: Companions in Magick.* St. Paul: Llewellyn Publications, 2002.

Ray, Sondra. *Pele's Wish: Secrets of the Hawaiian Masters and Eternal Life.* Novato: New World Library, 2005.

Redfield, James, and Carol Adrienne. *The Celestine Prophecy An Adventure.* New York: Warner Books, 1993.

Redfield, James. *The Celestine Prophecy: An Adventure.* Boston: Wheeler Publishing, 1994.

Redfield, James. *The Tenth Insight: Holding the Vision.* New York: Warner Books, 1998.

Reifler, Sam. *I Ching: A New Interpretation for Modern Times.* New York: Bantam, 1991.

Renard, Gary. *The Disappearance of the Universe: Straight Talk About Illusions, Past Lives, Religion, Sex, Politics, and the Miracles of Forgiveness.* Carlsbad: Hay House, 2004.

Richard, Webster. *Spirit Guides & Angel Guardians.* St. Paul: Llewellyn, 2000.

Robertson, Jon. *The Sacred Bedroom: Creating Your Personal Sanctuary.* Novato, CA: New World Library, 2001.

Roman, Sanaya. *Living with Joy: Keys to Personal Power and Spiritual Transformation.* Tiburon: HJ Kramer, Inc., 1986.

Roman, Sanaya. *Personal Power Through Awareness.* Tiburon: HJ Kramer Inc., 1986.

Roman, Sanaya. *Soul Love: Awakening Your Heart Centers.* San Fransico: HJ Kramer, 1997.

Ruechardt, Edward. *Light Visible and Invisible.* Ann Arbor: Univ. Of Michigan Press, 1958.

Ruiz, Don Miguel. *The Four Agreements: A Practical Guide to Personal Freedom.* San Rafael: Amber-Allen Publishing, 2001.

Rushnell, Squire. *When GOD Winks: How the Power of Coincidence Guides Your Life.* New York: Atria, 2002.

Russo, Steve. *The Devil's PLayground: Playing With Fire Can Get You Burned.* Eugene: Harvest House, 1994.

Sagan, Samuel. *Atlantean Secrets II: Forever Love White Eagle.* Roseville: Clairvision, 1999.

Salem, Cheryl, and Harry Salem. *An Angel's Touch: The Presence and Purpose of Supernatural Messengers in Yo ur Life.* London: Harrison House, 1997.

Salzberg, Sharon. *Faith: Trusting Your Own Deepest Experience.* Boston: Riverhead Trade, 2003.

Scarf, Maggie. *Secrets, Lies, Betrayals: The Body/Mind Connection.* New York: Random House, 2004.

Scully, Nicki. *Power Animal Meditations: Shamanic Journeys with Your Spirit Allies.* New York: Bear & Company, 2001.

Seligman, Martin E. P. *Authentic Happiness—Using The New Positive Psychology To Realize Your Potential For Lasting Fulfillment.* Sydney: Random House Australia, 2002.

Severn, Jessica, and Gwen Totterdale. *Teleportation!: A Practical Guide for the Metaphysical Traveler.* Miami Beach: Words Of Wizdom International, 1996.

Shafir, Rebecca Z. *The Zen of Listening: Mindful Communications in the Age of Distractions.* Wheaton: Quest Books, 2003.

Shepard, Leslie A. *Encyclopedia of Occultism and Parapsychology.* New York: Avon Books, 1978.

Shine, Betty. *The Infinite Mind: The Mind/Brain Phenomenon.* London: Harpercollins UK, 2000.

Shinn, Florence Scovel. *The Wisdom of Florence Scovel Shinn.* New York: Fireside, 1989.

Shinn, Florence Scovel. *The Writings of Florence Scovel Shinn (Includes The Shinn Biography): The Game of Life/ Your Word Is Your Wand/ The Power of the Spoken Word/ The Secret Door to Success.* Camarillo: Devorss & Company, 1996.

Siegel, Bernie S. *Love, Medicine and Miracles.* New York: HarperCollins Publishers, 1988.

Simon, Stephen. *The Force Is with You: Mystical Movie Messages That Inspire Our Lives.* Charlottesville: Hampton Roads Publishing, 2002.

Simons, T. Raphael. *Feng Shui Step by Step: Arranging Your Home for Health and Happiness—with Personalized Astrological Charts.* New York: Three Rivers Press, 1996.

Sirgany, Rosalee. *It Has Always Been Thus*. Bakersfield: Golden Eagle Publications, 2000.

Slate, Joe H. *Aura Energy for Health, Healing and Balance*. St. Paul: Llewellyn Publications, 1999.

Smith, Mark. *Auras: See Them in Only 60 seconds*. St. Paul: Llewellyn Publications, 2002.

Smith, Penelope. *Animal Talk: Interspecies Telepathic Communication*. New York: Atria Books/Beyond Words, 2008.

Soanes, Catherine, and Angus Stevenson. *Concise Oxford English Dictionary: 11th Edition Revised 2008 (Dictionary)*. New York: Oxford University Press, USA, 2008.

Spalding, Baird T. *Life and Teaching of the Masters of the Far East (6 Volume Set)*. Camarillo: Devorss & Company, 1986.

Stavish, Mark. *The Path of Alchemy*. St. Paul: Llewellyn Publications, 2006.

Stein, Diane. *We Are the Angels: Healing Our Past, Present, and Future With the Lords of Karma*. Freedom: Crossing Press, 1997.

Stein, Melissa. *The Wit and Wisdom of Women*. Philadelphia: Running Pr, 1993.

Stevens, Lena S., and Joseph Stevens. *Secrets of Shamanism: Tapping the Spirit Power Within You*. New York: Avon Books, 1988.

Stone, Joshua David. *Soul Psychology: How to Clear Negative Emotions and Spiritualize Your Life*. New York: Wellspring/Ballantine, 1999.

Stone, Joshua David. *The Ascended Masters Light the Way: Beacons of Ascension (The Ascension Series)*. Phoenix: Light Technology Publications, 1996.

Stone, Randolph. *Polarity Therapy The Complete Collected Works Volume 1*. Summertown: Book Publishing Company, 1999.

Subramuniyaswami, Satguru Sivaya. *Lemurian Scrolls: Angelic Prophecies Revealing Human Origins*. Malaysia: Himalayan Academy Publications, 1998.

Sullivan, Kevin. *The Crystal Handbook*. New York: Dutton Books, 1999.

Sussman, Janet I. *Timeshift: The Experience of Dimensional Change*. Fairfield: Time Portal Publications, 1996.

Sutphen, Dick. *With Your Spirit Guide's Help*. Malibu: Valley of the Sun Publishing, 1999.

Tanski, Mai. *Comprehensive Herbalism: A Foundation for Natural Health*. Kearney: Morris Publishing, 2005.

Targ, Russell. *Limitless Mind: A Guide to Remote Viewing and Transformation of Consciousness*. Novato: New World Library, 2004.

Taylor, Albert. *Soul Traveler: A Guide to Out-of-Body Experiences and the Wonders Beyond*. New York: NAL Trade, 2000.

Taylor, Sandra Anne. *Secrets of Attraction: The Universal Laws of Love, Sex and Romance*. Carlsbad: Hay House, 2001.

Taylor, Terry Lynn, and Mary Beth Crain. *Angel Courage*. San Francisco: Harper, 1999.

Taylor, Terry Lynn, and Mary Beth Crain. *Angel Wisdom: 365 Meditations and Insights from the Heavens*. New York: Harperone, 1994.

Taylor, Terry Lynn. *Answers from the Angels: A Book of Angel Letters*. San Francisco: H. J. Kramer, 1993.

Taylor, Terry Lynn. *Creating With the Angels: An Angel-Guided Journey into Creativity*. San Francisco: H. J. Kramer, 1993.

Taylor, Terry Lynn. *Guardians of Hope: The Angels' Guide to Personal Growth*. San Francisco: H. J. Kramer, 1993.

Taylor, Terry Lynn. *Messengers of Light: The Angels' Guide to Spiritual Growth*. San Francisco: H. J. Kramer, 1993.

Tennant, Catherine. *The Box of Stars: A Practical Guide to the Mythology of the Night Sky*. New York: Bulfinch Press, 1993.

Thurston, Mark A. *Synchronicity As Spiritual Guidance*. Totoras: A.R.E. Press, 1997.

Todeschi, Kevin J. *Edgar Cayce on Soul Mates: Unlocking the Dynamics of Soul Attraction*. Washington DC: A.R.E. Press, 1999.

Towler, Solala. *Chi Energy Of Happiness*. Kansas City: Andrews McMeel Publishing, 2003.

Trine, Ralph Waldo. *In Tune with the Infinite*. New York: Dodd, Mead & Company, 1897.

Trollinger, Dan. *Voices of Dawn*. Durham: Satori, 2002.

Tzu, Lao, and Ralph Alan Dale. *Tao Te Ching*. London: Watkins Publishing, 2006.

Tzu, Lao. *Tao Teh Ching*. Boston: Shambhala, 2006.

Villoldo, Alberto. *Shaman, Healer, Sage: How to Heal Yourself and Others with the Energy Medicine of the Americas*. London: Harmony, 2000.

Virtue, Doreen. *Chakra Clearing: Awakening Your Spiritual Power to Know and Heal*. Carlsbad: Hay House, 2003.

Virtue, Doreen. *The Crystal Children*. Carlsbad: Hay House, 2003.

Walsch, Neale Donald. *Bringers of the Light*. Ashland: Millennium Legacies, 1995.

Walsch, Neale Donald. *Conversations with God, Book 1 Guidebook: An Uncommon Dialogue*. Charlottesville: Hampton Roads Publishing Company, 1997.

Walsch, Neale Donald. *Conversations with God: Book 1*. New York: G. P. Putnam's Sons, 1995.

Walsch, Neale Donald. *Conversations with God: Book 2*. Charlottesville: Hampton Roads, 1997.

Walsch, Neale Donald. *Conversations with God: Book 3*. Charlottesville: Hampton Roads, 1998.

Walsch, Neale Donald. *Friendship with God: An Uncommon Dialogue.* Calgary: Berkley Trade, 2002.

Walsch, Neale Donald. *Home with God: In a Life That Never Ends.* New York: Atria, 2006.

Walsch, Neale Donald. *ReCreating Your Self.* Ashland: Millenium, 1995.

Walsch, Neale Donald. *The New Revelations: A Conversation with God.* New York: Atria, 2004.

Walsch, Neale Donald. *Tomorrow's God : Our Greatest Spiritual Challenge.* New York: Atria, 2004.

Warter, Carlos. *Recovery of the Sacred.* Deerfield Beach: HCI, 1994.

Wauters, Ambika. *Chakras and Their Archetypes: Uniting Energy Awareness and Spiritual Growth.* Freedom, California: Crossing Press, 1997.

Wauters, Ambika. *Life Changes With the Energy of the Chakras.* Freedom, California: Crossing Press, 1999.

Weber, Karl, and Muhammad Yunus. *Creating a World without Poverty.* Ashland: Blackstone Audiobooks, Inc., 2008.

Webster, Richard. *Soul Mates : Understanding Relationships Across Time.* St. Paul: Llewellyn Publications, 2001.

Weil, Andrew. *Spontaneous Healing : How to Discover and Embrace Your Body's Natural Ability to Maintain and Heal Itself.* Chicago: Ballantine Books, 2000.

Weiss, Brian L. *Mirrors of Time: Using Regression for Physical, Emotional, and Spiritual Healing.* Carlsbad: Hay House, 2002.

Weiss, Brian L. *Only Love Is Real: A Story of Soulmates Reunited.* New York: Warner Books, 1997.

Whitedove, Michelle. *Angels Are Talking: A Psychic Medium Relays Messages from the Heavens.* Fort Lauderdale: Whitedove Press, 2002.

Wilde, Stuart. *Sixth Sense*. Carlsbad: Hay House, 2000.

Wilde, Stuart. *Weight Loss for the Mind*. Carlsbad: Hay House, 1998.

Williamson, Marianne. *A Return to Love: Reflections on the Principles of A Course in Miracles*. Brattleboro: Harper Paperbacks, 1996.

Williamson, Marianne. *A Woman's Worth*. Chicago: Ballantine Books, 1994.

Williamson, Marianne. *Everyday Grace—Having Hope, Finding Forgiveness, And Making Miracles*. New York: Riverhead Books, 2002.

Williamson, Marianne. *Healing the Soul of America: Reclaiming Our Voices as Spiritual Citizens*. New York: Simon & Schuster, 2000.

Williamson, Marianne. *Illuminata: A Return to Prayer*.

Boston: Riverhead Trade, 1995.

Williamson, Marianne. *Imagine: What America Could be in the 21st century*. New York: NAL Trade, 2001.

Williamson, Marianne. *The Age of Miracles: Embracing the New Midlife*. Carlsbad: Hay House, 2009.

Wolf, Fred Alan. *The Yoga of Time Travel: How the Mind Can Defeat Time*. Wheaton: Quest Books, 2004.

Wolfe, Amber. *Druid Power: Celtic Faerie Craft & Elemental Magic*. St. Paul: Llewellyn Publications, 2004.

Wolff, Robert. *Original Wisdom: Stories of an Ancient Way of Knowing*. New York: Inner Traditions, 2001.

Woodward, Mary Ann. *Edgar Cayce's Story of Karma*. New York: Berkley, 1988.

Yancey, Philip, Billy Graham, and Joni Eareckson Tada.

Amazing Grace. Grand Rapids: Zondervan, 1999.

Yin, Amorah Quan. *The Pleiadian Workbook: Awakening Your Divine Ka*. New York: Bear & Company, 1995.

Young-Sowers, Meredith. *Spirit Heals: Awakening a Woman's Inner Knowing for Self-Healing*. Novato: New World Library, 2007.

Zukav, Gary. *Soul Stories*. New York City: Free Press, 2000.

Zukav, Gary. *The Seat of the Soul*. New York : Simon & Schuster, 1999.

ed., Lewis C. Henry. *Five Thousand Quotations For All Occasions*. New York: Doubleday & Company, Inc., 1945.

Classic Wisdom for the Good Life. Waco: Thomas Nelson, 2006.

Country Living The Peaceful Home (Country Living). New York: Hearst, 2001.

Earth's Birth Changes: St. Germain Through Azena. Scottsdale: Triad, 1993.

Periodicals*

Afar. San Francisco: A Media.

Boho. Upper Montclair: Oinabiz Media, LLC.

Brain Child. Lexington: March Press.

Dr. Andrew Weil's Self Healing. Watertown: Body & Soul Omnimedia, Inc.

Energy Times. Reno: Integrated Publishing.

EnlightenNext: The Magazine for Evolutionaries. Lenox: EnlightenNext Magazine.

Experience Life. Chanhassen: Lifetime Fitness, Inc.

Fitness. Des Moines: Meredith Corporation.

Green Guide. Washington, D.C.: National Geographic Society.

I-Shift. Petaluma: Institute of Noetic Sciences

Kosmos. Lenox: Kosmos Associates Inc.

MaryJanesFarm. Norwalk: MaryJanesFarmPublishing Group

Mother Earth News. Topeka: Ogden Publications, Inc.

Mother Jones. San Francisco: Mother Jones and the Foundation for National Progress.

Natural Health. New York: Weider Publications, LLC.

Ode. Mill Valley: Ode Magazine USA, Inc.

Reason. Los Angeles: Reason Magazine.

Reiki News Magazine. Southfield, Michigan: Vision *Publications.*

Sedona Journal to Emergence. Flagstaff: Light Technology Publications.

Scientific American. New York: Scientific American, Inc.

Shambhala Sun. Halifax: Shambhala Sun Foundation

Sierra. Washington: Sierra Club.

Spirituality & Health. Traverse City: Spirituality & Health Media, LLC.

The Sun. Chapel Hill: The Sun Magazine.

Tin House. Portland: McCormack Communications, LLC.

Tricycle. New York: Tricycle.com.

VegNews. San Francisco: The VegNews Network.

Venture Inward. Virginia Beach: Association for Research and Enlightenment.

What is Enlightenment? Lenox, Ma.: EnlightenmentNext.

Well Being Journal. Carson City: Well Being Journal.

World Ark. Little Rock: Heifer Project International.

Yes!. Madrona Way: Positive Futures Network.

Yoga Journal. El Segundo: Cruz Bay Publishing Inc.

*The Periodicals mentioned above are new magazines that I have recently been exposed to. I feel that these may offer subjects coming from a new vantage point, which may help transition the reader to the new world, offering mind-opening ideas on many different topics. This list is simply presented as one way to illustrate the evolving world. In no way is the list a complete list, but rather is a list of new beginnings to use as a springboard to other topics and exposure to new ideas. Contact individual magazines for e-zine information.

HELPFUL RESOURCES

Family Entertainment and Movies:

www.spiritualcinema.com—uplifting movies for the entire family

Metaphysical, Spiritual, Healing Tools, and Accessories:

info@shambhalahealingtools.com Website to purchase and explore different meditation healing tools and music, such as the etheric weaver and many other tools

www.chimes.com Website to purchase Zenergy Chimes—chimes used to cleanse and clear your space of negative or dead energy

www.goddesselite.com—crystals and healing tools

www.fs2000.com—Website to view feng shui materials

Masters and Professional Contacts:

Andy81857@yahoo.com Andrew Piece Keith: Medium, Healer, Spiritual Teacher. Andrew regularly channels information from spirit or groups and teaches others how to connect to spirit and manage their ability. Contact-1-440-341-6401

carolyn@angelharps.com or www.angelharps.com—Carolyn's Corner—Your Angel Connection: Long-distance healing and angelic information channeled—together with the use of the angelic harp—for healing and raising of vibrational frequencies. Contact: Carolyn *khall@starmuses.com* or *www.starmuses.com*—Astrological Services and Hypnotherapy

loveofanimals@cox.net Telepathic Animal Communications, Healing Touch for Animals, Reiki Master, TTouch, Bach Flower Essences, Color Harmonics. Contact: Diane

tmd11111@yahoo.com Medium of the physical, spiritual, mental, and emotional healing realms. Specializes in: Spiritual Development Classes, Aura Photography, Channeling, Hands of Light Healing, Light Color Harmonics Therapy. Contact: Theresa, A Guided Journey.

Healing Centers:

Colon Therapy Clinic : Contact: Allaesia Menard—Asheville, North Carolina. 1-828-777-1141; Contact: Alain Menard—Sarasota, Florida. 1-941-922-7744.

Ways of Wisdom: Consultation, Reprogramming, BioCranial, and Ion Detox Foot Baths. Contact: Dr. Bonnie Weston—e-mail: waysofwisdom@wowway.com or www.waysofwisdom.net

Training Center:

www.info@spectrahue.com : Sprectrahue Light & Sound, Inc., Toronto, Canada. Contact: Julianne Bien 1-416-340-0882. Training in Color Harmonics, healing with light.

INDEX

A

Angelic Energy, 35, 367
angelic influences:
    assemblage of commitment instructor, 135
    cabalistic arcana guide, 135, 193
    complenary guide, 37, 298
    eighth chakra assistant, 54, 135, 192, 214, 258, 322
    emotional realm coordinator, 90
    fifth-dimensional counselors, 76, 86, 120, 146, 193
    heart chakra assistant, 50–51
    lead messenger, 29, 135, 193
    removal-of-fear guides, 90, 98, 153
    single attribute guide, 29, 147, 286
    spiritual companion counterpart, 50
    twin soul, 50, 76, 193, 235
    creativity guide, 166
Angel Power (McConnell), 9
angels, 24
animals, 286–87, 307–9
archangels
    Chamuel, 25
    Gabriel, 25, 31
    Jophiel, 25
    Michael, 24–26, 29, 31
    Raphael, 29
    Uriel, 25, 31
    Zadkiel, 25
aromatherapy, 145, 181, 194, 267, 290, 298, 367
arrow technique, 206–7
Atlantian, 217–20, 222, 224
aura photography, 13, 126, 324
auric field, 76–77, 79

B

bagua, 281–82, 284, 288
body, 287–88, 330–34
Bonnie (healer), 59–60
Box of Stars, The (Tennant), 210
Brown, Simon
    Feng Shui Bible, The, 286

C

Cayce, Edgar, 18, 119, 349
Celtic bards, 69
center of reality, 105, 110
chakras, 135, 143–44, 192
    base chakra, 243, 280, 298
    communication chakra, 143, 215, 280

crown chakra, 135, 210, 243, 280, 321–22, 364
heart chakra, 51, 67, 76–77, 143
solar plexus chakra, 258, 280, 283, 321, 330
spleen chakra, 243, 280
vitae chakra, 64, 143, 208, 280, 283, 321
channeling, 13, 47, 54–56
trance channel, 17, 59, 302
cherubim, 24
chi energy, 150, 152, 215, 286, 291, 320
children
crystal children, 337, 339
indigo children, 336, 338–39
rainbow children, 337, 339
Chopra, Deepak, 63, 72, 151, 177, 280
Perfect Health, 72, 280, 288
circle of love, 118, 238, 341, 355, 360
colonics, 334
color, 53, 319–25
Colors and Numbers (Hay), 310
complenary guide, 37, 298
Conquering Bear, 60–61
consciousness
emotional body of, 40
mental body of, 119, 164, 178, 181, 206, 240
copper, 327–29
crystals, 125–26
crystals, stones, and metals, 327

D

da Vinci, Leonardo
Last Supper, The, 323
Diamond, John
Way of the Pulse Drumming with Spirit, The, 70
Diane (expert animal communicator), 58–59, 246, 276

dimensions
fifth dimension, 75, 78–79, 81–84, 91–92
first dimension, 18
fourth dimension, 16, 18, 62
second dimension, 18
third dimension, 66, 68, 188, 265
dolphins, 17, 269–78
dominion, 24
Donna (healer), 60

E

earth battery technique, 203, 211
emerging energy of light, 101, 103
Emoto, Masaru
Hidden Messages in Water, The, 350
energy of light, 101, 103, 107, 109, 111
etheric body, 79, 320, 323
exercises, 52
breathing exercise, 189, 361
charging a stone or crystal, 363
connecting to your higher self, 362
Kirunda: energy balancing during transition to ascension, 364
sitting in the silence, 51, 312, 317, 361

F

faith, 83
fear, 77–78
feng shui, 279–81, 284–88, 290–91
Feng Shui Bible, The (Brown), 286
frankincense, 145, 181

G

geometry, 117, 157, 246
gold, 327–28, 342
gold, copper, and silver, 327

H

Hamilton, Claire, 69
  Tales of the Celtic Bards, 69
Hay, Louise L.
  Colors and Numbers, 310
healing, 32
Hidden Messages in Water, The (Emoto), 350
higher self. *See* oversoul
home, 288–90

I

Indiana Jones, 95
inner child, 62–68, 88
inner child processing, 161
integration, 103, 108, 193–95

K

Kirunda, 351

L

Lancelot, 18, 250, 256
Last Supper, The (da Vinci), 323
Lemurian, 216–20, 222, 224
ley line, 76, 126, 215, 246, 297, 356
lightbody, 109, 116
Little Engine that Could, The, 229
love
  infinite love, 83
  self-love, 81, 83, 90, 206
  universal love, 81, 83, 200, 202, 205–7
Love Is in the Earth - A Kaleidoscope of Crystals (Melody), 326

M

magic, 126–28, 130, 239–44, 246–49
major arcana guide, 76, 153, 193, 239–40, 247, 259

manifestation, 125, 181, 228, 230, 240
manifestation techniques
  arrow technique, 206–7
  earth battery technique, 203, 211
  purple energy technique, 204
  white light technique, 202
Markas (class moderator), 16–20
master numbers, 313, 315, 327
Mastertakes, 293
materialization, 125, 181, 202, 228, 230, 242
McConnell, Janice T.
  Angel Power, 9
Medicine Cards (Sams and Carson), 274
meditation, 51
Melody
  Love Is in the Earth - A Kaleidoscope of Crystals, 326
Merlin, 240, 247
metals, 327–29
Michael, 27
Mother Earth, 60, 203, 223, 278, 331, 340–41, 349
motion of energy, 92
music, healing properties, 62, 65–70, 72–74

N

new-fashioned way, 137, 193, 230, 338
nonlinear way, 102, 141, 191, 237, 242, 280, 293
numerology
  master numbers, 313, 315, 327
  personal day, 310–11, 313–14
  personal month, 310–11, 313–15
  personal year, 310–13
  universal year, 312, 314

O

Ones That Flow Like The River, 60
Orion, 18, 200–201, 203–4, 206–10

Orion's energy technique, 207
oversoul, 204, 252, 346

P

past-life regressions, 17, 138–39
patterns, 202, 215, 222, 263–65, 271–72, 290
pendulum, 48, 52, 55, 117, 165, 248, 320
Perfect Health (Chopra), 72, 288
Pleiades, 128–30, 302
Power Animal Meditations (Scully), 274
principalities, 24
pulsing, 81
purple energy technique, 204

R

realms
  emotional realm, 29, 90, 134, 153
  physical realm, 25, 30–31, 33
  spiritual realm, 29, 50, 121, 153, 183, 204, 227, 239–40
  universal realm, 134–35, 153

S

Sai Baba, 47
Scully, Nicki
  Power Animal Meditations, 274
self, 7, 54, 148, 171, 223, 284
seraphim, 24
Severn, Jessica, 17, 302
silver, 327, 329
soul-searching, 75
spirit communication, 46, 272, 285
spiritual gifts
  discernment of spirits, 49–50
  faith, 43, 50, 53, 236
  interpretation of tongues, 47
  messages of wisdom, 45
  miraculous powers, 47–48
  music, 62
  prophecy, 48, 53–54, 58–59, 100, 108
  speaking in tongues, 46, 57
  universal knowledge, 42–43
  wisdom, 45–46, 54, 60
stair-step effect, 201
stones, 325–27, 349
superconsciousness, 108, 121, 127, 178, 180, 182, 362

T

Tales of the Celtic Bards (Hamilton), 69
tarot, 42, 48, 54–55
teleportation, 241, 263, 272, 296, 300, 302–3
Teleportation, A Practical Guide for the Metaphysical Traveler (Tatterdale and Severn), 302
Tennant, Catherine
  Box of Stars, The, 210
Theresa (aura photographer, teacher, and healer), 13–14, 17, 58–59
totem, 72, 249, 274, 276, 307–9
Totterdale, Gwen, 16–17, 59, 304
transmigration, 145, 207, 263, 272, 296, 300
traveling, 296
  astral travel, 102, 129, 241, 296, 300–302, 367

U

unconditional and universal love, 200, 202, 205–10, 213
Universal Law of Attraction, 8
Universal Olympics, 159–60, 165, 176
universal principles, 134, 200, 208

V

vibrational frequency, 30, 122–25, 127, 144–45
visualization, 228, 231, 298, 316, 363
vortices, 194, 215, 280

W

Way of the Pulse Drumming with Spirit, The (Diamond), 70
white light technique, 202
Wizard of Oz, The, 144
work environment, 290